Benign Neglect

The Quakers and Wales *c*.1860–1918

BENIGN NEGLECT

The Quakers and Wales *c*.1860–1918

Owain Gethin Evans

Benign Neglect – the Quakers and Wales c.1860–1918
First published in Wales in 2014
on behalf of the author
by
BRIDGE BOOKS
61 Park Avenue
WREXHAM
LL12 7AW

A CIP entry for this book is available from the British Library

ISBN 978-1-84494-097-4

Printed and bound
by
Gutenberg Press Ltd
Malta

Er cof am fy rhieni
Meinir a Sadie Evans, Ardwyn, Llanrug gynt,
a'm hynafiaid, ddysgodd i fyw a marw yng nghysgod
a llwch y 'Garreg Lâs'.

'Beth yw byw? Cael neuadd fawr
Rhwng cyfyng furiau.'

Waldo Williams

Contents

Acknowledgements

There are many people to be thanked for having encouraged, assisted and supported me in the evolution and completion of this book. I feel that to name them all might result in me overlooking someone which would be unforgivable. Hence, my thanks to all – family, F/friends, academic, technical, everyone who gave such invaluable assistance.

All errors are mine and I am deeply conscious of my own short-comings and there will, I am sure, be criticism for overlooking them and not being vigorous enough in my editing.

In reflecting on giving thanks then it's not those immediately involved that my mind turns, but rather those from my past who shaped and influenced me.

That I come from a fast vanishing background and culture is an undercurrent that underpins the emphasis of the book. I do not apologise, but can say that Britain Yearly Meeting is now much changed and more sensitive to those issues that challenge me – although I remain unconvinced that all Friends in Wales wish to identify with Wales and its future.

From the past come the whispers of things given, provided, taken and lost, tears and laughter. The sweet memory of the following in particular, amongst many, remain with me:

Rev. E. Goronwy Williams
Rev. Prof. Harri Williams
Annie Baines Griffith, H. Garrison Williams, Emlyn Jones, Tom Jones, Leslie Larsen, Miss Parry – all teachers at Ysgol Gynradd Llanrug
Ysgolion Sul Capel Mawr, Llanrug, Mynydd Seion, Abergele and Capel Hirael, Bangor
Nain a Taid, Gwynllys, Llanrug
Walter Ruffle Evans, Llanrug
Tom and Lellie Evans, Y Felinheli
Owena Lewis Parry and her parents

ACKNOWLEDGEMENTS

Mary and Alun Jones, Bryn Hyfryd, Llanrug

Mary and Jessie Mackinnon, Plas Tirion, Llanrug

Gwilym, Rita and Margaret Roberts, Ffordd Caerdydd, Pwllheli

H.C. Evans, Friars Grammar School, Bangor

Brain and Barbara Rodgers, University of Manchester

Evelyn Evans, Bangor, Quaker

Michael and Dorothy Shewell, Dyffryn Conwy, Quakers

Gwen Loney, Richhill, Armagh, Quaker

Doreen and Hereward Armstrong, Llanidloes, Quakers

If these now provide memories then there are my fellow postgraduate Interpol students from the 2000-2001 class at Aberystwyth and my former students at Brummana High School, Lebanon who deserve mention, as do *'Pentrefwyr Trefor* and *Plwyfolion Clynnogfawr, Gwynedd,'* and the former members and staff of Cyngor Dosbarth Dwyfor – *'Angor yr Iaith'* – neither should many former colleagues from the old Gwynedd County Council be over-looked.

Finally, to the Quakers amongst whom I have made my home since 1971. I have been involved in some aspects of their work within Wales and in Britain as a whole. Some developments within now cause me concern with an evolution of a type of Quakerism with which I struggle. That probably sums up the condition of all of us facing change.

> *Beth yw bod yn genedl? Dawn*
> *Yn nwfn y galon.*
> *Beth yw gwladgarwch? Cadw tŷ*
> *Mewn cwmwl tystion.*

Waldo Williams

Gethin Evans

11.2.2014

Abbreviations and translations

The following abbreviations are used throughout, both in the main text and in the footnotes:

BYM:	Britain Yearly Meeting
CA:	Ceredigion Archives
CLS:	Ceredigion Library Service
CN:	*Cambrian News*
CJ:	*Carmarthen Journal*
CPM:	Cardiff Preparative Meeting.
DHMM:	Devonshire House Monthly Meeting
DQB:	Dictionary of Quaker Biography, Friends House Library, London
DWB:	*Dictionary of Welsh Biography (Y Bywgraffiadur Cymreig)*
ECWQM:	Evangelistic Committee, Western Quarterly Meeting
ETS:	Extracts from the diaries of Elizabeth Trusted Southall
FAU:	Friends Ambulance Unit
FFDSA:	Friends First Day School Association
FTA:	Friends Tracts Association
GA:	Gloucestershire Archives
GRO:	Glamorgan Record Office
HMC:	Home Mission Committee
HMCEC:	Home Mission Committee, Executive Committee
HMEC:	Home Mission and Extension Committee
HMECEC:	Home Mission and Extension Committee, Executive Committee
HRMM:	Hereford and Radnor Monthly Meeting
HRO:	Herefordshire Records Office
LCQM:	Lancashire and Cheshire Quarterly Meeting
LRO:	Lancashire Records Office
LSF:	Library of the Society of Friends, London
LlWPM:	Llandrindod Wells Preparative Meeting
LYM:	London Yearly Meeting

M:	Where followed by a number denotes the minute as recorded in the relevant minute book of whatever meeting is being referenced.
MfS:	Meeting for Sufferings
MM:	Monthly Meeting
NLW:	National Library of Wales
NPM:	Neath Preparative Meeting
PCAO:	Powys County Archives Office
PM:	Preparative Meeting
PMDB:	Minute Book, Pales Mission and Day School
QFP:	*Quaker Faith and Practice*
QM:	Quarterly Meeting
RCLW:	Royal Commission on Land in Wales and Monmouthshire
RE:	*Radnor Express*
SPM:	Swansea Preparative Meeting
SUWL:	Society for the Utilisation of the Welsh Language
SWDN:	*South Wales Daily News*
SWMM:	South Wales Monthly Meeting
SWMOC:	South Wales Monthly Meeting, Ministry and Oversight Committee
TC:	*The Crusader*
TF:	*The Friend*
TT:	*The Times*
WCM:	Welsh Calvinistic Methodists
WLMM:	Westminster and Longford Monthly Meeting
WG:	*Welsh Gazette [Aberystwyth Chronicle and West Wales Advertiser]*
WM:	*Western Mail*
WQM:	Western Quarterly Meeting
WRO:	Worcestershire Record Office
YBC:	*Ye Brython Cymreig*
YFAC:	*Y Faner ac Amserau Cymru*
YMP:	Minutes and Proceedings of the Yearly Meeting of Friends
YUC:	*Yr Undebwr Cymreig*

Translation

All translations from the Welsh are mine and are given fully in the footnotes to assist proper understanding, given that translations are subjective.

Chapter 1
Wales and London Yearly Meeting

The activities and development of the Religious Society of Friends (Quakers) in Wales during the Victorian and Edwardian periods deserves attention. To date there has been no such study and this perhaps because of a feeling there was little to write about. Yet it was a period when, most historians are agreed, Wales saw a resurgence of its national awareness,[1] when Nonconformist activity and influence was both loud and successful. The relationship between London Yearly Meeting (LYM), the supreme constitutional body for Friends in Britain,[2] and Wales is therefore important and its comprehension of issues is necessary to understanding its contribution to the life of Wales. What were the reactions and sensitivities within LYM to matters relating to Welsh national identity, and did it recognise that Quakers in Wales had a distinct identity? The answers may offer some understanding as to why, when other Nonconformists in Wales grew in strength, the Quakers remained as a very small and unimportant group within the denominational demographic.

This was the period when Wales was transformed into an industrial powerhouse as it was gripped and reshaped by the processes of urbanisation and industrialisation; the demographic changes that followed, even though accompanied by greater Anglicisation, created new loci of activity. Its population nearly doubled between 1800 and 1851, with a 51% increase amongst Nonconformists[3] giving to Wales the stamp of being a 'religious society.'[4] The rise of militant Nonconformity, in its call amongst other things

1. The following texts are of particular interest: Mathew Cragoe, *Culture, politics, and national identity in Wales, 1832–1886*, 2004; John Davies, *A History of Wales*, 1993; D.Gareth Evans, *A History of Wales, 1815–1906*, 1989; Geraint H. Jenkins, *Hanes Cymru yn y Cyfnod Modern Cynnar, 1530–1760*, 1983; Philip Jenkins, *A History of Modern Wales 1536–1990*, 1992; Gareth Elwyn Jones, *Modern Wales: A Concise History*, 1999; K.O. Morgan, *Rebirth of a Nation: A History of Modern Wales*, 1981; K.O. Morgan, *Wales in British Politics, 1868–1922*, 1991; Gwyn A. Williams, *When Was Wales?*, 1985.
2. Since 1994 redesignated as Britain Yearly Meeting (BYM).
3. Jones, *Modern Wales*, 1999, 273.
4. E.T. Davies, *Religion in the Industrial Revolution in South Wales*, 1965, 141.

for land reform, disestablishment of the Church of England, and 'Welsh home rule,' provided a focus for aroused passions, which further cemented the transformation of Welsh identity in the political sphere. Overall, by the end of the nineteenth century, 'Welshness had become a distinct and respectable political theme.'[5]

The literature on the Quakers in Wales during the period of this study is sparse. This is not surprising given that by the mid–nineteenth century the Society in Wales was deeply enfeebled. Material, scholarly and otherwise, before the period of this study is more abundant, primarily focused on the seventeenth and eighteen centuries. Two broad overviews on the history of the Quakers in Wales are available, one in English by the Congregationalist minister, T. Mardy Rees, and the other in Welsh by the Baptist minister, Richard Jones. Both were entries in a competition set for the National Eisteddfod in 1923, but neither now can be described as disciplined scholarly studies, although Rees' study has proved to be a valuable source of information. Both offer more story than analysis.[6] The following year, an American descendent of the Lloyds of Dolobran, published *The Quaker Seekers in Wales*, more as a novella than historical scholarship.[7]

The most important work is Richard Allen's study of Quakers in Monmouthshire. It offers a comprehensive scholarly analysis of the Quakers in Wales from their establishment up to 1836.[8] M. Fay Williams's 1959 thesis on the Quakers in the old county of Glamorgan offers some description of activity up to 1900,[9] and H.G. Jones' 1938 examination of John Kelsall's journals[10] which, covering part of the eighteenth century, locates Welsh Quakerism within a broader national context. His subsequent essay[11] offered an assessment of the state of Quakerism then and after. Martin Williams concentrates

5. K.O. Morgan, *Modern Wales: Politics, Places and People*, 1995, 6.
6. Rev. T. Mardy Rees, *A History of the Quakers in Wales and their Emigration to North America*, 1925; Richard Jones, *Crynwyr Bore Cymru*, 1931.
7. Anna Lloyd Braithwaite Thomas, *The Quaker Seekers of Wales: A Story of the Lloyds of Dolobran*, 1924.
8. Richard C. Allen, *Quaker Communities in Early Modern Wales: From Resistance to Respectability*, 2007.
9. M. Fay Williams, 'The Society of Friends in Glamorgan, 1654–1900', unpublished M.A Thesis, University of Wales, Aberystwyth, 1950.
10. H.G. Jones, 'John Kelsall: A Study in Religious and Economic History', unpublished M.A Thesis, University of Wales, Bangor, 1938.
11. H.G. Jones, 'Dyddiau Olaf y Crynwyr yng Nghymru' in *Y Traethodydd*, viii, 1939, 78–87.

on the Quakers of Radnorshire during the period of this study, offering valuable local vignettes.[12] Emyr Wyn Jones provided a sketch of one Victorian Welsh Quaker, whose focus was not on Wales or Welsh issues.[13] Two published 'county' studies touch the period to a limited extent.[14]

Primary material, such as minutes and reports generated by various Quaker meetings, do not provide a complete picture, proving often to be mere signposts to nowhere, since it is not always possible to be sure how issues arose and what was their conclusion. Articles and materials in the principal Quaker periodicals of the time, *The Friend*, a publication more inclined to favour the evangelic wing within the yearly meeting, and *The British Friend*, more modernist in its approach, are useful, especially the former, but their indexes provide no clue to Welsh affairs, and one has to dig to find reports which are relevant to Wales. In addition, some might be cautious about reliance on these magazines since they were not official Yearly Meeting publications and therefore offered the partisan viewpoints of contributors and editors. Nevertheless, both magazines are invaluable, providing insight as to how Quakers and the Yearly Meeting saw their own and the wider world. Published biographies and personal correspondence by Quakers living in Wales commenting on the life and activities of the Society within Wales are sadly lacking. The exceptions are some brief archived papers by Neath Quaker and industrialist, Frederick Joseph Gibbins, who was interested in the history of the Society in Wales.

An important contribution to the history of the Society in Britain during the period is B.D. Phillips' study of Edwardian Quakers,[15] but its anglo–centrism, especially in relation to the 1902 Education Act, where he makes no reference to the serious and institutional agitation in Wales, diminishes its contribution. Neither does he make any reference to disestablishment, an issue that challenged the assumed homogeneity within the political life of Britain. Similarly, Elizabeth Isichei's seminal study of Victorian Quakers[16] is

---

12. Martin Williams at http://www.hmwquakers.org.uk/Radnorshire_evangelical_Friends_from_19th_cent.pdf.
13. Emyr Wyn Jones, 'William Jones: Quaker and Peacemaker,' in *The National Library of Wales Journal*, XXVI, 4, 1990, 401–426.
14. Stephen Griffith, *A History of Quakers in Pembrokeshire*, 1990; Trevor Macpherson, *Friends in Radnorshire*, 1999.
15. B.D. Phillips, 'Friendly Patriotism: British Quakerism and the Imperial Nation, 1890–1910', unpublished PhD Thesis, University of Cambridge, 1989.
16. Elizabeth Isichei, *Victorian Quakers*, 1970.

not concerned with Welsh matters. As does Phillips, she locates her study within the broader 'British' framework. Kennedy focuses on changes and the transformation within LYM, during most of the period, concentrating on the shift to a more liberal understanding of theology and action, which affected the overall social and internal witness of the Society, but without reference to any national sensibilities.[17]

Therein perhaps is part of a problem, that in the story of Quakers in Wales, LYM became an English institution, and not the 'British' body that it imagined itself to be. Possibly because even as late as 1830–67, 'British' remained an elusive concept, and what was dominant was the 'hegemonic cultural identity'[18] of England, highlighting a British/English identity that was submerged in an imperial racist discourse. This hegemonic relationship does not alter or negate the fact of diversity and plurality within the British state, but it does mean that the history of Wales, Ireland and Scotland are conceived as largely determined by their response to England.[19] Englishness then is not so much a category as a relationship, able to bestow the identity of the core on the periphery.[20] Thus England stands as proxy for the others, following the logic of English developments.[21] The culture of the core assumed a 'higher' prestige, and the peripheral cultures, survived and adapted,[22] often as forms of 'hidden resistance'[23] i.e. expressions of beliefs and practices, which have a subterranean existence, hidden from those in power, giving the use of Welsh and Gaelic a particular potency. These were the people of the 'savage frontier'[24] the earliest members of the English empire.[25] Consequently, and perhaps not surprisingly, LYM failed to have any

17. Thomas C. Kennedy, *British Quakerism 1860–1920: The Transformation of a Religious Community*, 2001.
18. Catherine Hall, *Civilising Subject: Metropole and Colony in the English Imagination 1830–67*, 2002, 22.
19. J.G.A. Pocock, 'British History: A Plea for a New Subject,' in *Journal of Modern History*, 4, 4, 1975, 601–628.
20. Philip Dodd, 'Englishness and the National Culture,' in *Englishness: Politics and Culture 1880–1920*, Robert Colls and Philip Dodd, eds., 1986, 12 & 14.
21. J.C.D. Clark, 'English History's Forgotten Context: Scotland, Ireland, Wales,' in *The Historical Journal*, 32, 1, 1989), 211–228.
22. Neil Evans, 'Internal Colonialism? Colonisation, Economic Development and Political Mobilisation in Wales, Scotland and Ireland,' in *Regions, Nations and European Integration: Remaking the Celtic Periphery*, Graham Day and Gareth Rees, eds., 1991, 235–264.
23. James C. Scott, *Domination and the Arts of Resistance: Hidden Transcripts*, 1990.
24. Ronald Hutton, Debates in Stuart History, 2004), 182.
25. R.R. Davies, 'Colonial Wales,' in *Past and Present*, 65, November 1974, 3–23, and *The First English Empire: Power and Identities in the British Isles, 1039–1341*, 2000.

distinctive ownership of Welsh affairs and remained Anglo–centric in attitude, with what one senses was a patronising attitude to Welsh affairs. This is in keeping with a narrow view of the British state that did not recognise its multinational character. Doing so would have exposed the political domination of England[26] in which the history of Britain was 'the history of England, apart from [the] occasional interruptions from the periphery.'[27] LYM regrettably fell into that trap and treated Wales with ambivalence redolent of benign neglect. Indeed the paucity of material about Quakers in the evolving modern Wales provides an indicator of the way the Yearly Meeting operated in relation to Wales, essentially that its activities and interest were limited especially after 1797 with the demise of Wales Yearly Meeting. The focus of its enterprises was on what it perceived as the broader 'British' canvass, with little attention paid to aspirations in Britain's constituent parts. For the early Quakers national sensibilities were not a primary concern, their principle satisfaction and objective came, as for all evangelists, from seeing that

> the people were turned to the divine light of Christ, and his spirit, by which they might come to know God and Christ, and the Scriptures, and to have fellowship with them, and one with another in the same spirit[28]

acknowledging the message of the Quaker truth about the nature of the church and its mission.

This ambivalence entails looking at how the Society's organisation and structures evolved. The early Quaker missionaries, often referred to as the 'Valiant Sixty,'[29] travelled widely and overseas, gathering converts. As the movement grew, organisational discipline became important in response to persecution, imprisonment and internal disagreements over doctrine and practice. The imposition of this discipline turned the movement into an institution, and as it centralised its discipline, so inevitably, this affected relationships and communications, and the growing institutionalization in

---

26. Richard Kearney, *Postnationalist Ireland: Politics, Culture, Philosophy*, 1997, 10.
27. Keith G. Robbins, 'Wales and the 'British Question' in *Transactions of the Honourable Society of Cymmrodorion*, 2002, New Series, 9, 2003, 155.
28. *Journal of George Fox* (JGF) John L. Nickalls, ed., 1975, 339–340.
29. See Elfrida Vipont, *George Fox and the Valiant Sixty*, 1975.

itself, as Ingle acknowledges, 'became the object of widespread attack.'[30]

From 1652 the Quaker organisational structure evolved from a mere gathering of Seekers, to become, by 1678, a fully representative Yearly Meeting, a body that assumed final constitutional authority over its members throughout, by then, the restored kingdoms.[31] In June 1671, at a meeting in London, Friends took the decision to establish a central body both to advise and manage their public affairs. This was to meet annually in London during Whitsun week, a body of ministers and representative Friends from the 'counties.' George Fox, credited as founder and principal leader of the Quakers, refers to this meeting as a Yearly Meeting where 'many came from all parts of the nation, and a mighty meeting it was.'[32] Fox had similarly used the word nation for a meeting held in Bedfordshire in May 1656 which he described as 'a General Yearly Meeting for the whole nation ... This meeting lasted three days, and many Friends from most parts of the nation came to it.'[33] In Skipton, Yorkshire in June 1659, Friends from the north of England had gathered to consider how best to support, financially and otherwise, those travelling in the ministry or in gaol. They agreed to meet again in the same place in October. Friends in Durham gathered to prepare for this meeting and wrote a letter to it. They touched upon the need for firmer structures so 'that truth itself in the body may reign'[34] with practical proposals that all business amongst Friends, especially in the north, should be set in proper order and that a general meeting should gather twice or thrice annually. This was endorsed, but they went further, 'we wish the like may be settled in all parts, and one General Meeting of England.'[35] This proposal was forwarded to the leadership based in London and a meeting on these lines was convened on April 25th 1660 again in Skipton, where according to Fox, 'some Friends did come out of most parts of the nation, for it was about business of the church both in this nation and beyond the seas.'[36] The fact that it was representatives from meetings across England that attended these

---

30. H. Larry Ingle, *First Among Friends: George Fox and the Creation of Quakerism*, 1994, 259.
31. England, Scotland and Ireland – the three kingdoms.
32. *JGF*, 579.
33. *JGF*, 339. Fox's description that there were 'three or four thousand people were at it' is probably an exaggeration.
34. William C. Braithwaite, *The Beginnings of Quakerism*, Henry J Cadbury, ed., 1955, 329.
35. Ibid., 330.
36. *JGF*, 373.

gatherings provides substance to the interpretation that by nation, Fox was referring to England.

Such an implication should be understood in the context given to nation at that time. Before the revolution, and after 1660, the Crown embodied and gave substance to the 'nations' – the three kingdoms. Conrad Russell high–lighted the different constitutional and religious structures and traditions in each kingdom, a multiplicity that gave rise to instability.[37] Attempts at uniformity, especially in religion, was destined to fail since the monarch had no British façade, and Charles I's push for a 'British' dimension of identity was not viable, and in 'British' terms, the English parliament was as much a local assembly as the *cortes* of Castile.'[38] As for Wales, it existed as a princi-pality nestling under the wing of the English Crown, preserving its national identity through language, memory and myth. Britain did not yet exist.

Between 1671 and 1677 the 'Morning Meeting,' the new central body, was confined to those designated as ministers, and it was only in 1678 that the intentions of 1671 were fulfilled, when male representatives chosen from the counties (women were excluded) met alongside the Meeting of Ministers which served as an advisory body.[39] This concentration of meetings on London must have been a hindrance since in practical terms the oversight of the Society meant that it was Friends who lived in or near the city, or were frequent visitors there, who dominated the deliberations of the Society. Christine Trevett, exploring the relationship between the London based meetings with women and Wales, in particular the Morning Meeting, is right to comment that, 'Women had no place in the decision–making of the Meeting and almost all Welsh Friends were peripheral to this new kind of leadership … for reasons of 'class', language and mores.'[40] This did not mean that Wales, or anywhere, was ignored – the Morning Meeting was open to all Ministers present in London. Since it met weekly, by default, it suggests a certain restriction. She should have added distance!

Between 1652 and 1678 a hierarchy of monthly and quarterly meetings

37. Conrad Russell, 'The British Problem and the English Civil War' in *History*, 72, 1987, 395–415.
38. Ibid., 404.
39. William C. Braithwaite, *The Second Period of Quakerism*, 1961, 276–77.
40. Christine Trevett, in 'Not Fit To Be Printed: The Welsh, the women and the Second Day Morning Meeting,' in the *Journal of the Friends Historical Society*, 59, 2, 2001 (Issued 2004), 119.

had been set up with the counties forming the political units within which they primarily operated.[41] By 1691, 151 monthly meetings (MM) were established. Each monthly meeting in Wales was based on the historical counties, with the exception of Anglesey, where no meeting was ever established.[42] There is uncertainty about Caernarfonshire and Breconshire, but both had Quaker converts there in the early period.

In May 1670, during Fox's visit to Ireland, 'to visit the Seed of God in that nation,'[43] a Half–Yearly or National Meeting was established, to meet twice annually and to send representatives to LYM, this in the view of one author reflecting the Society's progress there.[44] Through the efforts of people such as William Edmondson, the Quaker message had been sown in Ireland since around 1654, in English amongst the Protestant settlers in the country their success was almost reliant on the areas of the Cromwellian settlement, and the conversion of settlers and soldiers. The Quakers were an important part of the Protestant community and concerned for its ascendancy. Fox preached and moved then amongst a well–settled Quaker community who showed little sensitivity towards Gaelic, the principal language of the Irish Catholic population. The Quaker message was never widely preached in that language and there was little contact with the Gaelic speaking population. Maurice Wigham refers to the efforts of one particular Gaelic speaker in 1678, adding that there were never many Irish–speaking Friends and that, 'the language must have been a greater barrier than upbringing and culture to the advance of Quakerism among the Irish of Gaelic origin,'[45] indeed that there was no evidence 'a Celtic–Irishman becoming a Quaker' because the principles of Friends found little acceptance amongst them.[46] Grubb concurs 'very few of its members have been of Celtic race.'[47] The Quakers contributed to the linguistic repression of Gaelic that sprang from the Reformation,[48] and there is no reason to believe that they were any the less prejudiced than their

41. Braithwaite, *The Beginnings*, 251–289 and *The Second Period*, 306–342.
42. Braithwaite, *The Second Period*, 256 fn. 1.
43. *JGF*, 536.
44. Isabel Grubb, *Quakers in Ireland: 1654–1900*, 1927.
45. Maurice J. Wigham, *The Irish Quakers: A Short History of the Religious Society of Friends in Ireland*, 1992, 27–28.
46. Ibid, quotes Arthur Cook Myers, *The Immigration of the Irish Quakers into Pennsylvania, 1682–1750*, 1902.
47. Grubb, Quakers in, 1927, 17.
48. See Victor Edward Durkacz, *The Decline of the Celtic Languages*, 1983, 6– 23.

fellow Protestants, or any more tolerant of Catholics.

In 1797 this Irish body assumed the name, Dublin Yearly Meeting, abandoning the twice annual meeting. It was subordinate to LYM, endorsing its recommendations and advice. Nevertheless, it pursued its own petitions, lobbying directly to the Irish parliament, but joining with LYM in dealing with Westminster. It was a competent body to represent Irish Quakers, acquiring as it did particular attributes relevant to itself.[49] The establishment of this National Meeting reflected the unique political and national position of Ireland, which LYM Meeting respected and acknowledged.

Quaker progress in Scotland was far more laboured, where the hostility of the Presbyterians was harsh and successful, such that for Braithwaite those who became Quakers in Scotland were 'men of power'[50] because they had walked away from Presbyterianism. Quakerism belonged to another cultural milieu so that, in the opinion of one Scottish Quaker historian, it 'always suffered from the imputation of alien origin,'[51] i.e. that it came from England. Development in Scotland was not as unified as elsewhere, and it was only in 1786 that efforts were made to bring together its two existing yearly meetings, one based on Edinburgh and the other on Aberdeen, and amalgamated as General Meeting for Scotland in 1807.[52]

By 1878, the total number of Quakers in Scotland was 182, not so markedly different, as we shall see, from Wales. Henry Lees of Huddersfield, visiting Scotland in late 1884, reported to his monthly meeting that there were only six meetings in the country with a total of 193 members, and half of these were at Glasgow Meeting. One Friend commenting on this was however optimistic about the future, remarking with a tinge of theological and Anglo-centric judgement that:

> it was a fact that religious beliefs, like plants and cereals, thrive better on some grounds than on others, and the Scotch mind up to now had encouraged the hard and cold tenets of Calvinism and predestination, rather than the gentler side of redeeming grace so clearly set forth by George Fox and others.

49. Wigham, *The Irish Quakers*, 145.
50. Braithwaite, *The Second Period*, 328.
51. G.B. Burnet, *The Story of Quakerism in Scotland: 1650–1850*, 1952, 196.
52. Ibid, 164 and 195.

Nevertheless there were indications that changes are coming over the religious thought of Scotland, and it behoved us to be on watch.[53]

George Fox made his first visit into Wales in 1657, making two shorter visits in 1663 and 1667. All the Welsh counties were visited in 1657, not only to spread the message, but also 'to repair the damage caused to the reputation of the movement by James Nayler's celebrated debacle at Bristol the previous autumn.'[54] Nayler, an able and charismatic Quaker preacher who had Welsh supporters, and who was in many ways a rival to Fox, had been accused and convicted of heresy by Parliament. Fox's visit was largely concentrated,[55] but not exclusively, on the larger towns which had military garrisons where he was able to preach openly in English, the dominant language amongst them. Many Quakers were drawn from the ranks of the Parliamentarian Army. Christopher Hill comments that, 'the number of Quakers who had been in the Army and Navy, until they were forced out, is legion.'[56]

Fox was accompanied by Welsh–speaking ministers such as John ap John[57] and Edward Edwards,[58] both Denbighshire men. John, of Trefor near Froncysyllte, had been a follower of Morgan Llwyd, the Independent minister at Wrexham, who had sent him and another to Swarthmore to visit Fox in 1653, and who came back a Quaker. As they progressed through Wales meetings were established, such that it is not unrealistic to think that most meetings were dominated by Welsh–speaking Friends, with Welsh used extensively in the meetings. J. Gwyn Williams is emphatic, that 'the greater majority of Welsh Quakers were Welsh speaking, but since Quaker-ism came from England into Wales the consequence of Babel's Tower cannot be avoided.'[59]

53. TF, 11th month, 1884, 292.
54. Geraint H. Jenkins, *Protestant Dissenters in Wales, 1639–1689*, 1992, 36.
55. *JGF*, 290–306.
56. Christopher Hill, *The Experience of Defeat: Milton and Some Contemporaries* (London, Faber and Faber, 1984), 127.
57. See 'John ap John and Early Records of Friends in Wales,' compiled by William Gregory Norris, *Journal of the Friends' Historical Society*, Supplement 6, 1907.
58. See Some Brief Epistles, *Testimonies and Counsel given by that Ancient and Faithful Servant of the Lord, Mary Edwards, Recommended to Friends, called Quakers in Gloucestershire, Wales, Bristol and elsewhere concerned*, London, J. Sawle, 1720. Written by his wife and contains a testimony to him.
59. J. Gwyn Williams, 'Crynwyr Cynnar Cymru: Cipolwg,' in *Y Gair a'r Genedl: Cyfrol Deyrnged R Tudur Jones*, E. Stanley John, ed., 1986, 126–271 ('*Hyn yn wir a wyddom,*

Fox's journal reflects the fact that he acknowledged Wales' unique national character and recognised that Welsh had to be used to reach the largely monoglot population. By 1801, in a population of about 600,000, nine out of ten people in Wales spoke Welsh; seven out of ten were monoglot. By 1891, the figure was around 30% monoglot, with higher proportions in certain districts.[60]

In 1666 he claimed that he spoke the language.[61] At Dolgellau 'The people were attentive so I was moved to speak to John ap John to stand up and speak in Welsh to them, and he did. So the meeting broke up in peace.'[62] Despite this almost none of the records of Welsh Friends were written in Welsh; English was the language of administration. The only existing records written in Welsh belong to Monmouthshire MM. Allen discussing the use of Welsh within that MM, notes that Friends 'for the most part failed to recognise the importance of the language as the main means of communication.'[63]

Young examines how English was enforced on Wales in a determined effort to replace Welsh as the language of instruction, remarking that Englishness is unequivocally British, 'a cunning word of political correctness invoked in order to mask the metronymic extension of English dominance'.[64] Welsh culture was submerged and assimilated:

> The fusion of all the inhabitants of these islands into one homogenous, English speaking whole, the breaking down of barriers between us, the swallowing up of separate provincial nationalities, is a consummation to which the natural course of things irresistibly tends; it is a necessity of what is called modern civilisation, a modern civil is a real, legitimate force; the change must come, and its accomplishment is a mere affair of time. The sooner the Welsh language disappears as an instrument of the practical, political social life of Wales, the better, the better for England, the better for Wales itself ... the language of a Welshman is and must be English.[65]

Cymry Cymraeg oedd mwyafrif Crynwyr Cymru ond gan mai o Loegr y treiddiodd Crynwriaeth i Gymru ni ellid osgoi canlyniadau Twr Babel.')
60. Geraint H. Jenkins ed., *Language and Community in the Nineteenth Century*, 1998, 1–2.
61. *JGF*, 505.
62. *JGF*, 303.
63. Allen, 'The Society of Friends,' 1999, 476– 478.
64. Robert J. C. Young, *Colonial Desire: Hybridity in Theory, Culture and Race*, 1995, 3.
65. Matthew Arnold, 'On the Study of Celtic Literature,' in *Lectures and Essays in Criticism*, 1962, 297.

In Matthew Arnold's search for that plain of high culture, the existence of minority languages and cultures was a hindrance to assimilation and the creation of a modern culture, where he 'saw culture as a binding and unifying agent,'[66] underpinning the unity of the British state. Many Welsh speakers would have identified with Arnold; the 'respectable bourgeoisie anglophile social engineers,'[67] anxious to uphold the Hegelian reverence for the state, fearful that upholding Welsh and Wales undermined the concept of the unified state. Arnold and his Welsh sympathisers saw social progress embedded in an English discourse, an imperialistic view, even if it was never verbalised as such. Such pronouncements affected attitudes to the way Welsh and Wales were perceived and treated. The infamous *Encyclopædia Britannica*, 1888 edition, entry for Wales was simple, 'For Wales see England.' Indeed, the England–Wales relationship, if only because of geographical proximity, meant that Wales was considered psychologically, politically and culturally from the thirteenth century to be part of England.[68]

English was the language of LYM and this was never questioned. Welsh belonged to Wales Yearly Meeting, but was not elevated by it. Despite their pronouncements, and their desire to ensure publication in Welsh, their output can only be described as disappointing; no original work was produced and those published were translations from English. Trevett demonstrates that there were structural obstacles.[69] All publications were subject to approval of Second Day Morning Meeting of men ministers meeting in London, established by Fox circa 1673. Part of its function was to ensure that anything published by Friends in defence of their teachings was acceptable. The meeting had little enthusiasm for Welsh–language publications, and was 'ill–equipped to deal with writings which derived from authors whose first language was Welsh.'[70] Trevett concludes that lack of patronage might have been an added factor, whilst the ability of Welsh Friends to make their case before a meeting held in London must have had some bearing, especially since it was unlikely that any members of the committee would have been able to read Welsh. Indeed, LYM had

66. Nicholas Murray, *A Life of Matthew Arnold*, 1996, 231.
67. Emyr Humphreys, 'Arnold in Wonderland' in *Miscellany Two*, 1981, 81–100.
68. Jocelyn Hackforth–Jones, 'Re–Visioning Landscape, c 1760–1840,' in *Cultural Identities and the Aesthetics of Britishness*, Dana Arnold, ed., 2004, 35–52.
69. Trevett, 'Not Fit', 2001, 115–144.
70. Ibid, 129.

little knowledge of the peculiar needs and difficulties of Wales. In particular, they failed to appreciate the significance of the difference in language. From the outset, the use of English predominated.[71]

In some ways this was perhaps inevitable if the focus of mission was to be about saving souls, language was utilitarian, something Fox acknowledged in an introduction he wrote to a book published in 1660 on the Quaker usage of 'thee' and 'thou' and its defence of a practice which was seen to undermine social convention attracting much criticism and opposition.

All languages are to me no more than dust, who was before language were, and am redeemed out of languages into the power where men shall agree: but this is a whip and a rod to all such who have degenerated through pride and ambition from their natural tongue and languages; and all languages upon earth is but natural [i.e. undivine] and makes none Divine, but that which makes divine is the Word which was before languages and tongues.[72]

An attitude that would no doubt have reverberated throughout the Society.

Dodd, makes a perceptive comment about the Quaker emigrants to Pennsylvania, that their commitment to the language was, unlike other dissenters, affected by the fact that they had no creed or hymns, which were written and collectively enounced. An analysis that is consistent with the idea that identity is preserved and imprinted through the use of text. The use of Welsh was not integral to Quaker worship, hence in the American setting their use of the language waned long before other denominations.[73] The same can surely be applied to what happened in Wales, there was no vibrant 'voice' with which they communicated their faith, and hence their identification with things Welsh was enfeebled, whilst being organisationally attached to a system that was essentially anglo–centric. Jenkins sees it more starkly, that in the quenching of their own fire they lost their ambition becoming mere 'objects of curiosity.'[74]

71. Williams, 'The Society of Friends', 1950, 69.
72. *A Battle Door for Teachers and professors to learn singular and plural*, 1660.
73. A.H. Dodd, 'The Background of the Welsh Quaker Migration to Pennsylvania,' in *Journal of the Merioneth Historical and Record Society*, III, Part II, 1958, 126.
74. Geraint H. Jenkins, *The Foundations of Modern Wales 1642–1780*, 1987, 381.

Fox's first Epistle 'To Friends in Wales,' of 1657 makes no direct reference to the country, merely exhorting Friends there to live in the faith, to know Christ and to 'walk in the light of the lamb.'[75] In his second epistle of 1685 he acknowledged the existence of the Wales Yearly Meeting and its epistle, which was

> received and publicly read out in our Yearly Meeting, and well accepted of in love and unity and with the spirit that give it forth. And Friends are very glad to hear, feel, and see your fellowship and unity in the Lord's blessed truth, and your communion in the holy ghost.[76]

Some might make play on the use by Fox of 'our' to describe the gathering in London, as though it were a body from which the Friends of Wales were excluded, but this was not the case. Any reading of Fox's theology highlights the fact that it transcends nationhood except that he was conscious of national sensibilities.

In 1682 the Yearly Meeting for Wales was established, but there are no comments in Fox's journal since it terminates in 1676. It had taken 35 years from the date of Fox's first visit for an all–Wales body to be created, although there had been a half–yearly meeting for Wales but no information as to when it was established. Seemingly the initiative to establish a Yearly Meeting had been taken by Richard Davies, the Welshpool Quaker, who records that at the Yearly Meeting in London in 1681 'it lay upon my mind to move for a yearly meeting in Wales, and after some consideration about it, it was left to friends in Wales to appoint their first yearly meeting.'[77]

The Yearly Meeting was responsible for overseeing the 'sufferings' of persecuted Friends, supporting them and their families practically in their predicament, upholding of the 'testimonies, that is the way Friends led their lives, and translating their faith into practice, the management of property, publications in Welsh and crucially, a concern for the state and life of the

75. G. Fox, *The Works of George Fox*, Vol. 7, Epistle 147, (New York, AMS Press, 1975), 138–139.
76. Ibid., Vol. 8, Epistle 496, 292–93. Emphasis added.
77. Richard Davies, *An Account of the Convincement, Exercises, Services and Travels of that Ancient Servant of the Lord, Richard Davies: comprising some information relative to the spreading of the truth in North Wales*, 1825, 111.

Society in Wales. They were 'more than assemblies for the conduct of routine business … exercising a widespread influence in the districts where the meetings were held.'[78] Like its Irish counterpart these national meetings were not meant to act as autonomous national bodies, but were conceived to represent and reflect national aspirations. In 1699 LYM had made it clear that they were to be only for worship, to strengthen witness and the spiritual community. Braithwaite[79] makes the point by calling them provincial, 'Circular' Yearly Meetings, pointing out that some were established within England. For example in 1691 a meeting for Friends in the west of England, based on Bristol, was inaugurated which met until 1798; in 1698 a meeting for Friends in Cumberland, Westmoreland, Lancashire and Cheshire was established. Wales, by this analysis was no more than a mere region.

The meetings of the Yearly Meeting for Wales were not confined simply to Friends in Wales, and Friends from Shropshire Monthly Meeting contributed fully to its meetings and its finances from around 1693. In 1718, the Yearly Meeting gathered at Shrewsbury and thereafter on eleven occasions met in western Shropshire, the clerkship being held for four periods by Friends from that county. Friends from England held the clerkship for at least 30 years. Whiting surmised that, 'It may be that the Welshmen who had at that time lived an almost entirely agricultural life, considered it a wiser course that a clerical task should be undertaken by men with greater business experience,'[80] men such as Abraham Darby, the iron master, of Coalbrookdale. This dependence on Shropshire Friends, and a comment on the perilous state of Welsh Friends and their disappearance from Merionethshire, is reflected in the fact that when in 1855 the meeting house at Tyddyn y Garreg, Dolgellau was sold the proceeds were assigned to Shropshire MM 'for the use of that meeting,'[81] not that Friends in Shropshire, by that time were any the stronger.

The minutes of the Wales Yearly Meeting offer a glimpse into those matters which exercised Friends in Wales. It concentrated on all the matters

78. E.S. Whiting, 'The Yearly Meeting for Wales 1682–1797,' in the *Journal of Friends Historical Society*, 47, 1, 1955, 67.
79. Braithwaite, *The Second Period*, 1961, 546–548.
80. Whiting, 'The Yearly Meeting', 60
81. Worcestershire Records Office (WRO), 898.2.1303, General Meeting for Herefordshire, Warwickshire and Wales, Minute 5, (M5) 4.4.1855.

defined for it, but sadly was never able to commission any original publications in Welsh, relying totally on translations from the English, this despite pronouncements to the contrary, and their 'failure to produce a regular and substantial corpus of Welsh literature' was in Jenkins' opinion a major factor in their demise.[82] Indeed their publication efforts in 1704 proved an enormous strain on their 'hard–pressed resources'[83] as their minutes confirm.

In the nineteenth century, described as the golden age of Welsh publishing,[84] this failure was even more pronounced. By the late 1880s there were over seventy English weekly and twenty–five Welsh weekly papers published in Wales, although 'targeted primarily at small audiences.'[85] Although each of the Welsh denominations published extensively, none of it was Quaker. The Wesleyan Methodists, for example, brought out their *Eurgrawn Wesleyaidd* in 1809, and the Unitarians, by 1847, were publishing their *Yr Ymofynydd*. By 1889 the Salvation Army were publishing 10,000 copies of *War Cry* in Welsh, although this was to be shortlived.[86] This failure meant that Friends were not identified with the Welsh collective; they did not contribute to its evolution. Literature was an important element in shaping and asserting Welsh identity.[87]

The Welsh yearly meeting originally met in the homes of Friends, but as time went on allowed for public meetings where the Quaker message was preached. The meeting increasingly began to depend on visiting ministers from across the country and abroad, and this was a further reflection of the decline of the Society.

By 1794 there was such a concern about the lowly state of the Yearly Meeting that it asked LYM to provide assistance and advice as to the way forward. LYM of 1795 appointed a committee to visit, and at the Yearly Meeting held at Llandovery in 1797 their minute was clear as to the advice received and the direction to be taken:

> The following answer to our proposition for discontinuing the usual Yearly
> and Quarterly meeting for the Principality and holding in lieu two Half Yearly

---

82. Geraint H. Jenkins, *Literature, Religion and Society in Wales 1660–1730*, 1978, 415.
83. Ibid 412.
84. Huw Walters, *Y Wasg Gyfnodol Gymreig 1735–1900/The Welsh Periodical Press*, 1987.
85. Aled Jones, Press, *Politics and Society: A History of Journalism in Wales*, 1993, 237.
86. Glen Horridge, 'The Salvation Army in Wales' in the *Journal of Welsh Ecclesiastical History*, 6, 1989, 51–70.
87. Emyr Humphreys, *The Taliesin Tradition*, 2000.

Meetings was brought to this meeting from the Yearly Meeting held in London: 'This meeting agrees to the proposition from Wales and leaves it to the adjournment of the Welsh Yearly Meeting to carry it into effect.' Agreeably thereto this meeting is dissolved and the business of the Yearly Meeting as well as that of the Quarterly Meetings for North and South Wales is referred to the Half Yearly Meetings now settled.[88]

The Yearly Meeting for Wales was laid down, having met continuously since 1682, its demise reflecting the gradual decline of the Quakers across the country. Their contraction was to be reflected in further amalgamation of business meetings. Merioneth and Montgomeryshire MMs were amalgamated in 1770, and met last in Llanidloes in 1829, being united that year with Radnorshire MM, as North Wales MM. Radnorshire MM had their doubts and the marriage did not last. Their comment offers insight to the challenges facing the ever–decreasing number of Friends:

> it appears to be the judgement of this Meeting that it cannot promote such an alteration on a review of its present weak state the very deficient attendance of Meetings for discipline by many of its Members and from the distance of the two meetings from each other.[89]

Radnorshire amalgamated with Hereford MM in 1834, as Hereford and Radnor Monthly Meeting (HRMM). In 1829, Pembrokeshire MM was united with Carmarthenshire and Glamorganshire MM, as the South Division of Wales MM, to which Monmouthshire MM was joined when it was laid down in 1836. But even earlier the activities of Friends in North Wales had come under the discipline of Cheshire Quarterly Meeting. Money collected at Rhuddallt meeting had been conveyed to it for example in 1681 and the marriage of Tryall Rider, a Wrexham Friend in 1688 recorded by it.[90] After 1742 Friends in Flintshire and Denbighshire transferred their membership to Cheshire. This must have affected the vitality of the Yearly Meeting.

88. Glamorgan Record Office, (GRO), Cardiff, GB 0214 DSF. Minute Book of Wales Yearly Meeting, 21/22/8.1797.
89. Powys County Archives Office, (PCAO), North Wales Monthly Meeting Minute Book 8, 8th month 1828.
90. Cheshire Records Office, (CRO) EFC1/1, Minute Book Cheshire and Nantwich Quarterly Meeting, 1676–1704.

The new Half Yearly Meeting met from 1798 until 1831, when it became a Quarterly Meeting, and united with Herefordshire and Worcester Quarterly Meeting as the General Meeting for Herefordshire, Worcestershire and Wales. This in 1869 became Western Quarterly Meeting (WQM)[91] – but did not include north Wales. In that same year Gloucester and Nailsworth Monthly Meeting joined this new Meeting, extending its area and prompting the change of name to a neutral geographical entity.[92]

WQM became the body that by default took on the wider responsibilities of the former Wales National Meeting but did not function as an all–Wales body. By 1869 the name of Wales as a national entity had been expunged from the Yearly Meeting nomenclature, except for the residual reference in the name of the South Division of Wales Monthly Meeting.

North Wales, during most of the late eighteenth and nineteenth centuries, was an area almost devoid of Quakers. There was probably a meeting in Ruthun from the mid–1840s but it was discontinued in 1866, even though in 1863 it had 24 members.[93] It had come under the authority of Hardshaw West Monthly Meeting, originally part of Chester and Staffordshire Quarterly Meeting[94] before it transferred to Lancashire and Cheshire Quarterly Meeting. In 1893 when a meeting was established in Colwyn Bay, to service it as a popular watering and retiring centre frequented by Quakers especially from the north west of England.[95] The interests of north Wales, c.1858, came under the care of Hardshaw West Monthly Meeting which was then centred on Warrington.

The perambulations of changed business meetings in Wales reflected the weak state of the Society in Wales. The demise being due to many factors, as several authors have outlined – the emigration of many able leaders to Pennsylvania, the lack of missionary zeal amongst those who remained in Wales, and the failure to attract the monoglot Welsh to their meetings, whilst the Methodist revival had an impact particularly on the isolated Friends in the rural areas.[96] Iorwerth Peate comments that whilst the Independents and

91. WRO 898.2.1303, M4, 18.3.1869, Minute Book Western Quarterly Meeting
92. WRO 898.2.1303, WQM, M4, 13.10.1869.
93. Lancashire Record Office (LRO), FRL 1/1/13/1, Records Lancashire and Cheshire Quarterly Meeting (LCQM).
94. Jones, 'William Jones: Quaker', 1990, 406.
95. LRO, FRL 1/1/1/41. LCQM M4, 15/16.4.1896.
96. See Allen, 'The Society of,' 1999; J. G. Williams, 'The Quakers of Merioneth during the

Baptists, 'espoused much of the Methodist theology and indeed aspects of its church government and while they tended to become 'methodized' the Quakers in Wales were squeezed out of existence.'[97] The fact that Friends settled increasingly in the towns, middle class, commercial in attitude and effort, also meant that place and class progressively alienated them from the greater part of the population.[98]

Fox referred to Scotland and Ireland, but not Wales, in several of his epistles, recognising their particular national status. In 1683, addressing Friends in Carolina, he reflected that in 'Ireland, Scotland, Holland, Germany and Dantzyck, we hear that Friends are in peace and quietness.'[99] All three countries were given some recognition under the umbrella of LYM, but it served implicitly as the all–encompassing body for England, where the majority of Quakers lived. The dominance of England within LYM meant that it came to exercise itself as an English entity, although never expressed as such. The nomenclature LYM shielded it from the vagaries of national nomenclature and aspirations. Overall, however, the development of the Society in all four countries followed the same trajectory.

What then was the condition of the Society in Wales by the mid–nineteenth century, did 'Truth prosper' amongst them? This was the query first addressed to the YM in 1682. It was used by the early Quakers as 'an alternative word for 'Gospel' (and) developed a special resonance describing their personal faith and its realization in their lives,'[100] it was a distinctive appellation to describe both faith and behaviour, which was to be reflected in their lives amongst themselves and in the wider community.

The Religious Census of 1851 provided a general picture of the state of every denomination in Britain. Whatever may be said about the its technical weaknesses it was

---

Seventeenth Century,' in *Journal of the Merioneth Historical and Record Society*, VIII (Two parts) 1978, 122–156 and 1979, 312–339.

97. Iorwerth C. Peate, *Traditions and Folk Life: A Welsh View*, 1972, 84–85.
98. Sheila Wright, *Friends in York: The Dynamics of Quaker Revival 1780–1860*, 1995), 109–112. Isichei's thesis in her *Victorian Quakers*, particularly, 171–181 pursues the same point.
99. Fox, *The Works*, Epistle 386, Vol. 8, 1975, 234.
100. Rosemary Moore, *The Light in their Consciences: The Early Quakers in Britain 1646–1666*, 2000, 82.

for all its faults, … a valuable source of information. Recent historians, whilst not failing to expound its inherent drawbacks, have defended its essential accuracy and usefulness.[101]

The census did not give membership figures for each place of worship, but provided a picture of the number of worshippers in attendance on the designated Sunday, and the seating places available to worshippers ('sittings'). It was vulnerable to subjective interpretation because of the way information was recorded and collated. The census revealed that a large section of the population did not attend any place of worship – some 60%, and that close to half the worshippers were not Anglicans. Wales emerging as 'having religious characteristics which often set it apart from England'[102] with seating for 75% of its population, and an average attendance of 34% compared to 24% for both England and Wales.[103] In Wales, 87% of attendees were Nonconformist, 9% Anglican and the chapels made up 71% of all places of worship.[104]

The census provides an independent overview of LYM's lowly state. Snell and Ell remark that the figures show a denomination in decline, and that their provision was not under pressure anywhere. The census recorded 372 Quaker places of worship in 265 of 624 enumeration districts. In Wales there were 6.5 Quaker 'sittings' for every attendee, and there was a distinctive mismatch between total sittings and attendances amongst them, 'when one examines attendance data, it is worth emphasising that, compared to other denominations with a similar geographical coverage, the Quakers were weak almost everywhere'.[105] Their decline across Britain had challenged the Society for some time, as one Quaker observed in 1859,

In 1761 London Yearly Meeting deputed a large committee to visit all the

101. T. Larsen, *Friends of Religious Equality: Nonconformist Politics in Mid–Victorian England*, 1999, 20.
102. K.D.M Snell and Paul S. Ell, *Rival Jerusalems: The Geography of Victorian Religion*, 2000, 18.
103. Evans, *A History of Wales*, 1989, 219
104. Ieuan Gwynedd Jones and David Williams, *The Religious Census of 1851: a calendar of returns relating to Wales, South Wales*, Vol. 1, 1976) xxiii.
105. Snell *et al*, *Rival Jerusalems*, 111.

meetings throughout England, in the hope of reviving the health of the body, which had long showed signs of debility and disease.[106]

In 1859 J.S. Rowntree's essay on the causes of decline was published which influenced thinking and analysis, and eased the way to reform of practice and procedure.

Table 1: Religious Census 1851 from Wales: Attendance at worship: Religious Society of Friends[107]

	a.m.	p.m.
Denbighshire:		
Ruthun	4	4
Glamorganshire:		
Cardiff	5	3
Neath	40	16
Swansea	22	1
Pembrokeshire:		
Haverfordwest	5	Nil
Radnorshire:		
Pales	16	Nil
Presteigne	23	7
Old Radnor	7	7
Hay	3	Nil

The Census for Wales (Table 1) shows one Quaker meeting in north Wales, Ruthun, none in Anglesey, Breconshire, Caernarfonshire, Flintshire, Merionethshire or Montgomeryshire, the latter once a stronghold, had lost the Llanwddyn meeting by 1749, and by 1791, Dolobran was no more.[108] There were eight meetings in the rest of the country. In these nine meetings, there were a total offering of 824 'sittings' but in the morning there were 125 worshipping with Friends and 50 in the evening. In this context, Williams's description of the Religious Society of Friends in Glamorganshire is apt, applicable across Wales, not just for the 18th century but also for the greater part of the nineteenth century:

106. *TF*, 8th month, 1859, 138.
107. Jones and Williams, *The Religious Census of 1851* Vol. 1 (1976) and *North Wales*, Vol. 2 (1981).
108. Melvin Humphreys, *The Crisis of Community, Montgomeryshire, 1680–1815*, 1996, 174.

The 18th century forms a depressing episode in the history of Glamorganshire Quakers. All the older meetings except one had dwindled onto extinction. [They were] seized by a growing paralysis which showed every sign of proving fatal as it had already been elsewhere ... Quakers in South Wales appeared to be a completely spent force.[109]

A useful comparator of Quaker strength is that in Swansea 36 Jews worshipped at the synagogue on the relevant Saturday morning[110] and 157 Unitarians at their Sunday gathering.[111] A later Quaker analysis of the census highlighted the many decaying meetings, with forty having a morning attendance of five, three meetings only had one Friend, one meeting had two; 'Such records tell a pathetic story of faithfulness amid discouragement,'[112]

In 1859 Swansea Meeting had been visited by a Nonconformist minister. His publication offers an unique, if not the only description of a Quaker meeting in Wales by an outsider at that time. His observations were probably a true reflection of all the other meetings in the country. He saw a totally silent meeting adhering to the quietist tradition, such that,

In the small Swansea congregation there have been no preachers for a long time; consequently, in accordance with the principles that acceptable worship may be performed in silence the Quaker meetings have been conducted for years without speech and ceremony.[113]

There were about twenty present, all middle–aged and elderly, the men wearing their hats, 'then we all sat as still as death. Not a sound was heard. No one coughed.'[114] The visitor during his stay composed, in his mind, a sermon on the nature of silence; the pamphlet echoing the writer's sadness at a lost vibrancy.

Each year since 1737, when the Yearly Meeting codified and regularised the nature of its membership, each Quarterly Meeting was expected to

109. Williams, 'The Society of Friends,' 1950, 106.
110. Jones and Williams, *The Religious Census*, Vol. 1, 261.
111. Ibid., 263.
112. *TF*, 23.9.1904, 620.
113. *Sundays in Wales: Visits to the places of worship of the Quakers, the Unitarians, the Roman Catholics, and the Jews by a Week–Day Preacher*, n.a., 1859, 6.
114. Ibid., 7.

collate statistics on the number of members in all their meetings. Table 2 provides the breakdown of membership for a sample years between 1862 and 1897 of meetings in Wales. Added also are figures of membership across the Yearly Meeting, reflecting the same downward trend. The jump in membership between 1879 and 1897 is explored in the following chapter, reflecting successful attempts by the Yearly Meeting to reverse the decline.

Of the eight meetings in Wales in the 1851 census, by 1862 only four were extant. By 1862 Walton had opened and in all probability those worshipping at Presteigne and Old Radnor had transferred there. There was still only the one meeting in north Wales, Ruthun with its six male and one female member,[115] and a solitary Quaker, at Milford, represented west Wales. By 1862 there were 111 Quakers in Wales, and by 1867 the figure had dropped to 74. By 1897 the numbers had risen with 313 members in eight meetings, but by then of the 1851 meetings five had disappeared to be replaced by three new ones: Colwyn Bay, Aberystwyth and Llandrindod, the latter having the care of a new mission meeting at Llanyre. Pales had Penybont added to it, as a satellite or mission meeting. In south–east Wales, Newport was new.

Table 2: Tabular Returns from Quarterly Meetings regarding Wales[116]

Meeting	1862	1865	1866	1867	1873	1879	1897
Pales	2	2	2	2	7	46	60
Walton	12	5	4	4	–	–	–
Aberystwyth	–	–	–	–	–	–	9
Llan'dod & Llanyre	–	–	–	–	–	–	60
Swansea	18	13	8	8	4	8	37
Neath	34	41	35	34	57	43	20
Milford	1	1	1	1	1	–	–
Newport	13	10	7	5	3	11	27
Cardiff	–	–	–	–	12	29	81
No meeting	24	20	17	20	15	5	10
Total	104	82	73	74	99	142	295
Total: WQM	321	303	291	284	443	615	829
Ruthun	7	–	–	–	–	–	–
Colwyn Bay	–	–	–	–	–	–	18
Wales	111	82	73	74	99	142	313
Yearly Meeting	13809	13756	13786	13815	14085	14894	16854

115. LRO, FRL 1/1/13/1.
116. WRO, 898.2 1303 collated from Quarterly Meeting returns for the relevant years.

Compared to the other churches in Wales the 1897 Quaker membership figure of 313 verged on the insignificant. The *Royal Commission on the Church of England in Wales*[117] estimated that in Wales in 1905 there were 193,081 Anglican communicants and 550,566 Nonconformists, of whom 270 were Quakers. The total population of Wales was 2,012,917– Quakers then made up 0.05% of the dissenting population, and 0.01% of the total population. The Welsh Calvinistic Methodists by 1898 had forty–one chapels in Liverpool, ten in London and fifteen in Manchester, with a combined membership of 12,593, and 20,260 attenders or 'listeners'. Thus in England they had almost as many as the membership of LYM.[118]

It is significant that there were twenty–four Quakers who were not attached to any meeting in 1862, a fifth of the membership. In 1863 two Friends lived in Aberdare,[119] two in Cardiff and Friends were living in Cowbridge and Llantrisant.[120] The editor of *The Friend* commented on Thomas Rees' entry regarding the Quakers in his Nonconformity in Wales, that he had not taken the trouble to inform himself accurately on their numbers. Rees stating that there were in 1860 six or seven hundred Quakers in Wales, 'about five or six times the correct figures.'[121] In October 1871, WQM received a report from a committee appointed to visit its meetings. Its comments about meetings in South Wales was not surprising, recognising that things were not well:

> the only meeting of much size in Wales is Neath. Here there are between forty and fifty members. We have been comforted by the love in which they are united and by the evidence of care for the children who form a large proportion of the Meeting … We regret that Swansea meeting is so reduced and the circumstances under which it is maintained.[122]

Cardiff they noted had several members, but meeting for worship was held there but once a month, under the care of a committee, with no formal

---

117. Royal Commission on the Church of England and other Religious Bodies in Wales and Monmouthshire 1910, Report, Vol. 1, 20, Cmd. 5432.
118. Figures derived from denominational year–books quoted in *Y Cymro*, 6.1.1898.
119. *TF*, 1st month, 1863, 9.
120. *TF*, 8th month, 1863, 188.
121. *TF*, 1st month, 1862, 18–19.
122. WQM, Report, 18.10.1871.

meeting for church affairs recognised by the Monthly Meeting. By December 1874 a preparative meeting[123] was re–established in both Cardiff and Newport.[124]

The use of the word 'Wales' in this report has significance since it indicates that WQM still saw itself as the body responsible for the whole of Wales, in reality taking on the mantle of the former Yearly and Half–Yearly Meetings for Wales, of which in essence it was the inheritor body. In June 1874 it confirmed its care of graveyards at Llwyndu, Merionethshire, and Esgairgoch and Llangurig, in Montgomeryshire, even though there were at that time no meetings in either county. It was only in December 1891 that WQM formally consented to the arrangement 'that the counties of Caernarvonshire, Anglesey, Denbighshire and Flintshire be included in Lancashire and Cheshire Quarterly Meeting.'[125] This followed discussion at Meeting for Sufferings who minuted that 'care should be taken that every part of the country in included within the boundaries of some Monthly Meeting.'[126] Thus, by 1891, Wales was officially split between two Quarterly Meetings, and the decision formalised what was a *de facto* situation.

The impact of dissent and nonconformity, especially following the Methodist revival,[127] had cemented the relation between religion, language, text and national identity in Wales. Nonconformity provided the basis for Welsh social and political development during the nineteenth century, giving 'Welsh society its own characteristic ethos.'[128] Its influence was deeper than its politics, supplying 'much of its popular culture,'[129] but it was not a 'solid phalanx,'[130] denominational differences prevailed, but it was an adherence that gave many a primary sense of identity,[131] forming 'a vibrant Christian counter culture.'[132] It gave to Wales the means whereby its national

123. A worshipping group of Friends were designated as 'allowed' and 'recognised' by a Monthly Meeting, but did not conduct business, until it became a 'preparative meeting,' a group that carried out business, preparing members for a forthcoming MM.
124. WQM, M4, 9.12.1874.
125. WQM, M10, 9.12.1891.
126. WQM, M13, 16.9.1891.
127. See for example, E. Wyn James, ' 'The New Birth of a People': Welsh language and Identity and the Welsh Methodists, c.1740–1820,' in *Religion and National Identity: Wales and Scotland* c.1700–2000, Robert Pope, ed., 2001, 14–42.
128. Morgan, *Wales in British*, 1991, 13.
129.E.T. Davies, *Religion and Society in the Nineteenth Century*, 1981, 64.
130. E. T. Davies, *Religion in the Industrial*, 50.
131. D.W. Bebbington, *Victorian Nonconformity*, 1992, 21.
132. Ibid., 81.

identity was sharpened;[133] particularly since Welsh nonconformity was also overwhelmingly Welsh speaking, and without the use of Welsh there were no converts.[134] One result was that the chapel, in the popular imagination, became a representation of things Welsh, often inimical in its domination, affecting popular culture and recreation. Quakers belonged outside this experience.

The new industrial society of nineteenth century Wales was thus strongly Nonconformist, and in the first part of the nineteenth century, 'essentially working class in character'[135] an aspect that further alienated the Quakers given the dominant bourgeois nature of their membership.

An important backdrop to this relationship had been the publication in 1847 of the *Reports of the Commissioners of Enquiry into the State of Education in Wales*, which became known as the 'Treachery of the Blue Books'. They were seen as a slur on Nonconformity, critical of the use of Welsh and of monoglot Wales. The reports were perceived as an attack on Welsh nationhood, becoming tools for Welsh radical and nationalist politicians. Their publication

> marked a watershed in officially recognized images of the Welsh people and language, and of Welsh people's images of themselves which they might wish to reject but could not ignore. It has, directly or indirectly, made a major contribution in the shaping of such images and attitudes towards what it meant and what it means to be Welsh, and as such has played a significant role in the process of construction of a modern Welsh identity.[136]

One of the principal critics of the reports was Henry Richard, who as secretary of the Peace Society, was closely allied to Friends and their activities. Friends, however, made no public comments on the reports.

In national life the tussle between Nonconformity and Anglicanism served as a vital backdrop to much that dominated Welsh politics in the

---

133. D.W. Bebbington, 'Religion and National Feeling in 19th Century Wales and Scotland,' in *Studies in Church History: Religion and National Identity*, Vol. 18, Stuart Mews ed., 1982, 489–503.
134. Hugh McLeod, *Religion and the People of Western Europe, 1789–1989*, 1997, 42–43.
135. Davies, *Religion in the Industrial*, 18.
136. Gwyneth Tyson Roberts, *The Language of the Blue Books: The Perfect Instrument of Empire*, 1998, 3.

period, expressed especially by the campaign for disestablishment. In this shaping what was implied was that the Anglicans were identified as being 'non' if not anti–Welsh in their attitudes; an analysis that served the Nonconformist religious–political axis well, although an anti–Anglican rhetoric at the parish level was far less confrontational.[137] This hostile representation of Anglicanism is unjust given that many Anglicans in Wales supported disestablishment. Quakers identified with this objective but their voice was subdued. Whereas many Anglicans showed their devotion to Wales and its culture[138] the same cannot be said for the Quakers, who lacked any authoritative Welsh national figure or voice. Yet, the contribution of individuals within the life of the Society in Wales cannot be overlooked, since by their personalities and presence they ensured that the Society was not totally divorced from Welsh public life. They had their roles and reputations in their own locales, were 'public personae' in civic life and contributed to the ethos of public service.[139]

By the nineteenth century Friends were firmly established within society, assimilated and accepted by it, their 'otherness' and peculiarity a thing of the past. They were now part of the establishment. They accepted their responsibilities and allegiance to the state. Over time they became more firmly located and identified within the English setting, if only because this is where the majority of the members of LYM resided. Its language of administration and discipline was English. The Celtic countries were part of its periphery, not by any design, but because the numbers of Quakers who resided there was so small. Dublin Yearly Meeting retained an element of 'independence,' but by 1869, other than in the title of the South Division of Wales Monthly Meeting, the name of Wales had been obliterated from the organisational structures of the Yearly Meeting.

LYM Meeting had no need to question the problematic of British identity, because it did not impinge on its collective awareness. Similarly, the problematic of Wales was subsumed into the overall activity of the Yearly

137. Mathew Cragoe, 'Anticlericalism and Politics in Mid–Victorian Wales,' in *Anticlericalism in Britain c.1500–1914*, Nigel Aston and Matthew Cragoe eds., 2000, 179.
138. See Jenkins, *Hanes Cymru yn y Bedwaredd*, 1933, 113.
139. Julie Light, '…mere seekers of fame'? Personalities, power and politics in the small town: Pontypool and Bridgend, c.1860–95,' in *Urban History*, 32, 1, 2005, 88–99.

Meeting with no issues to be addressed; what was paramount was its own vitality. The question of what and where was Wales has been difficult even for those captured within it, shaped as it was by images of coal mines, choirs and chapels. Gwyn Alf Williams's question as to 'When Was Wales?' concerned as he was to discover a part of himself, solving the conundrum of being Welsh, within the complex canvass of Britain, explored an invented people, who constructed themselves repeatedly against the odds.[140] 'Welshness' was as elusive even within Wales.[141]

The Quakers were circumscribed in their focus on national identity within Britain because they felt that they had a greater calling to their divine mission and the needs of humanity, caught as they were in their testimonies, whose source 'was the Spirit of Christ ... a real and dynamic force which had a number of names: Inward Light, Seed, Grace or Word of God.'[142] These were powerful drivers for undertaking pioneering relief work, where nationality or political identity was irrelevant. In this context they turned to scripture and saw that all are one in Christ. In such a context national identity was irrelevant with little need for any overt nationalistic expression.

Nevertheless, in the nineteenth century, as many in the Yearly Meeting prospered and began to involve themselves in the political and institutional life of Britain, their patriotism was demonstrable. An interesting illustrator being the way *The Friend* reported and gave space, in several editions over the years, to the number of Quakers elected to Parliament. Information as to political affiliation was omitted, and the reports can be understood as a 'roll of honour' of the commitment of Quakers to their country.[143] For October 1900 the publication noted that seven members had been elected to parliament; the report adding triumphantly, 'Besides the forgoing, at least four other members are ex–members of the Society of Friends.' In 1904 the magazine published short articles by Quaker MPs on parliamentary life, listing 34 Friends who had served, or were serving as members, plus another 26 who had been closely associated with Friends, noting that 'Of these latter

140. William, *When Was Wales?* 1985, 6.
141. Dai Smith, *Wales: A Question of History*, 1999.
142. Dale Hess, *A Brief Background to the Quaker Peace Testimony*, 1992, 1.
143. *TF*, 26.10.1900, 693.

it would be almost impracticable to make an exhaustive list.'[144] This demonstrable patriotism, if not smugness, is surely to be seen as nationalistic expression.

The problematic of Welsh identity within the context of Britain, was never an issue in the early formative years of the Society. By the mid–nineteenth century Quaker presence in Wales had been so seriously eroded, that it was almost invisible. At a time when Welsh national aspirations were being rekindled, by a distinctive political agenda affecting the British political establishment there was to be no distinctive Quaker witness. For LYM issues of political and national identity remained as an unspoken discourse in its organisational life, and explicit expression of it was avoided, unless it was tied to Queen and empire.

The Quaker understanding of leadership also meant that no single Quaker could dominate and shape LYM's activities, thus it never produced a face or voice to represent its interests in Wales. Its public interface and voice was heard in collective witness and in its philanthropic and humanitarian endeavours; activity that was recognised by other denominations within Wales. The Rev. Herber Evans, Congregational minister at Caernarfon, taking the chair of the Congregational Union in City Temple, London in 1892, remarked in his first address to that body, that the Quakers were noted for 'their service not to a sect but to humanity.'[146]

LYM's response to matters Welsh was largely mute. Welsh political issues hardly touched its life, although disestablishment was allied to its view of the role of the church. Its attempts to recover and strengthen its presence in Wales, through its Home Mission Committee, was never a national co-ordinated effort, and paled when compared to the efforts of the other denominations. Given the importance of the 1904–05 Welsh Religious Revival to Christians internationally, its response to that outpouring, representing as it did a hoped for rebirth, was generally distant. All serve as prisms through which the activities of the Society can be viewed and examined.

Quakers in Britain exist as a denomination reliant on a membership without benefit of clergy, its visibility and tenaciousness is reflected in the contribution of those associated with it, without benefit of a visible, prominent

144. *TF*, 9.12.1904, 809–821.
145. See John Ormerod Greenwood, *Quaker Encounters: Friends in Relief*, Vol. I, 1975.
146. *Y Genedl*, 25.5.1892. (*'eu gwasanaeth nid i sect ond i ddynoliaeth'*).

leadership. Their theological understanding of leadership is that it is spiritual, with authority derived from unity with the leadings of the Spirit of God discovered within the worshipping group – reliant on the authority of the inward light. Leadership does not rest with specific people, 'The Headship of Christ in His Church necessarily precluded the idea of any body humanly constituted appointing any human being to be the head over any section of the Church,'[147] Leadership is dependent on the way the worshipping group, in unity, discerns the divine will and recognises the direction to be taken:

> not deciding affairs by the greater vote, or the number of men but ... by hearing, and determining every matter coming before you in love, coolness, gentleness and dear unity.[148]

Theoretically then the Society would not expect individuals to dominate within it. Inevitably however some had greater influence than others.

Isichei was clear from her examination of Victorian Quakers in session at Yearly Meeting that governance was determined by those who could afford and had the time to attend. Consequently decisions relied on a minority especially those 'whose power was symbolically indicated by the fact that they sat next to the Clerk's table, the emblem of authority.'[149] Such a minority was principally composed of middle–aged men, a gerontocratic elite,[150] principally those born into membership. She highlights the disparity between theory and practice. Decision–making and leadership depended on attendance, determined by means and leisure time, such that the nature of governance and its outcomes were skewed. Kennedy's analysis of the influence of evangelical Friends in the Yearly Meeting up to around 1888, hints at the same phenomenon, as he examines their efforts in shaping the agenda of the Yearly Meeting.[151]

---

147. TF, 11.11.1892, 746.
148. Edward Burroughs in *Christian Life: Faith and Thought in the Society of Friends*, 1923, 104.
149. Isichei, *Victorian*, 1970, 80.
150. Ibid., 81.
151. Thomas C. Kennedy, 'An Angry God or a Reasonable Faith: The British Society of Friends,' in *Journal of the Friends' Historical Society*, 57, 2, 1995. 183–198.

There were hardly any individuals from Wales who influenced the Yearly Meeting and the public face of Quakers in Wales was subdued. There were some individual Quakers in Wales who made a noteworthy contribution, although by today their names are largely forgotten. Their contribution balanced an otherwise unremarkable scene; Henry Tobit Evans, a lone Ceredigion Quaker, who was actively involved for a time in Welsh politics but an important journalist; Hercules Davies Phillips, a convinced Radnorshire Quaker journalist, who laboured principally in that county for most of his life as a Home Missionary, and who ensured that the Quaker presence, in that rural county, was robustly maintained, and finally, John Edward Southall, an English Quaker, domiciled in Wales, publisher, whose particular love for Wales and its language had an almost spiritual fervour, expressive of his own unique Quaker life. These were men who were important in their own spheres but who achieved limited prominence nationally and even within LYM they were minor figures. Their contribution deserves some attention. Sadly, no women Quakers made any mark on Welsh national life, and this was consistent with the profile women had within the society during the period at least in its public face. Women were equal in the ministry, and only became eligible in 1896 for appointment to Meeting for Sufferings, the executive committee of the Yearly Meeting, and it was only in 1906 that the separate Men and Women's Yearly Meetings were united into the one body, thus eliminating male domination of the instruments of governance.

In 1882 Frederick J. Gibbins addressed WQM. His views are illustrative of the issues and of the weakness of the Society in Wales. He was of the opinion that between 1800 and 1875 only 25 Friends had come into membership by convincement within South Wales Monthly Meeting (SWMM), and that the Society's fortunes in south Wales had, and did, rely on Friends coming into Wales to settle and work, and that there was 'scarcely a member whose grandparents were Welsh Friends.' The Monthly Meeting was of a 'migratory character' with no members over 25 years of age who had belonged to Friends during the whole of their lives. He noted that:

> Friends could not now get an audience among Welsh speaking people, as there are not now more than two Friends in South Wales who can speak the language. It is often said by those who understand both languages that they only tolerate an English address whilst they wait impatiently for the Welsh

which is a language of far grander sound to contain such greater fullness and variety of expression.[152]

Marwick came to the same conclusion in relation to Scotland, that growth there in the late nineteenth century 'seems explicable ... partly to immigration from England, probably outbalancing emigration.'[153]

Therein lies another clue to the complexity of denominational vibrancy: their roots in general society. Most Quakers coming into Wales would have been predominantly middle–class, petit bourgeois, reflecting the trend in their overall membership across the whole of Britain. This, alongside a linguistic barrier, would have set them apart from the majority of people in Wales, although they attracted some working class members but never in any noticeable number.

This issue of class needs to be understood alongside the concept of *gwerin* – 'all of the people, the folk,'[154] with its 'resonance ... in its undifferentiated nature, akin to the German idea of *volk*.'[155] It had become a marker of identity for the Welsh utilised, for example, by the Welsh Methodist leaders, and in the 1868 election as a marker victory over their Tory oppressors, with the emergence of *y genedl werinol* – (the nation of the *gwerin*). Here, in the Welsh, the word *gwerin* has become an adjective, such that the nation is something more than just its people.[156] This did not mean that the Welsh were classless, but *gwerin* became an 'idealistic salute ... (a) ... mobilizing myth for the middle class which had climbed out of it and found its identity.'[157] The *gwerin* was not a class, to be distinguished from the proletarian working classes, it was seen as an unifying force. *Gwerin* served as a powerful collective metaphor upon which much of the cultural nationalism of the Victorian and Edwardian relied, and which would have resonated with many people in Wales. It is doubtful that Friends would have been attuned to its potency.

152. National Library of Wales (NLW), MS 4859C/9.
153. William H. Marwick, 'Quakers in early twentieth century Scotland,' in the *Journal of the Friends' Historical Society*, 52, 1968–71, 211.
154. Iorwerth C. Peate, 'Diwylliant Gwerin,' in the *Transactions of the Honourable Society of Cymmrodorion*, 1938, 241–250.
155. Paul Chambers and Andrew Thompson, 'Coming to terms with the Past: Religion and Identity in Wales,' in *Social Compass*, 52, 3, September 2005, fn 1, 350.
156. Frank Price Jones, 'Gwerin Cymru,' in *Radicaliaeth a'r Werin Gymreig yn y Bedwaredd Ganrif ar Bymtheg*, 1975, 203.
157. Williams, *When Was Wales?* 1985, 152.

The Quakers in Wales were not then, like the other Nonconformist denominations in the country, embedded in Welsh life or imagination, and were largely divorced from it.

Chapter 2
Quakers and Welsh Politics,
circa 1860–1918

The renaissance of Welsh national identity as it was being reshaped within Imperial Britain is reflected in its politics. This renaissance underpinned the national life of Wales, particularly from the 1860s. The way that LYM responded to that development gives some indication as to how it saw Wales and Welsh issues, providing a gauge of its sensitivity to both. Denominations are not political bodies, and yet within them there will be diverse views where 'subjectivity and the social order are intricately bound up.'[1] Hence, locating LYM within the *politics* – those aspects of life, which relate to the establishment of social order and day-to-day decision-making – and the political – the frame of reference within which all this happens, and which defines those areas of life, which are not politics[2] – is important.

The disestablishment of the Anglican Church in Wales, the impact of the Education Act 1902, the 1881 Sunday Closing Act Wales are elements which are illustrative of how different Wales was politically, and that its politics deserved attention. These three issues were tied strongly to Welsh nonconformity, such that its effect on Welsh life should not be overlooked. Industrial unrest in Wales overshadowed the politics, and Welsh pacifist activity during the First World War, was also a harbinger of change in the political landscape.

Morgan sees the Welsh political revival emerging in the middle decades of the nineteenth century, highlighting the early 1880s as the time when this acquired a robustness which impacted on the national imperial scene,[3] to

---

1. Jenny Edkins, *Poststructuralist and International Relations: Bringing the Political Back In*, 1999, 7.
2. Ibid., 2–3.
3. Morgan, *Rebirth*, 1981, 90–122.

which Wales contributed enthusiastically.[4] The election of 1868 saw the beginnings of the 'Liberal Ascendancy,'[5] when Nonconformists began to permeate the electoral system, and the radical element within the Liberal Party eroded the hold of its Whiggish element, as political power shifted away from the gentry.[6] According to Jenkins this was the point at which the three forces of liberalism, nonconformity and nationalism effectively merged, 'to create a set of political assumptions and commonplaces.'[7]

Dissent shaped Liberal party politics, so that in its Welsh context, chapel and liberal politics became effectively fused. This nonconformity was radical only in so much as it reflected the aspirations of that constituency. It was not based on a liberal theology abandoning the 'peripheral elements of faith to make it more attractive to modern man'[8] but became so. For R. Tudur Jones, however, such developments allowed uncertainty and secularism to erode the Welsh nonconformist hegemony, introducing a philosophy 'that would not recognise the rights of religion over any part of life;'[9] a process that, through a burgeoning educational system, undermined the language of demonstrative faith – Welsh – the influence of England's culture threatened both the nationhood of Wales and its Christianity. Wales in the 1870s, like England, entered a 'spiritual tunnel,'[10] as its intellectual leaders embraced influences that dulled its Christian life and culture, deepening the chasm between them. What was unique to Wales was the way the language was affected as religious adherence declined.[11]

---

4. Aled Jones and Bill Jones, 'The Welsh World and the British Empire, *circa* 1851–1939' in *The British World: Diaspora, Culture and Identity*, Carl Bridge and Kent Federovich, eds., 2002, 57-81

5. Morgan, *Rebirth*, 1981, Ch. 2.

6. Morgan, *Wales in British Politics*, 1991, 38-39.

7. Jenkins, *A History of Modern Wales*, 1992, 302.

8. Steve Bruce, *A House Divided: Protestantism, schism and secularisation*, 1990, 117.

9. R. Tudur Jones, *Ffydd ac Argyfwng Cenedl* (Faith and the Crisis of Nation), 1982, 12. ('*blagurai seciwlariaeth, sef yr athroniaeth na fynnai gydnabod hawl crefydd ar unrhyw ddarn o fywyd.*')

10. Ibid., 17. ('*i'r twnnel ysbrydol.*')

11. See D. Densil Morgan, 'The Welsh Language and Religion,' in 'Let's Do Out Best for the Ancient Tongue:' *The Welsh Language in the Twentieth Century*, Geraint H. Jenkins, Mari A. Williams, eds., 2000, 371–96. A bleaker analysis is provided by Robert Smith, "'*Cadw'r Iaith yw Cadw Crefydd Cymru:' Yr Enwadau Ymneilltuol a'r Iaith Gymraeg*," 1918-1939, in *Llen Cymru*, 25, 2002, 105–29.

In political terms common interests and themes persisted. Even if spiritual vigour was being undermined a new type of political leadership emerged as the nationalist and radical wings within the Liberal Party merged with the nonconformist agenda particularly in the 1880s.

The 1874 General Election temporarily challenged the Liberal ascendancy when Disraeli took over as Prime Minister, and Welsh matters became more 'tranquil.'[12] Emyr Williams sees the1886 election as the crucial turning point, when 'henceforth Welsh nationalism would provide a framework for negotiating the demands of Welsh Liberalism with … the Liberal party in the UK,'[13] particularly with regard to disestablishment. In effect this is the point at which a Welsh mandate asserted itself within the political system, and nonconformity made its demands.

By the 1890s the campaign for Welsh Home Rule, pursued by the 'Cymru Fydd'[14] movement, provided for a far sharper political agenda with its objectives

> to facilitate the attainment of a National Legislature for Wales, with full control over all purely Welsh business, and a Welsh Executive responsible to it and the Imperial Parliament, where Wales would still be represented.[15]

The demise of 'Cymru Fydd' could be interpreted as the failure of the nationalist mandate, but also its phoenix. Its aspirations are reflected in the career of Lloyd George, epitomising the hopes of many in Wales, as for example in the matter of social justice for the language, which some Quakers such as John Edward Southall would have totally endorsed.[16]

Nevertheless, the debate over home rule amongst Welsh Liberals proved acrimonious and fractious. One Cardiff Alderman, Robert Bird, a shipping magnate, and prominent member of the United Methodist Free Church, who was no stranger to controversy since he opposed the Boer War and lost the Liberal candidature for Cardiff as a result, declared that,

12. Morgan, *Wales in British*, 1991, 39.
13. Emyr Wyn Williams, 'Liberalism in Wales and the Politics of Welsh Home Rule 1886–1910' in *Bulletin of the Board of Celtic Studies*, 37, 1990, 191–207.
14. 'Wales will be' but in English was often referred to as 'Young Wales.' See Dewi Rowland Hughes, *Cymru Fydd*, 2006.
15. *Manifesto of the Cymry Fydd Society* (Welsh National Association), n.d. (*circa* 1888).
16. See Emyr Wyn Price, *David Lloyd George*, 2006.

We will not submit to the domination of Welsh ideas ... Throughout South Wales, from Swansea to Newport, there were thousands of Englishmen, as true Liberals ... who would object to the ideas and principles, which Lloyd George has enunciated.[17]

Not surprisingly he reflected the attitudes from the more cosmopolitan anglicised Welsh districts, those areas where the Quakers had their meetings, although there is no evidence that they contributed to this debate, even if many of them might have identified with the 'English' ethnic reference. When Bird stood for election in 1883 for the Roath Ward, one of his nominees was a prominent Cardiff Quaker, Arthur Sessions.[18]

The shift in the Welsh political debate in the 1890s was to a more focused political nationalism, with strong linguistic and cultural characteristics – around feelings of national pride, past historical, literary and Bardic glory. Some care is necessary that cultural nationalism is not interpreted as being inherently 'soft,' it also creates its own particular resistances relevant to the struggle for national identity.[19]

It was within this overall scenario that Quakers in Wales would have contributed, but given their very small numbers their involvement was minimal, locally and nationally. The Yearly Meeting did not participate directly in political activity, although many prominent members were involved, especially in promoting the Liberal Party across Britain and the Liberal Unionist cause on its formation. Both the Cadburys and the Rowntrees acquired interests in newspapers championing Liberal causes.

The Quaker political commitment was overall equivocal towards political reform, compared to their interest in philanthropy. Isichei's considers that their contribution to philanthropy outweighed their political contribution, James Walvin agrees, that they were to be best remembered for their philanthropy rather than their politics, thus 'Parliamentary Quakers tended to be more interested in philanthropic reforming matters,' adding that 'their

17. Quoted by Price, David, 2006, 174.
18. *Western Mail* (WM), 23.10.1883.
19. See for example, Katie Trumpener, *Bardic Nationalism: The Romantic Novel and the British Empire*, 1997.

worthy, high-minded speeches were famous for rapidly emptying the House.'[20]

There has already been reference to the numbers of Quakers elected to parliament in 1900, and the importance that this bestowed, in the eyes of many Friends, on their standing in the country. Yet one Quarterly Meeting bemoaned lack of political activity and influence amongst Friends 'few … serve on Town Councils, School Boards and other public bodies … direct personal influence of Friends on public affairs [is] but small.'[21] The most prominent Quaker family in Wales during this period, the Gibbins' of Neath, involved themselves but slightly in electioneering. In March 1910, Frederick William Gibbins was returned to Parliament in a by-election, replacing S.T. Evans, as Liberal member of parliament for Mid-Glamorganshire, defeating by 2,710 votes, the Labour candidate, Vernon Hartshorn, who was to become a cabinet minister under Ramsey Macdonald. Hartshorn was seen as a militant, since he disagreed with the 'Progressive' attitudes of the South Wales Miners Federation, who had prevented him from standing against the Liberals in the elections of 1906 and 1908. Gibbins' candidature had an element of controversy to it. The party at Westminster wanted the seat conceded to Labour, but this was rejected by the local Liberals.[22] Gibbins seems to have been part of the machinations to ensure this. D. Brynmor-Jones, member of parliament for Swansea District writing to S.T. Evans said that Mid Glamorgan was 'a heritage of embarrassment' and that Gibbins was asking for help.[23] Hartshorn surmised that the 1910 by-election had been conducted in terms of Christianity versus socialism, declaiming that 'a more sordid or unscrupulous contest had never been waged in the history of the county.'[24] A sad judgement and to which presumably Gibbins, as a candidate, must have contributed.

Gibbins did not seek re-election in the general election of December 1910, suggesting that his original candidature was more strategic than serious. He

20. Isichei, *Victorian Quakers*, 1970, 21 and James Walvin, *The Quakers: Money and Morals,* 1997, 147.
21. Lancashire and Cheshire Quarterly Meeting (LCQM), M13, 16/17.4.1902.
22. Morgan, *Wales in British*, 1991, 251.
23. NLW Sir Samuel T. Evans Papers, 28. Letter dated 19.3.1910.
24. Quoted by Peter Stead, 'Vernon Hartshorn: Miners' Agent and Cabinet Minister,' in *Glamorgan Historian*, Vol. 6, Stewart Williams, ed., 1968, 90.

'was quickly tired of parliamentary life and would have preferred, as he put it, to pay his office boy to walk through the Lobbies.'[25] Thus ended the parliamentary career of the only Welsh Quaker ever elected to Westminster. His work as an industrialist and philanthropist, served his memory far more effectively. The only other Quaker to achieve prominence in Welsh politics was Henry Tobit Evans, who although never elected to national public office, made an impression especially at the county level, although his name is not now so well remembered buried as it was under a Liberal avalanche, a cause which he abandoned.

During the Victorian and Edwardian period those political issues affecting Wales never permeated the life of the Yearly Meeting, but neither were they totally ignored. They were not, however, taken up actively in contrast to the other Welsh denominations. For the Quakers home rule had proven to be challenging, Irish Home Rule especially so, 'perplexity was strongly marked within our Society … rarely, if ever, were the Friends so divided at the polling booths, in some instances father and son taking different sides.'[26] In 1914 E.T. John, Liberal member for East Denbighshire, introduced the first Welsh home rule measure, which never progressed beyond its first reading, and Welsh Home Rule proved different from its Irish cousin, and was not a substantive political issue for any denomination, but proved to be a resilient, resurrective sub-text. Thus in *Y Drysorfa*, the Calvinistic Methodist monthly:

Self-government for Wales: There is no need to spend any time proving that Wales is a nation, and that she possesses her own unique and different attributes: but the Welsh nation cannot give her best to the world until she is free, until she can settle her own issues without interference from outside. We do not mean a divorce from the Empire but freedom within the larger body to which she belongs … the Welsh are mature, without doubt, to reject intoxicating drink. If so, why should an enlightened Wales be tied to the less enlightened people of England, giving both the same legislation.[27]

25. Thomas Jones, *Welsh Broth* (London, W. Griffiths, 1951), 130.
26. *TF*, Editorial, 1st Month 1887, 2.
27. *Y Drysorfa*, 'Nodiadau Misol', October 1917, 392–4, ('*Ymreolaeth i Gymru: Nid oes eisiau ymdroi i brofi fod y Cymry yn genedl, ag iddi ei nodweddion neillduol a gwhaniaethol: ond nis gall cenedl y Cymry roddi ei goreu i'r byd hyd nes y bydd hi yn rhydd, hyd nes y ca hawl i drefnu ei holl faterion ei hun heb ymyriad neb o'r tu allan. Nid ysgariaeth oddiwrth yr Ymherodraeth a olygwn ond rhyddid o fewn i'r corff mwy i ba un y mae yn perthyn … Y*

This emphasis, sentiment and language, except those relating to the Imperial project, would not be found in Quaker speak or for that matter in their publications.

The Boer War extinguished much of the Welsh political debate, and the First World War similarly, 'triggered a major ideological reaction as the need to defend British interests took a grip on the popular consciousness, effectively submerging the cause of Welsh home rule.'[28]

There are three issues and two themes in Welsh political life where the interest of LYM would have been expected, given that they were issues around which Quakers demonstrated some affinity. These deserve attention.

i. Disestablishment in Wales

For LYM separating the Church from the State was a matter of principle. William Penn's words remained true, 'no human law can make a true church. A true church is of Christ's making.'[29] Nevertheless, the Yearly Meeting did not actively engage in the disestablishment debate in the period after 1833 when the 'United' Committee established by the Dissenting Deputies first met to further the disestablishment cause and replicating what Quakers had already done in terms of political action. Friends kept aloof from it. Nevertheless, following the formation of the Voluntary Church Association in 1834 it was William Howitt, 'an energetic Quaker,'[31] who acted as spokesperson before the Prime Minister, Earl Grey to argue for disestablishment. When in 1842, a national conference was held in London from which the Anti-State-Church Society emerged to become known as the Liberation Society.[32] Friends attended as individuals, with such national figures as

---

mae Cymry yn aeddfed, o bosibl, i llwyr waharddiad y diodydd meddwol. Os felly, paham y rhaid rhwymo gwerin oleuedig Cymru wrth werin llai goleuedig Lloegr, a rhoddi yr un mesur i'r ddwy.')

28. Williams, *Liberalism in Wales*, 1990, 206.

29. William Penn, 'Good Advice to the Church of England, Roman Catholick, and Protestant Dissenter,' in *The Political Writings of William Penn*, 2002, 340.

30. See N.C. Hunt, *Two Early Political Associations: The Quakers and the Dissenting Deputies in the Age of Sir Robert Walpole*, 1961.

31. William H. Mackintosh, *Disestablishment and Liberation: The Movement for the Separation of the Anglican Church from State Control*, 1972, 7.

32. See Ieuan Gwynedd Jones, 'The Liberation Society and Welsh Politics,' in *Explorations and Explanations: Essays in the Social History of Victorian Wales*, 1981, 236–68.

Joseph Sturge and John Bright taking and active part.[33]

Isichei noted ambivalence amongst Friends concerning the Liberation Society, ascribing this to the legacy of quietism with its aversion to militancy, and the desire to cultivate influence as a means to seeking solutions.[34] When in 1871 Edward Miall introduced his first disestablishment motion not all the Quakers in parliament supported him. Four Quaker MPs abstained and two voted for the motion.[35] The Quaker members never voted as a block, and played little part in the politics of dissent and were merely 'conscientious but obscure backbenchers.'[36] This is somewhat ironic given that by 1681, the Quakers 'were showing every sign of becoming an effective and closely built political association'[37] whose techniques and characteristics later organisations, such as the Anti-Corn Law League, emulated. Bebbington contends that by 1883 the Liberation Society and its activities in England was 'running out of steam,'[38] having seen its zenith between 1868 and 1871. A wilting, because it opted to become more involved with Liberal party politics 'rather than the purity of the moral crusade.'[39] From the Welsh perspective disestablishment developed into a national campaign, separate from the Liberation Society, which some in Wales saw as an alien foundation since it did not press for Welsh disestablishment.[40] Knight saw Welsh disestablish-ment as covering four phases; the first from 1847, following the publication of the 'Blue Books,' in which the Church was seen to be implicated; the second, from around 1868, followed the extended national franchise, when the Liberation Society had 55 branches in Wales; the third, after 1886, when it assumed a nationalistic guise, and finally the final phase, after 1904, when despite signs of decline in Nonconformist strength, legislation was finally introduced. Thus by 1886 disestablishment 'had emerged as a major factor in

33. Mackintosh, *Disestablishment*, 1972, 28.

34. Isichei, *Victorian*, 1970, 198–200.

35. Ibid., 200.

36. Ibid., 204.

37. Hunt, *Two Early*, 1961, 11.

38. D.W.Bebbington, *The Nonconformist Conscience: Chapel and Politics, 1870–1914*, 1982, 19.

39. Gerald Parsons, 'Liberation and Church Defence,' in *Religion in Victorian Britain* II, Controversies, Gerald Parsons ed., 1988, 156.

40. K.O. Morgan, 'The Campaign for Welsh Disestablishment,' in *Modern Wales* etc, 1995, 175.

the context of British politics as a whole,'[41] allied as it was to the dominance of the Liberals in Wales, giving the campaign momentum and representation.

One of the most prominent of Liberationists was Henry Richard, Congregational minister and Member of Parliament for Merthyr Tydfil (1868–88), who, as secretary of the Peace Society was well connected to Friends, and whose efforts would have garnered their interest and support. Thus, for example, the Women's Meeting of WQM in 1879 minuted:

> The subject of peace has been introduced at this time, and a memorial to the House of Commons in support of Henry Richards' intended motion for the reduction of European Armaments had been produced, which by the direction of the Meeting has been signed by the Clerk on its behalf.[42]

His association with the Liberation Society meant that his focus was on the wholesale disestablishment of the Anglican Church, such that Richard and his cohort looked wider, not simply focusing on Wales, even though many of his pronouncements gave the impression that he would have supported national Welsh liberation; more a question of tactic than principle. After 1886 that wider traditional view was an anachronism, and the English liberationist campaign no longer vibrant. The Liberal Party adopted Welsh disestablishment as policy in 1887.

In 1886 it was a Welsh member of parliament of Quaker descent, and another prominent Liberationist and radical, Lewis Llewelyn Dillwyn, who presented the first motion before the House calling for disestablishment in Wales, basing his case on the issue of Welsh nationality.[43] Friends would have been sensitive to the issue in its Welsh context by 1886, many would agree with Anthony Dell, the son of a Quaker, and in 1912 acting sub-chief editor of the *Daily Citizen* (the first newspaper to support the Labour Party) that the Anglican church in Wales was 'not the Church of the Welsh people' and for him the division between Church and chapel in Wales was also 'one between class and class to a greater extent than in England.'[44] The attitude of

---

41. Frances Knight, 'The National Scene,' in *The Welsh Church from Reformation to Disestablishment 1603–1920*, 2007, 318.

42. WRO 898.2 1303, WQM, Women's Meeting, M5, 10.12.1879.

43. Morgan, *Wales in British*, 1991, 67 and 77.

44. Anthony Dell, *The Church in Wales: A Complete Guide to the Disestablishment Question*, 1912, 27.

Friends can be cryptically inferred from an observation made by WQM, gathered at Neath, that:

> Here in spite of the influence of the Established Church, the chapel holds its own, and through the voluntary efforts of the Welsh people truth is preserved and proclaimed.[45]

By 1886 the tussle over disestablishment took a more assertive character through what became known in Wales as the 'tithe wars' (*Rhyfel y Degwm*), further highlighting calls for separation of church and state. These began in Denbighshire in August 1886 and continued until 1889, agitation was mainly concentrated in North Wales, and allied to the 'Anti Tithe League' (*Cynghrair Gorthrymedigion y Degwm*) established in 1886 under the leadership of Thomas Gee, owner/editor of *Y Faner*, a prominent Calvinistic Methodist, Liberal and supporter of disestablishment. The Welsh Land League was then formed in 1888 as 'The Welsh Land, Labour and Commercial League,' highlighting a stronger labourist element fitting in with a stronger political radicalism and nationalism.[46] Its objectives were similar to the Irish Land League. It league reflected, not only a dissenting position, but also the economic depression affecting agriculture at the time, and the agitation over tithes was part of Gee's campaign for disestablishment, 'the payment of tithes to this Church is considered to be a badge of conquest which we are determined to shake off.'[47] A call that would have echoed with Friends in terms of their own historical sufferings, an issue not altogether ignored by the Welsh press. Gee, remarking on the 1867 Yearly Meeting discussion on distraint, said, 'If we behaved similarly to the Quakers, there would be a different spirit in our country, politically and religiously.'[48]

The debate in Wales concerning disestablishment was never indifferent. In March 1893 an editorial in *The Friend* highlighted the old arguments. Government had no right to endow one denomination over another, and using statistics on the collections and contributions made within the chapels as proof of the domination of nonconformity, stated that it was 'manifest

---

45. *TF*, 8th month, 1886, 216.

46. Price, *Lloyd George*, 2006, 41.

47. Quoted in Frank Price Jones, 'Rhyfel y Degwm,' in *Radicaliaeth a'r Werin Gymreig yn y Bedwaredd Ganrif ar Bymtheg*, 1975, 90.

48. *Y Faner ac Amserau Cymru*, (*YFAC*), 14.08.1867.

that in some remarkable way the heart of the people of Wales has become alienated from the Church of England.'[49]

In February 1895, Herbert Asquith as Home Secretary, introduced for the second time, a Welsh Disestablishment Bill. Passed by a majority of 44, it fell, when in June, the administration resigned to be replaced by a Tory/Unionist administration. HRMM agreed to forward a memorial[50] in support of the Bill to Sir Francis Edwards, the Anglican, Liberal member for Radnorshire. Subsequently, WQM sent a similar memorial to the House of Commons, instructing its Clerk to sign a petition on its behalf,

> in favour of the disestablishment of the Church of England in Wales ... the Religious Body to which your petitioners belong has for more than two centuries firmly held that the union of church and state is derogatory to the government of Christ as the sole head of the Church and injurious to the spread of vital Christianity.[51]

Both bodies, taking action on the matter, did not pass the matter up to Sufferings even though they did so on some matters. Sufferings, for example, considered a minute from the Monthly Meeting regarding establishing a fund for the non-combatant victims of the South African War, and decided to set up a committee to take the matter further.[52]

The Yearly Meeting had a parliamentary committee, but it assumed a restricted and selective remit. It monitored legislation that affected the standing and assets of the Yearly Meeting. In 1877–8, for example, it kept a particular eye on a valuation Bill brought before Parliament, because it sought to exempt curates from having to pay general rates. This was 'considered to involve the objectionable feature of favouring a State Church at the expense of the general ratepayers,'[53] and seen as 'an infringement of the principles of religious equality, and manifestly unjust to the body of ratepayers, upon whom an increased burden will be thrown.'[54] This echoed the general

49. *TF*, 10.3.1893, 145.
50. Hereford Record Office (HRO), HRMM, M11, 10.4.1895
51. WRO, 898.2 BA1302, WQM, M2, 17.4.1895.
52. Minutes of Meeting for Sufferings (MfS), Friends House Library, M6, 1.12.1899.
53. MfS, Report from the Parliamentary Committee, 7.9.1877.
54. MfS, M7, 6.9.1878.

concerns of the Yearly Meeting about the Established Church, but overall Welsh demands never merited its attention.

Neither did the Parliamentary Committee concern itself with Irish Home Rule, and in its report to Sufferings for 1883 noted only that the attention of the legislature had been almost exclusively occupied with legislation affecting Ireland, such that 'little room was left for ordinary legislation, and no Bills affecting the Society of Friends especially became law.'[55] For 1885 and 1886 there were no references to Irish Home Rule, despite its dominance on national legislation, but this was an issue, that had it been discussed by the Yearly Meeting, would have created division and dissension, undermining unity.

For 1889, and again in 1890 the Parliamentary Committee could report that 'nothing material to report as to the measures of the Session, which proved to be a very barren one.'[56] In 1891 it reflected on the Marriage of Nonconformists Bill, which would have allowed all Nonconformists to marry without a state registrar, but their watchfulness was more to do with protecting the interest and position of Friends, more than it was to give equality to their nonconformist brethren. Lord Hardwicke's Act, 1753, meant that Friends could marry according to their own practices, as could Jews and Anglicans and no others. Friends were defensive of their privilege and wary of change that might affect them. Hence, the minute read that, 'amendments were introduced which made it desirable that Friends' marriages should be excepted from the scope of the Bill, and Lewis Fry gave notice of intention to move an exemption with this aim in mind.'[57] The focus of the Yearly Meeting was somewhat selfish and not particularly supportive of equity.Hence, when the Nonconformist Marriages (Attendance of Registers) Bill received Royal Assent in 1897 the Parliamentary Committee commented on its responsibility, 'In order to make it clear that the measure if passed would not affect the Society of Friends an amendment was proposed by John Edward Ellis M.P., which was added to the bill.'[58] Yet, it was not as though that committee was totally divorced from broader social concerns. In 1875,

55. MfS, M5, 5.1.1883.
56. MfS, M5, 3.10.1890.
57. MfS, M8, 4.9.1891.
58. MfS, Report of the Parliamentary Committee, 7.1.1898. Ellis, was a Quaker and Liberal M.P.

for example, Sufferings asked it to monitor and provide guidance on vivisection.[59]

Usually when the Parliamentary Committee reported to the Yearly Meeting its comments as for 1896, were not unusual, 'No measures have been brought forward (in the preceding 12 months) requiring the attention of the Committee.'[60] An examination of the minutes of Meeting for Sufferings from 1875 to 1912 reveals no discussion on Welsh disestablishment even as it dominated Welsh politics. *The Friend* upheld the Quaker position, that a church 'supported by the State [was] manifestly doomed'[61] especially when nonconformists provided for more sittings than the Established Church. The same theme was picked up in September 1906, where, on the basis of an analysis of church membership in Wales, it concluded that 'it is clearly shown that Wales is a nonconformist nation.'[62]

In the election of 1906 the Liberals swept into power capturing all Welsh seats, and in June the government established a Royal Commission to inquire into the state of religion in Wales, namely,

> to inquire into the origin, nature, amount and application of the temporalities, endowments and other properties of the Church of England in Wales and and into the provision made, and the work done, by the Churches of all in Wales and Monmouthshire for the spiritual welfare of the people, and the which the people avail themselves of such provision; and to report thereon.[63]

As there was no reference to disestablishment in its remit many in Wales were suspicious and mistrustful of the commission's direction and terms of reference. The rigid interpretation and approach of the Chairman of the Commission, Lord Justice Sir Roland Vaughan Williams, did not help, since he was anxious to ensure that the commissioners did touch on questions regarding the relationship between Church and State, for him political issues not falling within the remit. In one exchange he challenged a commissioner because he was 'going directly to the question of the relations between

59. MfS, 2.7.1875.
60. Extracts from the Minutes and Proceedings of the Yearly Meeting of Friends held in London, (YMP) 1896, 113.
61. *TF*, 24.1.1902, 50.
62. *TF*, 14.9.1906, 621.
63. *Royal Commission on the Church of England*, (RCCE), Vol. 1,1910, Cmd. 5432.

Church and State ... Please do not let us get any nearer; let us have nothing to do with the question of Church and State.'[64]

The Commission's progress from October 1906 was never smooth. In April 1907, three Nonconformist members resigned.[65] *The Friend* sympathised with its tribulations but was reassured by statements made by the government. It was however anxious about the attitude of the Lords reflecting that

> Wales has no confidence in the Lords, and it will not blame the Government
> for whatever happens in that House ... Wales has been long suffering (and)
> the claims of the Principality to special treatment in this matter have been
> fully demonstrated.[66]

Its English dimension forgotten. It was not until 1912 that the first version of a Bill was introduced; a delay that reflected other priorities, such as the introduction of the Parliament Act to thwart the Lords, and the fate of the Peoples' Budget and National Insurance.

Friends appeared before the Commission on May 13th 1908, Hercules Davies Phillips, a 'recorded minister of the Society of Friends and clerk of Hereford and Radnor Monthly Meeting'[67] giving evidence on their behalf. He was cross-examined by four commissioners, and fully reported in a complimentary light by *The Friend*.[68] It quoted the *South Wales Daily News*, that Phillips had been 'about the only witness who has been able to induce the Lord Justice to accept any historical matters at all' but his submission, the Chairman said, 'must not be taken as precedent; it is let in for its shortness'[69] possibly because, compared to the other denominations, the voice of Friends was less hysterical. Phillips' evidence related to the historical persecution of Quakers in Wales, and their present circumstances, highlighting the fact that there were now only 302 Quakers in Wales, compared to the 18,760 within the Yearly Meeting. True to his beliefs Phillips took exception to the use by the Commission of the word 'communicants' to

---

64. RCCE, *Minutes of Evidence*, Vol. 3, 1909, paragraph 42, 285, p. 856.
65. See Morgan, *Wales in British*, 1991 231–74.
66. *TF*, 12.7.1907, 461.
67. RCCE, *Minutes of Evidence*, Vol. 3, 1909, para. 42, 228. For Phillips see chapter 3.
68. *TF*, 22.5.1908, 331.
69. RCCE, *Minutes of Evidence*, Vol. 3, 1909, para. 42, 239, p. 854.

describe Friends, explaining that he had used it only because it was convenient to do so.

A copy of the Yearly Meeting's *Book of Christian Discipline* was given to the Commissioners, and they were referred to pages 137–42, where views on the nature of an Established Church were set out. The Chairman was anxious to pursue the question of regulation and order within the Society, highlighting his understanding that 'the Society of Friends, who have gone further than any people have in the assertion of individualism in the matter of religion,'[70] but also had rules for order and discipline. Phillips replied positively, whilst trying to reflect the doctrinal position of the Yearly Meeting:

> Yes; for instance there may be Friends who are very much inclined towards Unitarianism. It would be very doubtful if one who openly proclaimed himself a Unitarian could retain his membership of the Society of Friends. There must be a limit somewhere.[71]

Archdeacon Owen Evans was anxious to demonstrate that it was not the Anglicans who had led the persecution of Friends. Phillips concurred, but his responses to Owen on factual matters relating to Welsh Quaker history highlighted some uncertainty. He gave the commissioners a copy of the journal by Richard Davies of Cloddiau Cochion, Welshpool, *An account of the convincement, exercises, services and travels of that ancient servant of the Lord, Richard Davies*, but was unsure of this Quaker's friendship with Bishop Lloyd of St Asaph, but no doubt aware of the debates held between the two. Neither did he seemingly know much about Morgan Llwyd of Gwynedd, a serious omission given his importance as a Welsh literary figure, and as someone who had some sympathy with Friends. Phillips was not a Welsh speaker and, having been brought up in Knighton, it is unlikely that he had a deep understanding of Welsh history and literature, but his commitment to Wales never wavered.

One outcome of Phillips' testimony reflected the standing of Friends in Wales as understood by the press. The *Welsh Gazette*, an Aberystwyth paper, had two items relating to his evidence, one in Welsh, the other in English, which was pointed in its challenge:

70. Ibid., para. 42, 489, p. 857.
71. Ibid. para, 42, 489.

interesting evidence in reference to the Quakers was given before the Welsh Church Commission last week. It was stated that the number of Friends at Aberystwyth was seventeen. Where are they?[72]

The Welsh version[73] was gentler, pointing out merely that they had no meeting house, and that the Unitarians were now using their old meeting place. The Quakers never built or owned a meeting house in Aberystwyth but had used an old building in the town centre, which in December 1904 the Unitarians leased and eventually purchased.[74] The Quakers used the building again in the 1950s.

Once the Commission reported, *The Friend* had an article quoting extensively from a book published by the Rev. J. Morgan Gibbon, Congregational minister at Stamford Hill Church, London, one of the Commissioners. He had refused to sign the final report because of his dissatisfaction with the conduct of the inquiry with respect its terms of reference and the treatment, as he saw it, of Nonconformists.[75] The Commission's report avoided any reference to endowments, a matter of some interest to Friends, and what should be done with them explicit. They had been 'given by the people, long ago, ... should be returned to the public treasury. In that way, the people would benefit greatly to the extent that they would be relieved of the public taxes and impositions which these funds would replace.'[76] Immediately following publication of the Commission *The Friend* had little to say informing its readers that,

The Prime Minister informed a deputation of Welsh Members that it was the intention of the Government on the assumption that the Parliamentary Bill was carried into Law that year, to give the Welsh Disestablishment Bill such a position next year as would enable it to override the veto of the Lords during the present Parliament.[77]

72. *The Welsh Gazette* (WG), 21.05.1908.
73. Ibid.
74. Islwyn ap Nicholas, *Heretics at Large: The Story of a Unitarian Chapel*, 1977.
75. *TF*, 14.4.1911, 236.
76. Robert Barclay, *Barclay's Apology in Modern English*, Dean Freiday ed., 1967, 230.
77. *TF*, 17.3.1911, 178.

By 1912 *The Friend*, conscious that parliament was about to reconsider this 'burning topic,'[78] introduced Friends to two recent publications on the subject, both favourable to disestablishment. In February 1913 it reported the sympathy shown to the Welsh Church Bill by the Bishop of Oxford in the Lords,[79] and outlined the speech in June by W.G.C. Gladstone, highlighting the repugnance shown by many across the whole country to the opposition shown to the Bill.[80] Disestablishment became law in May 1914, having been twice rejected by the Lords. *The Friend* noted the royal assent briefly in its 'Day to Day' column.[81] George Cadbury, given his personal conviction, 'I believe that our Society still has an important place to fill as a living protest against a State Church, and the tyranny connected with it,'[82] was no doubt delighted that the whole of the church in Wales was now to be free of state control, even though the contribution of the Religious Society of Friends to that achievement was never vocal.

ii. The 1902 Education Act

Another major issue in Wales, and closely aligned to its Nonconformist conscience and culture was the struggle over education. According to Bebbington it was the one issue that most prominently brought the whole of Nonconformity into politics in the late and early twentieth century.[83] Education was much favoured by Friends, both for children and adults, although within Wales their contribution was limited. Joseph Lancaster, a Quaker by conviction, had been instrumental in developing nationally, the 'monitorial system,' whereby older pupils were appointed to to teach the younger pupils in small classes. The Royal Lancastrian Society for Promoting the Education of Children of the Poor, was then established in 1808 with Quaker support. In 1814 it was renamed the British and Foreign Schools Society, encouraging the building of what became known as the British Schools, the nonconformist element in voluntary education across England and Wales. Lancaster visited Cardiff, Neath, Swansea and Carmarthen in 1806–07. Richard Phillips, a London-based Quaker, born in Swansea, the

78. *TF*, 5.4.1912, 218.
79. *TF*, 21.2.1913, 115.
80. *TF*, 27.6.1913, 424.
81. *TF*, 25.9.1914, 717.
82. *TF*, 1.1.1892, 5.
83. Bebbington, *The Nonconformist*, 1982, 127.

son of a disowned Swansea Quaker, who then joined the Society when he was 34 years old, was closely involved in the management of the 'Lancastrian Schools' and also prominent in the abolition of the slave trade, and was one of Thomas Clarkson's closest collaborators.[84] In 1806 the Swansea Society of the Education of Children of the Poor was established with Quaker support, supported by Phillips along with 'T. Bigg, L.W. Dillwyn and R. Eaton well known townsmen from Quaker families.'[85] In 1821 Phillips, discontented with the way the Girls School was being managed in Swansea established another school for girls at Swansea, funded exclusively by Quakers. In 1808 Quaker industrialists organised a school in Cardiff, at the Melingriffith Tinplate by John and Samuel Harford, Bristol Quakers, whose family name, but non-Quaker, would latterly reverberate around Lampeter.[86] An earlier school was established at the Quaker owned Neath Abbey Ironworks by J. Tregelles Price, one of the founders of the Peace Society. According to the Rev. William Roberts ('Nefydd'), agent to the British and Foreign School Society in South Wales, 'This institution is the oldest, I think, in Wales, as an unsectarian school. It was established in 1802 by the late respected Joseph Price.'[87]

The passage of the 1870 Education Act satisfied many Friends, given that its architect was W.E. Forster, a birthright but disowned Friend, 'not voluntary on his part,' because he had married, contrary to the discipline of the Society, a non-Quaker, Jane, Matthew Arnold's sister. He was however to be buried in 1886 in a simple Quaker funeral.[88] Forster's Act created a national non-sectarian elementary state school system for those aged between 5–13, in publicly-funded schools, built and managed by elected school boards, for which women could vote and become candidates. In 1870 nine women were elected onto the boards, this had risen to 24 by 1876, 41 in 1879. No women were elected in Wales in 1870.[89] The elections to these

---

84. See David Painting, 'Swansea and the Abolition of the Slave Trade,' in *The Swansea History Journal: Minerva*, 15, 2007–08, 10–18.

85. A. L. Trott, 'The British School Movement in Wales, 1806–1846,' in *The History of Education in Wales*, Vol. 1, Jac L. Williams and Gwilym Rees Hughes, eds, 1978, 86.

86. Ibid., 87.

87. E. D. Jones, 'The Journal of William Roberts, (Nefydd) 1853–1862,' in *The National Library of Wales Journal*, IX, 1955-56, 95.

88. T. Weymyss Reid, *Life of the Honourable William Edward Forster*, 1888, 266.

89. Patricia Hollis, *Ladies Elect: Women in English Local Government, 1865–1914*, 1987, 131–2.

boards became a sectarian affair, and in Wales the more so, where they were 'more strenuously contested'[90] as Nonconformists struggled with the Established Church.[91] The board schools supplemented the voluntary schools, and were built in those areas 'where voluntary effort was not sufficient to supply the local demand.'[92] The Act was seen as 'a compromise upon compromise,'[93] as the government struggled to extend and improve provision, whilst containing the conflicting sectarian interests. The boards could remit the costs of poorer children from local rates, both in their own schools and in the voluntary sector, since this was not universal free education.

Sectarian teaching in board schools was prohibited, the Bill being amended to include the Cowper-Temple Clause so that 'no religious catechism or religious formulary which is distinctive of any particular denomination shall be taught.'[94]

The religious controversy in education hinged not on an issue of theology, but whether or not public money from the local rates, or the exchequer, should be given to denominational schools which taught religion from that viewpoint. Since Anglican schools dominated the voluntary sector, attending nonconformist children were exposed to Anglican teaching. It was then for the Quakers an issue of religious liberty. John Edward Ellis noting that

> the State in its corporate capacity has no concern with the religious opinions
> of the individuals who compose it … In State schools religion has no place.[95]

It was this theme and the nature of state support for education that underpinned the debate. The underlying themes were the hegemony of the Anglicans and their fears about the dominance of dissent. It is not then insignificant that much discussion, during this period, hinges on statistical headcount, such as the numbers of nonconformists in the country compared

90. H.G. Williams, 'The Forster Education Act and Welsh Politics,' in *Welsh History Review*, 14, 2, 1988, 263.

91. See N. J. Richards, 'Religious Controversy and the School Boards 1870–1902,' in *British Journal of Educational Studies*, 18, 2, 1970, 180–96.

92. H.C. Barnard, *A History of English Education from 1760*, 1964, 119.

93. Attributed to the Secretary of the National Education League, and quoted by John Lawson and Harold Silver in *A Social History of Education in England*, 1973, 316.

94. Section 14.2, Education Act 1870, quoted Lawson and Silver, *A Social History*, 1973, 317

95. *TF*, Letter 5th month, 1870, 110–110.

to Anglicans. Much of the debate in Wales was coloured by concern about the numbers of members and attenders in the chapels and churches, to demonstrate their majority over the Anglicans. Yet, neither the Non-conformists nor the Anglicans would support another religious census as in 1851. The former because they did not want a simple question as to religious profession, since this intruded onto right of conscience, and the latter because they were concerned as to how any statistics might be used.[96] LYM was similarly challenged by the annual returns of its membership –the Tabular Statement – and the implications the statistics had about denominational vibrancy.

This issue of religious liberty was visible in 1843, when James Graham introduced legislation to regulate the employment of women and children in factories, seeking at the same time to allow working children, and those living in workhouses, to be educated in Anglican schools supported by state funding. The Yearly Meeting opposed the Bill organising a petition against it based on the issue of conscience, that public funds should not be used to support denominational teaching even when part of a more noble objective; it was signed by 861 men 18 of these from Herefordshire, Worcestershire and Wales Quarterly Meeting.[97] In the same vein, Neath Friends objected to the appointment of a chaplain to the local workhouse, petitioning the Poor Law Board, 'we feel strong objections to such appointment, as imposing upon Dissenters from the Established Church, the hardships of having to pay a proportion of the stipend for a ministry from which they conscientiously dissent.'[98] One of the few examples, in this period, of Welsh Quakers acting politically. The 1843 Bill failed.

Despite compromises, the 1870 Act was still heavily criticised by nonconformists, because they saw it as preserving Anglican domination. The Act recognised the centrality of the voluntary sector to the provision of education, and that no other course would have proved tenable politically or practically at the time.[99] The voluntary schools were the backbone of what

---

96. See Snell and Ell: *Rival Jerusalems etc*, 2000, in particular appendix F, 449–52.

97. See A. Neave Brayshaw, 'The Society of Friends and the Education Bill' in *TF*, 26.9.1902, 624–6.

98. *TF*, 2nd month, 1843, 1–2.

99. Lawson and Silver, *A Social History*, 1973, 314.

was still a rudimentary educational system. In addition, the act allowed for national grants to the voluntary bodies to build more schools, avidly taken up by the Anglicans, who by 1880 had added a million places to their portfolio.[100] Opposition to the Bill came primarily from Joseph Chamberlain and his National Education League. In Wales, a parallel but much weaker body was established, the Welsh Education Alliance, representing the voice of Welsh nonconformity, into which Quakers seem to have had no input.[101]

The Bill proved problematic for the Liberal administration, 132 Liberal MPs voting for the bill, 133 abstaining, with less than a hundred in support.[102] It carried only with Tory support. John Bright, the leading Quaker politician of the day opposed it, although by 1873 when in the cabinet, he was to praise the principles embodied in the act and its provision for state education. By 1876 he proclaimed the act to be a 'remarkable success,'[103] a view endorsed later by many, in the light of the threat they perceived to come from 1902 legislation. In reality the nature of nonconformist opposition was spilt. Some strove against any sectarian education in the schools, others were prepared to have what was known as non-denominational religious teaching outside the curricula. Thus in Wales the secularist position was represented in the main by the Independents and Baptists, who opposed any religious instruction, and the Calvinistic Methodists who were supportive.[104]

Between 1870 and 1900 the number of schools in Wales doubled, with 1,709 in receipt of grants. In the new industrial areas of Wales where the church schools had not been able to keep pace with population expansion, Board Schools accounted for 82% of school places, and in Glamorganshire and Merthyr 74%.[105] Ironically, in the rural areas where Nonconformists predominated, their children had to attend the National Schools because these were the only ones available. This added to the sectarian tensions and divide.

Williams' analysis of the Act's impact in Wales, is clear that its passage revitalised Anglicans, and shifted Nonconformists into a more radical

100. S.J. Curtis, *History of Education in Great Britain*, 1948, 169.

101. Leighton Hergest, 'The Welsh Educational Alliance and the 1870 Elementary Education Act,' in *Welsh History Review*, 10, 1980–1, 172–205.

102. See Eric E. Rich, *The Education Act 1870: A Study in Public Opinion*, 1970.

103. Herman Ausubel, *John Bright: Victorian Reformer*, 1966, 195.

104. See Williams, *The Forster Education*, 1988.

105. See Jones and Roderick, *A History of*, 2003, 79–82.

position in demanding non-sectarian provision. At the same time its passage was a challenge because it

> crystallised those links between nonconformity, social class and nationality ... and marked a significant stage in the emergence of the 'Welsh' dimension in late nineteenth century Welsh politics.[106]

Hence, through education the Anglican/nonconformist struggle was further embedded politically. Nonconformists through the School Boards gained an element of control, a factor that influenced their response to the 1902 Act, and in effect compromised their original opposition to the 1870 Act.

In 1889 the Welsh Intermediate Education Act had been passed by a Tory administration supported by politicians across the party divide. It established local county-based committees – the local education authorities – who could prepare schemes for intermediate education in their areas, the 'county schools.' By 1902, there were 94 such schools in Wales. These were non-denominational and received rate support and treasury grants which probably benefited Welsh nonconformity because 'their ethos was Nonconformist.'[107] It meant in effect that Wales, unlike England, developed a more rational system of secondary education. Bevan Lean, who became headmaster of the Quaker school at Sidcot, was full of praise for the Act and its impact on secondary education in Wales. He described a visit in the summer of 1901 to one such school in a mining village that had 'a strange name, unpronounce-able by a Saxon' where he had watched the science master with his class, and to his 'amazement I find that all but one are the children of the labouring and artisan classes.'[108] His surprise reflects a certain prejudice, but his professional admiration of the system was obvious.

The Central Welsh Board of Education was created in 1896 to oversee the intermediate schools and develop an examination system, set up as a co-ordinating body – made up of 80 members drawn principally from the county and county borough councils, who financed it in conjunction with the treasury. As a quasi-national body it accommodated some nonconformist unease about an educational system still dependent on Anglican schools, but

106. Williams, *The Forster Education*, 1988, 268.
107. Davies, *Religion in the Industrial*, 1965, 146.
108. *TF*, 25.4.1902, 261.

it meant that education in Wales had acquired a distinct voice worthy of protection, with local authorities that had experience of managing secondary education.[109]

The 1902 Education Bill brought turmoil to education following the failed 1896 Education Bill that had aroused much fury amongst nonconformists,[110] an act that 'should be titled the Church Party Act since it represented a great victory for the supporters of Anglicanism.'[111] The Bill had proposed the abolition of the Cowper-Temple clause, so that religious instruction could be allowed 'in the Board schools to those children whose parents desired it,'[112] challenging their non-sectarian status. Meeting for Sufferings in January 1896 agreed a memorial to the government on the matter stating that if

> the compromise of 1870 is to be disturbed, we unite with other Nonconformist Churches in the demand that an unsectarian school under public management shall be established within reasonable distance of every family.[113]

Sufferings had been much exercised similarly in 1894 when it felt that the balance within the educational system was being threatened.[114]

The 1902 Bill sought to introduce a more equitable educational system across the whole of England and Wales, particularly as the denominational schools could no longer compete with the resources available to the Board Schools. It envisaged abolition of the Board system, with the establishment of education committees across the country, introducing to England what was already proven to work in Wales with regard to secondary education. In other words all schools, irrespective of their denominational status, should receive direct rate support. This continued to be unacceptable to Nonconformity, because it implied state support for religious instruction. The principle of maintaining voluntary schools on the rates dominated the

---

109. See Gareth Elwyn Jones, 'Policy and Power: One Hundred Years of Local Education Authorities in Wales,' in *Oxford Review of Education*, 28, 2/3, Jun–Sept 2002, 343–58.
110. See J.E.B. Munson, 'The Unionist Coalition and Education 1895–1902,' in *The Historical Journal*, 20, 3, 1977, 607–45.
111. Tony Taylor, 'The Politics of Reaction: The Ideology of the Cecils and the Challenge of Secular Education 1889–1902,' in *Educational Administration and History Monographs*, no. 20,1997, 1997, 2.
112. Curtis, *History of*, 1948, 186.
113. MfS, M8, 3.1.1896.
114. MfS, M9, 2.11.1894.

argument, with the 'fiercest response coming from Wales, where Lloyd George led a national revolt.'[115] Such was the scale of the revolt in Wales that the appellation, 'Welsh Revolt' is both appropriate and telling, and helped to regalvanise Welsh Liberals.[116]

The Quakers reiterated their principles on education in relation to the new Bill, viewing it with regret,

> many of [its] proposals ... as being prejudicial to the efficiency of education and opposed to the principles of representative control, *and of religious liberty and equality.*

WQM considering the Bill to be retrogressive handing education over to those who did not have it as their primary concern and would 'increase dissension on grounds of religious belief. Public funds will be ... appropriated to schools in which sectarian teaching prevails.'[118] There were two principal strands of opposition, firstly, the perennial provision of state funds to denominational schools, and then the fact that local control, brought in by the 1870 Act, was affected with the abolition of direct elections to the school boards. Kevin Manton argues that what the 1902 Act did was to abolish direct democratic control of education and 'strengthened the hold of elitists and traditionalists' from which the educational system has never recovered, reinforcing class domination. The school boards, elected every three years, had between five to fifteen members, and were the 'most advanced democratic bodies of their day.'[119] Membership of the new education committees was by nomination, a factor that could affect the role of women, with fears that Anglicans would dominate. Overall the legislation sought to ensure that education provision was brought under unified control, albeit dominated by Anglican voluntary provision. In Wales this was a factor that weighed heavily especially in the rural areas, and the pride taken in the success of the

115. Gareth Elwyn Jones, *Controls and Conflict in Welsh Secondary Education 1899–1944*, 1982, 48.
116. Morgan, *Wales in British*, 1991, 181.
117. *TF*, 13.6.1902, 384–5, emphasis added.
118. *WQM*, M20, 16.4.1902.
119. Kevin Manton, 'The 1902 Education Act,' in *History Today*, 52, 12, December 2002, 18–19.

county schools was important, some undoubtedly seeing these now being sucked under clerical control.

Some care needs to be taken that arguments over the Act simply reflected a tussle between Anglican and Nonconformist. The nature and complexity of opposition should not however be oversimplified, the Bishops of Hereford, Manchester and Winchester, for example, voiced Anglican opposition. More radical Anglicans were fearful, 'because the Act seemed to bolster a quasi feudal clerical control especially in county districts,'[120] whilst the National Protestant Church Union[121] representing the evangelical wing of Anglicanism, was concerned that it might encourage greater collaboration between Roman Catholics and High Church Anglicans. Socialists on the other hand, such as Sidney and Beatrice Webb, were supportive seeing sectarian education as unavoidable.[122]

Across the whole of England and Wales Nonconformist opposition to the act was united, but in Wales the political institutions were mobilised more effectively, with practical implications. Most Welsh nonconformists would have echoed the pronouncement of the writer in the Baptist, *Seren Gomer* that the Bill was 'one of the most unjust acts amongst a host during the last fifty years.' The writer saw it as a call for dissenters to awaken, having been lured into sleep by the compromise of the 1870 Act. What the government was doing, he argued, was taking advantage of its majority gained in the shadow of the South African War, and legislating for the Church of England and the Papacy.[123]

In August 1903 the Union of Welsh Congregationalists, meeting at Dowlais, voiced their opposition to the Act declaring that they would fight for free non-sectarian education.[124] The Union, alongside their 1902 annual convention, had organised a conference in Caernarfon that supported a resolution to each of their quarterly and county meetings encouraging opposition to the legislation.[125]

120. N.T. Gullifer, 'Opposition to the 1902 Education Act,' in *Oxford Review of Education*, 8, 1, 1982, 85.

121. Since 1950 known as the Church Society.

122. Gullifer, *Opposition*, 1982, 91.

123. W. Morris: '*Deddf Addysg 1902*' in *Seren Gomer*, January 1903, 1, 24, 1–8, ('*un o'r deddfau mwyaf annuniawn ymhlith lleng yr hanner can mlynedd diweddaf.*')

124. *Y Dysgedydd*, August 1903, 315.

125. R.Tudur Jones, *Yr Undeb:Hanes Undeb yr Annibynwyr Cymraeg 1872–1972* , 1975, 181–4.

This bond of opposition between Welsh Liberalism and nonconformity was firm, without it, the cohesion particularly at the level of the county councils would not have been as robust.[126] A good illustration of the link between the Liberal Party and nonconformity was the 'Conference of Welsh Progressives' held at Bangor, in September, 1903, chaired by J. Herbert Lewis, M.P. (Liberal, Flintshire Boroughs), and convened by the Liberal Associations and the Free Church Councils.[127] The opposition was a clear example of the way Lloyd George, especially,[128] and the Liberal Party cultivated nonconformity, culminating in the sweeping Liberal success of the 1906 election, where Nonconformity expended considerable funds and energy to return a Liberal majority with 200 Nonconformist members.[129] Wales returned no Conservative members at the election.

The importance of nurturing political connections was not lost on *The Friend*. In its overview of events in 1896 and mindful of the need for nonconformists to be on their guard against what it saw as encroachments on their liberties, it saw the 'growing influence of the National Congress of the Evangelical Free Churches, which this year adopted the title Council,'[130] as an important safeguard: in effect seeing nonconformity as a political power to be utilised. In terms of the 1902 Act, however, the Council did not lead on any active opposition, pursuing a highly erratic but vocal course.[131]

Welsh resistance was based on the County Councils refusing to provide funds to the voluntary schools, exploiting weaknesses in the Act. *The Friend* reported on their actions in refusing to give aid to schools 'not provided by or under the full control of the Council,'[132] referring to steps taken by Flintshire and Carmarthenshire. In December 1903, it noted that many voluntary schools were in financial difficulty, because of withheld rate aid, and that most county councils were refusing to hand out grants to 'any

126. See for example Mathew Cragoe, 'Conscience or Coercion: Clerical Influence at the General Election of 1868 in Wales,' in *Past and Present*, 149, Nov 1995, 140–69.

127. NLW, T. Llechid Jones, *Collection*, 125.

128. See Stephen Koss, 'Lloyd George and Nonconformity: the last rally,' in *The English Historical Review*, 89, No. 350, January 1974, 77–108.

129. G.R. Searle, *The Liberal Party: Triumph and Disintegration 1886–1929*, 1992, 41.

130. *TF*, 1.01.1897, 3.

131. Bebbington, *The Nonconformist*, 1982, 142–4.

132. *TF*, 31.7.1903, 502.

voluntary schools which continues to be privately managed.'[133] The same article noted that Cambridgeshire had passed a similar resolution, but direct action by the authorities in England was less intense. West Riding County Council did deduct money from voluntary schools to reflect what they estimated were the costs expended on denominational teaching.[134]

By the end of 1903, Breconshire and Radnorshire were the only counties administering the Act in Wales. The County Council elections of 1904 changed that. *The Friend* stated that the effect of the Act was to give the 'Progressives' control in every County, noting that in Radnorshire, a 'Sectarian' majority of six had been turned into a 'Progressive' majority of ten, commenting, 'Thus Wales in answer to sectarianism.'[135] The nature, intensity and resolve of Welsh resistance proved variable but the impact was visible and effective, and was not mere gesture.[136]

Such was the magnitude of the 'Welsh Revolt' that the government introduced the 1904 Education (Local Authority Default) Act, 'the Coercion of Wales Act as it came to be known,'[137] to control the rebellion, allowing the Central Welsh Board to deal directly with affected schools. In its May 5th editorial for that year *The Friend* made an explicit statement about the nature of Welsh nationality, as reflected in the educational tussle, noting that,

> The Welsh objection to the Act is precisely the same as that which obtains in England, only on account of the preponderating Nonconformity of Wales the injustice is more glaring … We may well pray the Lord to deliver the Welsh people from this great evil.[138]

The article acknowledged the deep interest education generated in Wales and the heroic sacrifices made to promote education, conscious of the way, for example, finance had been raised from ordinary people across Wales for

133. *TF*, 1.1.1904, 2.

134. Gullifer, *Opposition*, 1982, 91.

135. *TF*, 18.3.1904, 189.

136. See Eirwen Griffiths, 'Monmouthshire and the Education Act 1902: The Welsh Revolt of 1902–05: A Study of Conflict between National and Local Government in the Field of Education', unpublished M.Phil Thesis, University of London, 1994; Gareth Elwyn Jones, 'The Welsh Revolt Revisited: Merioneth and Montgomeryshire in default,' in *Welsh History Review*, 14, 3, June 1989, 417–38.

137. Jones, *Controls and Conflicts*, 1982, 481.

138. *TF*, 6.5.1904, 290.

the establishment of the university colleges, especially through the chapels. The 'University of Wales Temporary Sustentation Fund Report and List of Subscribers 1875–76,' shows no evidence that any Quakers, and certainly not Neath Meeting, the largest meeting in Wales at the time, made any contribution that was publicly acknowledged. The list demonstrates graphically how the chapels and ordinary people across Wales contributed significant amounts to the fund. Obviously, the absence of Quakers from the list does not mean that no Quaker ever contributed. However, given their propensity for demonstrating their financial contributions to other causes, then their absence is revealing.

In May 1902 Sufferings established a committee to consider the implications of the new Bill. Their Parliamentary Committee, felt that the matter deserved closer scrutiny but by the parent body. A small committee of seven was established which reported on its findings to an adjourned meeting of Sufferings later in the month. The committee believed that the Yearly Meeting should make a more strenuous protest than had been the case for the 1896 Bill, 'chiefly but though not exclusively on account of its serious infringement of religious liberty and equality.'[139] The issue of democratic control figures large in their concerns.Their report to the Yearly Meeting highlighted the Bill's infringement of religious liberty and equality. To give support to denominational schools from the rates, without at the same time having managerial control over them, was iniquitous, whilst the appointment of teachers by sectarian managers should not be tolerated

> to compel the whole community to pay the costs of schools placed under strictly sectarian management seems to us even more objectionable than was the enforcement of Church rates.[140]

The discussion at the Yearly Meeting was expansive with five members of the committee speaking to their report. Varied comments were made by at least 29 Friends[141] all concerned with the traditional stance taken by Friends on sectarian education, but there was caution. Bevan Lean felt the committee

---

139. MfS, M32, 22.5.1902.
140. 'Report of the Committee appointed to consider what action should be taken by the Meeting for Sufferings as to the Education Bill,' YMP, 1902, 59.
141. *TF*, 6.6.1902, 372–5.

report was too negative, feeling that it was the removal of defects in the Bill that was important, since there were elements within it, from an educational viewpoint, that were to be welcomed, such as the creation of single education authorities. Lucy Morland, a member of the committee, endorsed this concerned as she was about how education was organised and managed. Lean, acerbically referred to the fact that there was in fact one Quaker school in the North of England that already received rate support, and that overall it was important to improve the standard of education provided by all voluntary schools to over three million children. Lean's attempts to draw discussion and decision towards the pragmatic needs of education were endorsed. T.M. Ormston Pease welcomed Lean's analysis, but felt it important to 'raise voice against the serious imperfections' and similarly T. Theodore Harris felt it was best to 'improve a bad Bill.'[142] Theodore Neild, another educationalist, was disappointed with provisions in the Bill for secondary and higher education. Richard Reynolds Fox, another member of the committee, was clear that representation to parliament was important but not to 'encourage a ferment of agitation'[143] especially, as in his view, the Federal Church Council had already lost its head on the matter.

Crucially, it is important to remember that the government responsible for the Bill, was also made up of Liberal Unionists, hence Joseph Chamberlain, a member of the cabinet, was keenly aware that the government needed to tread carefully if only to protect 'the remnants of his nonconformist support.'[144] There were Liberal Unionists amongst the Yearly Meeting whose views would have been influenced by their political allegiance. One such was Thomas Hodgkin, who proclaimed to the Yearly Meeting that what was needed was compromise, and that in this Friends had a mediatory role to play,[145] such also was the call of another weighty Friend, Joseph Storrs Fry, the head of Fry's Chocolates. A lone Welsh Quaker voice was that of Henry Tobit Evans, editor of the *Carmarthen Journal*, and a noted Liberal Unionist. In his editorial column he commented that the Bill

142. Ibid., 374.
143. Ibid., 374.
144. Denis Judd, *Radical Joe: A life of Joseph Chamberlain*, 1993, 235.
145. *TF*, 24.10 1902, 694.

... consolidates and unifies the system of education throughout the land ... it practically annihilates the religious differences. We hear mutterings of a stubborn Radicalism opposed to the Bill... fractious and partisan, and is not in the true interests of education.[146]

He echoed this in October outlining what he saw as the 'malice and misrepresentation raised' against the Bill.[147]

As for the decision of the Yearly Meeting, its Clerk, J. Morland Fry, felt that the meeting could go largely in the direction of the committee report, noting in the minute, that a memorial be prepared, which should then be circulated amongst Friends across the country. A group was appointed and given liberty to alter the report, where this improved it. The memorial emphasised principle and pragmatic needs, and was endorsed. It high-lighted Friends' commitment to education, but viewed with regret many of the proposals contained within the Bill, and considered to be prejudicial to educational efficiency, and asked for amendments. Control of education should be made more democratic, sectarian schools should not debar employ-ment and promotion of teachers on sectarian grounds, and all training colleges supported by the rates should be open to candidates irrespective of their denomination. There should also be an effective conscience clause for any who did work in sectarian establishments, so that they were not obliged to promote any sectarian expectations.[148] The actual minute of the Yearly Meeting was a call to action,

> we would encourage Friends to take such action as they are able in their own localities to influence their fellow citizens and their representatives in Parliament in opposition to the Bill as a whole, and in the event of its being pressed forward, to urge the removal of those provisions of the Bill which would infringe liberty of conscience, or which would remove education from popular control.[149]

The discussion during Yearly Meeting was overshadowed by the knowledge that the Bill had already had its second reading. Once the Act was passed the

---

146. *Carmarthen Journal* (*CJ*) 4.4.1902.
147. *CJ*, 10.10.1902.
148. *TF*, 13.6.1902, 384 - 385.
149. *YMP*, M65 1902, 58.

debate took another direction, since it no longer reflected the principal objections and concerns of the Yearly Meeting.

The pages of *The Friend*, after the Yearly Meeting, are replete with reactions to the changed circumstances. The issue now was what should be done since the legislation was considered offensive to religious conscience? Roland Reynolds writing[150] from his home outside Cardiff summed it up, as he sought the opinion of Friends – should they now pursue a policy of non-payment of the rates in protest at the Act, since such an action could be considered to be in line with their traditional principles on religious liberty? Reynolds would have been aware of national deliberations by individuals to pursue 'passive resistance.' Inevitably Friends responded to his appeal for advice. Viewpoints were expressed within two polarities. Those who felt Friends had to act as their ancestors had done, resist and suffer the consequences, and those who took the view that it was impossible to withhold money from the general rates and taxes, since to do so undermined general civic responsibilities. Indeed, writing in another letter in October, Reynolds took up these issues, recognising the dilemmas inherent in the payment of general taxation to uphold 'civil government,' but that it was legitimate not to pay where circumstances indicated.[151]

This was Roland Exton Reynolds, who had moved to Cardiff in 1892 to work for the Quaker firm of Sessions & Sons, with whom he remained until his early death in 1922. He remains the only Quaker living in Wales who had a biography written about him. outlining, in particular, his activity with the Boy Scout movement, noting that when established, this was an organisation which, 'In common with many other members of the Society of Friends he shared a prejudice against ... believing that its tendency was alien to the peace testimony of the religious society.'[152] Reynolds went on to become a leading Scout leader in the Cardiff area, giving up his connection with the Junior Section of the Cardiff YMCA to undertake this task. This biography is the only one for a Quaker living in Wales during the period of this study, but sadly gives no insight into the activities of the Quakers in the Cardiff

150. *TF*, 4.7.1902, 444.

151. *TF*, 3.10.1902, 651.

152. Joan Reynolds, *The Book of Roland: Being the Life of Roland Exton Reynolds: Boy Lover and Scoutmaster 1871–1922*, Written by his sister and her friend, Ashford, 1923, 129.

and area, other than to mention that he was instrumental in the success of the Literary Society, which attracted a wider circle than its immediate membership of Quakers.

Yearly Meeting in 1903 continued their deliberations focusing their attention on further legislation abolishing the London School Board, and creating an all London Education Authority. By then the 'Passive Resistance Movement and Citizen's League' was established and campaigning against the Act. The prominent Baptist, Dr John Clifford, chaired its executive committee and Dr Rendel Harris its only Quaker member, but not representing the Yearly Meeting. As for Harris he perhaps reflected a particular view of Quakers, 'His entire bearing in the pulpit denoted the dreamer and teacher, rather than the practical man of the world.'[153] The committee membership read like a roll of honour of nonconformity. The only representative from Wales was the Methodist, Robert Bird, J.P., Cardiff.

The organisation's objectives was to 'band together all those who on religious grounds, feel bound to oppose the principles embodied in the Education Act 1902,'[154] providing legal and other assistance to members suffering as a consequence of withholding payment of that portion of their rates considered to be for education. Full membership was open to those resolved to offer passive resistance, with associate membership to those willing to further the objectives of the League, but hesitant about illegal activity. It was more active in England many there being inspired by the 'Welsh Revolt', such that when Lloyd George addressed a demonstration in the Albert Hall in July 1903, he was 'greeted with an ovation that was renewed again and again (demonstrating) how much Free Churchmen realised the debt they owe to this gentleman.'[155] Wales was the beacon. Clifford declared as the struggle progressed that 'Wales must stand to her guns. Wales is in the front of this fight. If you fail, England will be lost to the cause of liberty.'[156]

Many Friends would have been conscious of these developments and that by October 1902, both the Congregational and Baptists Unions in England

---

153. *The Crusader*, (*TC*) 6.11.1903.
154. *TC*, 15.5.1903.
155. *TC*, 15.7.1903.
156. *TC*, 3.3.1904.

and Wales had recommended passive resistance to their members.[157] They would also have been aware of hesitations amongst some local Free Church Councils, indeed with some 384 Councils, 48% of the them, including some important councils, such as Macclesfield, Ipswich, Monmouth and Nelson opposed passive resistance.[158] Since the National Free Church Council felt such a campaign, 'not expedient,' it was such reluctance that led Clifford and his allies to establish the Passive Resistance Movement. Friends attending the Yearly Meeting would have been well aware of the opposition amongst them to passive resistance. George Cadbury, a prominent supporter of the Free Church Council, had threatened to resign from it when the ferment of the Education Bill came before it. Cadbury took the view that national righteousness, 'in the endeavour to bring Christ's teaching to the vast majority'[159] and the saving of souls was the priority, and not political action.

Many Friends were associated with this body notably George Cadbury and Rendel Harris. The National Council of Evangelical Free Churches or the National Free Church Council as it was more commonly known, was created in 1895 as part of an attempt to ensure that nonconformists continued to influence national policy. It was not a representative body, drawing its support from varied sources, including individual congregations and in effect was a loose network of local councils. In 1919, the Federal Council of Evangelical Free Churches was established to complement the work of the older body, but it was composed of representatives chosen by their respective denominations, with the aim of encouraging organic unity amongst the churches. It was avowedly non-political, and partly established because of the other body's political inclinations. Friends were not represented officially on the Federal Council.

The 1903 Yearly Meeting had no difficulty agreeing a memorial against the London Bill, some such as J.B. Braithwaite Jun., supported amongst others by Silvanus P. Thompson, a noted physicist and electrical engineer, wanted a stronger memorial to the one issued in 1902, but others were reluctant. A memorial was brought in and after slight modifications by a

157. Bebbington, *The Nonconformist*, 1982, 143.
158. J.E.B. Munson, 'A Study of Nonconformity in Edwardian England as revealed by the Passive Resistance Movement against the 1902 Education Act', unpublished PhD thesis, University of Oxford, 1973, 177.
159. A.G. Gardiner, *The Life of George Cadbury*, 1923, 186.

small group accepted by the gathering. Its wording was almost identical to the 1902 memorial, and called 'upon Parliament to reject the Bill, as being opposed to those principles of civil and religious liberty which it has ever been the duty and privilege of the Society of Friends to uphold.'[160]

The Yearly Meeting discussion was predictable, touching upon the principle of corporate action and support for civil disobedience through passive resistance. The Clerk drafted a minute but was unable to have it accepted, and so formal support for resistance was withheld, eliciting the comment that, 'LYM very properly declined to express any judgement on the question of Passive Resistance.'[161] The Epistle from the Yearly Meeting hints at inevitable compromise:

> The provisions of the Education Act 1902 and of the Education Bill for London … have received our careful consideration … We recognise in some of these provisions a serious menace to that civil and religious liberty for the preservation of which in the past members of our Society have suffered loss and imprisonment. Our testimony against State intervention with religion has suffered no abatement, and so far as these measures interfere with rights of conscience which we consider to be sacred, we urge our members to maintain their protest against the injustice of this legislation.[162]

Phillips sees this as part of a softening in the Quaker position, reflecting its struggle between the different identities with which it contended, 'wedged uncomfortably between the rock of Edwardian respectability and the hard place of militant opposition.'[163] In the process forfeiting their historic reputation amongst some Nonconformists[164] that Friends no longer 'testify against wrong as once they did.'[165] This did not prevent action by individual Friends, and the Yearly Meeting had recognised this possibility.

By June it was reported that probably the first Friend in the country had been summoned for non-payment of the rate.[166] This was J. Gundry

160. *TF*, 12.6.1903, 388-89.

161. *TF*, 6.5.1903, 371.

162. *YMP* 1903, 80.

163. Phillips, 'Friendly Patriotism', 1989, 113.

164. Ibid. 137.

165. Munson, 'A Study of Nonconformity' 1973, quotes William Robertson Nicoll, editor of the *British Weekly*, 201.

166. *TF*, 12.6.1903, 387.

Alexander of Tunbridge Wells, who would be in Norway representing the Yearly Meeting when his summons would be heard. By the end of the month, J.B. Braithwaite Jnr.,[167] who had joined Rendel Harris on the executive committee of the Passive Resisters Movement, reported that three members of the Society had been summoned.[168]

The position of those suffering for conscience sake now became an issue for Meeting for Sufferings. At its July meeting it agreed to set up a committee to offer 'advice, on doubtful points of law or technical matters, which may enable Friends to follow their own conscience.'[169] By having J. Bevan Braithwaite Jnr. as its Clerk, and adding J. Gundry Alexander[170] and Rendel Harris to its membership,[171] all resisters, it indicated that it was being supportive and sensitive of Friends despite the reluctance of the Yearly Meeting.

In their report to Yearly Meeting in 1904 the Committee noted that it had placed an advert in *The Friend* to inform members of its existence and had received 128 responses.[172] This was unwelcome to some and one, Edward Garnett, who had no sympathy with direct action, questioned the need for the committee since it encouraged, 'a course which if the methods it involved were widely adopted would lead to anarchy.'[173]

Despite the intensity of the 'Welsh Revolt' this did not deflect some individuals from taking action on grounds of conscience. Passive resistance committees were established across Wales, by July1903 in Abergavenny, Barmouth, Brynmawr, Cardiff, Llanelli, Swansea and Radnorshire – presumably Llandrindod Wells. The first Welsh summons was issued in Carmarthen.[175] Bassett notes Baptist passive resistance in several places. The report of Sufferings' committee to Yearly Meeting in 1905 indicated that it had had enquiries from three places in Wales – Glamorgan, Radnorshire and Penybont (Radnorshire!).

167. Munson, 'A Study of Nonconformity,' 1973, 408.

168. *TF*, 26.6.1903, 429.

169. MfS, M14, 3.7.1903.

170. MfS, M13, 2.8.1903.

171. MfS, M18, 2.10.1903.

172. YMP, 1904, M81, 86 with reference to report on pages 200–01.

173. *TF*, 9.6.1905, 378.

174. *TC*, 15.7.1903

175. *TC*, 15.8.1903.

HRMM, in May 1903, expressed their feelings about the Act, and wished 'to unite with members of the Free Church Council in their protest against it.'[177] Llandrindod Wells Meeting had considered a request for, 'the use of the meeting house for a prayer meeting in connection with the prosecution of those whose conscience do not allow them to pay the education rate.'[178] They deferred the matter in the hope that the group would be able to use another facility, presumably reflecting some unease amongst its members. But by 1903 they minuted the injustice of the Act and wished to 'unite with members of the Free Church Council in their protest against the Act.'[179]

In February 1904, J. Owen Jenkins, Penybont Meeting, a magistrate and Chair of the Penybont bench, was summoned for non-payment of the rate. He vacated the chair to

deliver his conscience against a summons for the non-payment of 7s 6d, a sum representing the portion of the poor rate to be used for the purpose of sectarian education.[180]

In April, Jenkins was serving on the bench at Llandrindod, when nineteen persons were summoned for non-payment of their rates, amongst them Hercules Davies Phillips, described as a 'minister of the Society of Friends,'[181] and secretary of the Llandrindod Free Church Council, who had been instrumental in the formation of the Radnorshire Free Churches and Citizen's League.[182] In view of Jenkins' stand he was released from service for the hearing. The *Radnor Express* reported on the deliberations in detail. Phillips, to applause, stated that he believed that he would have been false to his conscience if he had paid the rate. The Chairman wished to know whether he had any legal objection, to which Phillips responded, again to applause, that the Education Act had been passed in defiance of the will of the people, and that some of the clauses succeeded only because of the votes

---

176. T. M. Bassett, *Bedyddwyr Cymru*, 1977, 358–9.
177. Herefordshire Record Office 9 (HRO), A85/9–16, HRMM, M8, 7.5.1903.
178. PCAO, RNC/2B, Llandrindod Wells Preparative Meeting, (LlPWM) M6, 18.1.1903.
179. LlWPM, M8, 6.5.1903.
180. *Radnor Express*, (RE) 11.02.1904.
181. *RE*, 24.4.1903.
182. *RE*, 5.6.1903.

of Irish Roman Catholics.[183] (There was a strong anti-papist, Unionist discourse embedded in the Passive Resistance crusade.[184]) At this point the Chairman, having already warned about applause, ordered the court to be cleared, ' an order which was carried out to the great public disappoint-ment.'[185] In Jenkins' and Phillips' case goods were distrained. In April a coffee set distrained from Jenkins was sold at auction in Llandrindod, and Phillips' bicycle was sold for 40s.

As far as can be ascertained these were the only prosecutions against Quakers in Wales. There are no minutes of South Wales or HRMM recording any suffering. WQM, as noted, had expressed its viewpoint, and took an interest in educational matters. In June 1900 it protested strongly against encouraging military practices and the possible introduction of military drill into schools, preparing a memorandum on the subject. This was translated into Welsh, the first such gesture by the body, by 'Our Friend Henry T. Evans of Aberayron ... and sent ... to all the papers in the Principality several of whom willingly inserted it.'[186] This emanated from consideration by the YM, circulating their stance to 560 newspapers and periodicals and 576 Free Church Councils. As for the Welsh appeal, the Quarterly Meeting of the Calvinistic Methodists in Merioneth discussed it, wishing to encourage wide distribution of its contents.[187]

As for the general resistance across England, *The Friend* reported that Samuel Southall of Leeds, aged 76, and formerly of Leominster, had in March 1905 been sentenced to three days imprisonment, for 'refusing to pay the portion of the poor rate which they calculated would be devoted to sectarian purposes.'[188] It further noted (mistakenly) that, as far as it knew, he was the first Quaker to go to prison because of resistance to the Act. The Crusader had reported a week earlier that Dr Alfred Salter was in prison for the third time, 'the only one of that body (Religious Society of Friends) to suffer imprisonment up to the present time.'[189]

183. *RE*, 24.04.1903.

184. Munson, *A Study of' Nonconformity*, 1973, 145

185. *RE*, 24.4.1904.

186. WRO, 898.2, BA 1303,WQM, M2, 27.6.1900.

187. *YFAC*, 14.11.1900.

188. *TF*, 24.3.1905, 184.

189.*TC* 16.3.1905.

Salter, a doctor in Bermondsey, reflects certain ambivalence amongst the establishment concerning passive resistance. He refused to pay his rates six times and was sentenced on each occasion to three days in prison. The resisters made the maximum propaganda of this parading the streets with posters, 'Dr Alfred Salter is in PRISON today for Conscience Sake.'[190] When he was imprisoned efforts were made to ensure that this did not inconvenience his patients, and so he would arrange with the police that he be arrested when the pressure of work was light. He was always arrested on a Friday night because that made him due for discharge on Sunday – it being prison practice to liberate Sunday discharges on the Saturday.

Quaker contribution to the 'Welsh Revolt' is unquantifiable since so little is minuted. Action by individual Quakers in Wales was subdued. In April 1904 two conferences were held at Llandrindod, one associated with the Free Church Council, where no doubt Hercules Phillips, as secretary of its Llandrindod Council would have been involved.At the other a conference with representatives of the Welsh County Councils, *Y Diwigiwr* noted that it was amongst the most important ever held in the town

> and in any other place in the history of the Welsh nation ... the banner of freedom and educational and religious equality has been raised, and the greater majority of the Welsh nation enlisted under it.[191]

In such a clamour the Quaker voice would have been barely heard. Thus Edward Grubb, in his Presidential Address to the Friends' Guild of Teachers, in January 1903, made no reference to the turmoil surrounding the Act, addressing himself to the loftier and more spiritual question.'[192] The agitation was quietened by the spectacular Liberal victory of 1906, when all the Welsh seats fell to the Liberals or their Labour allies, but followed by disappointment with the failure to improve, amend or repeal elements of the Act. A failure considered a marker in the death of political nonconformity.[193]

---

190. Fenner Brockway, *Bermondsey Story: The Life of Alfred Salter*, London, 1947, 27.
191. *Y Diwigiwr*, May 1904, 133–7. ('*ac mewn unrhyw le arall yn hanes y genedl Gymreig ... y mae baner rhyddid a chydraddoldeb addysgol a chrefyddol wedi ei chodi, a mwyafrif aruthrol y Genedl wedi listio tani.*')
192. *BF*, February 1903.
193. See Noel J. Richards, 'The Education Bill of 1906 and the Decline of Political Nonconformity,' in *Journal of Ecclesiastical History*, XXIII, No. 1, January 1972, 49–63.

iii. Temperance – 1881 Wales Sunday Closing Day Act

Temperance, nonconformity, and sabbatarianism became strongly identified with Welsh national aspirations. These were aspects of Welsh life that would have appealed to many Quakers, who despite their small numbers in Britain produced far more teetotal leaders than any other denomination – 24% of those whose religious affiliations were known to be Quakers.[194] Temperance was an issue that evangelic Friends took up vigorously. Indeed, Henry Stanley Newman had proudly proclaimed that 'Mission work and total abstinence were inseparably connected together in our country.'[195]

The temperance movement was not a homogeneous and united effort. Within it was a spectrum of emphasis, from total abstinence to those who sought reasonable control over the industry. Friends had proven supportive to the movement when other denominations had been more reluctant. They were important not simply for their numbers, but because of their generous financial support. Similarly replicated in the struggle against the Contagious Diseases Act, where the Quakers were the largest of the nonconformist groups represented on, for example, the Ladies National Association for the Repeal of the Act. Here again Quaker money was important, such that that organisation, 'never had to worry about money. Rather, its problem was one of how to spend its income.'[196]

As in the case of disestablishment Harrison highlights the same strong identification between temperance and Welsh national aspirations. Whereas, according to him, English prohibitionism by 1870 was stagnating this was not the case in Wales, and the United Kingdom Alliance, established in 1853 by a group of Mancunian nonconformists headed by the cotton manufacturer and Quaker, Nathaniel Card, 'continued to expand in Wales until the late 1880s.'[197] Quakers in Wales played a significant role in the expansion of temperance in the Principality. The Swansea temperance movement in 1836, for example, was promoted by a group of Quakers, and Frederick Joseph Gibbins, the Neath industrialist, was such a renowned and esteemed campaigner that at his funeral the taverns of Neath were closed for the day.

194. Brian Harrison, *Drink and the Victorians: The Temperance Question in England 1815–1872*, 1971, 156.
195. *TF*, 6th month, 1877, 179.
196. Paul McHugh, *Prostitution and Victorian Social Reform*, 1980, 192.
197. Harrison, *Drink*, 1994, 235.

His testimony before the Yearly Meeting in 1907 in YMP, 1907, 206–8. The testimony read that the 'President of the Local Victualers requested all the public houses to be closed upon the occasion of his funeral.'[198] His son, the short-lived Member of Parliament, was to carry on his endeavours opening a temperance bar at his Melincrydden works.[199]

There was overwhelming support from Welsh Members of Parliament for temperance; in 1885, 36 members were teetotallers and their voting on temperance matters consistent.[200] In such a context, and given that the issue figured prominently in election addresses in 1880,[201] it was not surprising that in 1881 Parliament passed the Wales Sunday Closing Act, the first time that the 'Imperial Parliament had sanctioned separate legislative treatment for Wales.'[202] This was seen, by some, as the first part of the movement towards Home Rule, one correspondent noting that on the day the Act was passed, 'Little Wales raised her head on that day in the Counsels of the Legislature higher than any other time in her whole history.'[203] In that light it should be seen as a defining moment in the furtherance and consolidation of Welsh national political identity.

The Act was principally the result of an alliance between sabbatarian and temperance reformers,[204] evangelical belief rather than political fervour being the principal motive. Scotland had had Sunday closing since 1853 and Ireland since 1878. Whether the Act was successful was doubtful and its outcome 'lay in its underlying principle rather than in its operation.'[205] One of its effects was the creation of more clubs and illegal shebeens. The 1890 Royal Commission on the workings of the Act had to acknowledge that it had reduced drunkenness in rural areas but had been 'constantly evaded and defied in some urban areas.'[206]

198. *YMP*, 1907, 206–08.

199. Rees, *Welsh Hustings*, 2005, 107.

200. W. R. Lambert, *Drink and Sobriety in Victorian Wales*, 1983, 212.

201. Morgan, *Wales in British*, 1991, 42.

202. Ibid., 223.

203. Daniel Rowlands, 'Y Fasnach Feddwol' in *Y Traethodydd*, xxxvi, 1881, 336–50. ('*Fe gododd Cymru fechan ei phen diwrnod hwnnw yn Nghyngor y Wladwriaeth yn uwch nag ar un adeg arall yn ei holl hanes.*')

204. Lambert, *Drink*, 1983, 213.

205. Morgan, *Wales in British*, 1991, 43.

206. Lambert, *Drink*, 1983, 230.

Quakers in Wales, through their Monthly Meetings said nothing about the workings of the Act, and WQM was similarly silent. There was one Quaker witness before the 1890 Commission: Frederick J. Gibbins of Neath. He considered the Act to have been a success in promoting temperance, and felt that the greater number of arrests for drunkenness was as a result of greater vigilance by the police for evasions. His own workmen, (he employed about 50 men) supported the Act. Gibbins supported it also because it meant that women servants, on Sunday evenings were no longer forced to use the public houses, as had been the case when they had nowhere else to go![207]

Meetings were actively involved and sympathetic to the objectives of the temperance movement. The Women's Meeting of WQM, consistently returned to the subject during their deliberations, 'The strong claims of the Temperance cause have been afresh before us at this time. We earnestly desire that this important subject should receive increased attention from the Women's Yearly Meeting.'[208] *The Friend* found no reason to report on the Act, but in 1885, in relation to the impending election, referred to it as an example of the good work done by the House of Commons,[209] highlighting the importance of the issue of local control of licensing. This was something that temperance campaigners were keen to see across the country, since they saw it as an opportunity to extend prohibition.

When in September 1906 a summer school for Friends was held at Llandrindod and of an 'experimental nature'[210] – it was hoped it could draw people in from the 1500 to 2000 attending the various evangelic events in the town – the vice-chairman of Radnorshire County Council chaired a meeting on temperance with consideration of another temperance Bill before parliament. Henry Southall, Ross Meeting, was anxious that temperance should proceed in a moderate way, expressing doubts about certain elements in the Bill, echoed by Richard Watkins of Swansea Meeting. Percy Thomas, of Cardiff, was anxious to press the claims of Wales for the local veto, paying

---

207. The Welsh Sunday Closing Act: Evidence: Report of the Royal Commissioners appointed to enquire into the operation of the Sunday Closing (Wales) Act 1881, 1890, Cmd. 5994, 6013–44.

208. WRO 898.2, 1303/14, M2 12.12.1883.

209. *TF*, Ninth Month, 1885, 216.

210. *TF*, 7.9.1906, 607 and 14.9.1906, 619.

tribute to J. Herbert Roberts, member of partliament for Flintshire, who had originally introduced, as a private measure, what became the 1881 Act.

Theodore Neild addressed the summer school on the subject, and in 1908 wrote an article on another licensing Bill going before parliament to bring Monmouthshire into the compass of the 1881 Act, commenting that 'Monmouthshire was to be reckoned as a county of Wales for the purposes of Sunday opening.'[211] He at least realised that this was an issue that had some importance to Welsh sensitivities, the exclusion of Monmouthshire from the original bill had caused considerable unease. Its omission from the original 1881 Act reflected considerable debate as to the historical status of Monmouthshire as part of Wales. By population, language and history it was Welsh, but since it had been omitted by Tudor legislation from Welsh organisational arrangements it had acquired an anomalous status. The 1908 Licensing Act went part of the way to correct this position, bringing Monmouthshire within the Welsh ambit.

The Friends' Temperance Union (FTU), originally established in 1852, to spread 'Temperance principles and practice amongst members of the Society of Friends throughout the area of LYM.' Its membership was limited to total abstainers, and the aim was to form a branch in each meeting with a correspondent, with an aggregate meeting within each Quarterly Meeting, with an annual meeting during Yearly Meeting. It was reconstituted in 1877, from which time it reported directly to the Yearly Meeting, not for discussion, but rather to simply record, that it had held its meeting during the time of YM.[212] Despite its status it paid no heed to the passage of the 1881 Act.

As an organisation it was primarily concerned with reclamation and moral improvement within the Society and was not forward looking. The FTU spent some time considering the needs of pupils in Quaker schools. Between 1877 and 1884 they showed no interest in the politics of temperance. Its minutes reveal that this was a London dominated organisation, conservative in attitude, whose meetings were relatively short and undynamic. When its members considered whether women should join the committee in November 1881, they minuted:

211. *TF*, 6.3.1908, 148.
212. *YMP* 1877, 32.

The Committee would gladly have the company of women Friends at the Committee meetings, but owing to the time at which they are held, and the short time that they often last, it is not thought desirable to ask for their company except on special occasions.[213]

They willingly gave money to the Women Friends Union of Abstainers, agreeing to grant them in September 1881, £5 to cover expenses incurred.[214]

By the 1890s the temperance movement no longer had a strong political voice and was much weakened with most working people having greater concerns. FTU and other temperance organisations were no longer as relevant. After the First World War, 'temperance reformers of all kinds were no longer *avant garde* among social reformers.'[215] Harrison refers to the work of two Quakers, Joseph Rowntree and Arthur Shewell, as an example of the shift to a more constructive consideration of social problems[216] and temperance had 'lost its distinct identity in the face of the advance of the twentieth century welfare state.'[217]

The FTU would no doubt have read with regret, and yet with satisfaction, a report on temperance works in Swansea in March 1906, an area still gripped by the effects of the Welsh Revival. It was noted that about fifty taverns had closed in the town, and that the Quaker Band of Hope was a great success, in a town where

> there is much drinking ... amongst men and women. Women are often seen staggering drunk with infants in their arms ... Our Band of Hope numbers about 140 and the children largely of these drinking parents.[218]

The 1881 Act, despite its importance in Welsh national life, was not a corporate issue for the Yearly Meeting, which had always been equivocal about temperance and abstinence. The 1861 *Christian Doctrine, Practice and Discipline*, which set out the rules governing the life of meetings, and the social behaviour of Friends, included only reference to advice issued in 1691

---

213. LSF, temp MSS 893, FTU, M2, November 1881.
214. Ibid., M5, 2.9.1881.
215. Harrison, *Drink and the Victorians*, 1984, 382.
216. Ibid., 382. This was their *Temperance Problems and Social Reforms*, published 1899.
217. Lambert, *Drink*, 1983, 248.
218. *TF*, 30.3.1906, 209.

on language, habit, deportment and behaviour; the 1703 advice on being spotless and blameless, modest and sober, and from 1751 a warning to abstain from every appearance of evil to include excess of drinking. From 1791 the discipline expected of Friends was more specific:

> As to the frequenting of public houses, we desire that all under our name may be cautious of remaining in them, after the purpose of business or refreshment is accomplished, but to make them a resort for any other purpose, may it never need to be named among a people who profess the practice of Christian sobriety.[219]

The 1883 version of the book repeated the same advice, with no call for total abstinence, rather encouraging self-denial, reflective of the importance of individual conscience, and quoted from an 1870 epistle that,

> We attempt not to define the limits of individual duty; but we desire that all our members may be willing … to take a calm view of this great subject [and] to press home to every one of our members his individual responsibility.[220]

Frederick Sessions of Gloucester, home mission worker and brother of Arthur Sessions, Cardiff Meeting, was an active worker for temperance. He summed up the position of the YM succinctly in a lecture he gave to the FTU in 1893, that the Meeting 'has never made any unmistakeable emphatic pronouncements in its corporate capacity in favour of Total Abstinence as a rule of life for its members, although it has several times implied that its leanings are in that direction.'[221] Yet the Yearly Meeting was defensive of its reputation and standing in the matter of alcohol. In 1904 Sufferings, for example, approved action in the Courts seeking to prevent a brewer from labelling one of his products as 'Quaker Stout.'[222] The case was dismissed, the Judge depending on a previous judgement by the Quaker judge, Sir Edward Fry, that any 'grievance had to have a legal and not a sentimental one.'

---

219. *Christian Doctrine, Practice and Discipline* (London, Friends' Book Depository, 1861).
220. *Book of Christian Discipline of the Religious Society of Friends in Great Britain*, 1883, 104–14.
221. Frederick Sessions, *Two and a half Centuries of Temperance Work in the Society of Friends, 1643–1893*, 1893.
222. *TF*, 15.7.1904, 473.

Whether or not the Yearly Meeting had an official position regarding temperance, it is apparent that within Wales, the general efforts of Friends in the movement were much appreciated. In 1881 *Y Traethodydd* reported that

> Members of the Society of Friends have always been in the forefront in efforts in this country against the harm of intemperance. Many of the most able and influential proponents for the principles of temperance are, and have been Friends; the annual meeting of the Friends Temperance Union is amongst the most interesting meetings held by the denomination during the year. Most of the Friends are notable abstainers.[223]

This serves as an example of the way the Quakers caught and held the imagination of others, and in the process contributed to their own self-satisfaction, if not self-aggrandisement.

iv. Industrial disputes

One theme of interest to Friends, so far as the general life of Wales was concerned, was the growing number of industrial disputes affecting it. This was reflected threefold; entrepreneurial and economic, the fact that wealth exercised conscience – there were a 'disproportionately large number of Quaker entrepreneurs' whose wealth challenged their consciences, often expressed in paternalistic outpourings,[224] and the conviction, derived from their peace testimony, that negotiation and conciliation was preferable to militancy, and that common ground should be found. Indeed,

> The Quaker abhorrence of conflict manifested itself in the belief that cooperation was the true basis of business. The custom of 'taking the sense of

223. T.M. Williams, '*Yr Enwadau Crefyddol a Dirwest*' (The Religious Denominations and Temperance), in *Y Traethodydd*, xxxvi, 1881, 462. ('*Mae aelodau Cymdeithas y Cyfeillion wedi bod bob amser ymysg y rhai blaenaf yn yr ymgyrch yn y wlad hon yn erbyn y drwg anferth o anghymedroldeb. Y mae llawer o amddiffynwyr mwyaf galluog a dylanwadol egwyddorion dirwestol yn, ac wedi bod yn Gyfeillion; ac fe gyfrifir cyfarfod blynyddol Undeb Dirwestol y Cyfeillion ynun o gyfarfodydd mwyaf dyddorol a gynhelir gan yr enwad yn ystod y flwyddyn. Mae y mwyafrif mawr o'r Cyfeillion yn ddirwestwyr amlwg.*')
224. T.A.B. Conley, 'Changing Quaker attitudes to wealth, 1690–1950,' in *Religion, Business and Wealth in Modern Britain*, David J. Jeremy ed., 1998, 140 – 142.

the meeting' also encouraged the search for consensus in the factory. Business was a trust. Workers had the first claim on their employers' benevolence.[225]

Disputes were not of course unique to Wales. However, given their scale and impact, the Penrhyn Quarry Strikes, or lockouts, at Bethesda, Caernarfonshire deserves attention.

The first began in September 1896, lasting until August 1897, and the second, from the 22nd November 1900 to November 1903, *Y Streic Fawr* (The Great Strike), when 2,800 men walked out and 1,000 never returned. This was, according to one historian, a gigantic 'struggle for the rights of trade unionism'[226] and therefore of national significance. In 1885–6, the quarrymen of the Dinorwic Quarry, Llanberis had struck, reflecting general unease across the industry, but the refusal of Lord Penrhyn to recognise his workers' rights to collective bargaining at Bethesda, led to what was for many years the longest strike in Welsh and British history.

The Penrhyn Relief Fund collected over £88,000[227] to help the devastated communities of the Ogwen Valley, and it is hard not to imagine Quakers contributing, given the hardships. The editorial in *The Friend* on the subject in February 1897 would have resonated with many. It described Lord Penrhyn's refusal to recognise the North Wales Quarrymen's Union as a denial of liberty, and his stubbornness in not accepting the assistance of the Board of Trade, under the 1896 Conciliation Act, as 'not only un-English but un-Christian.'[228] The editor could have easily omitted the reference to England.

The principles behind the dispute were of universal importance, and the second dispute in particular struck at the heart of a close Welsh community tearing it apart. *The Friend* in June 1901 reported that, after being locked out for seven months, some 400 workmen had voluntarily returned to work, pointedly adding that only 100 'were quarrymen proper.'[229] This resulted in signs in Welsh appearing in the windows of many homes across the area,

225. Charles Dellheim, 'The Creation of a Company Culture: Cadburys, 1861–1931,' in *The American Historical Review*, 92, 1, February 1987, 33.
226. Merfyn Jones, *The North Wales Quarrymen 1874–1922*, 1982, 267.
227. Ibid., 270.
228. *TF*, 5.2.1897, 81.
229. *TF*, 21.6.1901, 417.

'There is no traitor in this house.'[230] The ill feeling created entered Welsh folklore. *The Friend* did not pick up on this issue, but there was some understanding of the tragedy and the sadness inherent in the dispute. The editor referred to 'the pathetic situation at Bethesda'[231] that had again come before the House of Commons. No notice of the end of the strike or its impact appeared in its pages, but in a somewhat sad report in September 1903, two months before the strike came to an end, it reported that the North Wales Quarrymen's Union had received notice that the monthly subsidy of £3,000 from the General Federation of Trade Unions was to cease.[232]

The *British Friend*, whose editor William Edward Turner was similarly enraged about the Penrhyn strike, noted in May 1903 that the 'dispute seemed endless, a striking exhibition of the persistence of feudal ideas,'[233] agreeing with the Quaker M.P., John Edward Ellis, that the quarrymen had the right to join together in a union, an essential prerequisite to modern industrial relations. The monthly sought to soften personal criticism of Lord Penrhyn, hinting that his stubbornness was a problem, but pursuing a political line that it was time, 'that such power over the lives and happiness of the many was taken from the few.'[234]

There are several references to other Welsh industrial disputes in *The Friend* at the beginning of the twentieth century, reflecting the shifts that were happening in the social, economic and political life of the country. On 7th September 1900 it described the Welsh railway dispute, which led to the Taff Vale judgement. The Taff Vale Railway Company sued the Amalgamated Society of Railway Servants for losses incurred during a strike. The union was fined and failed on appeal to the Lords. This meant that unions were then liable for damages caused to employers during a dispute, thus weakening the efficacy of the strike. The Liberal government's, Trade Disputes Act 1906, nullified the effect of the decision, and the importance of the Board of Conciliation established as a practical approach to Christian peacemaking. When William Abraham, the Liberal-Labour M.P for the

---

230. Jones, *The North Wales*, 1982, 234. '*Nid oes bradwr yn y tŷ hwn.*' Cards were issued to each striker in June 1901.
231. *TF*, 13.3.1903,159.
232. *TF*, 25.9.1903, 644.
233. *BF*, May 1903, 106.
234. Ibid.

Rhondda, popularly known by his bardic name 'Mabon', and who in 1907 became the leader of the Welsh Miners Federation, visited the USA, *The Friend* reported, with satisfaction, his comments when '… he tells the people of the Rhondda Valley that the interests of working men and capitalists, instead of being necessarily antagonistic, are in reality parallel.'[235] Mabon's conciliatory attitude would have resonated and be welcomed by Quakers.

In September 1910 there was a lockout at the Ely pit, part of the Cambrian Collieries, followed by a mass walkout by all 12,000 miners in the group, which dragged on until August 1911. This was the strike that saw Winston Churchill authorising military support at Tonypandy. In Llanelli in 1911, during a national rail stoppage, troops shot and killed two men, and much looting and rioting followed this.[236] The overall ugliness of industrial unrest was to be seen in riots against Jews in some areas of south Wales. There were also attacks against gypsies in Llanelli in 1912, and in 1919 there were racial riots in Cardiff.[237] None of this was reported in *The Friend* or commented upon by any meetings.

The deteriorating working conditions within the coal industry were naturally of considerable importance to south Wales, and Quaker concern shaped by genuine sympathy. A key to understanding the scale of Quaker relief offered in south Wales from 1926, compared to action in the other British coalfields. In 1912 a national coal strike was called in support of a minimum wage. The plight of the workers was recognised and in an article on the 5th April, 1912 *The Friend* reported that 'a well known Friend has received from a former domestic servant in her employ, now married and living in the Rhondda Valley, a statement of the circumstances from the miners' point of view,'[238] an extract which the editor felt would be informative to some readers. The following week Caroline E. Ferris, of Penarth – she and her sister Lydia ran a private school in Penarth, and was Clerk of SWMM for an unbroken period of 30 years, which she dominated by her very presence, steadfastness and perseverance – wrote to confirm the verity

235. *TF*, 18.4.1902, 243.
236. See Deian Hopkins, 'The Llanelli Riots, 1911,' in *Welsh History Review*, 11, 1982–3, 488–511.
237. See Colin Holmes, 'The Tredegar Riots of 1911: Anti Jewish Disturbances in South Wales,' in *Welsh History Review*, Vol. 11, 1982–3, 214–25.
238. *TF*, 5.4.1912, 218.

of the statement about miners' low wages, referring to a young miner from the Forest of Dean who had visited her:

> He has sometimes had nothing at all for a whole week's work, when getting out stones and rubbish. Yet this has to be done, as coal may be behind. No wonder they struck.[239]

This compassionate tone was similarly evident in 1898 during another dispute. The editor was concerned about the hardships in south Wales,[240] and the following week noted that Sir Edward Fry,[241] had been appointed as conciliator in the dispute. The following week, John Edward Southall of Newport wrote to express his concern about the poor pay of miners that they 'deserve our sympathy.'[242]

Disasters in the mines were reported but nothing to reflect their scale and frequency. According to one chronicler[243] there were at least 164 disasters in Wales between 1849 and 1925, each claiming five or more lives accounting for 5,650 deaths which represented only a small proportion of Welsh miners killed at their workplace, less than 17% of all mining deaths.

William G. Hall of Swansea Meeting was among the mourners at Wattstown, where 119 miners were killed, in July 1905, his sadness is palpable, but neither can he escape his evangelical leanings, commenting that 'It was a pleasure to find that many of those killed had experienced changed lives during the [Welsh] revival.'[244] The tragedy at the Universal Mine in Senghenydd in October 1913, when 439 were killed, was also reported, *The Friend* recognising the broad issues and problems facing the coal industry, especially the issue of coal dust as a factor in accidents.[245]

Such events contributed to changes in awareness challenging Welsh nonconformity and the old Liberal hegemony with its complacent cultural nationalism. Pope remarks that the decline of Nonconformity was aligned to the ascendancy of the Labour Party at both Welsh national and local levels,

239. *TF*, 12.4.1912, 237–8.
240. *TF*, 1.7.1898, 416–17.
241. *TF*, 8.7.1898, 430.
242. *TF*, 15.7.1898, 457–8.
243. www.welshcoalmines.co.uk accessed 22.02.13
244. *TF*, 28.7.1905, 487.
245. *TF*, 17.10.1913, 697 and 24.10.1913, pp. 700–01.

such that:

> Socialism was to be associated increasingly with progress and the English language whilst the Welsh language, especially in the valleys of the industrial south, became identified with the Nonconformist and Liberal past.[246]

The decline of Nonconformity was not of course unique to Wales, reflecting as it did the processes of secularisation and urbanisation. Jeffrey Cox analyses the process of change in Lambeth, noting that the long-term failure of the churches to recruit was a major issue, although in Wales the impact of the 1904-05 Revival stemmed this temporarily. He was clear that the churches failed to respond to the implications of material improvements and prosperity, and that it was not merely a response to intellectual debate or socialistic ideals. The chapels had been hit by 'the emergence of new philanthropic, administrative, and educational bureaucracies which destroyed their claims to social utility.'[247] Religion had to compete in a free market of ideals. Friends were not immune from this.

This is a different world, providing new directions, and a move to class politics away from cultural politics where chapels and Quaker meetings remained stuck and 'formed in some degree an enclave of cultural politics in a period when class politics had become the norm.'[248] This presents a picture of castles under siege, but Packer is cautious, believing that overall the situation, particularly before the First World War, has been exaggerated.[249] Using the Rowntree family, and the Quakers, he demonstrates that new Liberalism was responsive, and that moral issues, such as temperance and sabbatarianism, orientated some Liberals towards social reform. The 'New Evangelicalism' meant less emphasis on atonement and more on the example of the life of Christ, noting that as a result many evangelicals retreated into holiness.[250] Koss saw the politics of the early 1900s reviving nonconformist

---

246. Robert Pope, *Building Jerusalem: Nonconformity, Labour and the Social Question in Wales, 1906–1939*, 1998, 28.

247. Jeffrey Cox, *The English Churches in a Secular Society*, 1982, 253.

248. D.W. Bebbington, 'Nonconformity and Electoral Sociology, 1867–1918,' in *Historical Journal*, 27, 1984, 656.

249. I. Packer, 'Religion and the New Liberalism: The Rowntree Family, Quakerism and Social Reform,' in *Journal of British Studies*, 42, 2003, 236–57.

250. Ibid., 241.

vitality, the establishment of the National Council of Evangelical Free Churches, 1895, and the Federal Free Church Council in 1916, part of this trend.[251]

All this reflected aspirations that were not perhaps totally comprehended by those in its midst. In Wales the one aspect that was most visible to the chapels was the decline of the language, an issue that barely affected Friends since there were no Welsh-speaking meetings, and explains why they ignored the matter, either then or subsequently. The exception was John Edward Southall. Friends would not have identified with one evaluation of the 1901 linguistic census, that some of the larger cities of England had more Welsh spoken in them than Cardiff or Newport.[252]

Others perceived the threat to the life of Wales in far starker, if not by what today would be construed as racialist terms. The Rev. W.F. Phillips, Tenby writing about indications of national decline in what was for him a religious nation, attributed it to foreign elements, which had slipped into the country:

> Into our midst have come some of the worst characteristics of England and other countries, they have brought their corrupting influences with them ... and the workers are being led by foreigners, and from the mouths of these leaders come the sharpest attacks on our country, our language and our nation.[253]

Sentiments that would not have found their way into Quaker talk given that by this analysis they were part of a problem.

v. War and pacifism

The South African War submerged the debate about Welsh Home Rule but opposition to the conflict in Wales was particularly vocal, principally through

---

251. Stephen Koss, *Nonconformity in Modern British Politics*, 1975.

252. J. Williams, 'Cofrifiad Ieithyddol Cymru' (Welsh Linguistic Census) 1901,' in *Y Traethodydd*, Vol. LIX, 1904, 452–9.

253. Rev.W.F. Phillips, '*Arwyddion Dirywiad Cenedlaethol*' (Signs of National Deterioration), in *Y Traethodydd*, October 1914, 2, 8, 321–34. ('*... elfennau estronol lithrodd i mewn i fywyd y wlad. Daeth i fyw i'n plith rai o gymeriadau salaf Lloegr a gwledydd eraill, a daethant a'u harferion llygredig gyda hwynt ... cymer y gweithwyr eu harwain gan estroniaid, ac o enau'r arweinwyr hyn y ceir yr ymosodiadau ar ein gwlad, ein hiaith a'n cenedl.*')

Lloyd George's leadership, an effort that would help transform him from a Welsh into a national British politician. His opposition was according to Price influenced by both Nonconformist and nationalist sympathies for the Boers.[254] Welsh opposition to the war, as Morgan comments, was initially confined to a vocal minority with the Nonconformist and predominantly rural Welsh speaking areas most hostile.[255] Nevertheless, the 'bulk of articulate opinion in Wales was strongly pro-war and sympathetic to imperialism.'[256] There was no unity within LYM about the war, and it in many respects was ambivalent.[257] Phillips contends that the attitude of Edwardian Friends towards peace was posture driven,[258] and there were many prominent Quaker public voices heard in support of the war, such as John Bellows, Gloucester and Dr Thomas Hodgkin, but both were Liberal Unionists.[259] Indeed the war made political compromise amongst Friends inevitable, and the stance of many in support of it paving the way for more flexible attitudes during the First World War when it arrived. As Hodgkin wrote:

> I am inclined, therefore, to think that if our Saviour now returned to earth, and if one of His disciples asked for His guidance on the question whether he might use police force to protect property or military force to repel unjust attack by a foreign power, He would not withhold the required permission ... any such use of force ... would have to be made under a stern and solemn sense of absolute duty.[260]

Amongst Welsh Quakers, Henry Tobit Evans proved to be a prominent supporter of the war and the Imperial cause.

The opposition to the war within Wales was not entirely lost on Friends. In 1901 the YM Peace Committee distributed 190,000 copies of a leaflet *Christianity and War* which had been published by the 1900 YM, and

254. Price, *David Lloyd*, 2006, 187.

255. Morgan, *Wales in British*, 1991, 178–9.

256. Morgan, *Modern Wales*, 1995, 'Peace Movements in Wales 1899–1945,' 87.

257. Kennedy, *British Quakerism*, 2001, 253–61.

258. Phillips, 'Friendly Patriotism', 1989, 153–259, see Hewison, *Hedge*, 1989.

259. See H.H. Hewison, *Hedge of Wild Almonds: South Africa, the pro-Boers and the Quaker Conscience 1890–1910*, 1989).

260. Louise Creighton, *Life and Letters, Life and Letters of Thomas Hodgkin*, 1917, 245.

arranged for 5,000 copies to be printed in Welsh. The translation 'being kindly undertaken by a Congregational minister, Ivan T. Davies of Corwen, a descendent of Friends, who volunteered for this service and also gave valuable assistance in the matter of distribution and procuring insertion in Welsh newspapers.'[261] This reflected the resilience of Welsh anti-war sentiment, led not only by Lloyd George but also by such men as Bryn Roberts the member of parliament for south Caernarfonshire. One obituary of him noted that he 'praised the Quakers with deep reverence, and said more than once that if he were young, and the Quakers within reach, that he would have joined them.'[262] At a peace conference held in Cardiff on the war in January 1901, Frederick J. Gibbins of Neath seconded one resolution to promote the ideals of peace in Wales, in the course of which he read from the minute of protest agreed by Meeting for Sufferings in December 1900, 'which was very cordially received by the conference.'[263]

The Peace Society had been founded in London in 1816 with Joseph Tregelles Price, the Neath Quaker, as one of its principal founders. Despite this Welsh connection it never took deep roots in Wales,[264] even though its first four secretaries were Welsh of whom two were Quakers, Evan Rees from Neath and William Jones, originally from Ruthun; then there was Henry Richard and Dr W. Evans Darby, born in Saundersfoot, Pembroke-shire.[265]

The dominant role of Henry Richard, not only in the Peace Society but also within the Liberation Society, allied to his status as a member of parliament, must have conveyed to many Quakers that Wales was somewhat more pacifist than elsewhere in Britain, helping to create a pacifistic representation for Wales. A factor in the opinion of one author that helped

261. YMP, 1901, 28–9.
262. Y Drysorfa, 1208, August 1931, 309, ('Canmolai'r Barnwr y Crynwyr gyda pharch dwfn, a dywedodd fwy nag unwaith pe bae ef yn ieuengach, a'r Crynwyr o fewn cyrraedd iddo, y buasai yn ymuno â hwy.').
263. TF, 11.01.1901, 28.
264. T.H. Lewis, 'Y Mudiad Heddwch yng Nghymru, 1800–1899,' in the Transactions of the Honourable Society of Cymmrodorion, 1957 Session, 87–127. See also, Bob Owen, 'Cymru a'r Mudiad Heddwch, 1814–1824,' in Y Genninen, xliii, 1925, 201–10.
265. See Goronwy J. Jones, Wales and the Quest for Peace (Cardiff, University of Wales Press, 1969).

reshape Welsh political life, since on the back of it, Keir Hardie secured his election in 1900 giving socialism a foothold in Wales.[266] Although in reality Welsh pacifism was far from being pacific embedded as it was in a radical discourse.[267] But the pacifism of Wales was as individualistic as elsewhere, led by political and sermonic rhetoric; there was never a sustained national debate around the subject, whilst the Quaker contribution to any such debate in Wales, was minimal. Thus Dewi Eurig Davies in his study of the response of the Welsh church to the Great War makes no reference to the Quakers.[268]

What developed from the debate over the South African War was that 'Welshness' acquired a greater pacifist construction, encouraging 'a process of selective amnesia ... presenting the Welsh as an inherently pacific people,'[269] who extolled Christian peace, piety and quietism that would have appealed to the Quakers. Evans gives some support to this view, that during the nineteenth century and up to the First World War, military recruitment was at a lower level in Wales compared to the rest of the country and the Welsh underrepresented in the army. An image of Wales as an unpatriotic, anti-militarist, pacifist nation that suited two sets of politicians. It upheld the Nonconformist in their determination over their rights and role and justified accusations by the Tories (and Anglicans) that nonconformists were unpatriotic.[270]

With the advent of the First World War, Wales was pulled into a vortex, entering a period of decay, with attendant loss of purpose and national identity.[271] A small number in Wales opposed the war, enthusiasm for it reflective of the general European experience.[272] Aled Eurig hints that the official statistics of the time, 21.5% of eligible Welsh men enlisting compared

---

266. Ibid., 160.

267. See Geraint H. Jenkins, 'Rhyfel yr Oen: Y Mudiad Heddwch yng Nghymru 1653–1816', in Cadw Tŷ Mewn Cwmwl Tystion, 1990, 27–50.

268. Dewi Eurig Davies , Byddin y Brenin – Cymru a'i Chrefydd yn y Rhyfel Mawr, 1988.

269. John S. Ellis, 'Pacifism, militarism and Welsh Identity,' in Wales and War: Society, Politics and Religion in the Nineteenth and twentieth centuries, Mathew Cragoe and Chris Williams, eds, 2007, 32.

270. Neil Evans, 'Loyalties: state, nation, community and military recruiting,' in Cragoe and Willliams, Wales and War, 2007, 39. (58).

271. Tecwyn Lloyd, 'Welsh Public Opinion and the First World War,' in Planet, 10, 1972, Feb/March, 25.

272. Evans, 'Loyalties,' 2007,46.

to 24% in England, 23.7% in Scotland, as evidence that the Welsh were not as enthusiastic.[273] Gregory attests that in early August 1914 there was no real fervour for the war in Wales, Welsh miners for example, initially refusing to cut short their annual holiday entitlement.[274] The overall situation was of course far more complex. Thus at the by-election held in the Merthyr Boroughs in November, 1915, following the death of the anti-war Keir Hardie, the seat was won by Charles Stanton, standing as an independent pro-war Labour candidate, against the ILP candidate and president of the South Wales Miners Federation, James Winstone.[275]

In October 1916, until November 1919, some leading nonconformists and academics published an anti-war monthly non-denominational, strongly nationalist and labourist newspaper, *Y Deyrnas*, because: 'We have been driven to shame by the failure of Christianity of Europe that it did not to serve as a strong bulwark against destructive impulses.'[276] It also relied on that romanticism about Wales that the, 'Welsh were the most peaceful in spirit on the earth.'[277]

The paper had a circulation of up to 3,000, but was dependent for this level of sales on strong personal connections in certain locales.[278] It had no Quaker contribution during its short-lived existence and made no reference to the witness of the Society of Friends, not even when officers of the Friends Service Committee were imprisoned for contravening the censorship regulations in 1918.[279]

It was the issue of conscription that sharpened the debate about the war. This was an issue that, according to Pope, 'demonstrated that [Nonconformists]

273. Aled Eurig, '*Agweddau ar y Gwrthwynebiad i'r Rhyfel Byd Cyntaf*' (Aspects on opposition to the First World War), in Llafur, Vol. 4, No 4, 1986, 58–68.
274. Adrian Gregory, 'British 'War Enthusiasm' in 1914: a reappraisal,' in *Evidence, History and the Great War: Historians and the Impact of 1914–18*, ed., Gail Braybon, 2005, 67–85.
275. See Barry M. Doyle, 'Who Paid the Price of Patriotism? The Funding of Charles Stanton during the Merthyr Boroughs By-Election of 1915,' in the *English Historical Review*, 109, 434, Nov 1994, 1215–22.
276. *Y Deyrnas*, 1, Oct 1916.
277. Ibid., January 1917.
278. Eurig, *Agweddau*, 1986, 63.
279. See Punshon, *Portrait*, 1984, 232.
280. Robert Pope, 'Christ and Caesar? Welsh Nonconformity and the State,' in Cragoe and Williams, *Wales and War*, 2007, 166.

had very little influence over government policy,'[280] even though in Wales, from the outset, they gave wide support to the war effort. Conscription, even within that most conservative of denominations, the Calvinistic Methodists, saw them at their General Assembly in May 1916 declare that conscription was unacceptable. The resolution presented by the Rev. John Williams, Brynsiencyn, well known for his recruiting vigour, who had been given the honorary rank of colonel and chaplain in the Army, declared that 'they [the church] adhered to their principles, with a view to peace and the true rights of conscience.'[281] The Calvinistic Methodists weekly newspaper, *Y Goleuad*, was also critical of conscription and certain aspects of the war effort, and post 1918 was particularly anxious to promote reconciliation with Germany critical of the punitive reparation demands.[282] Conscription proved to be a catalyst.

Eurig estimates that between 1916–8 there were, across Britain, 16,500 applications for conscientious objection of which 6,500 were excused on grounds of conscience. There were to be 985 absolutists – those refusing any type of service, including approved alternative service – 142 of whom were Quakers.[283] The number of objectors in Wales was small. Gleaning through the pages of *The Friend* for 1916–8, an inadequate mechanism for a proper understanding of the scale of activity since it did not report all acts of conscience, it is possible to identify thirteen men who sought exemption and who were attached to meetings in Wales. Of these two seem to have been absolutists, B.H. Cudbird, Cardiff who was released from his second sentence in July 1919, and Samuel Broomfield of Newport, who insisted on keeping his hat on in court, indicating his allegiance to the tradition of 'plain' Friends.[284] Offered absolute exemption with condition he refused, and by June was in Wormwood Scrubs sentenced to six months hard labour. One other Welsh-born absolutist was Harold Mostyn Watkins, originally from Llanfyllin, but in membership at Worcestershire and Shropshire Monthly Meeting. He served four periods of imprisonment.

281. Quoted by Densil Morgan, 'Y Ffydd yng Nghymru yn yr Ugeinfed Ganrif: Profiadau 1900–1920' in 'Ysbryd Dealltwrus ac Enaid Anfarwol:' Ysgrifau ar Hanes Crefydd yng Nghymru, ed., W.P. Griffith, 1999, 202.

282. See Robert Smith, 'Methodistiad Calfinaidd a Gwleidyddiaeth Cymru: 1918–1939' in Historical Society of the Presbyterian Church of Wales, 26–7, 2002–03, 49–66.

283. Eurig, Agweddau, 1986, 65.

284. TF, 24.3.1916, 188.

Cardiff Preparative Meeting spent time on war related issues but there is an ambivalence about its reflections. It decided not to subscribe to the Aliens Relief Fund, but encouraged individuals to do so, presumably because some within the meeting had reservations about collective action.[285] Many Friends had enlisted and this must have had some bearing on their attitudes. The Evangelistic Committee of WQM made enquiries about who had joined the armed forces, discovering that from Gloucester and Nailsworth Monthly Meeting, two members had joined, from HRMM, three members and three attenders non-members, and from SWMM, two. They went on to record and to ask that no disciplinary action be taken and 'deferred until the war is over and peace declared.'[286] One Cardiff Friend, writing to *The Friend*, felt that all Quakers in uniform should be disowned, that

> the retention of military Quakers can and ought only to mean that the Society professes no principle against war; whereas I believe no comprehensive presentation of our special tenets will be without it, its importance only increasing with the lapse of time.[287]

When asked by Sufferings to support a memorial on cessation of hostilities three months later, Cardiff hesitated, deciding 'to take no official action in the matter at present, this meeting feeling that the time for such action had not yet arrived.'[288] By December 1915 they were renting a room to the Fellowship of Reconciliation, and by June 1916 to the No Conscription Fellowship.[289] Despite this in February 1916 at a Special Preparative Meeting, called in response to Military Service Act, they could not agree to the placing of an advert in the local press offering help to conscientious objectors:

> But though the proposal was favourably considered no Friend could be found able and willing to undertake the work. The matter was therefore left in abeyance.[290]

285. GRO, S/S SF 462/2. Cardiff Preparative Meeting (CPM) M9, 21.1.1915.
286. WRO, WQM, M6, 21.4.1915.
287. *TF*, 19.3.1915, 226,
288. CPM, M4, 25.4.1915.
289. CPM, M5, 16.4.1916.
290. CPM, M5, 13.2.1916.

They did donate to a local fund set up in response to conscription establishing a committee to visit objectors in prison,[291] visits not presumably confined to Quakers. In July 1916 they sent two delegates to a conference convened in Swansea by the National Council for Civil Liberties.[292] General relief to the dependents of conscientious objectors was fully supported, Caroline Ferris being a delegate to a meeting setting up of a local 'Macdonald Committee' – the local branch of the Committee for the Relief of Dependents of Conscientious Objectors, established by the No Conscription Fellowship under the chairmanship of J. Ramsay Macdonald – agreeing to collect funds for it; Charlotte M. Elliott served on the committee in November 1917.[293]

In Llandrindod Wells the meeting discussed how to support conscientious objectors arranging for occasional visits to those held at a Home Office camp, but with no record of decision.[294] Similarly SWMM where two of their members did visit – B.J. Elsmere and Richard Watkins, from Swansea Meeting, visited those held at Llanddeusant.[295] Llandrindod co-operated in arranging religious services at the meeting house for soldiers in local hospitals, 'The weekly service for soldiers was held at the Friends Meeting House on Sunday morning ... Owing to the snowstorm, a number of men were unable to leave their hospitals.'[296] It also concentrated on helping Belgian refugees, one of their members, C.M. Binyon, was presented with a handsome letter wallet because 'for over twelve months has performed, the duties of honorary organiser'[297] of the local committee, which in 1914 had 25 refugees under its care.[298]

Twenty-nine individuals from Wales were listed as having worked with the Friends Ambulance Unit (FAU) in 1919, not all Quakers.[299] The involvement of Friends in Wales as witnesses against the war was consistent with the vigour shown by the Yearly Meeting, and something that did not please everyone. One Friend from Wrexham in membership through Chester

291. CPM, M1, 14.5.1916.

292. CPM, M3, 30.7.1916.

293. CPM 18.11.1917.

294. LlWPM, M8, 16.1.1917.

295. SWMM, M11, 8.9.1917.

296. *RE*, 25.4.1918.

297. *RE*, 6.1.1916.

298. *TF*, 13.11.1914, 836.

299. *Friends Ambulance Unit, List of Members and Addresses*, London, FAU, 1919.

Meeting, along with three others, wrote protesting against the decision of Meeting for Sufferings in challenging the censorship regulations, noting that Friends 'stood for truth and liberty, not for license of liberty.'[300] The Assistant Clerk of Chester Preparative Meeting wrote in reply, supporting the decision of Sufferings, noting with wonderful understatement that three of the four signatories

> Are so placed that they can never attend either meeting for worship or discipline, and can therefore hardly be expected to appreciate the difficulties that beset those Friends who are now in active work in our Society.[301]

The experience of total war brought its horrors closer to home, such that as a result the peace movement attracted greater support, allowing for growth in what Caedel[302] defines as 'pacificism,' the ethic of responsibility, where prevention of war is primary, but where controlled use of force is sanctioned. In this regard the popularity and growth of the League of Nations Association in Wales is proof. The Yearly Meeting in 1918 had however failed to support the League because its constitution envisaged the use of military force to deal with international incidents. The Yearly Meeting Clerks felt that a report by the Peace Committee, which recommended support for the formation of the League, could not be pursued.[303] Subsequently, some Friends established a League of Nations Committee, but not as an official arm of the Yearly Meeting; some local and Quarterly meetings minuted their support for it. Llandrindod Wells Meeting minuted that two of their members, including Hercules Phillips should represent the meeting on the local committee of the Union[304] and Phillips became involved at the Welsh national level. Three Friends were elected onto the Council of the League of Nations Union, and one, Joseph Bevan Braithwaite Jnr, served on its executive committee.[305]

Caedel contrasts his 'pacificism' with 'pacifism,' with the personal

---

300. *TF*, 11.1.1918, 31.
301. *TF*, 25.1.1918, 67.
302. Martin Caedel, *Pacifism in Britain, 1914–1945: The Defining of a Faith*, 1980.
303. *TF*, 31.5.1918, 347.
304. LlWPM, 30.5.1920.
305. *TF*, 31.1.1919, 65.

conviction that war is not justified under any circumstances a distinction that is important in relation to Friends given that within LYM, according to its own analysis, 33.6% of its members of military age enlisted to fight.[306] Three members of SWMM were killed in action: Private Llywelyn Benjamin Elsmere, Llangennech, King's Own (Royal Lancaster Regiment) a member of Swansea Meeting (died 3rd November 1917, aged 31, in France) and Lieutenant John Herford Vivian Sessions, Newport, 13th Welsh Regiment, a member of Cardiff Meeting (died September 1918).[307] Elsmere was probably a conscript and, given his medal roll entry, went overseas to France after 1st January 1916. Sessions was a volunteer and joined the Honourable Artillery Company, a Territorial unit that drew its recruits from the middle-class men of the City of London, a major source for officers for the New Army (Service) battalions. He probably responded to Kitchener's appeal and did not see active service before 1916 as he was only awarded the British War Medal and the Allied Victory Medal.[308] The third Friend was Private Alan Corder Cunningham, who enlisted whilst living in South Africa. One member from South Wales was to be awarded the Military Cross for conspicuous gallantry and devotion to duty.

In April 1918 Hercules D. Philips addressed WQM about the growing peace movement in Wales 'both among Free Church ministers and among members of the Independent Labour and Socialist Parties.' The meeting minuted that this provided 'probable opening for the service of Friends in the near future,'[309] Phillips, as a home mission worker was ever hopeful.

Conclusion

The reawakening of Welsh national awareness belongs to the last decades of the nineteenth century. The issues around which this was centred related closely to the ideological claims nonconformity made on the life of the country, particularly in its tussle for parity and equity with the Established Church. In such a context nonconformity was a crucible from which Welsh historical, linguistic and cultural life drew succour. The triggers for such emergence are no doubt manifold, but what arouses the voice? The

---

306. YMP, 1923, 231–2.
307. SWMM minutes 1918.
308. Private correspondence with W. Alister Williams, military historian.
309. M16, WQM, 24/25.4.1918.

'Treachery of the Blue Books' was important,[310] since it helped undermine the traditional claims made by Anglicanism. Indeed

> The Welshness of Victoria's reign could be very fierce and passionate, but this is because it had to contend with so many enemies. To survive, Welshness had, in the 1860s and 1870s, to transfer itself subtly to the new world of radicalism and nonconformity.[311]

Even though nonconformity was a genuine hegemonic condition, political mobilisation also depended on opportunities offered through franchise reform. If Nonconformity was the prism through which class, privilege and power were refracted[312] then it also depended, as Hempton elaborates, on such factors as wealth from new industries, social mobility, and the balance that evolved between urban and rural religion.[313] If as Morgan enunciates Wales had been captured in a 'druidic mould' possessing an 'air of a colonized society, on the periphery,'[314] then the marriage between Nonconformity and Liberalism provided a genesis for reinvention and solidarity, reflective of changes, not only in Wales, but across Britain. In the Welsh context the vitality injected by religion cannot be ignored, including an Anglican input. Despite the demonisation of Anglicanism by radical nonconformists some Welsh Anglican clergy shared their sentiments about the religious condition of Wales. Rev. T.J. Jones, rector of Gelligaer writing: 'But our environment in the Principality differs from that of England, in as much here the mass outside is professedly religious, whilst there it is not.'[315]

The question to be asked is what contribution, if any, did LYM make to this marriage of religion and politics. In terms of general principle, Friends identified with the claims for disestablishment and disendownment, issues that affected their notion of the Church. They identified with the world of

---

310. Prys Morgan, 'The Hunt for the Welsh Past,' in *The Invention of Tradition*, E.J. Hobsbawm and Terence Ranger eds, 2002, 43–100.
311. Ibid. 98–9.
312. David Hempton, *Religion and political culture in Brtian and Ireland: From the Glorious Revolution to the decline of Empire*, 1996, 58.
313. Ibid., 60–3.
314. Morgan, *The Hunt for*, 2002, 3 & 22.
315. Rev.T.J. Jones, *Some Thoughts on How to Improve the Condition of the Welsh Church*, 1893, 1.

Welsh nonconformity and saw themselves as part of it. The close involvement of Quakers in the establishment of the ecumenical instruments, especially at the local level across Britain, provides proof of this.

The debate around religion in education tied into the tensional challenge between dissent and the State, called to the Quaker understanding of conscience and pragmatism. This is especially true if the thesis is accepted that the Education Act of 1902 was a determined attempt by influential Tories to keep Anglicanism within the school system, and stem the rise of secular schools, ensuring a

> denominational system of ideological instruction and indoctrination [providing] the kind of political acquiescence that the Tory party believed was necessary for the formation of correct political attitudes and behaviours.[316]

In this context, the battle over the 1902 Education Act meant that the Yearly Meeting, since it gave tacit support to resisters, touched upon what was in effect a political tussle, and in Wales a revolt. This was a revolt where Lloyd George 'frankly admits that the real objective is disestablishment in Wales,'[317] emphasising that in the Welsh context, the major issues could not be disentangled. Many Quakers would have agreed that the act was not about improving education but 'mainly concerned with the question of who shall manage the elementary schools,'[318] and in Wales, Friends would have been alive to wider the political implications of the struggles. Indeed if Jones is correct and the 1902 Act had no roots in the Welsh situation that 'it was a piece of legislation painted in the political colours of the English shires [that] it was the needs of the greater neighbour which dominated,'[319] then Friends had some legitimacy in being aloof from Welsh strategy and developments.

Overall, as the Quakers and others championed the cause of non-sectarian education, they were unwittingly diluting their own position, and opening the way to greater secularisation. This struggle in Wales was part of broader resistance against the privileged position of the Anglican Church

316. Taylor, *The Politics of*, 1997, 28.
317. Quoted by Munson, 'A Study of Nonconformity', 1973, 309, Morant to Balfour in September 1905.
318. Liberal Party, *The Parliamentary History of the Education Act 1902*, 1903, 1.
319. Jones, *The Welsh Revolt*, 1989, 436.

and a direct challenge to the religious establishment. The 'Welsh Revolt' entailed recourse to legal procedure and technical devices. The argument about education was however moving away from the churches and into the legal and secular realm, and into a more regulatory environment. In one sense the churches were allowing and inevitably encouraging the state, albeit in the interest of improved education (a point not lost on the Anglicans and Roman Catholics who supported the legislation) to extend control over part of what they had perceived to be their area of operation. Inevitably as the nonconformists challenged the Education Act, defending their Protestant legacy from the Reformation, with its call to independent enquiry and the questioning of ecclesiastical control, it also meant that their campaign carried within it 'the seeds of secularization.'[320]

There is no doubt that the moral questions around temperance aroused many within LYM, but there is no evidence that the political implications of the 1881 Sunday Closing Act was ever appreciated. It is however surprising, given the strong wish by the FTU to promote abstinence, that the fact that public houses were closed on Sundays in Wales, but not in England, did not appeal to its collective imagination. But the Yearly Meeting found it difficult to cross that boundary between the morality of drink and of total abstinence, the matter being left to individual conscience.

As for industrial unrest and war the Quaker response was predictably traditional, their responses could be described as feeble. It was pragmatic in relation to the First World War and largely paternalistic to industry. In these matters the position in Wales was no different, and not deserving of particular attention from the Yearly Meeting.

In 1906 it was the state of the Society of Friends in Wales that was of concern to one Welshman. Referring to Thomas Rees's history of nonconformity in Wales and his estimate that in 1715 there were about 3,000 Quakers in Wales, asked, 'Why is it we are gone back and other Protestant sects have increased? Perhaps some of our Friends may be able to explain,'[321] in so questioning he touched upon the one major weakness of Friends in Wales. They were simply too small a denomination to influence any Welsh

---

320. Thomas Albert Howard, *Religion and the Rise of Historicism: W M L de Watte, Jacob Burckhardt, and the theological origins of nineteenth century Historical Consciousness,* 2000, 17.

321. *TF*, 23.2.1906, 127.

debate, engaged in it as insignificant observers. This was further compounded by the fact that amongst them there were no prominent national figures. Some care is necessary here, F.W. Gibbins for example was peripherally involved, member of parliament for a few months and was concerned about social conditions in Wales. His contribution to Welsh politics was not however so outstanding as to have any resonance. Tobit Evans was never able to capitalise on his political ideals, belonging to the 'The Paper Unionists' who had been buried out of sight, had little history, and who 'were, as a rule good Liberals who had faith in Mr Chamberlain as a Radical leader.'[322] Evans never emerged as a leader, despite the intimations.

322. CN, 25.01.1889.

Chapter 3
Mission and Convincement, *circa* 1860 – 1918.

The activities of LYM in Wales at the end of the nineteenth century can best be described by examining the activities of the Home Mission Committee (HMC), especially after 1882, when the Yearly Meeting assimilated it into its structures. The work of the Committee must be set against a background of a weak, enfeebled Society struggling to maintain its presence in Wales. Its enterprises in no way gave LYM any claim to having a distinctive Welsh focus: it remained as a marginal player in the life of a country rediscovering its own identity. The activities of the committee can also be reflected in the life and work of its appointed workers or home missionaries. One such was Hercules Davies Phillips of Llandrindod Wells. His endeavours show a valiant attempt to rediscover, for Wales, part of its lost Quaker heritage.

If 'Welsh society ... was historically informed by a close relationship between Nonconformist religion, language and ethnicity,'[1] then the Quakers are situated within the same tradition. However, the demographic changes which were taking place in Wales as industry expanded, and urbanisation gathered pace, also began to remodel the Welsh religious topography especially after the 1840s. Thus, by the time of the religious census of 1851, Wales' population had doubled, but with the rural counties showing steady decline.[2] The expansion of the Roman Catholic Church in Wales, accompanied by 'perpetual bigotry,'[3] is illustrative of this, reflecting in particular Irish in-migration.[4] Considerable hostility was shown to Catholics up to the 1960s, when it was realised that they were a major Welsh denomination, and no longer seen as a threat. However, this increase in Catholic numbers

1. Paul Chambers, 'Religious Diversity in Wales' in *A Tolerant Nation: exploring ethnic diversity in Wales*, Charlotte Williams, Neil Evans and Paul O'Leary, eds., 2003, 125.
2. Jenkins, *Hanes Cymru*, 1933, 53.
3. Trystan Owain Hughes, *Winds of Change: The Roman Catholic Church and Society in Wales, 1916–1962* , 1999, 4.
4. See P. O'Leary, *Immigration and Integration: The Irish in Wales 1798–1922*, 2000.

'contributed to the Anglicisation of traditional Welsh society'[5] and was another factor in the hostility shown towards the Church, largely because most Catholics moving into Wales, especially the Irish immigrants, were primarily English by language. This process was aided by conversion from amongst the Welsh, helping to establish and strengthen a new Catholic middle class, and hastening the reintegration of the Church into the life of Wales.[6] The Quakers were not as visible and faced no such hostility.

The Jews in Wales, despite their small numbers, faced prejudice (there were anti-Semitic riots in Tredegar in 1911)[7] but generally speaking they had become well accepted in south Wales, where their appearance reflected expansion in the iron and steel and coal industries.[8] By 1911 there were 135 Jews living in Brynmawr,[9] forming 2% of the population, a town that was in the 1930s to be closely identified with Quakers, but whose numbers never reached any such proportions. The Jews, unlike the Quakers, were not an evangelising missionary body.

The Quakers could claim their roots as part of the Welsh nonconformist topography, perceived by the imaginations of the pulpit as being part of the Welsh historical tapestry. Despite this, the *Friendly Messenger*, a HMC publication published between 1904 to 1910, to inform the Society about its work and endeavours, commented with considerable truism in its editorial in July 1909, in relation to a three-part article appearing in the magazine entitled 'Quakers in Wales' and reproduced by permission of the *South Wales Daily News*, that 'the remark is sometimes heard in Wales to-day that Quakers in the Principality is a spent force.'[10]

Their story in Wales towards the end of the nineteenth century and the beginning of the twentieth was dominated by the efforts of the HMC. Mission was not unique to Quakers: in 1891 the Presbyterian Church of Wales established its home mission branch, the *Y Mudiad Ymosodol* – the

5. Hughes, *Winds*, 1999, 199.

6. See Trystan Owain Hughes, 'An Uneasy Alliance? Welsh Nationalism and Roman Catholicism,' in *North American Journal of Welsh Studies*, 2, 2, Summer 2002, 1–6.

7. See Anthony Glaser, 'The Tredegar Riots of August 1911,' in *The Jews of South Wales: Historical Studies*, Ursula R.Q. Henriques ed., 1993, 151–176.

8. Ursula R.Q. Henriques, 'Introduction,' in Henriques, *The Jews of South Wales*, 1993, 7.

9. Anthony Glaser and R.Q. Henriques, 'The Valleys Communities,' in Henriques, *The Jews*, 1993, 45–68.

10. *The Friendly Messenger*, July 1909. Article's author was Hercules D. Phillips.

Forward Movement, to promote evangelism. This development was described as necessary because,

> the advent of the English speaking foreigner with his different conceptions of life, his low moral ideals, caused much head and heartache to the spiritually sensitive sections of the Welsh community, and especially to the leaders who felt that something should be done to provide for the religious needs of the English immigrant.[11]

Not perhaps the way the HMC would have described its endeavours.

An important element which underpinned the witness of the Society in Britain was the tension that existed within it regarding how it projected itself theologically and practically, and was very much about where and how the nature of authority was explained within LYM. This can be more simplistically observed as a tussle between two broad camps, the 'evangelic' and the 'quietist,' the exposition of which was more visible in the schisms that occurred amongst Quakers in America, and which inevitably reverberated across the Atlantic.[12] Isichei highlights a tripartite division amongst Victorian Friends reflecting an additional trend – the Unitarian.[13]

Schematic representation of views within LYM[14]

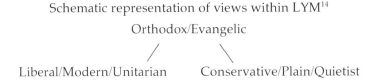

Orthodox/Evangelic

Liberal/Modern/Unitarian   Conservative/Plain/Quietist

These tensions were never a real threat to denominational unity, more a nuisance in the actions of enthusiastic individuals. Indeed Quaker evangelicalism, compared to the other mainstream churches, was always moderate.[15]

11. Howell Williams, *The Romance of the Forward Movement of the Presbyterian Church of Wales*, n.d, 12.
12. See Thomas D. Hamm, *The Transformation of American Quakerism: Orthodox Friends 1800–1907*, 1992, for a fuller exploration of these developments.
13. Isichei, *Victorian*, 1970, Ch. 1, 1–32.
14. Descriptions in italics are from Isichei, *Victorian*.
15. Grubb, 'The Beacon Separation,' 1988, 197.

The 'quietists' emphasised 'the primacy of the Holy Spirit, though not at the expense of abandoning the Bible ... espousing dependence on the Holy Spirit informed by Scripture,'[16] and relied on the writings of early Friends, tending to invest them, as Hamm sees it, with a certain level of infallibility.[17] These were the conservative or primitive Friends, sometimes referred to as Wilburites – adhering to the ideas and ministry of the American Quaker, John Wilbur. They were overall distrustful of evangelical outpourings based simply on scriptural authority. For them it was the leading of the spirit that sanctified and converted.

Evangelical efforts within LYM upheld the teachings expounded by such members as John Joseph Gurney, considered to be the 'single most import-ant figure'[18] in the British Quaker evangelical tradition. This upheld the general evangelical emphasis on individual conversion, reliance on scriptural certainty and authority, with an acceptance of Christ's substitutionary atonement. Gurney's teachings and emphasis had considerable influence on the course of schism amongst American Yearly Meetings, and in particular the split between Conservative-Wilburite and Orthodox Friends in 1845–6.

The endeavours of the Home Mission within LYM relied on Gurney's teaching co-existing alongside Friends who maintained the more traditional and quietist approach. Within the Yearly Meeting 'doctrinal differences ... were often not clearly stated or easy to detect'[19] and the tension between the two traditions, that of the quietist-mystical and the Biblical-evangelical, between reliance on inward rather than external authority, meant, as Punshon claims, that Friends in Britain were caught between spiritual streams, sharing a 'Divided Inheritance.[20] This did not lead to any meaning-ful schism – there was a co-existence of ideas, even though it was the evangelicals who took centre stage and dominated the public utterances of the Yearly Meeting. Newman strongly hints at this, that the evangelical influence was visible and noticeable, but not perhaps as dominant as one is

16. Wilmer A. Cooper, *A Living Faith: An Historical Study of Quaker Beliefs*, 1990, 22

17. Hamm, *The Transformation of*, 1992, 29.

18. David E. Swift, *John Joseph Gurney: Banker, Reformer and Quaker*, 1962, 254.

19. Edwina Newman, 'John Brewin's Tracts: The written word, evangelicalism and the Quaker way in mid–nineteenth century England,' in *Quaker Studies*, 9, 2, 2005, 238.

20. John Punshon, *Portrait in Grey: A short history of the Quakers*, 1999, Ch. 7.

lead to believe. Indeed, that for all Friends what was important was the nature of 'devotional practice that trusted to immediate and continuous revelation.'[21] This evangelical emphasis was not imbued with a simple arid theology of damnation and salvation, but also found inspiration 'in its prayerful concern for the spiritual estate of individual men and women and in its passion for social reform.'[22] Grubb highlights the fact that there were few, if any, differences between the evangelicals and conservative Friends in terms of theology.[23] They shared the same understanding about the fall of man, but the conservatives were fearful that the mystical basis of Quakerism, the supremacy of the Light of God in the soul, and the paramount need of His inward work of cleansing and regeneration was being undermined.

Wilson believed that evangelical penetration of the Yearly Meeting in the nineteenth century was superficial rather than deep,[24] suggesting that their leadership was less certain than they imagined. J.B. Braithwaite, 'the Quaker Bishop of Westminster,'[25] and one of the leading evangelics in the Yearly Meeting, despite being one of the principal drafters of a basis of faith called the Richmond Declaration of Faith (1887)[26] adopted by many American Yearly Meetings, saw his own Yearly Meeting in 1888 refusing to endorse it. When the Yearly Meeting was in Leeds in 1905, at the opening session, a letter from Braithwaite was read out apologising for his absence, a measure of his standing amongst the membership, but also an indication that he was not a leader who could impose his will upon it. This supports Wilson's assessment of a visible evangelic leadership, but one that was devoid of individual authority, another indication that individual leadership within the Society is problematic.[27]

21. Newman, 'John Brewin's', 2005, 246.

22. Swift, *John Joseph Gurney*, 1962, 253.

23. Edward Grubb, 'The Evangelical Movement and its Impact on the Society of Friends (Presidential Address to the Friends Historical Society,1923),' in *The Friends Quarterly Examiner*, 1924, 1–34.

24. Roger Wilson, 'Friends in the Nineteenth Century,' in *Friends Quarterly*, October 1984, 23, 8, 357.

25. For Braithwaite see www.oxforddnb.com/view/article/4705 accessed 31.12.12.

26. See Hamm, *The Transformation*, 137–139.

27. See P. Dandelion, 'A Sociological Analysis of the Theology of Quakers', unpublished Ph.D Thesis, University of Brighton, 1993, Ch. 5, 271–328.

Home Mission and LYM

Home Mission efforts within LYM up to 1882 were not strictly under the supervision of the Yearly Meeting, and reflected rather the concerns and enthusiasm of individuals and groups of evangelically inclined Friends. The principal conduit for their collective ambitions was the Friends First Day Schools Association (FFDSA), who held their first annual meeting at Ackworth School in 1848. The society was, 'conducted chiefly by young men, in whose minds a lively feeling of interest had been excited on behalf of the more neglected portion of the community, leading to the establishment of First-day schools in various parts of the country.'[28]

In 1875 the Yearly Meeting established a committee, initially for a year, to assist Quarterly Meeting to arrange general meetings whose function it was to carry out concentrated evangelism especially to the un-churched. This was modelled on activity in Dublin Yearly Meeting, influenced by the endeavours of Moody and Sankey there, and drawing on developments amongst the American Quakers;[29] a departure not welcomed by everyone in the Yearly Meeting. Some general meetings continued amongst some Quarterly Meetings until 1886, when they were replaced by the overall endeavours of the HMC, which took over the work of the original General Meetings committee in 1883. Irrespective of doctrinal difference, the very survival of the Society was of deep concern for all Friends. Hence in November 1873 Meeting for Sufferings organised, at the behest of the YM, a Conference on the State of the Society, which proved popular, with Quarterly Meetings appointing 410 to attend. Falling membership figures and future prospects acted as a powerful stimulant. In 1821 the membership of the Society was 18,040. By 1870 it had fallen to 14,000 – a decrease of 22%.[30] The challenge was to reverse this trend, and the response led to 'steady but low growth'[31] compared with the greater vitality of the other Nonconformist denominations.

---

28. *TF*, 8th month, 1848, 141.
29. See Malcolm Thomas, 'The Committee on General Meetings 1875–83,' in *A Quaker Miscellany* for Edward H Milligan, David Blamires, Jeremy Greenwood and Alex Kerr eds., 1985, 133–144.
30. Robert Currie, Alan Gilbert, Lee Horsley, *Churches and Churchgoers: patterns of Church Growth in the British Isles since 1700*, 1977, 156–160.
31. Ibid., 35.

Home mission activities mirrored the work of the FFSDA, who brought together for the first time, at a national level, Quaker endeavours around what others called Sunday Schools. Isichei illustrates that the Quaker schools differed from those of other denominations in that they were established much later, responding slowly 'partly because of their quietist traditions,'[32] and their schools were intended for the uneducated of all ages, their schools reflecting the social strata of the locality in which they were based.[33] All the Sunday schools 'were crucial not only for the inculcation of literacy and basic education, but also for the related success of different denominations, and, indeed, for the future of religious adherence as a whole.'[34] The Sunday School was an especially important element in the development of education in Wales, crucial to the nonconformist hegemony, the survival of the language, and the demand for secular reading material in the vernacular. Although Bassett takes a more cautious view, that it is not easy to assess its actual contribution, and that it has 'suffered from too much eulogising and too little well-meant criticism.'[35]

In Charlton's judgement Friends invested happily in such schools knowing that they did not threaten 'the viability of their own meeting ... they were only too pleased to see that adult scholars remained separated from them';[36] an issue that was to challenge some Friends especially from the beginning of the twentieth century linked to the reawakening of purpose amongst Friends, alongside the influence of liberal theology, with concerns for broadening the understanding of Friends socially and theologically.[37] The objectives of the schools encouraged self-help, thrift, and temperance, and since they were not authoritarian about church membership, they offered 'a particular attraction for adult scholars'[38] and indeed their success testified to

32. Walvin, *The Quakers*, 1997, 152.

33. Isichei, *Victorian*, 1970, 258.

34. K.D.M. Snell, 'The Sunday–School Movement in England and Wales: Child Labour, Denominational Control and Working Class Culture,' in *Past and Present*, No 164, Aug 1999, 138.

35. T.M. Bassett, 'The Sunday School,' in *The History of Education in Wales*, Vol. 1, 1978, 78.

36. C. Charlton, 'Introduction,' in *A History of the Adult School Movement*, J. Wilhelm Rowntree and Henry Bryan Binns, 1995), liv.

37. Kennedy, *British Quakerism*, 2001, 270–311.

38. Michael Hibbert, 'Quaker Influence on Adult Education during the Victorian Era,1837–1901,' unpublished M.Ed thesis, University of Wales, Bangor, 1990, 48.

their popularity.[39] This did not mean that they ignored the needs of the soul. At the 1867 FFDSA Conference one paper focused on how best to encourage scholars to attend a place of worship. Their eventual approach to worship meant that their activities brought them to that 'point at which Quakers came to look more like the conventional Christian denominations than at any other time.'[40] Their missionary endeavours made Friends undistinguishable from other Nonconformist sects, as educational and salvific endeavours became intertwined.

In June 1881 at their annual conference, the FFDSA and the Bedford Institute, the Quaker centre based in Whitechapel, London for the education and relief of the poor in the East End, and founded in 1867, agreed to convene a conference in London 'to collect the experience of Friends in various parts of the country engaged in Home Mission work (especially in connection with our First Day schools).'[41] This November conference was convened with 'Christian fervour, and the hearty loyalty to the Society'[42] pervading every sitting. Some 200 Friends were present, but no town in Wales is listed as being represented.[43] The conference reflected upon the state of the Society, with Charles Hoyland reporting that since 1801 the number of Quarterly Meetings had fallen from 30 to 17,196 meetings had closed and 73 new ones opened. William Beck, using figures analysed from FFDSA returns, gave a paper on home mission endeavours arguing that there was considerable work to be done, of 126 meetings in five Northern England Quarterly Meetings, only 41 had first day schools and only seventeen had mission meetings. Two Friends from WQM presented papers. Frederick Sessions of Gloucester spoke on the challenge facing a home mission association in developing its work and the encouragement and assistance that workers needed. Henry Stanley Newman, Leominster spoke to, 'The Attitude of the Society of Friends towards Working Men and the attitude of Working Men towards the Society.' He claimed that there had been a revival amongst Friends because of the increased evangelical

---

39. Ibid., 29.
40. Ibid., 53.
41. *TF*, 10th month, 1881, 280.
42. *TF*, 12th month 1881: as a supplement with no pagination.
43. Conference on Home Mission Work in the Society of Friends held in London, 29–30 Eleventh Month, 1881, 1881.

emphasis within the Society, and because the 'removal of some of the moss-grown conventionalities of opinion and habit,' meant that they now had more in common with 'every other religious denomination around us.'[44]

The conference agreed to establish a provisional committee of thirty to oversee the interest of home mission work, agreeing to present the matter to the 1882 Yearly Meeting. At that meeting there was objection to the conference report being presented at all. Charles Thompson felt that the FFDSA had 'taken to itself a responsibility not contemplated by the Yearly Meeting' and that the report was not in proper ordering; William Graham noting that it had not come up through the agreed channels i.e. through a Quarterly Meeting, and reflecting his conservative sympathies, felt that the YM should 'see that before (it) endorsed singing, music and so forth, as they were asked to do, they must first consider whether they could do this consistently as Friends.' The Yearly Meeting Clerk, Joseph Storrs Fry, who was also secretary of the FFDSA, 'said the matter contained in the report must come under the notice of Friends at some time or other, and he thought they might just as well consider it now.'[45]

The Yearly Meeting considered and adopted the report of the conference, agreeing to establish a committee of men and women for one year, 'to form a bond of union between many whose work is now carried on in comparative isolation,'[46] and to review its future in 1883, thus reflecting a certain degree of hesitation. The committee had 44 members, 17 of whom were women, most members were evangelically inclined, such as John Bevan Braithwaite, Joseph Storrs Fry, Caleb T. Kemp, with Henry Stanley Newman and Frederick Sessions from Western Quarterly meeting. It had no Friends from Wales.

Punshon comments on this reluctance, that 'the heart of the Society of Friends was not really in it,'[47] reflecting the tensions which arose from differences in theological emphasis and practice within the Yearly Meeting.[48]

44. Ibid., 70.
45. *TF*, 5th month, 1882, 137–147.
46. Ibid.
47. Punshon, *Portrait*, 1999, 193.
48. See 'The Ancient Way: The Conservative Tradition in Nineteenth Century British Quakerism' Edward H Milligan in *The Journal of the Friends' Historical Society*, 57, 1, 1994, 74–101.

In his 1917 study Grubb highlighted the 'strong objections'[49] to any mission work, and the way in which the topic produced 'painful discussions in the Yearly Meeting.'[50] Although his evaluation may be considered partisan, in that his grandmother Sarah (Lynes) Grubb had been a prominent conservative Friend, who had tenaciously resisted the claims made by evangelical Friends on the life of LYM. The recurring theme of opposition centred in part on the question of a paid ministry – 'we consider the gift of ministry to be of so pure and sacred a nature, that no payment should be made for its exercise, and that it ought never to be undertaken for pecuniary remuneration.'[51] When Henry Stanley Newman had spoken at the 1881 conference, he had gone out of his way to address this particular issue, acknowledging that the 'working men of England respect a free and unpaid ministry, and loathe priestcraft,'[52] but that nevertheless the Bible justified some being set apart, and that some 'ministers' needed financial support. He acknowledged that most Quaker ministers, being in comfortable circumstances, could forego financial assistance, but that this led to certain complacency about how Quakerism spread its message, and the danger that 'lies in the direction of getting our work done by proxy.'[53] The issue of payments to missionaries in the foreign field seems not to have caused difficulty.

The HMC established in 1882 continued in existence. In 1892 it organised a conference to review its work and constitution, but the question of paid ministers remained as a principal criticism, and a powerful undercurrent in deliberations within the Yearly Meeting, the question of mission itself was not the issue, as Grubb would have it, but rather its methods. This was clearly outlined by J. Bevan Braithwaite Jnr, in his address to the Conference,[54] repeating what he had said to the 1887 Yearly Meeting, that

49. Edward Grubb, *What is Quakerism? An Exposition of the leading Principles and Practices of the Society of Friends, as based on the experience of the 'Inward Light,'* 1929 edition, 195.

50. Ibid. 196.

51. 'From the Address issued by the Yearly Meeting, 1841,' in *Christian Life: Faith and Thought in the Society of Friends,* 1923, 105.

52. Conference on Home Mission Work in the Society of Friends held in London, 29–30 Eleventh Month, 1881, 1881, 74.

53. Ibid., 75.

54. *TF,* 11.11.1892, 746

payments by the HMC to its workers meant that the Gospel was no longer being preached 'freely and without payment' a paid pastorate had been established, contrasting this with the unfortunate decline in the number of Friends travelling in the ministry on a minute from their Monthly Meeting.[55] Arthur Sessions of Cardiff, based on his experiences, sought to address some of the criticism: home mission work was a necessity, and the workers, he said, were not leaders, but rather 'helpers to the Friends in the town where they lived' that 'we wanted clever organisers in our meetings, and if these were also ministers of the Gospel, we could not object.'[56]

By 1892 the HMC had 42 workers, 16 of whom were new[57] and in 1893 the Yearly Meeting reconstituted it on a representative basis. The Quarterly Meetings were invited to nominate Friends to serve on a new committee. Grubb comments that this change reflected dissatisfaction in the way the committee worked, noting that the effect was to transfer any divisions of opinion from the Yearly Meeting to the Committee,[58] although such tensions are not reflected in the minutes of the committee. The HMC became an arm of the Yearly Meeting. Not everyone welcomed such centralisation; Henry Lees and William Robertson restated their continuing opposition, stressing that responsibility for mission should lie within each Quarterly Meeting.[59] Braithwaite Jnr, maintained, along with many others, a quietist inclination:

> I am one of those who believe that the surest way to reach the people and bring them to a saving knowledge of the Lord Jesus Christ is to invite them to join us in sitting down in reverent silence to wait upon the Lord Himself, and, with nothing to distract them from waiting upon Him, I believe that the Lord Himself will speak to the needs of the people in a way that we can never do[60]

insisting that the committee failed because 'it does not fairly represent the

---

55. *TF*, 6th month 1887, 149.
56. *TF*, 11.11.1892, 746.
57. *TF*, 27.5.1892, 353–357.
58. Grubb, *What is*, 1929, 196.
59. *TF*, 2.6.1893, 356.
60. *Report of the Proceedings of the Conference held at Manchester from the eleventh to fifteenth of eleventh month 1895*, LYM, 1895, 114. See Ch. 4, fn. 16.

opinion of the Society on Mission work, and second, because of its introduction of paid workers.'[61] There was for the Quaker only the headship of Christ. Within the Quaker meeting only a spiritual leadership was possible. No one could be set apart because this contravened a basic principle of the Quaker understanding of the nature of the Church, 'they would not concur in any Friend being separated to take charge of any particular meeting.'[62]

In controlling the home mission work the Yearly Meeting assumed responsibility for what Henry Stanley Newman had told the HMC in May 1886 was its one aim, 'the salvation of souls.'[63] According to one commentator, the missionaries were suited to the objectives set them, in that they

> were young, many were converts to Quakerism, all were extreme evangelicals. They tended to be of working class origin ...[and] were often anathema to long established communities of well to do conservative Friends.[64]

Her judgement may be slightly misplaced; some missionaries were well to do birthright Friends, amongst them for example, Frederick Sessions of Gloucester. He was more peripatetic than most, paid by the Committee who directed his service, and receiving £200 per annum, 'in addition to a moderate sum from his business' on agreement that he could 'resume his position at his business either in two years or on the death of either of his partners.'[65] Similarly Charles Edward Gillett, of Oxford, was a birthright Friend from a fairly well-off background.[66]

Mission as strategy
The minutes of the HMC from the 1880s provides no evidence that the committee had any strategic intent. It seems rather to have responded to requests for assistance from across the country, and would see how and in

61. *BF*, 4th month, 1893, 95.
62. *TF*, 11.11.1892, 746.
63. *TF*, 6th Month 1886, 169.
64. Isichei, *Victorian*, 1970, 100.
65. LSF, HMC Minute Book, M2, 21.5.1883.
66. *TF*, 19.2.1892, 130.

what way it could assist; parts of the country were hardly touched – Scotland in particular. For example in 1894 Scotland General Meeting had not sent a representative to the newly-constituted committee.[67] Investment seems to have followed the interests of particular members of the committee for their own areas, and possibly the weightier the Friend the greater the attention. Continuity of membership would then have been important.

Henry Stanley Newman served on the committee from 1882, and was influential in persuading the Yearly Meeting to take its decision of that year. As a committed evangelist and temperance worker, he had told the Home Mission and Total Abstinence Meeting at Yearly Meeting in 1877 that 'Mission work and total abstinence were inseparably connected together,'[68] and was prominent and active in both camps, nationally and in his own home area. Any reading of his life sees these as important foundations for his witness and life. In 1865 he published his 'Foreign Missions Reviewed', which was instrumental in the formation of the Friends Foreign Mission Association in that year,[69] of which he remained honorary secretary until his death in 1912. He supported the Adult School, founded in Leominster in 1858 by his father and uncle, and according to his biographer became 'one of the foremost leaders of the Adult School Movement amongst Friends, and was constantly in request as a speaker.'[70] As editor of *The Friend* from 1891 until 1912, Newman was influential and well placed.

By May 1900 there were 30 workers connected with the HMC, of these eight (almost 25%) were placed within WQM, and four (13%) were in Wales.[71] No Friend from WQM served on the executive committee at this time, and it made the recommendations as to the direction of work and placement of workers. Why then was Wales so prominent in the way the committee allocated its resources? The role of Henry Stanley Newman was probably crucial.

His involvement in Wales was first demonstrated by his efforts, with others, in establishing a school at the Pales. At the annual meeting of the

67. *TF*, 1.6.1894, 351.

68. *TF*, 6th month 1877, 179.

69. Newman, *Henry Stanley Newman*, 1917, 30.

70. Ibid., 11.

71. HMC Minute Book, Report, May 1900.

FFDSA in 1868 he commented that its efforts were confined to 60–70 meetings across the country, and that a large number of smaller meetings had never experienced any developments, 'many of them are like the unfruitful fig-tree, dying away, dwindling down year after year.'[72] This was a challenge to the organisation, and he spoke 'very feelingly of a meeting of five individuals in a large old meeting house [Pales], one of those memorials of the ancient vigorous life of our Society,'[72] whom he had recommended should start a First Day school to reinvigorate itself, and that this is what other meetings should also do to strengthen their witness. At Pales the ambitions were more than a mere First Day school.

As Clerk to Hereford and Radnor Monthly Meeting from 1869 to 1893, Newman was in a position to influence the direction of its affairs, and the way it supported efforts for example at the Pales. His testimony to Yearly Meeting, 1913 records that

> Radnorshire had a warm place in his heart … The opening of the meetings
> and the building of meeting-houses at Penybont and Llandrindod were in
> large measure due to his aggressive efforts and to his eagerness to ensure that
> causes once founded should in due time be established.[74]

This was allied to his general interest in mission, especially in Wales. Hercules Davies Phillips, one of the Home Mission workers at Llandrindod comments in a short unpublished memoir that, 'One of the ideas which Henry Stanley Newman had was that Llandrindod Wells should become a strategic centre for the spread of Quakerism in Wales.'[75] Phillips does not elaborate on why this was never achieved, commenting only that there were good reasons for it. These would probably be concerned with practical and financial considerations, and to the way the HMC operated.

Newman would have reflected the general concerns of his Quarterly Meeting as to its condition, and similarly in Wales, 'In some of our meetings both for worship and discipline there has been but little change to report

---

72. *TF*, Eighth month 1868, 206.
73. Ibid.
74. YMP, 1913, 254–259.
75. H.D. Phillips, 'The Growth of Llandrindod Wells Society,' unpublished paper, *circa* 1934, 2. Original presented to Llandrindod Wells Meeting in 1987.

except in the gradual decline of their numbers.'[76] It would be difficult to argue that there was ever a Welsh mission *per se*, rather what was taking place was general evangelic work, some of which happened to be located at Welsh centres. WQM would have been aware of the special circumstances pertaining to Wales, and at its meeting in April 1894, and in its triennial report to the Yearly Meeting, piously recorded:

> In the Welsh speaking districts of Wales the Society is at present practically unrepresented: but we think there is an opening for Friends, among a population so disposed as they are to the reception of religious truth in its more simple forms, if any could be found, imbued with the principles of Friends willing to devote themselves to the work, and at the same time possessing a competent knowledge of the language.[77]

This idea that a few Friends could provide a mission to the whole of Welsh speaking Wales is unarguably patronising, remarkable in its optimistic tenor, lacking realism. Thus Frederick Sessions' hopes were of that. He wrote, soon after he was recorded a minister in October 1869, that he had a vision to minister in Wales, 'I really was called to minister to the Welsh speaking population at the foot of Cader Idris' (i.e. Dolgellau), no doubt envisaging a reawakening in that area, adding an insightful comment as to the reasons for the demise of Friends in the area, 'when, because of unfaithfulness and 'quietism,' our candlestick was removed out of its place.'[78] Sessions had no Welsh and his efforts would have had limited effect.

The statement from WQM reflects a particular representation of Welsh religious sensibilities which might be considered audaciously arrogant in its presumptions. The Quarterly Meeting had lost sight of what Frederick J. Gibbins had told them, in 1882, as he presented a paper on behalf of the Home Mission Association:

> Friends could not now get an audience among Welsh speaking people, as there are not now more than two Friends in South Wales who can speak the

---

76. WQM, M1, 15.4.1885.
77. WQM, Report 18.4.1894.
78. *Friends Quarterly Examiner*, 1893, 27, 'A Home Missionary's Experiences,' 181–199.

language. It is often said by those who understand both languages that they only tolerate an English address whilst they wait impatiently for the Welsh which is a language of far grander sound to contain such greater fullness and variety of expression.[79]

It is hardly likely that within a matter of eleven years the Society would have gathered into its folds those whose Welsh was so proficient as to be able to undertake any mission work. Indeed the reverse was true. There were no meetings in any areas where the Welsh language was dominant, and it is unlikely that Welsh would have been heard, even in ministry, in the few meetings that existed. There is a revealing report on this question of language in *The Friend* in 1897 when Frederick J. Gibbins reported that at a the Swansea Cymmrodorion, a lecture to be delivered by W. Jenkyn Thomas M.A., headmaster of Aberdare Intermediate School on 'The History of the Quakers in Wales' was given in English 'When it became known that some Friends wished to hear the lecture.'[80] The hopes of the Quarterly Meeting were therefore written more from pious hope than practicality. None of the missionaries appointed by the HMC spoke Welsh, although one, B.J. Elsmere, told them prior to his appointment that he had some knowledge of the Welsh language.[81] Elsmere was never to serve in a community where Welsh was the principal language, although he did move to live to Llangennech once he resigned his position with the committee. Of all the missionaries who served in Wales only one was born in Wales, on the borders, in Knighton, Hercules Phillips, who served throughout at Llandrindod Wells, and who proved to be sensitive and supportive to all matters Welsh.[82] The HMC made no efforts to develop its work across the whole of Wales, and if they were aware of Gibbins' comments they made no efforts to respond to the implied challenge.

---

79. NLW MS 4859C/9. Paper 'Written at the request of a committee of the Home Mission Association and read at a conference held by WQM at Gloucester" 'South Division of Wales Monthly Meeting,' Frederick J. Gibbins 12th mo 1882.
80. *TF*, 5.2.1897,94. This lecture was probably the one Thomas had given in London in 1894, see Ch. 2, fn. 508.
81. HMC, Minutes 28.5.1892.
82. H.D. Phillips, 'The Personal Story of H.D. Phillips', unpublished manuscript, 1941. Original at Llandrindod Wells meeting house.

Despite its shortcomings WQM had a concern for the whole of the area which fell within its territory, including Wales. It was inevitably more concerned about the state of the meetings for which it had responsibility, and asked for assistance from HMC on that basis. The committee never defined any particular strategy, other than to uphold meetings and take Quakerism out to the world. Its efforts in Wales were focused on those meetings already in existence, and so its activities were confined to parts of South Wales and Radnorshire.

The condition of Quakers in Wales by 1867 can only be described as perilous, with a membership of only 73 across the whole country, such that even by 1881 WQM, in its report to Yearly Meeting, could declare that

> several meeting-houses no longer used by Friends, in a few cases these have been lent to other religious bodies – in some instances those occupied by Friends in the morning are lent to other persons in the evening.[83]

Sharing resources was not to be decried, but if the tenor of the report is one of sadness, it did not mean that the Quarterly Meeting was idle.

Welsh meetings and the HMC

i. Pales

Pales is located in the parish of Llandegley, Radnorshire off the road between Llandrindod and Kington. The 1861 Census showed the population of the parish to be 475, rising to 589 by 1871, by 1881 it was 398, and by 1901 had fallen to 292. If the two neighbouring parishes are added (Llanfihangel Rhydithon and Cefnllys) the population was still not large: 1861 – 1,248, 1871 – 1,475, 1881 – 1,429, with the growth in Cefnllys parish, containing the new town of Llandrindod Wells, which expanded after the 1860s. The population, in all these parishes, from which Friends could draw, was therefore relatively small, but Friends had been at the Pales since the seventeenth century and it was held with affection: 'Pales is one of the oldest Meeting-houses, dating back to 1673, and is certainly the spiritual home of Quakerism in Radnorshire.'[84] Its condition was however perilous, around 1860: 'The

83. WQM, Report, 19.4.1881.
84. Williams, 'Evangelical', 1992.

Meeting can hardly be said to exist. One infirm, old man, disowned by the Society, for marrying a non-member crosses the hills at the hour of worship to sit there alone with God.'[85]

The efforts to establish a successful day school at Pales in 1867 was to be a precursor to greater activity, allied as it eventually was to the stimulation generated through the activities of the Yearly Meeting's Committee on General Meetings; the school serving as an important symbol for continued Quaker interest in Radnorshire and the survival of Friends within it:

> The meeting at Pales had so long been an object of interest to Friends, from being kept up pretty much by non-members, and from the large number of friends formerly resident among the hills and dales of Radnorshire, that the Committee feel confidence that the school, the expense of which has rested on a limited number of Friends, will be cordially supported by the General Meeting at large. They believe that so long as it continues to be efficiently conducted, it will prove the means of doing much good in simple and inexpensive way.[86]

The impetus came from Friends in Leominster, focusing initially on the educational needs of children in the Llandegley and Penybont[87] area. Five of their numbers, Edward P. Southall, Samuel Alexander, Josiah Newman, John T. Southall, and Henry S. Newman sent a letter addressed to the local populace stating that they 'thought it right to commence a Day School at the Pales' where many had 'expressed the conviction that there is a great want of further accommodation for the good education of children.'[88] Hereford and Radnor Monthly Meeting almost immediately 'took the school more completely under its care' recognising that 'the subject of the need of education in the district of Pales has been brought before us and seriously

85. H.D. Phillips quoting Stanley Pumphrey (Henry Stanley Newman's brother–in–law) in 'The Beginnings of Quakerism in Radnorshire,' *The Transactions of the Radnorshire Society*, xi, 1941, 31–36.
86. Minute Book of the Pales Mission and Day School. (PMDB) PCAO, R/NC/2/A, Report 1868.
87. Penybont is a small hamlet on the A44 to Leominster, on the crossroads with the A488 to Knighton. Llandegley is the next hamlet to the east, about 2 miles from Penybont.
88. PMDB, R/NC/2/A.

considered, and it is agreed to establish a Day School at the meeting house'[89] using some money left in a trust,[90] but seeking subscriptions from across the country.[91] The meeting also added two other Friends to the original five to act on its behalf. They appointed the 22 year old William Knowles from Bentham, Lancashire to act as the first schoolmaster.[92] He was to be paid £50 per annum to include the 'school pence' – the contribution expected from each child attending the school. From reading the minutes and annual reports it becomes apparent that Knowles' focus was entirely educational and not missionary, and indeed the reports are so entitled, 'Report of the Day School.' Knowles proved successful, so much so that by July 1868 his salary was consolidated at £70 p.a.[93] but the relevant minute of October 1868 suggests that the basic salary was still £50 plus the school pence.[94] By 1870 he was to be paid by result, and by 1873 he was receiving £88 p.a. and the average attendance, reflecting the school's success, was 47.

There is a suggestion that Pales meeting had such an iconic position in the thinking of Friends, because of its history, that its existence resonated symbolically in the way Friends approached questions about its future. Their second annual report was direct:

> Friends' meetings continue to be regularly kept up, although so few of the attenders are in membership, and it is believed that the school is useful in confirming the attachment of the inhabitants of the district for the Society of Friends.[95]

The school's financial position was of permanent concern, and in 1869 the committee noted their wish that parents and local residents would 'assist more in the pecuniary support of the school.'[96] The committee observed and monitored the education offered, and were pleased that in 1872 the government inspector had found the school to be the best in the neighbour-

89. PMDB, M1, 18.2.1867.
90. HRMM, M9, 12.3.1867.
91. HRMM, M7, 29.1.1867.
92. PMDB, M1, 18.2.1867.
93. PMDB, M2, 18.7.1868.
94. PMDB, 1.10.1868.
95. PMDB, 2nd Annual Report 1869.
96. Ibid.

hood,[97] hinting at the potential that this good work would bring 'the result of which we trust, will hereafter more fully appear.'[98] This may refer to the educational advantages for the children but also the mission potential of the school for the Society.

In March 1874 Knowles announced his resignation, at which point the committee recommended to the Monthly Meeting that the school should be discontinued, 'unless a master comes forward.'[99] By June no suitable Friends had offered their services, and so in October, the Monthly Meeting minuted that: 'The final report of Pales School has been produced. The school being now given up, the Committee is discharged.'[100] Changes brought about by the Education Act of 1870 and the establishment of board schools had had an impact. The seventh annual and final report focused on the condition and future of Pales as a worshipping community. They were concerned at the 'state of Pales Meeting, which is very much reduced, and to express the desire that although the School is closed, Friends would maintain a continued interest in the Meeting.'[101] Obviously the school had not impacted greatly on the religious life of the Meeting attached to it.

In September 1876 a committee of four, all former members of the original school committee, namely Samuel Alexander, Josiah Newman, Henry Newman, and H.S. Newman met with the American Quaker, Yardley Warner[102] at Leominster. He proposed to reopen the school, believing that in 'making this offer he was following divine guidance.'[103] One Quaker historian believes that Warner's interest had been aroused by his contact with Samuel Pumphrey, who had travelled extensively in the ministry in the USA.[104] It is unclear whether the Monthly Meeting was consulted about this as there are no relevant minutes. However, in April 1876 it had minuted that, 'This meeting had been brought into feelings of much interest with the

---

97. PMDB, 5th Annual Report 1872.
 98. Ibid.
 99. PMDB, M20, 31.3.1874.
100. HRMM, M8, 26.10.1874.
101. PDMB, 7th Annual Report, 1874.
102. See Stafford Allen Warner, *Yardley Warner: The Freedman's Friend*, 1957.
103. PDMB, 30.9.1876.
104. Martin Williams, 'Evangelical Friends in Radnorshire from the late 19th Century', Unpublished paper 28.11.1995, 7.

account that has been given us respecting the religious state of the people around the Pales and we appoint John Tertius Southall to pay them a visit.'[105] Whatever the precise circumstances, Warner reopened the school in October 1876 with a wage of a £1 a week, in the first year, plus the 'school pence,' but with the added proviso that he agreed 'to consider it part of his duty to attend the meeting at Pales on First day,'[106] thus acquiring pastoral and mission responsibilities. Indeed from here on the annual report from Pales was entitled 'Pales School and Mission.' and with Warner's arrival 'now, in no uncertain way, evangelism had arrived in Radnorshire.'[107] He of course meant Quaker evangelism. What is clear is that Warner's enthusiasm saw him work closely with the Primitive Methodists and others in the area, to the discomfort of his Monthly Meeting colleagues. The reconstituted committee impressed on Warner, 'that the afternoon meeting on First Day, though of an open character should be held under his control, as a meeting for which the Society of Friends is responsible and which is under its care.'[108] By 1878 they felt the Primitive Methodists were taking over, recording their concerns about their continued dominance and 'that friends have to ask the permission of the Primitive Methodists before they feel at liberty to address the meeting.'[109] Neither was the educational element as proficient as it had been under Knowles. By June 1880 the committee recorded concerns about the educational standards, but by then their own surveillance might not have been as it should have been, since there are no minutes between June 1878 and June 1880, although they noted that committee had been held 'as occasions required … without any record being made.'[110]

Warner's import would have added to the importance of mission amongst certain Friends within the monthly and quarterly meeting. Thus WQM in April 1879 agreed to arrange a general meeting at Pales, appointing a committee of seven to organise the event,[111] with Anna Warner, Yardley's wife as a member. The rest of the committee drew heavily for its member-

105. HRMM, M6, 25.4.1876, HRMM.
106. PMDB. M7, 30.9.1876.
107. Williams, 'Evangelical', 1995, 4.
108. PMDB, M3, 10.9.1877.
109. PMDB, 6.2.1878.
110. PMDB, 25.6.1880.
111. WQM, M6 16.4.1879.

ship on Leominster Meeting, which by 1878 was flourishing, with its 88 members.[112] It had already been active with its own evangelic endeavours, and from 1872 had organised its own tent meetings.[113] Since 1859 it had had its own tract association to spread the word. HRMM minuted their support for a general meeting at the Pales in December.[114]

It was no surprise that Henry Stanley Newman was a member of the WQM committee, and his membership of the of the Yearly Meeting Committee on General Meetings was consistent with his views about mission, but also his practical experience of organising mission meetings.

After the 1872 tent meeting Leominster organised further similar meetings. In June 1877 four meetings were arranged, when apparently over 1,000 were present, with the American Friend, Dr Dougan Clark, Professor of Systematic Theology and Church History at the Quaker, Earlham College in Richmond, Indiana, and author of the popular *The Theology of Holiness*, speaking on the 'Pathway of Holiness, preaching that "consecration was man's part, and that sanctification was God's gift to be received by faith."'[115] Clark was also in Leominster for the 1875 General Meeting, focusing again on holiness.[116] It would then be with regret that Newman as editor of *The Friend*, wrote in 1894, that, 'we read in the American papers of the baptism with water of our honoured Friend, Dougan Clark took place in Ohio Yearly Meeting,'[117] and because of it forced to give up his role as instructor at Earlham College, and repudiated by his YM. An example of how some Quakers, especially in America, were overcome in their evangelic Holiness fervour to move towards more mainline Protestant positions.

The General Meeting at Pales drew on this experience, and the reputation of the school meant it could also draw on local goodwill. Newman was one of the principal leaders in the efforts, assisted by Frank Dymond of Neath Meeting, a member there since 1871, and who evangelised widely, a prime example of how individual Quakers, with the backing of their Monthly Meetings, travelled the country preaching to Quakers and non-Quakers. For

112. HRMM, Tabular Statement 1878.
113. HRMM, 12.12.1881: handwritten report.
114. HRMM, M8, 3.12.1878.
115. *TF*, 8th month 1877, 236.
116. *BF*, 8th month, 1875.
117. *TF*, October 12.10.1894, 656

example in 1874 he had a minute of service within South Wales; as noted, in 1875 he was involved in the General Meeting at Leominster and went twice to Berkshire and Oxfordshire Quarterly Meeting. In 1879 he returned a minute of service to the Monthly Meeting after another journey; in February 1880 he was at Bristol, in December at Yorkshire Quarterly Meeting in Leeds, whilst in 5th month 1881, he attended Warwickshire, Leicester and Staffordshire Quarterly Meeting.[118]

In June 1879, the 'Pales committee' presented a report on their activities to their parent body. The general meeting had been held for a whole week in a tent erected on Penybont Common, with additional meetings conducted in local chapels. On the Sunday evening 400 were present at the gathering, and it could be happily reported that,

> One old man, who we were told had not attended a place of worship for years, stood up and informed us how he had been reached by the Spirit of God in the meetings. He appealed to Friends and said, 'I am reminded of the ostrich, who lays his eggs in the desert and hatches them not, and entreated that some means might be devised for shepherding those who have been so much blessed.'[119]

The Quarterly Meeting forwarded a report from Hereford and Radnor Monthly Meeting on the fruits of their endeavours in their area to the 1880 Yearly Meeting. It highlighted the fact that of 40 people recently received into membership; 37 were now attached to the Pales, 'these converts are filled with love and zeal. Some of them are descendants of former Friends.'[120] Newman, addressing the Yearly Meeting, said that he was acquainted with all 37 and reassured them that the Monthly Meeting had not received these new members in bulk; each had been dealt with individually. This was a necessary qualification, reassuring Friends that the traditional disciplines had not been ignored. Each and every applicant had been visited and

---

118. Referenced in sequence as follows: *TF*, 1.8.1874, 216; *BF* 5th month, 131 and 8th month, 224; SWMM M1, 4.12.1879; *TF*, 2nd month 1880, 50; *TF*, 12th month 1880, 318; *TF*, 5th month 1881, 127.
119. WQM, 25.6.1879 report.
120. *TF*, 6th month 1880, 137.

interviewed. Indeed, whereas most Friends could not identify the day of their spiritual birth, this was not the case with these Friends.[121]

In 1882 *The Friend* reported that the Monthly Meeting had given each new member a certificate of membership, signed by the Clerk of the Monthly Meeting, Henry Stanley Newman, 'welcoming among us those who we trust have known true conversion of heart by faith in our Lord Jesus Christ.'[122] For evangelical Friends, far too many Quakers were lukewarm about their faith and membership, whilst the evangelical credentials of those in Hereford and Radnor Monthly Meeting were apparent and indisputable. In this context the efforts and leadership of Newman, amongst others, makes Leominster an important and significant centre of Quaker evangelical activity in the nineteenth century, an aspect that is worthy of further study. Its contribution, directly and indirectly, to the life and mission of LYM was significant, not only spiritually but also socially, as evidenced by the establishment in the town of the Orphan Homes (1869) and then, latterly, the Orphan Press (1872) which provided employment and apprenticeship for those from the home. It was a hub of considerable activity supporting and caring for several small country meetings 'originating from the efforts of scholars at Leominster First Day school.'[123] Yet by the 1960s Leominster meeting was closed.

Yardley Warner and his family left the Pales in April 1880 and by October, James Abbatt of Preston and his wife, Mary Hannah, and her sister Allis Lamb stepped in. He was to be paid £20 per quarter. For 30 years a woollen draper, he relinquished his work in 1875, 'believing that God had called him to devote his whole life to Christian work.'[124] He was recoded as a minister by Hereford and Radnor Monthly Meeting in 1884. The same year the school was discontinued, to allow Abbatt 'to pursue his evangelical path,' liberated so that his 'time is now fully occupied in Gospel work and hours to hours visitation.'[125] Pales became a centre of mission.

The annual reports from this period testify to Abbatt's fervour, and the figures on convincements and membership reflect this. Between 1881and

121. *TF*, 6th month 1880, 137.
122. *TF*, 1st month 1882, 21.
123. *TF*, 4th month 1882, 85.
124. DQB.
125. PMDB, 8th Annual Report, 1884.

1884, there were 65 new members and 36 attenders at Pales. Mission meetings were held across the area, and Friends from Pales were engaged in religious and temperance work.[126] All this missionary fervour seems to have had one negative outcome, funding was becoming problematic. In 1879 the work at Pales had 64 subscribers, all from England, providing an annual income of over £94. By 1880 there were 59 subscribers and an income of £78, 1884 saw 39 subscribers with an income of £82, and by 1885 the committee noted the need for further funds, feeling that it was time for Abbatt to leave because it could no longer afford him. Some subscribers no longer wanted to support the work because the school had been closed – 'owing to the day school having been given up we found that some Friends objected to continue their subscriptions;'[127] a reflection that evangelic work was not attractive to many in the Yearly Meeting. Abbatt left in June 1885 transferring to St Ives, Huntingdon in order to work under the auspices of the HMC. The Pales committee were not insensitive to Abbatt's future, the possibility of him offering his services to the HMC had been raised in April,[128] and a month earlier they were enthusiastic about him going to Cardiff temporarily, responding to a request for help from the HMC.[129]

Despite the financial strictures the committee decided to ask the widow Anna Warner to return to restart some educational work at Pales, offering her £60 a year, noting to the Monthly Meeting that she would be paid '£20 less than that received by James Abbatt.'[130] She reopened the day school and became 'actively engaged in visitation and reorganisation,'[131] supporting smaller meetings in the community based in the homes of members. For example regular meetings were held at Gwernalltcwm Farm near Builth from 1887 to 1888, the home of one Thomas Williams.[132] By 1886 the work at the Pales indicated greater participation by its new members who had 'become increasingly attached to the Society, and regularly support the whole expense of the Meetings held in the Iron Room,' a reference to mission

126. Ibid.
127. PMDB, M4, 31.7.1885.
128. PMDB, M5 & 6, 23.4.1885.
129. PMDB, M4, 10.3.1885.
130. PMDB, M3, 31.7.1885.
131. PMDB, 9th Annual Report 1885.
132. Macpherson, *Friends in Radnorshire*, 58.

meetings held at the Iron Room at Penybont.[133] This offers insight into how and why the new meeting house was built at Penybont in 1891 a far more accessible meeting point than the Pales.

Contact with the HMC by the local Pales committee seems to have been fruitful, speakers being sent to the district, especially during Anne Warner's absences. Her health was fragile and she had to leave the Pales sometime in the winter of 1888 to go to Somerset to recuperate, B.J. Elsmere of Swansea took over for part of the winter. Her prolonged absence saw various Friends cover for her, principally Monthly Meeting Friends. The HMC supported the work. In January 1887, William Collyer held a three-week gospel mission at Penybont.[134] Home Mission workers were sent; W.G. Hall, the Home Mission worker at Almeley, Herefordshire was at Gwernalltcwm and the Pales for two to three weeks during 1888, and George Ash of Gloucester, at the Pales in April/May 1889. Other visitors were recorded, amongst them Hannah Pearsall Smith, the American Holiness leader and Friend, now domiciled in England, who visited in the summer of 1888. Anna Warner's health would not however allow her to stay at Pales and she resigned in April 1889.[135] The school was now to be permanently closed and by 1889 the income from 48 subscribers had fallen to £52.

The MMs Ministry and Oversight Committee agreed in the same month that Pales and Penybont still needed residential help.[136] Thus in October 1889, Benjamin. J. Elsmere, took up permanent residence with his family as a missioner, fulfilling a request from at least one letter writer from Penybont that it was desirable for a man to fill the vacancy.[137] Elsmere was a native of Ledbury, a brick manufacturer who had worked on the Dinmore tunnel on the Shrewsbury to Hereford railway line when he was seriously injured, then moved to south Wales. He and his wife came into membership of the Society in 1884.[138] He took up the post with a salary of £60 a year, which the committee guaranteed, 'though if J.O. Jenkins is able to send us any additional sum from the neighbourhood ... we may possibly be able to add

133. PMDB, 10th Annual Report 1886.
134. PMDB, M4, 12.1.1887.
135. PMDB, M2, 13.4.1889.
136. PMDB, 13.4.1889.
137. PMDB, M3, 13.4.1889.
138. SWMM, M5, 9.10.1884

to it.'[139] Jenkins was to prove to be another leading and important Quaker evangelic in the county. He was the product of the school at the Pales, amongst the first cohort of pupils when the school was opened in 1867. His mother was an old scholar of the Quaker school at Sidcot, disowned for 'marrying out.' Jenkins was convinced and became a Quaker at the age of 23, with conversion at one of the Quaker tent meetings at Penybont. He was recorded a minister in 1886 and retained the same Quaker evangelic fervour throughout his life. He served as Clerk and leader at Pales and Penybont for about 60 years.[140] Prominent in the public life of Radnorshire, Jenkins served as a magistrate for 20 years, a member of Radnorshire County Council, Parish Councillor, school governor and on the Court of Governors of the University of Wales. He was a founder member of the Farmers Co-operative Society for Radnorshire.[141] A homespun Radnorshire Quaker, he ventured vigorously into mission out of his own area. During the Revival of 1904–05 he was active in south Wales and Herefordshire, and given a minute of service by his Monthly Meeting in February 1905 to work in Cardiff. He was committed to the peace testimony, freedom of conscience and his opposition to the introduction of military drills into schools would not have gone unnoticed within his county.[142]

Elsmere was a vigorous worker, who, during his period at Pales, also travelled in the ministry; hence sometime during and after July 1890 he visited Milford, Swansea, Neath, Cardiff and Newport.[143] But his stay at Pales was to be a short one. The 13th Annual Report (1889) noted that Pales meeting had been affected by death and affliction; the meeting at Gwernalltcwm had been discontinued, its Quaker tenant having left, as had a house meeting at Ty'n y Llan, Llandegley.[144] By August 1890 Elsmere, in a poorly punctuated and gloomy letter, noted that he was 'plodding on'

---

139. PMDB, Minute Ministry and Oversight Committee, HRMM, 9.4.1889.

140. Williams, 'Evangelical,' 1995, 7–8.

141. Florence Jenkins, 'John Owen Jenkins 1856–1944', private unpublished paper, edited and printed by Martin Williams, Llandrindod Wells, 1992.

142. *TF*, 14.9.1906, 619.

143. HRMM, M1, 10.7.1890 liberated for service by the Monthly Meeting and report 25.11.1890.

144. PMDB, 13th Annual Report 1889.

referring to the fact that 'sin and drink is doing its deadly work'[145] illustrating this with two sad incidents. He indicated that he and his family were thinking of leaving by March 1891, 'we do not feel happy here.'[146] The reasons for this are not listed, but the low salary may have had a part to play, not to mention the isolation. At a meeting in January 1891 the committee had agreed to reimburse Elsmere the costs of his travel to Monthly Meeting during the past year (30 shillings) suggesting, that financial reimbursement was important.[147] The question of isolation also affected Abbatt, since he described his years in Radnorshire as being 'very isolated but joyous.'[148]

In September 1890 the committee noted Elsmere's wish to be released and actively sought a replacement. Their 14th Annual Report (1890) reveals that local people were subscribing small sums of money to activities, indicating that they were responding to the challenge set by the committee. Despite this, the committee's efforts to find a replacement failed, although one Home Mission worker did visit Pales but was considered unsuitable.[149] Elsmere was to be the last residential worker based at the Pales.

In January 1891 Hereford and Radnor Monthly Meeting agreed to support Pales' proposal to build a new meeting house at Penybont, a few miles away, on land given by John Owen Jenkins, and thus much more accessible than Pales.[150] By March funds, at least £225, had been identified for the work, but this new development was not enough to hold Elsmere in the area. This new development meant in effect that the focus of activity moved away from Pales, which nevertheless retained its status as the Preparative Meeting, and onto Penybont, which became a mission meeting, and remained so. The meeting was architecturally built in the style of a nonconformist chapel. The last Pales committee minute hints at the change:

> We conclude not to advertise further for a mission worker at the Pales at present earnestly desiring that John O. Jenkins and his wife and our other Radnorshire Friends will do their utmost efficiently to sustain the work.[151]

145. PMDB. Letter to the committee dated 29.8.1890.
146. Ibid.
147. PMDB, 6.1.1891.
148. DQB.
149. PMDB, 13.4.1891.
150. HRMM, M4, 6.1.1891.
151. PMDB, M6, 13.4.1891.

The building at Penybont went ahead, and the new 'chapel' opened in November, testimony no doubt to Jenkins' determination. £395 had been raised for the building, without difficulty, 'so that the work commences entirely clear of debt.'[152]

Elsmere and his family moved to Leominster. In June 1891 the Monthly Meeting wrote to the HMC seeking a 'resident missionary,'[153] for Radnorshire, since there were already workers at Almeley and Hereford. In October the HMC minuted that they had failed to find anyone to go to Penybont.[154]

ii. Llandrindod Wells

In May 1892 Elsmere approached the HMC, supported by a letter from John Owen Jenkins, stating that he wished to work in Wales 'providing that I could do some itinerant work in the principality,'[155] Elsmere outlined his former mission work at Pales, and the fact that he had already conducted Gospel Meetings at Milford Haven. In June 1892 HRMM minuted that Elsmere had been appointed to work at Llandrindod, but also to help out at the Pales and Penybont, 'and in other parts of Wales.'[156] A placement in what was still a relatively new town, indicating that the HMC saw it as a centre from which work in Radnorshire could be supported. It reflected the town's growing popularity as a prosperous health resort, 'visited annually by some forty thousand visitors, amongst which number there has of late years been a good sprinkling of Friends.'[157]

By July 1892 Elsmere was in Llandrindod but was not formally appointed and interviewed by the HMC until October, suggesting that informal networking and contact between leading Friends was sufficient. His pay must have been somewhat greater than when at Pales, but it is significant that, from time to time, his living allowance, like that of all the other workers, would be supplemented. In March 1899, for example, he was given a grant of £10 because of his wife's illness, and in July an allowance of £18 per

152. *TF*, 9th month, 1891, 251–2.
153. HRMM, M2, 9.6.1891.
154. HMC, 4.2.1892.
155. HMC, 28.5.1892.
156. HRMM, M2, 14.6.1892.
157. *TF*, 4.3.1898, 138.

year for two years was agreed so that his son could go to the Quaker boarding school at Sidcot.[158]

Elsmere threw himself into his work with considerable energy, building up a new meeting in the town. The records show that the first meeting for worship was held at the Lower Assembly Rooms on August 7th, 1892, with further meetings on fifth day evenings. On the fourteenth a First Day school for adults was established and one for children in the afternoon.[159] By April 1893 he was interested in establishing a mission station at Llanyre, a hamlet a few miles outside Llandrindod, where a 'desire quickly sprang up for the erection of a meeting house.'[160] This was a place which could claim a Quaker graveyard dating back to 1656, where it was estimated 120 were buried.[161] This historical association, one of those strategic decisions determined by nostalgia, may explain why the mission was established there. By July 1893 Elsmere was writing to Bruce & Still of Liverpool, galvanizer and manufacturer of corrugated iron, for a quote for building a mission hall,[162] although, according to Macpherson, the corrugated chapel at Llanyre was not actually built until 1895.[163]

In June 1893 Pales asked the Monthly Meeting, as would have been the practice, to establish Llandrindod as a separate Preparative Meeting, and this was agreed to in September,[164] confirmed by the Quarterly Meeting, with a membership of nineteen including seven children. One Hercules Davies Phillips was appointed as clerk.[165]

In October 1893 the Preparative Meeting, despite its small numbers, agreed that a purpose built meeting house was necessary, and

> would be of service to Friends from various parts of the country ... our work is hampered for the lack of a meeting house and we believe that when we have this the work will progress still faster.[166]

---

158. LSF, HMC, Executive Committee (HMCEC) minutes: M3, 3.3.1899 and M4, 5.7.1899.
159. PCAO, RNC/2B/1 &2/3.
160. LlWPM, 23.4.1893. (Preamble to the minute book.)
161. *TF*, 17.7.1897, 'Glimpses of Friends' Work in Radnorshire, unauthored article,' 471–72.
162. GRO D/D SF 469/2.
163. Macpherson, *Friends in Radnorshire*, 1999, 58.
164. HRMM, M4, 7.9.1893.
165. LlWPM, 16.9.1893.
166. LlWPM, M15, 3.10.1893.

The Monthly Meeting agreed and sought permission from the Quarterly Meeting.[167] Plans were drawn up and the building designed, according to *The Friend*, by O. Morris Roberts of Porthmadog, chosen no doubt because he had gained a reputation as the designer of places of worship.[168] Roberts may not have personally designed the building since he died in 1896,[169] but his reputation was such that his firm were engaged, despite the distance from Llandrindod.

The new meeting house at Llandrindod was built of red Ruabon facing bricks, with stone quoins, the internal arrangements conveniently providing accommodation for about 200, with two classrooms separated from the meeting room by a movable partition, and 'the lighting will be by means of electric light. (Llandrindod has no gasworks).'[170] Unlike the other two new meetings in the area, it was built not merely to satisfy local need. The transient holiday population was also a factor. In reflecting on this the Monthly Meeting was aware that Llandrindod was also popular amongst the Welsh, and that with its seasonal influx, it was becoming 'an important centre for Christian work'. They also reflected on the broader Welsh implications, conscious of historical precedent:

> When we consider the success of Quakerism in Wales in the times of George Fox, and the present religious characteristics of the people, their partiality for Free Churches and great readiness to welcome the ministry of Friends it appears to be the duty of the Society to develop its energies in this direction. Our own well known historical tradition as sufferers for liberty of conscience, and the whole tendency of religious Welsh aspirations, present a wide and open door for us to enter, and gather in a spiritual harvest.[171]

This was a call to wider mission, a reflection on the wider implications of having a new meeting, and evidence of the type of vision Newman

---

167. HRMM, M14, 23.11.1893.
168. Personal communication from two Welsh architects connected to the firm established by Roberts.
169. *The Builder*, 26.12.1896.
170. *TF*, 4.3.1898, 138.
171. HRMM, Triennial Report 23.11.1893.

especially had for both the new meeting house and the town. He probably wrote the report.

Elsmere stayed in Llandrindod until 1896 when he asked to be transferred to Swansea, feeling a concern to go there 'in order to carry out work in Wales from that centre.'[172] The Preparative Meeting recorded his wish to leave in April 1896,[173] and the HMC considered a letter from him in October, when he asked to move 'to another centre where service in several towns of South Wales and the district might be possible.'[174] Removal to Swansea, with the support of South Wales Monthly Meeting, was approved, and he transferred there by the end of September 1896.

In December 1895, Hercules Phillips had written to the HMC of his 'clear conviction that he must offer himself for service in Wales in connection with this committee.'[175] In January 1896 he was interviewed, transferring to Northfield, Birmingham for a six-month trial period. Reading the various documents it does not appear as though Phillips was necessarily destined for Llandrindod. In February, when he had gone to Northfield, Llandrindod Meeting had given him a gift of £1-7s-10d and an illuminated address, and he was not in the town when Elsmere announced his wish to leave in April. Phillips himself says he was asked to consider returning to Llandrindod to succeed Elsmere[176] and did so in September.

The work associated with the building of the new meeting house at Llandrindod then fell on Phillips' shoulders. It was opened in February 1898, with ecumenical input. There were now three new meeting-houses operating within an eight mile radius of the town; Llandrindod meeting, the mission hall at Llanyre, opened in 1895, and Greenfield Chapel, Penybont opened in 1892.

The work at Llandrindod Wells can then be encapsulated through the life and efforts of Hercules Phillips.

172. WQM, M12, 9.12.1896.
173. LlWPM, M7, 30.4.1896.
174. HMC, M11, 1.10.1896.
175. HMC, M6, 6.2.1896.
176. Philips, 'The Personal Story,' 1941, 2.

iii. Swansea

The condition of Swansea meeting in 1859 has already been commented upon. In 1871 a report to WQM on conditions there was just as bleak, regretting that 'things were so reduced and the circumstances under which it is maintained'[177] but this was no spur to action. Between 1871 and 1896 the situation looked dire. In 1874 the meeting house had closed, the meeting transferring to the local YMCA[178] presumably because of low numbers; the tabular statement showing six members in that year. An examination of the Preparative Meeting minutes from 1870 to 1897 indicates that it only met, or at least recorded meeting, but once a year, with perfunctory minutes. In April 1893 they minuted with a certain inexactitude that, 'Our meetings for worship are regularly held and attended at or near the time appointed.'[179] They did touch on some issues of national importance but with little enthusiasm, a petition for 'the suppression of the opium trade in China had been brought to the notice of this meeting'[180] with no record of a response. No Preparative Meetings were seemingly held between 1893 and 1896, but this was possibly because they could not appoint a Clerk. In December 1893 their long serving Clerk, Joseph Fraley Rutter, who may have been ill for some time died aged 72.[181]

By 1896, when Elsmere arrived, Swansea had three adult members, meeting once a week. This was the figure quoted by *The Friend* and may refer to those regularly worshipping there.[182] The tabular statement for 1896 indicates that Swansea had ten members, seventeen in 1897, and eight members were present at the Preparative Meeting on the 18th October, 1896.[183] WQMs membership book for 1897, shows fifteen members with the Elsmere family making up for two adult and nine child members, hence there were only four other adult members. This was indeed a very weak meeting.

The HMC must have been somehow persuaded to support Swansea although this had not been their view in January when they had considered

177. WQM, Report 18.10.1871.
178. *TF*, 1.9.1894.
179. GRO, D/D SF 428, Swansea Preparative Meeting (SPM) minutes, 29.3.1891.
180. SPM, 29.3.1891.
181. *TF*, 5.1.1894, 16.
182. *TF*, 20.12.1898, 854.
183. SPM, minutes, 18.10.1896.

the matter and concluded, 'That the time is not ripe for encouraging the settlement of a resident missionary, but that a periodical visitation by Quarterly Meeting committee on small meetings'[184] would be helpful. Elsmere's removal to Swansea was supported in June/July by SWMM and approved by the HMC in October,[185] and by December he was working there.[186] By December 1897 the decision was taken to build a new meeting house at Swansea, a sign of enthusiasm, optimism and determination by the Monthly Meeting.[187] The HMC in September 1897 recorded that Elsmere,

> reports a morning meeting of 20 and an evening one of 30 to 40. A small children's school and an adult school have been begun. The Monthly Meeting is about enlarging the room and this is needful before larger numbers can be accommodated in the evening.[188]

Clearly between then and December the decision was taken not to enlarge but build anew, and the HMC must have had some influence on that decision. The meeting house had proved too small to contain the numbers attracted and a hall had to be rented. It was thus proposed to build, at a cost of £1,200, a new meeting house that could hold 450 people. Swansea Preparative Meeting recorded their request to have a new meeting house by minute of February 1897, weeks after Elsmere's arrival. The approval of the Monthly Meeting had to wait until December 1897, whilst the Quarterly Meeting in July 1897 had agreed to appeal for funds. The appeal leaflet explained that

> The number of non-members who now frequently come to meeting is evidence that there really continues to be a good opening for Friends in Swansea. There is now active religious work being carried on; but it is quite clear that this can only be very restricted unless there are better rooms, which should include those in which adult school, bible classes etc could be held.[189]

184. HMC, 20.1.1896.
185. HMC, M11, 1.10.1896.
186. SWMM, Triennial Report, 3.12.1897.
187. SWMM, M12, 2.12.1897.
188. HMC, 30.91897.
189. Quoted by Butler: *The Quaker Meeting-houses*, 1999, 865.

Frederick William Gibbins was the appeal's treasurer and reported that the total cost was £1,298 of which £1,287 had been received, £777 from subscriptions and £455 from the sale of Great Western Railway stock belonging to South Wales Monthly Meeting; £85 had been received from collections. In June 1899 the new meeting house was opened with seating for 250. The *South Wales Daily Post* report on the opening was not especially complementary: 'Its architecture – or more accurately the absence of it, is rigidly consonant with the Quaker spirit. Red brick relieved by some Bath stone outside, and high white plastered walls inside – that is all the architecture.'[190] Its report also provides clues as to how the Quakers were commonly perceived rich, well connected, not the church of the common people, another reason why the denomination did not appeal to the mass of the population.

> Woven with the history of Quakerism in Swansea is the history of the best people who ever lived in the town, as will be understood when it is stated that among the families who from time to time fulfilled their devotions at the simple looking building in High Street were the Baths, the Rutters, the Eatons, the Sibberings and the Birchalls.[191]

In the same vein the *Herald of Wales* could not avoid connecting the Quakers to its prosperous membership, and the fact that the graves of the Bevans of the 'Barclays and Bevans the great bankers of the present day' were to be found in the Swansea meeting graveyard.[192]

By February 1899, Elsmere informed the HMC that the evening meeting was averaging 70 and in the morning 25, whilst the Bible Class attracted 30, although it was noted that the adult school suffered from the migratory habits of the men of the port, indicating that the school was to some extent reliant on the sailors of Swansea.[193] The committee noted with satisfaction that one of Elsmere's converts was a soldier, who had been with the

190. *South Wales Daily Post*, 29.6.1899.
191. Ibid.
192. *Herald of Wales* 1.7.1899.
193. HMC, M22, 2.2.1899.

congregation for some time and had bought himself out of the army on conscientious grounds.[194]

Elsmere's work was not confined to Swansea. In October 1898 he was visiting several places, especially Milford Haven where he thought there was an open door 'and a local doctor of position and his wife desire Friends to begin a meeting there,'[195] as though this was sufficient reason in itself.

His stay at Swansea was none too cordial, despite the new meeting house. The records indicate that Elsmere's wife was unwell in March 1899, and in the following year the secretary to the HMC, Ellwood Brockbank, had to report to its executive on conditions at Swansea. The minutes do not tell the story in detail, only that Elsmere had had 'serious difficulties to encounter,' such that Frederick J. Gibbins, as Clerk of the Monthly Meeting, had written inviting Brockbank to a conference to discuss the problems. William A. Albright, from Birmingham, was asked to accompany Brockbank, and they were given the mandate to tell whoever was concerned that the committee could not

> continue to be responsible for the residence of any worker in a meeting where he does not receive the support of the Monthly Meeting and where individuals are allowed to persistently oppose his work.[196]

Whatever the issues, they seem to have involved the clerk to the meeting, Sidney G. Wayne. There may have been some personal animosity involved. In October 1893, the Monthly Meeting had considered an application from Wayne that he be allowed to undertake mission work in Swansea. They, 'despite being sympathetic,' did not support him in his desire, 'to which judgement he yields.'[197] Wayne had been Clerk to the meeting since 1897 resigned his clerkship in October 1899 and was replaced by Frederick W. Gibbins of Neath Meeting, a sign that Swansea meeting was not sufficiently robust to find a clerk from amongst their own, and that the presence of an

194. Ibid.
195. HMC, M42, 6.10.1898.
196. HMCEC, M15, 2.3.1900.
197. SWMM, 12.10.1893.

'outsider' might have an effect. Gibbins remained as clerk until April 1902.[198]

The tensions did not abate: thus in February 1900, Elsmere asked the Preparative Meeting to assert their confidence in his work, and he, having withdrawn from the meeting, the Clerk recorded that, 'the matter was fully discussed but there does not seem sufficient unity to make any minute on the matter at this time,'[199] an indication of continued disagreement. The outcome was the decision of the HMC to send a delegation to Swansea.

They saw Wayne, and no doubt others, and as a result Wayne, 'assented to the wishes expressed' by his visitors, the points of their conversation being sent to him in writing. The hope was that Elsmere for his part would show 'a kind of conciliatory spirit' and a care 'exercised that the right service of S.G. Wayne in the meeting may not be hindered.'[200] The tension, which was obviously personal, seems to have been resolved, in that the committee did not discuss Swansea again in any detail again until 1904. This did not mean that all was well; indeed in November 1902, the Monthly Meeting appointed visitors to see William Philip Thomas and his family and recommended disownment. Thomas apparently 'acknowledges that he is entirely out of sympathy with Swansea Meeting and as such does not see that he is called upon to show a spirit of love towards those to whom he had given pain.'[201]

In a census of average attendance at meetings for worship for October 1904 there were 28 Friends in the morning meetings at Swansea, 21 adults and 7 children. In the evening meeting 65, including 14 children, a measure of Elsmere's success, although the figures are not overwhelming.[202] In Llandrindod for example, a much smaller town, there were also 28 in morning worship and 80 in the evening.[203] The morning meeting at both centres would have been conducted in the traditional Quaker manner, based on silent waiting, the evenings would have been mission meetings accompanied by singing with a programmed approach.

---

198. SPM, 5.8.1899.
199. SPM, M13, 11.12.1900.
200. HMC, M6, 4.4.1900.
201. SWMM, 29.11 M14.
202. YMP, 1905, M25, Report on Census of Attendance at Meetings, 19–21. Figures are in an appendix, 118–119.
203. Ibid.

By February 1904 Elsmere wished to devote part of his time to business. He had been offered employment locally. He would maintain his mission work on Sundays and evenings, but would be unable to undertake pastoral duties. The policy of the HMC was also changing at this time, in that they were encouraging their workers to take up remunerative work locally. In 1906 the Yearly Meeting also agreed to a change in the name to the Home Mission and Extension Committee (HMEC) reflecting changing attitudes to the nature of mission within the Yearly Meeting,[204] as it sought to encourage Monthly Meeting and Quarterly Meeting to take more direct responsibility for encouraging new members and attenders. Even so, by 1908 the number of workers under its wing was 35,[205] five more than in 1900.

Employed Elsmere could not, as was required of him, attend Yearly Meeting and asked that his wife be allowed to attend in his absence. The Committee did not concur and Elsmere responded, in such terms, that the committee noted 'that in view of his letter that it would be well that his connection with this committee should shortly come to an end.'[206] By June he had resigned, the committee recording acceptance of his resignation 'believing that it will have a healthy effect on his own spiritual life that he should again take up his old handicraft, using his spare time in such religious work as he feels able to take up.'[207] On this sour note he left, and when he again wrote, the executive committee read his letter without discussion, laid it on the table merely noting its receipt. However, Swansea Meeting warmly recorded their appreciation of his efforts amongst them.

We desire to place upon record the Christian work of our Friend B.J. Elsmere in connection with our Religious Society in Swansea. Through his exertions a new meeting house together with a Schoolroom was erected, also a Business Premises attached. The shop connected is now a considerable source of income to the Funds of the Monthly Meeting. Through our Friends' labour many have become interested in the Society, and some have in consequence joined us in membership.[208]

204. YMP, Annual Report HMC, 1906, 30.
205. YMP, Annual Report, HMEC 1908, 35.
206. Home Mission and Extension Committee (HMEC), M19, 6.5.1904.
207. HMEC, M13, 30.6.1904.
208. GRO, D/D SF 469/1. Letter 30.8.1905.

It is difficult to interpret what and where things went wrong for Elsmere. By 1909 he wrote to the Monthly Meeting indicating his wish to resign his membership, and this was again probably linked to particular clashes within the Meeting relating to the role of W.G. Hall who had replaced him. The Monthly Meeting sought to change his mind and succeeded.[209] It was in 1925 that his disenchantment with Friends was such that he finally resigned his membership when the YM abolished the role of recorded ministers.

Elsmere may be unique amongst British Friends. In 1925 he applied to the Presbyterian Church of Wales, through the South Wales Association, for admission to their ministry. A committee considered his application but could make no recommendation, but the Association agreed that he be recommended to the Brecon Presbytery as a preacher. That Presbytery in April 1930 supported his resubmitted application, which was referred to the Ministerial Candidate Board. They considered the matter, and recommended to the Association that it, in session, should decide. A sub-committee was appointed which noted that since Elsmere

> was appointed to the full work of the ministry amongst the Quakers in 1884, and because of that, and because – once he was united with the Association – he recognises the administration of the Ordinances, we recommend his acceptance as a minister amongst us.[210]

The recommendation was confirmed; Elsmere came forward, and was presented with the usual questions addressed to aspiring ministers. He was welcomed, and ordained simply on the basis of his past ministry amongst Friends, without benefit of rigorous academic study.

By October 1904 William G. Hall had transferred to Swansea as the new HMEC worker. Hall had been a mission worker from the HMC's early days, transferring to Swansea from Woburn Sands (now part of Milton Keynes). He was not unfamiliar with WQM since he had been a mission worker at

209. SWMM, M5, 13.10.1909.
210. NLW Calvinistic Methodist Archives, 30 (*'Neilltuwyd Mr B.J. Elsmere i gyflawn waith y Weinidogaeth ymhlith y Crynwyr yn 1884, ac oherwydd hynny, a chan – ar ol iddo uno a'r Cyfundeb – y cydnebydd weinyddiad yr Ordinhadau fel rhan o waith gweinidog, cymeradwywn ei dderbyn fel gweinidog yn ein plith ni.'*)

Almeley, Herefordshire, when Woonton Mission Meeting, now closed, was opened, and had been an employee of Henry Stanley Newman.[211]

In late 1904 and 1905 the Welsh Revival was to reinvigorate the religious life of Wales, and Hall proved enthusiastic about its prospects and implications. His stay at Swansea was not entirely harmonious either. It seems to have been a troubled meeting, even though the Triennial Report of WQM to 1909 Yearly Meeting reported that it 'has maintained a steady ingathering. There has been a decided increase in the interest shown in attendance at morning meeting' and could add that 'for the size of the meeting, compared with surrounding churches, Friends have in all probability the best Christian Endeavour Society in Swansea.'[212] This latter reference relates to the international interdenominational movement started in Portland, Maine in 1881, to train and equip young people to become leaders within their churches, indicating that for Hall at least there was an ecumenical dimension to his role.

In February 1910 the executive committee of the HMEC considered a letter from Richard Watkins of Swansea Meeting, in which he pointed out the difference which 'he believes exists between the actual practice of our workers in several meetings which have come under his notice and the aims of the Committee.'[213] He had written to Rachel Bevan Braithwaite, as secretary, in December to which she had responded, 'In the meanwhile attention is being paid very carefully to many of the points which thou has brought before us.'[214] Watkins seems to have been pointing the finger at Hall, with whom there might have been a personality clash or perhaps jealousy, because Watkins was to prove just as enthusiastic about mission work. Thus, in March 1907 he invited over seventy people, 'being the guests of Richard Watkins' to an 'at home' event at the meeting house in Swansea, when 'all the Christian work came under review.'[215]

Braithwaite communicated with the Clerk of SWMM regarding developments at Swansea on the same day which suggests previous dialogue and

211. *TF*, 27.6.1913, 431.
212. YMP, Triennial Report WQM 1909, 212.
213. Home Mission and Extension Committee Executive Committee (HMECEC), M5, 1.2.1910.
214. HMEC correspondence FHL. Letter 11.12.1909 (146).
215. *TF*, 29.3.1907, 205–206.

seemingly gently admonishing them possibly for their inaction and inability in coming to grips with the difficulties,

> It is, however, the custom to appoint an Advisory Committee of the Monthly Meeting from where a HM worker is settled to sympathize with or advise them from time to time. The names of the Advisory Committee of your Monthly Meeting are as follows: Caroline E. Gibbins and Arthur Sessions.[216]

Rachel Braithwaite was asked to visit Swansea. In March of 1910 the HMECs executive considered her report regarding meetings within WQM, and were so concerned about Swansea that they appointed a committee to visit.[217]

In April, Swansea Meeting had minuted, at Hall's request, a record of their appreciation of the way he approached his work, alongside another minute that it was not time 'for our worthy William G. Hall to leave Swansea.'[218] an indication that Watkins did not have the full support of the meeting. The visiting committee of the HMEC reported back in May, and again in June. The minute of the executive committee was precise and overrode what the local meeting had agreed,

> we are of the opinion that the service of W.G. Hall in that Meeting is finished. He does not seem to have the mental and physical strength to meet the difficulties of the situation and it has also been ascertained from him that he would be willing to leave, if the meeting were adequately provided for, and he would be glad of service in the neighbourhood of London where his eldest son is living in lodgings.[219]

They also decided that it would be better for Swansea if no other resident worker be placed there for several months. They felt that Hall should move on, and Swansea meeting encouraged to take greater responsibility for the work of the meeting.[220] Whatever the circumstances they did not let go of

216. Ibid. Letter 11.121909, (147).
217. HMECEC, M8, 4.3.1910.
218. SPM, M5, 20.04.1909.
219. HMECEC, M6, 6.6.1910.
220. HMEC, Secretary's report, 3.6.1910.

Hall and he was asked to transfer to Evensham, which he declined. By September he was in London working at the Bedford Institute. He was the last HMEC worker placed in Swansea and indeed in Wales. Frederick Sessions tribute to Hall's endeavours, on his early death in 1913, said of Swansea that, 'There were difficulties here, which the Quarterly Meeting failed successfully to grapple with, but which it is not worthwhile to enlarge upon.'[221]

The executive of the HMEC remained concerned about Swansea, with their sub-committee visiting at least three times up to November. The minutes of the Preparative Meeting reflect the unease within the meeting. There was obviously considerable tension and backbiting amongst the members – much of it seemingly directed against and from Richard Watkins, one minute stating that he had been 'the sole means of getting William George Hall from Swansea.'[222]

Richard Watkins was fifty when he became a member of the Society in November 1906.[223] Born in Myddfai, a village near Llandovery, he would have been Welsh speaking, and was, like his father, a builder and a Congregationalist. He had spent time as an evangelist in Australia and Tasmania, and had apparently served two chapels in Swansea as an organist. Interestingly, despite this musical inclination, he was accused of having described the formation of a singing class within the meeting as 'permitting the Devil to come in,'[224] thus indicating some ambivalence on his part regarding the use of music in meeting. This might have been part of Watkins' disagreement with Hall. In a paper to HMC workers in 1899, Hall had defended singing as an important part of Friends' missions by reference to the practices of early Friends. He felt from his own observations that most people considered Quaker meetings 'dull and unattractive,' for two reasons, the lengthy silent pauses and the absence of singing.[225]

221. *TF*, 21.6.1913, 431.
222. SPM, M9, 12.10.1910.
223. SWMM, M4, 14.11.1906.
224. SPM, M9, 12.10.1910.
225. A Plea for the Return to the energetic Faith and Practice of the Founders of the Society of Friends, A paper read before the HM workers in London, Nov 3rd 1899, W.G. Hall, Friends Tracts Association.

A tribute to Watkins in *The Friend* after his death highlighted his fervent prohibitionist views stating that he was 'responsible for the extinction of scores of licences'[226] over the years in Swansea. He had been a Guardian of the Poor, involved in ecumenical affairs, and described as a man who 'made his mark in any body of people.' Not slothful in business, 'he was fervent in spirit, carrying his business-like ways and methods in matters of religion.'[227] Regular in attendance at Yearly Meeting, he served on Meeting for Sufferings, the HMEC and on the Council of the FTU. Similarly, he was involved in the affairs of his Monthly Meeting as treasurer and as Registering Officer for Marriages. Watkins served as treasurer to his Quarterly Meeting and was Clerk of its Committee on Trusts and Awards.[228] Watkins was by any measure a prominent Friend, and if the descriptions of him are to be believed, determined and resolute, if not stubborn.

Watkins as a member of his Monthly Meetings Committee on Ministry and Oversight was in an influential position to pursue his own agenda and seemingly did so. In July 1910 they again discussed the situation at Swansea listening to Watkins' concern 'at the absence of a spirit of love and unity among certain of our Friends in Swansea Meeting.'[229] They had left matters to the Swansea elders but they had not met and indication again of some disunity amongst them. In view of the problems three Friends[230] were appointed to visit, two of whom were members of the HMEC's advisory committee. They were to enquire into the causes of disunion and seek a solution. After this, subsequent records of the committee indicate that Richard Watkins was not present at any of their meetings during 1911.

In September 1910 Swansea held a special Preparative Meeting in response to the disharmony. A minute was prepared – minute five. At the next business meeting in October, Watkins objected to the reading of that minute with non-members present. Their withdrawal was agreed but Watkins refused to leave the meeting when asked to do so and stayed. The issues involved Watkins and the events as described are not complementary to him. The matters discussed were about relationships and behaviour, with

226. *TF*, 22.08.1930, 767.
227. Ibid.
228. Ibid.
229. GRO, D/D SF 446/1, SWMM, Ministry and Oversight Committee (SWMOC), 13.07.1910.
230. Arthur Sessions, J.H.S. Elliott and Caroline E. Gibbins.

suggestions of impropriety.[231] In November 1910 at Swansea PM, after Hall's departure, a letter was read from SWMM elders and overseers declaring that they were

> deeply pained to hear of the disunity in your Meeting which is dishonouring to our Society, and above all unworthy of the followers of Christ. The change must come from within the Meeting, not from without.[232]

Swansea PM made no minute as a result of this intervention, and the last sentence indicates that the HMEC still had some interest in events there.

At a Preparative Meeting held on January 9th, 1918 – eight years after – the Meeting 'agreed that the Clerk be authorised to delete Minute 5 of the Preparative Meeting held 13th of the 9th Month 1910 as that minute is deemed to be improperly included in our Minute Book.'[233] A highly unusual, and unacceptable procedure for Friends, since although decisions may be subsequently changed, there cannot be justification for the deletion of a minute if it is a true record of discernment at the time of its writing. This would seem to testify to the authority and standing which by 1918 Richard Watkins had attained.

The disharmony and mutterings at Swansea persisted into 1911. At a Preparative Meeting in November 1911 it had noted in a report on the condition of the meeting that a

> large number of those who used to attend our meetings, have ceased to do so and there is considerable slackness on the part of many of those more closely associated with us and our work and also on the part of some of our own members.[234]

At a special Preparative Meeting in December 1912, fourteen attenders and members were removed from the meeting list. This all appears as a somewhat depressing endnote to the efforts and work of the HMEC in the

231. SPM, M9, 12.10.1910.
232. SPM Minute Book, 23.11.1910.
233. SPM, M5, 9.1.1918.
234. SPM, M7, 11.10.1911

town, and that Swansea was a meeting under judgement.

In March 1915 the Monthly Meeting, Ministry and Oversight Committee felt that it would be helpful to the meeting if Friends from other places visited Swansea more often,[235] perhaps because it had become isolated. In March 1916 the same committee discussed yet another minute from Swansea complaining that a large number of their Members seldom attended Meeting.[236] They asked their Clerk to spend a weekend in Swansea during April, presumably to see what was what.[237]

Developments in Swansea, and the impact of the investment made by the HMEC, can be gauged by an analysis of the tabular statement returns for the meeting. In 1861 the membership at Swansea stood at 18 but by 1878 had gone down to 3. When Elsmere arrived in the town membership stood at 10. Three years later it was 35, but the highest it ever reached was 38 in 1901. The Welsh Revival of 1904–05 seems to have had little impact on membership, and by 1906 it was back down to 34. From 1906 to 1918 the figures show a further gradual decline until in 1918 it stood at 17, the same as in 1885 and 1897 and one fewer than in 1861. Of course these raw figures mask any ebb and flow and give no indication of the stability of membership, nor do they show numbers of attenders. Despite the investment and the input of two mission workers from 1896 to 1910, the building of a new meeting house Swansea cannot be described as having a thriving Meeting.

Swansea meeting to-day remains open, in 2012 with 42 members.[238]

iv. Cardiff

Williams[239] in her study of Quakers in Glamorganshire outlined their growth in Cardiff, highlighting the city's contribution to the growth of dissent in Wales. She estimates that by 1815 there were probably no Quakers in Cardiff, but that by 1836 there had been some recovery.[240] From the 1851 religious census we know that five attended meeting for worship on the morning of

---

235. SWMOC, M3, 17.3.1915.
236. SWMOC, M3, 15.3.1916.
237. Ibid.
238. SWMM, List of Members and Attenders, 2012.
239. Williams, 'The Society of Friends,' 1950.
240. Ibid. 31. This from an electronic privately edited version of the thesis with editorial additions by Martin Willson.(2005)

the census, but by 1854 the meeting was held in the home of Samuel Bevington. The meeting house was reopened in 1870 largely through the efforts of Samuel Pumphrey Jnr and Edwin Octavius Tregelles.[241] For a substantial period before this it was solely used by the United Methodists, who in March 1863 wrote a 'memorial' to the Monthly Meeting asking that they be allowed to purchase the building, since they had used it for six years, and had in 1860 spent £150 on 'alterations and enlargements' to it.[242] By 1872 the meeting house at Charles Street, was let as a school, but with reservation for occasional meeting of Friends.

In April 1871 WQM established a committee to visit all of its meetings and report back on their circumstances. It did so in October, noting that 'At Cardiff we found several members and others connected with our Society. Some there are longing for the privilege of worshipping as Friends. These claim the exercise of pastoral care.'[243] This was then a concern for the proper management of a meeting in line with the expectations of Church Government, and they recommended that a Meeting for Worship under the care of a committee be held once a month in the city, indicating that the meeting itself did not have the resources to furnish its own elders and overseers. In January 1872 such a committee was appointed.[244]

The growth and attraction of Cardiff as a major city and port as well as its historical connection for Friends, made it an important attraction, and was also a place which offered business opportunities for some amongst them. In 1851 the population was around 20,000, but by 1872 it had risen to 82,761, and by 1891 it stood at 128,915.[245] The re-establishment of Quakerism there mirrors the growth of the city. Thus one family associated with the meeting at Cardiff during this time were the Sessions from Gloucester. They had established branches of their merchant builder enterprise in both Cardiff and Newport. In 1869 Arthur Sessions, Frederick Sessions brother, had moved to Cardiff taking over the management of the business after the early death of their other brother.[246] Arthur's input has some bearing on the way the

241. Williams, 'The Society of Friends', 1950, 40.
242. GRO, D/D SF 90.
243. WQM Report 18.10.1871.
244. WQM M3, 17.1.1872.
245. M.J. Daunton, *Coal Metropolis: Cardiff 1870–1914*, 1977, 10.
246. Private correspondence from C. Pitt Lewis, Arthur Session's great–grandson, July 2007.

meeting developed, and as a scion of a very notable and evangelic family he had access to a robust network of concerned Friends. From the minutes of SWMM and Cardiff Preparative Meeting it is obvious that Arthur Sessions input over the years was considerable. He served as Clerk and treasurer of Cardiff meeting, and for a substantial number of years was the Monthly Meeting's registering officer for marriages. His name appears in appointments to various committees and he was clearly a backbone to the meeting as it developed and settled. In 1879 he was one of WQM representative at Yearly Meeting and from 1901 to 1903 was a member of Meeting for Sufferings.[247]

By 1875 the tabular statement showed twenty seven members were attached to Cardiff. Two historians of Nonconformity note that the meeting house was reopened in 1874, adding that 'Prominent among those who have helped the cause since its revival are Messrs, Arthur Sessions and Henry Rees.'[248] It remained a meeting that was not however self-sufficient despite what would appear to be a healthy number of members. As Williams notes, they could not sustain a Preparative Meeting, and had to join with a smaller meeting at Newport for that purpose.[249] Sadly there are no minutes relating to Cardiff available until 1897.

In April 1879, WQM discussed their concerns about the state of Cardiff Meeting and set up a committee to investigate.[250] It did not report until April 1880 and its conclusions were far from positive. They had visited three or four times and felt that little or no permanent help could be given to the Friends there 'unless some experienced and judicious F to whom they could look for personal help and counsel should reside amongst them.'[251] They then arranged for a letter to be published in *The Friend* in the hope that this might lead to someone to move to Cardiff. They then requested that they may disbanded.

This must have been Frederick Sessions letter of January 1880. He wrote that although the disused meeting house there was a 'most unattractive and

247. YMP 1901, 43; 1902, 57; 1903, 55.
248. J. Austin Jenkins and E. Edwards James, *The History of Nonconformity in Cardiff*, 1901, 203.
249. Williams, 'The Society of Friends,' 1950, 40.
250. WQM, M3, 16.4.1879 and report *TF*, 5th month 1879, 133.
251. WQM, M2, 21.04.1880.

woe begone little building' through the efforts of a solitary Friend, referring to his brother Arthur,

> a company of Christians was gathered, and one by one they were received into membership ... but they are for the most part among the poor and illiterate of this world, and unused to our methods of church government and discipline. Since the removal of their Friend who gathered them in Western Quarterly Meeting has striven to aid them.[252]

Support could not however be guaranteed by the committee appointed because of problems of distance for those involved. Sessions appealed for an experienced and well-qualified Friend to go and live in Cardiff to support the fledgling group. There is no record of any actual response to this appeal.

The meeting seems to have remained lethargic, despite attempts to inject life into it, Arthur Sessions and George Carter organising mission meetings on Sunday evenings.[253] But by January 1882 the first day-school at Cardiff had been discontinued owing to circumstances 'which seemed unavoidable.'[254] Between 1882 and 1885 activities little is heard of Cardiff.

In May 1885, Henry Stanley Newman reported to the HMC, taking up the case for Cardiff. His report hints at the fact that he himself had recently evangelised there, aided by George Wood of Sudbury who had been directed there by the Committee, and 'they had some genuine cases of conversion.'[255] Wood had been at Cardiff since January 1885, and the Monthly Meeting had sought his stay but Newman had indicated to them that this was not possible. Newman, with some feeling of regret, given the fervour of his own convictions, had been given a list of the members in the Cardiff area and was 'struck by their numbers as well as by the fact that they did not seem to know each other ... Friends actually living close to each other were strangers.'[256]

In November 1885, William Hobson, an Ulsterman, who had been evangelising in England since 1873, was asked to take up residency in

252. *TF*, 1.01.1880, 11.
253. Williams, 'The Society of Friends', 1950, 40.
254. FFDSA, M11, 29.1.1883.
255. SWMM, M2 12.2.1885.
256. *TF*, 6th Month 1885, 161.

Cardiff. The HMC had responded to a minute from WQM of April 1885 who had agreed that they would contribute £20 per annum to the costs of a missioner.[257] Hobson had served in Bristol from July 1882 to the autumn of 1883, where he had been warmly supported in his work by Frederick Sessions.[258] Hobson was well known for his energetic efforts; before moving to Cardiff he had also served in Norwich, Dover, Cambridge and St Ives, Huntingdonshire. His motivation and enthusiasm is well reflected in a statement of his, which also no doubt represented the views of many Friends, especially those of a more evangelic inclination, 'The Baptists succeed, the Methodists prosper, and the Salvation Army increased rapidly. Why do Friends ALONE recede?'[259]

His advent to Cardiff drew some opposition, which according to his biographer 'came to nought.'[260] which was probably an understatement. Hobson himself, reflecting on his time at Cardiff, recognised that matters were never that simple commenting that within six months of arriving there was

> much that hindered the work and barred progress … six years of continuous struggling told on us, especially on my wife. It will never be possible to describe what we had to pass through in holding the fort.[261]

He was received warmly by the Nonconformist Ministerial Union, soon contributing to the local community, joining the committee of the YWCA and YMCA, conducting weekly dinner-hour meetings amongst the employees of the Taff Vale Railway, Spiller's Flour Mills (originally a Quaker firm), and organised Bible classes amongst the local police, and for a time served as the Nonconformist chaplain to the workhouse. He also published a monthly paper, *The Friendly Messenger*, with a circulation of about 2,000, with no indication as to why it ceased.[262] A mission room was rented in, 'the heart of a district largely occupied by the labouring population and he hoped that it

257. HMC, M6, 18.5.1885.
258. William King Baker, *A Quaker Warrior: Life of William Hobson*, 1913, 73.
259. *TF*, 10th month, 1883, 249.
260. Baker, A Quaker, 95.
261. Ibid., 95–96
262. Ibid., 129.

would act as a feeder to the Friends meeting.'[263] Establishing mission meetings amongst the poor was important, but the question of how they were then drawn into full membership perplexed many Quakers. In Cardiff some effort seems to have been made to provide adequate support to their poorer members, and thus encourage membership, as illustrated by this somewhat patronising report from WQM:

> One Friend, of Cardiff, and his family had the privilege of attending through the benefit of a Club established in that meeting, into which its poorer members pay regularly, and receive a certain sum for expenses and loss of time, as they are appointed to Quarterly and Monthly Meetings.[264]

Hobson's presence gave heart to the Quarterly Meeting, such that by 1887 it began to discuss the possibility of building a new meeting house in the city, Hobson of the view that the old meeting house 'was discreditable to Friends' cause.'[265] The treasurer to the building appeal concurred seeking 'accommodation worthy of our Society in the midst of the great metropolis of Wales.'[266] The building would cost £1,400; £550 had already been identified from within WQM, £180 coming from SWMM and £100 from Coalbrookdale Preparative Meeting Funds, another reminder of the contact between Shropshire Friends and Wales. The optimism of the Monthly Meeting was no doubt contagious and by December 1887 it could record that there had been an increase of thirty-six in its membership, partly attained through the movement of Friends from other parts of Britain, but that twenty had joined by convincement in Cardiff, reflecting the investment made by HMC in the city.[267]

The new meeting house was completed and opened in February 1889. £1,192 had been collected, from a total of 209 subscribers; the building costing £200 more than the original estimate,[268] in part probably because during the

---

263. *TF*, 1st Month, 1886, 22.
264. *TF*, 10th month, 1889,227.
265. King, *A Quaker*, 1914, 94.
266. *TF*, 3rd month, 1888, 63.
267. SWMM, M2, 1.12.1887.
268. *TF*, 2nd month 1889, 42–44.

construction 'the contractor failed and subsequently absconded, adding £180 to the cost.'[269]

Hobson's endeavours in Cardiff were substantial but the HMC noted that even by October 1889 he still drew opposition:

> The conduct of two or three Friends there has greatly interfered with the work, and the matter has been dealt with by the Quarterly Meeting on Ministry and Oversight, so that it is hoped that a better state of things may prevail.[270]

Hobson could not have expected everyone in Cardiff to welcome his arrival. The case of William Mills highlights these tensions. In December 1887 William and Florence Mills had been accepted into membership having been interviewed by F.J. Gibbins and by B.J. Elsmere both of whom believed that, 'William Mills is convinced of the views held by the Society of Friends, and others who know him being of the same opinion.'[271] By September 1889 the Monthly Meeting, Ministry and Oversight Committee had to consider Mills' situation, in so far as he was no longer in unity with his meeting. He published a leaflet to this effect, *A Testimony for the Welfare of Zion*,[272] in which he challenged the validity for Hobson's ministry and his paid standing by the HMC, but did not name him:

> It is with the greatest sorrow that I have witnessed and heard these principles of Truth sold for nought by your chief paid minister in this town; who has openly denied the Lord of Life and Glory, which is Christ's light within.[273]

He went on to highlight the way early Friends were guided by that 'light that was in them,' feeling confident that God would awaken his people, 'To your tents, O Israel! … blow ye the trumpet of Zion, for the enemy is upon you, and has broken down your ramparts, and is laying waste the heritage

269. *TF*, 5th month, 1888, 111.
270. HMC, M7, 6.10.1889.
271. SWMM, M6, 1.12.1887.
272. William Mills, *A Testimony for the Welfare of Zion*, 1889.
273. Ibid., 3.

of the Lord!'[274] The Monthly Meeting took no action against Mills, but he was to be visited by Friends. However, but in August he wrote to the meeting, and such was the content of the letter that it was felt not 'desirable to be read,'[275] and Mills was warned again about his behaviour at Cardiff meeting. Interestingly, in April 1890, despite his disagreements, Mills sought his children's entry onto the list of members, but this was not agreed.[276] By August 1890 the Monthly Meeting considered a letter from Henry Rees, on behalf of the ministry and oversight committee of Cardiff Meeting, with regard to Mills who had

> directly and publicly disturbed and produced disorder and shown open opposition in our Meeting for Worship ... to the detriment and damage of the cause of Christ and the discredit of the Truth.[277]

In tolerance the Monthly Meeting took no action, but gave full support to Cardiff Meeting. The next reference to Mills is the birth of his son in August 1891, but by April 1892, his wife had indicated her wish to be removed from the list of members.[278] A letter from four Friends at Cardiff in this month again highlighted Mills' continued and unacceptable behaviour causing 'great dissatisfaction to Friends' reflecting the fact that in February 1892 a minute noted that Mills had been given a note by the Elders at Cardiff asking him, 'not to take any public part in future; the ground being that his ministry gave uneasiness and dissatisfaction to Friends.'[279] The Monthly Meeting considered the position and concluded 'As this is disorderly and greatly disturbs the meeting we hereby disown William Mills as a member of our Society.'[280] The Quarterly Meeting confirmed this,[281] Mills appealed to the Yearly Meeting which they rejected, Mills was disowned.[282]

---

274. Ibid., 8.
275. SWMM, M8, 8.8.1889.
276. SWMM, M4, 10.4.1890.
277. SWMM, M6, 14.8.1890.
278. SWMM, M14, 14.4.1892.
279. SWMM, M17, 14.4.1892.
280. Ibid.
281. WQM, M3, 22.9.1892.
282. YMP 1893, M15, 15.

But Mills was not the only problem, so was Tonnes Andreasen, another convinced Friend. He was accepted into membership in November 1875 and his wife, Mary Ann, in February 1876, thus predating the arrival of Hobson. He worked for some time at the Cardiff docks as a manual worker, and was at one time a foreman in a slate yard. His working class status would have set him apart from the overall membership of Cardiff Meeting, but Mills was also from a similar background.

In 1880 Andreasen resigned from the Friends Christian Fellowship Union. Precise information on this organisation is sparse, but it would have been something that Hobson would have valued and organised. The few references shows it to be an organisation for fellowship and witness amongst younger evangelically inclined Friends. Andreasen outlined his reasons in a pamphlet declaring that the Union was not consistent with the views of Friends.[283] He then published six further leaflets all expounding similar views consistent with those of conservative, plain Quakers, witnessing to the 'backsliding from the Truth'[284] within LYM. Two leaflets are undated but it is not unrealistic to think that these were both published before Hobson arrived in Cardiff. The second undated leaflet, *A Warning: Concerning the Ministry in the Society of Friends* was published by John Edward Southall in Newport,[285] who was prominent in the conservative cause, and undoubtedly one of the influences on Andreasen and his departure from the orthodox Quaker position. In 1881 Southall published a leaflet in similar vein to Andreasen.[286]

Alongside Southall was the influence of Charles Allen Fox who was to become another thorn in the flesh of Cardiff meeting; Fox and Andreasen were both witnesses to Southall's marriage at Cardiff Meeting in September 1882. Southall and Fox were birthright Friends whose families were well embedded in the life of the Yearly Meeting.

---

283. Tonnes Andreasen, Resignation of Membership in the so–called Friends Christian Fellowship Union, Cardiff, 11th month 1880.
284. Tonnes Andreasen, *The Truth*, (Cardiff, no date, publisher or pagination).
285. See Ch. 4 on Southall.
286. John Edward Southall. *A Faithful Warning to those Calling Themselves Friends more particularly in Western Quarterly Meeting, England* (Gloucester, J.E. Southall, 1881.)

Once Hobson was in Cardiff, Andreasen published three more leaflets, all similarly critical,[287] but it was only after Hobson had gone from Cardiff that the Meeting took action against Andreasen and others. Unlike in the case of Mills, the threat of disownment, was not applied to Andreasen, suggesting that former was more vocal and vigorous in his denouncements which paralleled those of Fox.

These difficulties highlight the divergence that existed within the Yearly Meeting with regard to the work of the HMC, and the difference of emphasis existing between the evangelistic and the conservative, quietist Friends. The sequence of events in Cardiff provides local insight into this aspect of the life of the Yearly Meeting, although the extravagance of personality involved in Cardiff cannot be overlooked.

Fox was a descendent of the Fox family of Falmouth, and brought up in a plain, conservative Quaker household, his father being a London surgeon, Joseph John Fox, who attended Stoke Newington Meeting, part of Devonshire House Monthly Meeting. The father in early life wore the plain costume, and had been

> brought up amongst the older influences of Friendly thought, and his mind retained some of their colouring to the end. He has said that his grandmother, Hannah Fox (née Forster), a recorded minister, used to exhort him to 'mind the inward Monitor.[288]

This plain Quaker approach obviously influenced his son.

Once qualified, Charles was apprenticed to a Dr Leahy at the Llynfi and Ogmore Coal and Iron Works in the Maesteg–Bridgend area, certainly between 1869 and 1872.[289] There is little evidence of this early period of

---

287. Tonnes Andreasen, *Where are the 'Quakers' gone to?* (Cardiff, J. David, 1887); *A Guide to the Truth as held by the People (in scorn) called Quakers* (Cardiff, J. David, Steam Printer, 1889); *The Famine or the State of the Society of Friends at the present day, with extracts from Samuel Fothergill and Sarah (Lynes) Grubb* (Cardiff, J. David, Machine Printer, 203 Bute Road, 1890.)

288. *TF*, 7.1.1898, 6.

289. Charles Allen Fox, *Leaves of a Review of Life*, 1911, 7; Letters WM, 14.10.1898 and 9.11.1893.

residence in south Wales. At some point he was also in Australia.[290]

Fox regularly attended LYM and contributed to its deliberations on several occasions, revealing his conservative attitudes. *The Friend* records his attendance at seven YMs,[291] although in 1873 he had supported liberalising the query on tithes, being pragmatic as to how Friends should deal with these,[292] and in 1874 decried the formality that had set into the way queries were handled.[293] He was, however, critical of General Meetings[294] and clear about the inspiration of the Spirit in the mission of the 'ancient Friends'[295] whose stance he admired.

> It is a common practice to talk of our highly favoured Society, but this is because we do not suffer persecution: would rather that we were persecuted, and as the early Friends were! 'Stand in the old paths.'[296]

and pleaded for adherence to the old testimonies in the life of the Yearly Meeting.[297]

In 1874 he attended the Oxford Holiness Movement conference,[298] where he had his Damascene experience attesting to Jane M. Guyon, the French mystic, as his 'spiritual mother and aid:'[299] Not surprisingly he was also influenced by Asa Mahon the author of *On Christian Perfection*[300] and by the Pearsall Smiths and the Higher Life movement, defending their approach.[301]

For a period he lived in Derbyshire, a member of Chesterfield Monthly Meeting from *c*.1883 to *c*.1891.[302] As he lived not far from Fritchley, the home

---

290. Ibid., 10.

291. 1873, 1874, 1878, 1879, 1880, 1887, 1892.

292. *TF*, 6th month, 1873,141.

293. *TF*, 6th month, 1874, 119 and 143.

294. *TF*, 6th month, 1879, 171.

295. *TF*, 6th month, 1878, 139.

296. *TF*, 6th month, 1880, 141.

297. *TF*, 6th month, 1892, 347.

298. Fox, Leaves, 1911, 8.

299. Ibid., 12.

300. Ibid., 10.

301. *BF*, 10th month, 1874, 330.

302. Richard C. Allen, 'An Example of Quaker Discipline: The Case of Dr Charles Allen Fox and the Cardiff Quakers,' in *The Journal of Welsh Religious History*, 1, 2001, 46–73.

of the only independent conservative Quaker meeting in the UK, which in1868 had been established as Fritchley General Meeting. Fox would probably have links with them. By 1886 he had returned to south Wales, since in March he gave evidence at an inquest at Blaenafon, Monmouthshire[303] suggesting that he might have gone back to the coal mining areas before moving to Cardiff, where he gave evidence at an inquest there.[304] By this time his eccentricities were visible. He gave evidence at another inquest, implicating a husband in the violent death of his wife. The *Western Mail*, incensed by the jury's verdict of accidental death, and convinced of the husband's guilt, felt that the jury's decision arose from the fact that Fox as a Quaker through 'his eccentric attire had a prejudicial effect upon the minds of those who had to deal with his evidence.'[305]

By 1888 Fox saw himself as a specialist in mental health. That year he had been attacked and stabbed in the neck by a disturbed friend in London whom he had visited to treat, the newspaper reporting that the doctor was 'a specialist in mental disease and has a treatment peculiar to himself.'[306]

By any measure Fox was becoming more outlandish in his attitudes. In 1890 he wrote that compulsory vaccination was dangerous[307] and by 1913, in a newspaper article about him,[308] he claimed that he had returned to live in 'ancient simplicity', devised his own dress, a white cotton wrap leaving the arms and legs bare, advocating the abolition of clothes as then worn, and propounding pole twirling for the 'cultivation of grace.' He was linked to theosophy and believed in the mystery of the Great Pyramid, seeing the Britons as one of the lost tribes of Israel. Less unusually he was a vegetarian, an anti-vivisectionist, member of the Humanitarian League, the Land Nationalization Society, and the Purity League and supported the suffragettes. He advocated the 'Simple Life' as expounded by Charles Wagner, whose approach to living was to be influential in the USA (much admired by

---

303. WM, 22.5.1886.
304. WM, 29.8.1886.
305. WM, 2.10.1886.
306. WM, 24.12.1888.
307. Charles Allen Fox, *The Question of Compulsory Vaccination* (London, E.W. Allen, 1890).
308. *Daily Mirror* ,25.4.1913,article entitled, 'Savage Simplicity for Real Health: Man of Sixty Four Takes Five Baths Daily, Skips, Runs and Cycles; wash in morning dew.'

Theodore Roosevelt).[309] Some of his eccentricities, but not all, arose from his interpretation of being a conservative Quaker.

In 1881 his plain Quakerism led him to write a pamphlet rejecting any notion that the Salvation Army was inspired by George Fox, accusing them of misrepresentation.[310] When William Mills published his *A Testimony to the Welfare of Zion*, Charles Allen wrote the preface, identifying closely with its contents; he wrote at least one other pamphlet whilst in Cardiff.[311]

In April 1892 he and Mills together had caused a disturbance at Cardiff Meeting, and it must have been one of many since the Monthly Meeting decided to ask Devonshire House Monthly Meeting to consider the circumstances where Fox was now in membership since he must at some time have transferred his membership back there from Chesterfield,' We ask his Monthly Meeting to make such enquiry respecting him as may result in their dealing with him as they might find needful.'[312] The following month SWMM authorised their overseers to visit him,[313] but by August 1892, he had apparently left south Wales, and was living at Ross Herefordshire,[314] hence no further action was taken. By 1898 he was certainly back in Cardiff and probably there before then. In October the *Western Mail* published a long article where he expounded his views on several subjects related to his beliefs; he supported the Protestant Truth Society, founded by John Kensit in 1889 to 'oppose the growing influence of Romanism within church and the country, indeed he was one of a party that said its farewells to Kensit after his visit to Cardiff in 1898.[315] This stance appears contradictory given the fervent evangelicalism of the Society, but highlights Fox's distrust of Catholicism. He expounded on his Quakerism,[316] and his statements were

309. Listed and reported in Charles Allen Fox, *Of My Writings and of the Simple Life*, 1911.

310. Charles Allen Fox, *George Fox: No precursor of the Salvation Army* (so called, and that Sect no Quakers; its foundation tried and discovered to be on the sand; with a warning to all 'Friends'). In answer to G.R's 'George Fox and his Salvation Army of 200 Years ago') Written at Crick, Derbyshire, 12th month 1881, 1881.

311. C. A. Allen, *The Christian's Duty upon Politics*, 1886, but not traced.

312. SWMM, M18, 14.4,1892

313. SWMM, M11, 12.5.1892.

314. WM, 8.2.1894.

315. WM, 2.9.1898.

316. WM, 14.10.1898.

corrected in a letter from the Clerk to SWMM, F.J. Gibbins who was anxious to correct any misinterpretations arising from Fox's colourful expansions.[317]

A few days later the same paper reported that Fox was organising meetings in Cardiff for a 'number of select spirits around whom he proposes to import some portion of a Life's investigation … into the realm of mysticism and philosophy' which were attended by 'young men of many creeds and temperaments.'[318] It must have been these meetings that in 1899, described as a 'Quaker Class,' and advertised in the newspapers and in the meeting house, that again exercised the Monthly Meeting. This, especially since Fox had publicly announced that he was no longer in unity with Friends, and critical of all their endeavours, especially the new Cardiff meeting house,

> I cannot associate with them. The modern so-called Friends do not maintain the old principles, and here in Cardiff they have taken down an excellent sound meeting house, which was very useful and testified against all the showy places, and erected a most elaborate one, not like a hours of worship at all, and when it was not required Friends all over the country were appealed to, and were led to believe that a new meeting house was needed. Nor would they have had such a grievous place built as this … I have testified to the Society of Friends in Great Britain in their 'Yearly Meetings' at which I am like an Ignatius at the Church Congress. Friends are now chiefly philanthropists, but this is not their call primarily. The mode of worship and what takes place I could not own, nor could they be a Quaker's testimony.[319]

As to the class, Friends saw it as a libertarian group of 'low character,' since it met where 'intoxicating liquor is sold and where although its meetings are also held on First Day subjects are discussed … which are certainly not religious, even if not a doubtful moral character.'[320] The meetings apparently discussed free love, whether marriage was moral, and Fox did not support temperance; at Yearly Meeting in 1880 he had said that Friends should not

---

317. WM, 18.10.1898.
318. WM, 18.10.1898.
319. WM, 14.10.1898.
320. SWMM, M8, 16.2.1899.

'give up the use of alcohol, if we did not see its use to be wrong.'[321] The meetings were a source of outrage to the Monthly Meeting, who noted that Fox's conduct was 'injurious to the welfare of this meeting.'[322]

There may also have been tensions of a political nature between Fox and the Meeting. Fox supported the Labour Church Movement, established in 1891, as an attempt to fuse and reconcile socialist and Christian ethos in pursuit of emancipation of the working classes and closely linked to the Independent Labour Party.[323] Such a Church was established in Cardiff in January 1893 with S.G. Hobson as the presiding member, although 'the attendance was but small' and the absence of known Labour leaders in the city conspicuous.[324] Fox attended the Church.[325] If the Labour Church was unpopular with some Cardiff Friends the fact that William Hobson's son was closely associated with it might explain why this did not become an issue for the Meeting to condemn Fox – S.G. Hobson in fact became a member of the Council of the Labour Church Movement. The church in Cardiff must have been short lived since in 1898 attempts were made to revive it because it had 'fallen somewhat into abeyance.'[326]

Fox was sympathetic to the conditions of workers, supporting strikers at the Spiller Flour Mills in 1889, but consistent with his own viewpoint, 'strongly counselled moderation in all their actions.'[327] He supported the strikers in the Taff Vale railway dispute[328] attending one of their meetings, and expressing surprise that the workers in their negotiations had given 'up rights of representation.'[329] In 1898 he arranged what were described as classes with 'Readings from the Poets' (it is not clear whether these were the same meetings that drew the opprobrium of Friends) declaring, that, 'The poor will be admitted free, and will not be relegated to the back seats either, but be equally respected with those who chance to be better off among the

---

321. *TF*, 6th month, 1880, 151.

322. SWMM, M1, 4 4.1.1899.

323. See Stanley Pierson, 'John Trevor and the Labour Church Movement in England, 1891–1900,' in *Church History*, 29, 4, Dec. 1960, 463–478.

324. WM, 30.1.1893.

325. WM, 4.12.1893.

326. WM, 11.10.1898.

327. WM, 2.12.1889.

328. WM, 27.8.1900.

329. WM, 30.8.1900.

attendants at these meetings.'[330] Yet, in 1899 he was elected president of the Cardiff Ratepayers Association, a body not usually identified with progressive politics.[331] Allen, is of the opinion that Fox's 'upper-middle class professional background and his 'conservative' Quaker temperament based upon 'old principle' may have conflicted with those of the working-class members who sought to define their religious experiences' otherwise.[332] In fact the clash was more likely to be with the more middle class and birthright evangelically inclined Friends. Indeed two of the more 'conservative' convinced Friends at Cardiff were, as observed, working class. Fox was a man of complex motives and personality who was obviously not afraid of controversy, might perhaps have revelled in it, and was not troubled attacking renowned public figures, such as Lord Kitchener following his visit to Cardiff in December 1898.[333]

SWMM again asked Devonshire House Monthly Meeting to deal with Fox. It took no disciplinary action, largely because Fox had told them that he had discontinued his meetings and associations.[334] Nevertheless, by April 1900, WQM agreed to appoint a committee along with SWMM to consider what was obviously a continuing problem.[335] Two months later the Quarterly Meeting agreed to suggest to DHMM that Fox 'should be disunited.'[336] By February 1901, SWMM was informed that this had happened.[337] DHMM appointed a committee of twelve to advise them on what action should be taken.[338] By this time Fox had left Cardiff, moving to Somerset.[339]

In addition to these three Friends, there are other indications of disquiet in the Monthly Meeting minutes. In April 1892, Hannah Field had been visited and had expressed herself dissatisfied in that 'she did not agree with Friend Home Mission work,'[340] and that she would not attend meeting for

---

330. WM, 28.10.1898.
331. WM, 14.3.1899.
332. An Example, 2001, 52,
333. WM, 5.12.1898.
334. SWMM, 9.4.1899, minute from DHMM entered into the minute book.
335. WQM, M20, 18.04.1900.
336. WQM, M1, 27.06.1900.
337. SWMM, M4, 14.2.1901.
338. DHMM, M8, 15.11.1900.
339. DHMM, M13, 14.2.1901.
340. SWMM, M14, 14.4.1892.

worship. At the same meeting it was minuted that Thomas Evans would not attend because he could not, 'get clear of certain Friends whose particular views he does not agree with.'[341] In March 1897, F.W. John resigned his membership because he could no longer 'remain in membership with a body who are not candid enough to admit their intention of putting forward a paid ministry;'[342] a clear remonstrance to the efforts of the HMC.

By April 1892, William Jesper Sayce had moved to Cardiff as the new Home Mission worker replacing William Hobson who had moved away in May,[343] thus inheriting the turmoil that had exercised his predecessor. Sayce was Australian by birth, born in Melbourne in October 1857, his father, Alfred Edward Sayce, being considered an important figure in the establishment of Quakerism in the Antipodes, with his wife establishing the Melbourne meeting at their home in 1843.[344]

Sayce had offered himself to the service of the HMC in June 1882, having decided not to pursue his ambition to become a missionary to Madagascar.[345] By November he was in Hereford, a meeting within WQM, and by July 1883, HRMM in an obvious sign of his acceptance amongst them recorded him as a minister. His health may not have been robust, and the committee noted that a period away from Hereford

> seems to have benefited his health and to have drawn some of the Friends at Hereford nearer to him. With renewed health he has recommenced work that he had given up, and he reports so much encouragement that he does not see that he could suitably leave Hereford for the present.[346]

This is another hint that the task of the home workers was not easy and that they faced some resistance.

The HMC noted in October 1887 that the way had not yet opened for 'the

341. Ibid.
342. SWMM, M9, 24.3.1897.
343. SWMM, M13, 12.5.1892.
344. Charles Stevenson, 'Germs of Good: The Growth of Quakerism in Australia,' in *Journal of the Friends' Historical Society*, Vol. 59, No 1, 2000, 55–66.
345. HMC, M2, 27.6.1882.
346. HMC, report 3.3.1887.

removal of W.J. Sayce from Hereford,'[347] suggesting that they were contemplating his move. Sayce remained in Hereford until October 1890, when he asked to be liberated for service in Australia. This was agreed by Meeting for Sufferings, such that the costs of his service abroad and until his return in December 1891 were borne by the Yearly Meeting. The HMC in October 1890 decided that Sayce would not return to Hereford where Charles B. Cox was 'to remain there where he had done good work.'[348] However, it was clear that Sayce was held with some affection in Hereford, since he was back there in December 1891, with 250 present at a welcome home event, including Henry Stanley Newman and Frederick Sessions.[349] By April 1892 he was working in Cardiff and in that year published his only book, based on an address he had given in Australia, which reflected his evangelic leanings, but was also insightful of the challenges facing Quakers as they sought new adherents.[350]

His period at Cardiff was never comfortable. By May 1893 he withdrew for a few weeks because of ill-health, but announced in October through his Monthly Meeting that there were prospects in Cardiff but things in the city were challenging:

> Cardiff Meeting House is at the centre of a great variety of work, though it is all on a very small scale … the problem of how to get the people into our Meeting House is felt to be one easier to be discussed than solved in a particular manner.[351]

By February 1894 he reported slow progress, but by October was greatly encouraged again, with 52 attending the Adult School, 'the greatest number recorded for some years.'[352] Despite this optimism, by February 1895 the situation was such that the HMC minuted:

347. HMC, M12, 6.10.1887.
348. HMC, M19, 1.10.1890.
349. *TF*, 8.1.1892, 26.
350. W.J. Sayce, *What the Society of Friends Believes, and Why*, 1892.
351. SWMM, M12, 7.12.1893.
352. HMC, 4.10.1894.

> We have entered into sympathy with Wm. J. Sayce as regards his position
> and work in connection with this committee at Cardiff. The extreme difficulty
> and delicacy of his service there has been strikingly brought before us in this
> interview.[353]

Sayce wished however to stay, but the committee felt that discussion with
Friends in south Wales was necessary and that Sayce should remain there
pending the outcome of these negotiations.[354] They agreed to a Committee
of Conference with SWMM, the HMC being represented by some weighty
Friends, Joshua Rowntree, Mary S. Braithwaite, Sarah S. Bell, Jonathan Handley,
and W.C. Braithwaite, but their consultations did not see Sayce leave Cardiff
immediately and with B.J. Elsmere he was on a mission to Milford Haven in
October 1895. The following month the Monthly Meeting recorded that
Sayce himself had approached the HMC about the possibility of moving to
Newport.[355] He had already been doing some work there. It was in January
1896 that a committee, appointed by WQM, reported to the HMC, following
their consultation with the Monthly Meeting. By February 1896 Sayce's
health was again a cause of concern. In the meantime, temporary help was
provided to Cardiff Meeting with Sarah S. Bell and Sarah Y. Lury moving
there, to be replaced until the end of March by Caroline Langdon.[356] The
HMC recommended that Sayce be encouraged to go to Newport where he
would be welcome but

> connection [with Cardiff] shall entirely cease and that in accordance with the
> strongly expressed judgement of the South Wales Special Committee (in
> which we entirely unite) some Friends should be with the assistance of the
> Friends Home Mission Committee encouraged to reside there … Someone
> with a gift of eldership would seem to be essential.[357]

This is a strong hint that possibly Sayce's gifts were found wanting, his
health must have been a factor, and it's possible that his particular zeal might

353. HMC, M10, 7.2.1895.
354. HMC, M10, 7.2.1895.
355. SWMM, M12, 28.11.1895.
356. WQM, M8, 6.2.1896.
357. HMC, M3, 1.5.1896.

not have been welcome amongst more than those who supported Mills and his supporters.

By 1895 Cardiff had 78 members, with 25 regular attenders, so that Sayce's efforts were not insubstantial. He contributed to the civic life of Cardiff. In 1894 he was secretary of the Cardiff branch of the National Vigilance Association with its concern for social purity,[358] a subject upon which he had addressed the Yearly Meeting in 1896 which,

> he felt … to be one of the most important questions of the day … he knew there was a need for plain speaking amongst the young men who were gathered together in hundreds in large centres of population. These centres were often hot beds of impurity.[359]

In 1895, with other Nonconformist ministers, he signed a manifesto to the Cardiff School Board Elections on behalf of Friends.[360]

By the end of 1896 Emma Bishop had replaced Sayce. She was born into a Quaker family in Ipswich and her cousin, Robert Bishop, was a member of Cardiff meeting, and on their Finance Committee in December 1899. However, his application for membership for his infant daughter was refused by the Monthly Meeting in 1890[361] probably because his wife was not in membership. The HMC had asked Emma Bishop in October 1896 to visit Cardiff 'with the hope that if she appeared to find her right place there, she might be encouraged to prolong her stay.'[362] She had served at the Quaker mission and school at Ras el Metn, Lebanon, but ill-health had forced her to give up work in the foreign mission field.

By September 1897 she informed the Committee that she did not feel that a much longer residence in the town would be useful, but was unclear as to when she should leave, suggesting that after twelve months she was not fully settled.[363] Thus in November 1897, the HMC appointed a sub-committee

358. WM, 3.4.1894.
359. *TF*, 29.5.1896, 345.
360. WM, 23.12.1895.
361. SWMM, M11, 13.3.1890.
362. HMC, M8, 1.10.1896.
363. HMC, 30.9.1897.

to discuss the situation in Cardiff with the Quarterly Meeting.[364] In an article in April 1898 the needs of Cardiff and its scattered membership of 76 members and 24 attenders in their 'commodious premises in Charles Street' was explored. It appealed for someone to go to assist the meeting, a person, 'wise and judicious eldership combined with competent help to the Adult School and mother's meeting which have been in existence for some time,'[365] anyone desiring further information to contact Henry Stanley Newman. Emma Bishop, however, remained in Cardiff, despite any misgivings and made an impact despite her uncertainty and insecurity about remaining in the city. Cardiff Preparative Meeting considered her position, noting great appreciation of her work and hoping that the HMC would allow her to remain there.[366] By July 1899 she had lived in Cardiff for two and a half years and was again encouraged by the HMC to continue there.[367] The outcome was that she stayed until the summer of 1900, when she decided to accompany Henrietta Brown on her visit to Australia;[368] a visit supported by Meeting for Sufferings. She came back to Britain in 1903, returning her minute of service to Australia, as issued by SWMM to them in August 1905.[369]

Reading reports about Cardiff Meeting, it was far from moribund. In December 1900, it was reported that at the New Year's celebrations the meeting house at Cardiff a hundred had gathered.[370] In January 1899, the Cardiff Friends' Literary Society held their meeting at the Free Library indicating that this was an organisation that had life beyond the walls of the Meeting, taking an interest in varied subjects, not merely the religious. It met most often in the homes of Friends. In January 1900 they had discussed miscellaneous essays and, at the meeting house at the end of the month, an 'hour's chat' was held on the subject 'Black Diamonds' (coal and its products). On February 28th, a social evening was held at the meeting house.[371] Yet, in 1880 the Monthly Meeting had not allowed them to hold

364. HMC, M4, 3.2.1898.
365. *TF*, 15.4.1898, 231.
366. CPM, 4.6.1898.
367. *TF*, 14.7.1899, 454.
368. HMC, report, 5.7.1900.
369. *TF*, 14.8.1905, 543.
370. *TF*, 12.1.1900, 27.
371. *BF*, 10.1.1900 and 31.1.1990.

their gatherings at the meeting house[372] so there had been a liberalisation of attitudes. But overall there were strong hints that the meeting tended to be orthodox in its attitude; hence in November 1899 they did not allow attenders into their Preparative Meetings, rather that they were, 'continually invited to our Meetings for Worship and specials meetings, social evenings and lectures.'[373]

The departure of Emma Bishop was an opportunity for the HMC to review its investment in Cardiff, and justify the decision reported to the Yearly Meeting, that it had been decided to leave Cardiff Meeting without further resident help. Cardiff was the sixth Meeting which the HMC had left as 'self-supporting, and in several others less help is now given them than formerly although the work is larger,' although it still had 34 working for it, and it had 'never been clear of applications for assistance from meetings.'[374] Bishop was to be the last resident Quaker worker in the city.

This did not prevent Cardiff Meeting from calling for further assistance. In March 1904,[375] it asked for help with a series of meetings.[376] In January 1905, the Preparative Meeting again discussed its needs, and obviously did not feel self-sufficient enough to be able to deal with their own problems, and stating that they needed at resident worker. The meeting noted particular reasons for their request:

> The special reasons which make such a step desirable, are the long distances at which many of our members reside from each other, which makes visiting very difficult as nearly all are actively employed in business pursuits. The importance of Cardiff as a Commercial Centre towards which people will always be drifting for Commercial motives. The somewhat varied nature of our membership from the foregoing and other causes.[377]

Another request for assistance must have been made after this, such that in October 1906, the HMEC noted that a request for help from the Monthly

372. SWMM, M5, 12.2.1880.
373. CPM, M1, 14.11.1897.
374. YMP 1901, 36.
375. HMC, M1, 6.10.1904.
376. CPM, M6, 24.7.1904.
377. CPM, 29.1.1905.

Meeting for Cardiff had been withdrawn, and they were now asking for occasional visitors.[378] Yet, it appeared as though the Meeting was in good health, being filled to overflowing at a meeting on March 18th, 1906 when Frederick Sessions delivered a lantern lecture on the life of George Fox and William Penn.[379] By 1916, Cardiff meeting had 67 members, and was the largest meeting within the Monthly Meeting area.[380]

v. Newport

By the end of 1896 Sayce was in Newport, which had had a small meeting since 1885. No meeting was recorded there in the religious census of 1851, and the demise of Quakerism in Monmouthshire is a telling story given past vibrancy in the county. Monmouthshire Monthly Meeting was integrated with the South Division of Wales Monthly Meeting in 1836, and one Preparative Meeting established for the whole of the county lasting until 1870.[381] By 1868 they were unable to supply representatives to the Monthly Meeting.[382] Records at Friends House, London indicate that the meeting was discontinued c.1867. In the tabular statement for 1870, three Quakers were noted to be associated with the county.[383] The Quarterly Meeting in 1874 agreed to unite Newport with Cardiff as a Preparative Meeting that by 1876 could claim 10 members, meeting in a room at Newport Savings Bank[384] but by 1880 it had apparently closed. The town never had its own meeting house, but by March 1890 a new meeting were using premises made available to them by Arthur Bland, one of their members.[385] There are no records describing the life of Newport meeting at this time, but the one notable member was John Edward Southall.

The tabular return for 1896 showed 14 members attached to Newport

---

378. HMC, M1, 8.10.1906.

379. *TF*, 23.3.1906, 189.

380. See Appendix 3. In 1916 the largest meeting in Wales was Llandrindod Wells with 77 members.

381. See Allen, 'The Society of Friends', 1999, 498, also Reginald Nicholls, 'Early Quakers in Monmouthshire,' in *Monmouthshire Medley*, Vol. 1 Reginald Nicholls, ed., 1976, 79–88, and 'More about Early Quakers,' in Vol. 3, 1978, 58–74.

382. Allen, 'The Society of Friends', 1999, 507.

383. See appendix 3.

384. WQM, M12, 19.4.1876.

385. SWMM, M12, 14.11.1889.

meeting, with 14 attenders.[386] In February 1897 the HMC agreed that Sayce should stay at Newport, since they had being keeping his position under review.[387]

He maintained an interest in developments within the Yearly Meeting, and in January 1898 wrote, appealing as a missionary worker of some fourteen years experience, for a type of membership in the Society 'of a merely local character,'[388] suited for attenders at mission centres. He would have been aware of the mixed feelings about any such scheme, and his own Quarterly Meeting in September 1893 had decided not to support membership of a 'preliminary or associate character,'[389] even though the previous year SWMM had supported a form of membership of 'a probationary character'[390] which no doubt Sayce had influenced.

This issue was to be settled by the Yearly Meeting 1899 introducing what became known as 'associate membership'. This allowed a preparative meeting to give their attenders, more often than not in mission meetings, membership of the meeting but not of the Monthly Meeting, since that entailed formal application and visitation approved through and by it.[391] It was in other words a 'lesser' form of membership, reflecting what was in essence some prejudice, resting on the belief that those in mission meetings might not perhaps be able to cope with the rigours and sophistication of full membership and attendance at the traditional meeting for worship and one for business. At Cardiff this duality was reflected in a minute from November 1899, when they agreed to set up a committee to facilitate arrangements that could give

> special personal invitations to any attenders who in their judgement they think would be suitable to have and would value the privilege of attending Preparative Meetings of that year only during which the committee holds appointment.[392]

---

386. HRO, BG 63/1, 1897.
387. HMC, M8, 1.10.1896.
388. *TF*, 7.1.1898, 13.
389. WQM, Report 20.9.1893.
390. SWMM, M10, 1.12.1892.
391. *Christian Discipline of the Society of Friends: Church Government*, 1906, 31.
392. CPM, 26.11.1899.

Newport was amongst the meetings that by 1902 had adopted associate membership. Swansea and Llandrindod acted similarly but as a method of engaging members of the mission meetings it never proved popular across the Yearly Meeting, and by 1902 the HMC in its annual report revealed that only eleven meetings had adopted the convention; in 1901 it was twelve.[393] All the meetings in Wales who had home mission workers used the scheme, and to a degree was a measure of their success. 'The system of Associate Membership has now been in operation in two meetings for some years; but in only one Meeting – Llandrindod Wells – has it been widely adopted.'[394]

In 1899 the HMC reported to the Yearly Meeting that in Newport worship was held in rented premises, and like Cardiff efforts had been made to establish Adult Schools 'but without success.'[395] The following year they highlighted the fact that morning attendance at meeting for worship was about 20 with 30 to 40 in the evening. There must have been some concern about progress at Newport, Sayce telling the committee in February 1900 that he still felt that there was service for him there,[396] commenting that the work had not 'increased as much as he had hoped for. The Adult School is small, five or six, as is often the case in Wales.'[397]

In January 1900 the HMC granted Sayce leave to work for Sessions and Sons, 'thinking the change of employment will be useful to him'[398] – hinting at some difficulties. Indeed, the report behind the minute was stronger in that it expressed 'the feeling that it will be helpful to [Sayce] and his work to engage in regular business employment for a substantial period of his time.'[399] By April this had happened. Sayce had taken up paid work at thirty shillings a week with a local Newport firm whose owner had assisted Sayce in his tent work in the town. Consequently his allowance from the HMC was cut from £180 to £129 per annum, with payments for the schooling of his children continuing,[400] and it was noted that his partial employment should

393. YMP, 1901, 38.
394. WQM Triennial Report to YM, 1906, 126.
395. YMP 1899, 30.
396. HMC, report 1.2.1900.
397. *BF*, 3rd month 1900, 60.
398. HMC, M10, 1.2.1900.
399. HMC report, 1.2.1900.
400. HMCEC, M2, 4.4.1900.

be seen in a positive light as help in 'the furtherance of his service for his Lord.'[401]

It is difficult to gauge Sayce's impact in Newport. By 1903 there had been very little change in the numbers in membership with its twenty three members and twelve regular attenders.[402] He was involved in the life of the town, and had been, for example, President of the local Postal and Telecommunication Christian Association for three years[403] having taken up 'new openings amongst the postal and telegraph men' in the summer of 1899. He had organised tent meetings, such as the one in 1899,[404] when for two weeks William Hobson and John Oyston were the missionaries.[405] Matters at Newport must have continued in good spirit.

Things did not however run smoothly for Sayce. In May 1903 the committee decided to give him an allowance of £15 per month because he had lost his job, the firm was apparently downsizing and they had given his post 'to a daughter of the firm.'[406] At the same time, he requested, supported by his Monthly Meeting, that he be allowed time off from his mission work. Whatever the details and timeline, by the end of 1903 his connection with the committee was terminated, this apparently without consulting Newport Preparative Meeting,

> This meeting hears with great regret the severance of William Jesper Sayce from his position as representative of the Home Mission Committee in Newport. It is the desire of this meeting to place on record their appreciation of his services for the years he has been resident amongst us, his faithful preaching of the Everlasting Gospel has been a blessing to all who attend the meeting. We feel it would have been impossible to continue our Meeting without his presence and guidance.[407]

In March the committee agreed to provide a grant for one year towards the education of the Sayce children, and continued paying his allowance until

401. HMC, M2, 5.4.1900.
402. WQM tabular returns 1903.
403. *TF*, 22.11.1901, 771.
404. *TF*, 14.7.1899, 454.
405. *TF*, 8.9.1899, 591.
406. HMCEC, M6, 1.5.1903.
407. HMCEC, M14, 14, 3.2.1904.

March 1904,[408] the Monthly Meeting and the Quarterly Meeting agreeing in May to support Sayce financially for six months.[409] He then moved to Sunderland staying there until 1942. He died at The Retreat, York, the Quaker mental hospital founded in 1796 for the care of Friends suffering from mental illness in 1944, aged 87, suffering from senile dementia.[410]

In its triennial report to Yearly Meeting for 1906 WQM reported that Newport Meeting had closed 'owing to the removal of the worker.'[411] The Monthly Meeting in August 1904 had been clear that with Sayce's departure and the 'weakening of the meeting the unanimous feeling (was) that it should be closed.'[412] An 'allowed meeting' – a meeting sanctioned by a Monthly Meeting, without the formal sanction of its Quarterly Meeting and which met not less frequently than once a month – was opened again in the town in 1911. At a meeting held on September 15th twelve were present and it was decided to experiment for three months with a reopened meeting. The meeting's short-lived existence gives some credence to a view, that the experiment was not founded in unity with perhaps tensions amongst the members around the determination of John Edward Southall.[413] The meeting closed the following year, reopened in 1915, but was reported as closed by Yearly Meeting 1923. Reopened in 1924, it was closed again in 1931.[414]

vi. Neath

Neath was the only meeting in Wales not to receive the direct attention of the HMC, and yet by the 1890s it was palpably weak. The religious census of 1851 showed it to be the strongest meeting in Wales. By 1861 it had thirty three members, 38% of the total of the whole of SWMM, and by 1870 had seventy one members, constituting 64% of the Monthly Meetings membership, more a reflection of the Monthly Meetings' weakness than of the strength of Neath. WQM recorded in 1871 that 'the only meeting of much

408. HMCEC, M15, 3.2.1904.
409. SWMM, M1, 4.5.1904.
410. Correspondence from the Borthwick Institute for Archives, York, 15.08.06.
411. YMP, Triennial Report WQM 1906, 127.
412. SWMM, M1, 31.8.1904.
413. SWMM, M22, 18.10.1911.
414. YMP reports for the respective years.

size in Wales is Neath.'[415] Williams provides a picture of a thriving meeting in the late eighteenth century, blossoming in comparison to its neighbours.[416] Numerically it is in the 1880s that change becomes apparent, as the efforts of the home mission workers affected the balance between the various meetings. By 1887 membership at Neath had fallen to below 30 for the first time, indeed by 1890 only 20% of the Monthly Meeting membership was assigned to it.[417] By 1899 it was eclipsed by both Swansea and Newport, although the latter had closed by 1904, and by 1914 Neath again outstripped Swansea, which had lost its permanent worker.

Neath was the backbone of Welsh Quakerism well into the 1880s, the meeting maintaining its core membership largely through family adherences. From the 1850s the Gibbins' became more visible in the activities of the Meeting,[418] and were to provide the Clerkship of South Wales Monthly Meeting almost unbroken from 1880 to 1916 – with three generations serving in that capacity – H. Bevington Gibbins then his son F.J. Gibbins, and then his son F.W. Gibbins. Caroline Gibbins, F.J. Gibbins' wife, also served as clerk. Neath, as noted, also supplied Swansea Meeting with its clerk from 1899 to 1902. More importantly F.J. Gibbins was clerk to WQM from 1873 until 1898.

The Monthly Meeting triennial report for 1905 indicated that Neath, 'lies under the discouragement of a gradually lessening membership, the chief cause of this has been the removal of Friends from the neighbourhood.'[419] In 1907 it recorded that it could no longer meet the financial requirements laid upon it by the Monthly Meeting,[420] and its numbers so small 'that it cannot invite the Monthly Meeting to be held here next year.'[421] Yet, in 1880 and 1881 Neath hosted the Monthly Meeting for ten of their twelve meetings in each year.

By 1887 the drop in membership at Neath was detectable, but the focus was to be elsewhere within the Monthly Meeting; it may well be that the

415. WQM report 18.10.1871.
416. Williams, 'The Society of Friends', 1950.
417. HRO, BG 63/1, 1897 Membership List: Neath had twenty six members, five of whom were Gibbins'.
418. Williams, 'The Society of Friends', 1950, 32.
419. SWMM, 15.11.1905, Triennial Report to WQM.
420. GRO, D/D SF 17, Neath Preparative Meeting (NPM), M3, 18.8.1907.
421. NPM, M4, 18.8.1907. 1908.

reason for this was some reluctance in acknowledging the trend and some inherent conservative resistance about asking for help. Despite the reduction, the meeting had in January 1893 opened a new room for the 'Sunday School conducted by Friends.'[422] The Meeting was not without those offering service to the wider Quaker community, such as noted already, Frank Dymond. When the Quarterly Meeting asked the HMC for input in 1895, appointing a committee to this end, Neath was not targeted. In 1900 SWMM established committees to support home mission work in the three meetings, but Neath was not included.[423]

F.J. Gibbins, interested in Welsh Quaker history, may have been conservatively inclined, but as Clerk to the Quarterly Meeting he was central to the decisions made to invite the HMC to work within its area. His testimony hints that he might have been less amenable at a certain time in his life noting that he

> sympathised with the more progressive efforts of Friends and others in recent years. He had witnessed the growth of a remarkable Christian work in his own town, first as an unsectarian mission, (temperance) and then afterwards in connection with one of the larger Religious Societies in Wales, and this had broadened his outlook in connection with Christian activities.[424]

In this context the word 'progressive' may be assumed to indicate interest in evangelic effort, if so, it was not focused on his meeting.

By 1907, and in the shadow of the revival, Richard Watkins of Swansea seemingly volunteered, as a recently convinced Friend, to hold gospel meetings in Neath on Sunday evenings, which was accepted with 'diffidence.'[425] The meetings were abandoned by April 1908.[426] Richard Watkins had been discouraged since he had 'spent much time in visiting the poor homes around and inviting the people to come, but as they could not be induced to attend, it was decided to discontinue the meeting.'[427] In 1897, answering the

---

422. *TF*, 27.1.1893, 61.
423. SWMM, M14, 3.5.1900.
424. WQM, M9, 18.04.1907, Testimony to Frederick Joseph Gibbins, a Minister deceased.
425. NPM, M4, 1411.1907.
426. NPM, M5, 14.11.1907.
427. SWMM, 11.11.1908, Triennial report.

queries from the Yearly Meeting, Neath had been negative about mission work,[428] nevertheless in 1911 they organised Bible classes and a Sunday school for children.[428] By 1917 a feeling of fatigue seems to have overcome the Meeting since they suggested that no Monthly Meeting be held there in April, and that for June the venue should be Cardiff.[430] The minute reads that they made the suggestions because of the increased cost of travel but at the same meeting they had also recorded their inability to appoint a representative to YM that year.

vii. Smaller Meetings

Attention was given to the needs of some smaller towns by the HMC but not in any systematic way. WQM had by 1898, if not earlier, appointed a committee to have care of its smaller Meetings.[431] Milford Haven meeting had been re-established by Quaker whalers who had left Nantucket during the American War of Independence before being enticed to Wales. They arrived in Milford in 1793 from Nova Scotia where they had originally settled. The Starbucks being the most prominent amongst them.[432] By 1843, 'Quakerism in Pembrokeshire had reached a level at which it ceased to be viable.'[433] Its continuation seems to have been maintained through the presence in Milford of one solitary Quaker, George Phillips, who had come into membership in 1857, aged 36, having been born a Wesleyan, before turning to the Moravians.[434] In his will he left £10 to the Monthly Meeting, then used to purchase the book of discipline for distribution.[435] There were to be several mission meetings at the town For example in July 1889, HRMM liberated John Owen Jenkins for service in Milford Haven and similarly B.J. Elsmere in December 1890.[436] However, it was only in 1898 that the Quarterly

---

428. NPM report, 4.11.1897.
429. NPM, M1, 8.10.1911.
430. NPM, M4, 11.3.1917.
431. WQM, M10, 20.04.1898.
432. Rees, *A History of the*, 1925, 264–267.
433. Griffith, *A History of*, 1990, 27.
434. *Pembrokeshire County Guardian*, 9.1.1914, article entitled 'The Quakers in Pembroke-shire' by the Rev P. D. Morse, Wolfcastle
435. SWMM, 16.12.1889.
436. HRMM M2 23.7.1889 and M1, 10.7.1890.

Meeting decided that the Meeting at Milford was to be reopened,[437] after a series of special mission meetings held there during September of that year, William Hobson being one of the missionaries assisted by Hercules Davies Phillips.[438]

It is not, however, until 1909 that the Yearly Meeting was informed that the meeting house had been reopened, through the efforts of WQM Extension Committee, but it noted with some pessimism that its 'distance from other Meetings, from which available help is forthcoming, makes the work difficult, and it is too early to say if the Meeting can be permanently re-established.'[439] By 1912 Milford, as an allowed Meeting, was still functioning and has done ever since, even though its fortunes have waxed and waned. Efforts to establish a Meeting at Tenby proved difficult. There was a meeting in Tenby in 1897, meeting at rooms in the YMCA, two members were assigned to SWMM, whilst another family, the Lidbetters, and their three children were still attached to Saffron Walden Meeting.[440] The meeting does not appear in the Tabular returns for 1898. *The Friend* has an intriguing report in relation to Tenby, it reported the death of John Lewis of Tenby who had died in 1898, a member of the Town Council and manager of Walters' (now Lloyds) Bank at Haverfordwest, who had been treasurer of Haverfordwest Corporation and was

> a Friend in spirit, though not actually in membership and was strongly attached to the Society, in whose welfare and future progress he was deeply interested, and earnestly hoped that a way might open for the erection of a meeting house in Tenby.[441]

South Wales' Committee Ministry and Oversight encouraged Arthur Dickinson to set up a Meeting there in May 1912, and the tabular statement returns indicate that there was a Meeting recorded in the town from 1912 to 1914, with 5 members.

437. WQM, M20, 14.12.1898.
438. *TF*, 30.9.1898, 635.
439. YMP, HMEC Report 1909, 24.
440. WQM List of Members, 1897.
441. *TF*, 1.7.1898, 421.

During June and July of 1899 a series of meetings were held at Welshpool, where two Quakers had settled, with William Hobson and his wife, now living in London,[442] giving service along with others, amongst whom was William Henry Brown (1839–1907) who as a member of the Friends Tract Association, was well known for his travels with pony and cart distributing tracts across the country from Land's End to John O'Groats.[443] The Monthly Meeting appointed a committee to have care of the Welshpool endeavour 'with liberty to visit Welshpool and to make suggestions to our Monthly Meeting.'[444] The Meeting was still active in March 1901, when it was reported that Ellen Graham of Malvern[445] visited, but the meeting was not long-lived, despite the town's strong Quaker associations from the seventeenth century. WQM triennial report to YM 1900 noted: 'A slight attempt to open work has been made at Welshpool the home in the early days of the Society of an energetic Quaker propaganda.'[446]

John Henry Salter (1862–1942) a birthright Friend, had taken up appointment as assistant lecturer and demonstrator at Aberystwyth University College and from 1899–1908 was their first professor of Botany; a great walker and diarist with 21 volumes of diaries, which say nothing at all about his personal or Quaker life but a huge amount about the weather and plants.[447] In May 1898 he made an appeal for someone to go and live in Aberystwyth for the summer,[448] so as to give support to the Meeting established there in 1894, and recognised by the Monthly Meeting the following year. In November 1893, Henry Newman had brought to the attention of HRMM the fact that living in Aberystwyth were five members of the Society, suggesting that 'a visit from one or two women Friends would be desirable and helpful.'[449] The gender suggestion was made because the members were women students at the college. The matter was deferred for further consideration especially since Aberystwyth was considered to be 'one of the

442. *TF*, 21.7.1899, 475–76.
443. DQB.
444. HRMM, M16, 18.5.1899.
445. *TF*, 29.3.1901, 205.
446. YMP 1900, 119.
447. *Nature*,12.9.1942 and NLW MS 14432B–14452B Diaries of J.H. Salter.
448. *TF*, 13.5.1898, 294.
449. HRMM, M9, 23.11.1893.

most distant spots in this widely extended Monthly Meeting.'[450] Salter noted 'the few Friends here, all of them students in or otherwise connected with the college, began to meet for worship in an informal manner.'[451] The centrality of the college is obvious from the list of members for 1897, of the ten members five were students, four of them women.[452] Two families of Friends had moved into the town, one being that of William and Clara R. Fearnside. They had moved from Leominster in and around 1895, they left Aberystwyth during 1898 but returned there in 1902 remaining in the town until 1924 when William retired as secretary of the Aberystwyth Gas Company – returning to live to Leominster.

HRMM minuted at its May meeting that it wished to support Salter's appeal and in the event of no response to his letter that the HMC be asked to give 'temporary assistance.'[453] The Committee arranged for two workers, George S. Davidson and William H. Burton to spend three weeks each at the town, but that no further help could be given, indeed they asked the Monthly Meeting to contribute half the cost of the lodgings, costed at eight guineas. Regretfully, despite the investment, by October 1898 the Monthly Meeting had to record that Aberystwyth meeting had discontinued, the tenancy of the meeting room had expired and the members felt unable to continue. Yet, in June 1896, Henry Tobit Evans had written on the possibility of having a meeting house built in the town, the concern for the 'visitor' and the way the meeting was being upheld from afar.[454] His enthusiasm must have been somewhat dampened by the response of one of the student members who wrote, 'The suggestion about building a meetinghouse sounds very delightful to us, if only it were feasible.'[455] She was right, as Salter's letter mirrors. By September 1902 Aberystwyth had reopened as an allowed meeting. It was a meeting that had a chequered history.

On the last day of 1899 the first meeting for worship had been held at the new meeting house at Colwyn Bay; a development that had nothing to do

450. *TF*, 18.10.1895, 680.
451. *TF*, 13.5.1898, 294.
452. WQM, 1897 list of members.
453. HRMM, M10, 12.5.1898.
454. *TF*, 19.6.1896, 413.
455. *TF*, 26.6.1896, 429. The author of the letter was one Helen Grubb.

with home mission. A meeting was established in the town around 1892,[456] and by 1894 it was reported that it had at last succeeded in finding a place to worship.[457] Those worshipping were principally Friends who were on holiday. The new meeting house had been financed by Thomas Barlow, a rich Manchester-based trader, whose plans, since he died in 1897, were finalised by his widow Mary Ann Barlow, and who conveyed the property under the care of Hardshaw West Monthly Meeting, for the use of the Society. The meeting house was not formally and finally transferred into the actual ownership of the Monthly Meeting until 1988.

With the building at Colwyn Bay, two new meeting-houses had been built and opened in towns in Wales in two years where there had previously been none, Llandrindod being the other, along with two mission meetings in Radnorshire. All four resembled Victorian nonconformist chapels in design and style. It is significant that both Colwyn Bay and Llandrindod were popular holiday resorts for Quakers. Indeed a report in the British Friend went further, stating unequivocally, that the new meeting house at Colwyn Bay 'will no doubt be appreciated by the numerous visitors belonging to the Society, who resort to Colwyn at various seasons of the year in search of health and pleasure.'[458] In August 1907, *The Friend* noted the 'Special Addresses' arranged during 'the Season' at Llandrindod, probably taking advantage of speakers who were holiday makers, adding, that the support of such Friends was important because of competition from other churches, 'and in every case the very best talent of the churches has been sent to Llandrindod in the season, and all the services are largely advertised;'[459] an element of denominational competition. Colwyn Bay also attracted well-off Quaker retirees, particularly from the north west of England.

Another intriguing development was the attempt to establish a meeting in Merthyr Tydfil, the only example of a meeting in the valleys of south Wales. In their report to Yearly Meeting for 1899 the HMC, reflecting a particular view of society and of its own makeup, commented:

456. *BF*, January 1900, 15.
457. *TF*, 27.4.1894, 268.
458. *BF*, January 1900, 15.
459. *TF*, 30.8.1907, 577.

We have next a group of large and busy centres on the coast, where shipping industries and their accompanying trades gather thousands of artisans and labourers. Has Quakerism a message for these classes? We need only to mention the names of the towns to suggest the importance of the openings viz. Cardiff, Swansea, Newport (Mon).[460]

The fact that they had not yet turned their attention to the needs of the industrial valleys of south Wales was indicative of the fact that they no longer had a foothold there. This was an area that, at the time, was beyond their experience, and beyond their ability to assist, whereas the larger more anglicised coastal towns had their Quaker connections from the early days of the movement. It was to these towns that the socially mobile Quakers migrated.

There are indications that a little mission work was undertaken in the valleys, but nothing of any intensity. Quakers Yard near Merthyr seems to have been one place where such an endeavour was made, nostalgia influencing endeavour since it did have a Quaker graveyard. In October 1890, the HMC recorded that William Hobson had arranged a series of meetings there.[461] His son, S.G. Hobson, wrote to the press that, 'the inhabitants of Quaker's Yard may be glad to learn that the cause of Quakerism is going to be re-kindled in their midst during the coming summer [1891].'[462] In February 1891 a child's burial, the first such Quaker burial there for over 80 years, had taken place which had attracted a procession of 1,000. A Welsh minister, speaking in Welsh, took part in the proceedings, deploring 'the treatment early Friends had received at the hands of rough men there, and promised us a friendly reception'[463] referring to the forthcoming tent meetings that summer; Hobson commenting that Friends 'greatly appreciated the open kindness shown to perfect strangers and look forward with real interest to tent meetings in the summer.'[464] SWMM recorded in June 1892 that the Friends Christian Fellowship Union was to undertake a three-month mission at Quakers Yard, with W. J. Sayce

460. YMP, 1899, 30.
461. HMC, 1.10.1890
462. WM, 21.1.1891.
463. *TF*, 2nd month, 1891, 36
464. Ibid.

offering his support.[465] Interestingly this connection with Treharris/Quakers Yard had some resonance in 1894, when B.J. Elsmere asked HRMM for permission, which was given, to visit the area where apparently a group of young men met regularly 'somewhat after the manner of Friends.'[466] He was to be disappointed, for he reported that the group were in fact Baptists.[467]

In March 1894 SWMM recorded a certificate of removal from Dublin Monthly Meeting to Merthyr Tydfil of Thomas and Mary Anne Bentley and their six children. The Evangelistic Committee, of WQM of which H.D. Phillips was convenor, minuted in September 1903 an invitation from the Bentleys

> to hold a meeting or meetings for worship at that town ... Our friends offer the use of a large hall for this purpose, and we agree to report these facts to the Quarterly Meeting and to invite its judgement thereon.[468]

The outcome was not promising in that by December the same committee considered a letter from Mary Bentley, signifying, that because of her husband's health the proposal for holding meetings at the Central Hall had to be deferred, to which they agreed.[469] By March 1908 the Monthly Meeting was considering a request from Alfred Young that Merthyr Meeting be made an allowed meeting, since 'average attendance is ten or eleven.'[470] This seems not to have been agreed, since the name of Merthyr does not appear in the tabular statement returns. This mirrored developments of an Adult School in the town; a report for August 1907[471] indicates such a development under the presidency of Alfred Young. The Annual Report of the FFDSA for 1906 noted that there was a centre in Merthyr, listed as meeting at Bentley's Temperance Hotel, with Alf Young, as secretary.[472] The FFDSA report for 1907 explained that Merthyr was new to their list, 'giving evidence of growth

465. SWMM, 9.6.1892.
466. HRMM, M1, 8.1.1894.
467. Ibid., 8.3.1894.
468. WRO, WQM Evangelistic Committee, M3 24.9.1903.
469. Ibid., 6.12.1903.
470. SWMM, M20, 4.3.1908.
471. *TF*, 23.8.1907, 565.
472. Annual Report, FFDSA, 1906.

in that it had a membership of 150 at the end of the year.'[473] The description for October 1907 was heartening outlining some success, 'This school is showing signs of life and vigour.'[474] It had a membership of 89, with 15 on the probationary register, meeting at a hall lent to them by Thomas Bentley free of charge.

In December 1907 the school was still active. Percy Alden M.P amongst others had addressed the school, and the members had paraded in the streets headed by a volunteer band, making a collection for the local hospital. They marched to Hope Street Chapel where the pastor, the Rev. J.M. Jones, had 'uttered strong statements on deterioration at Merthyr – drunkenness, the sordid character of professional football.'[475] Marching or demonstrating with a band appears to have been important since this is similarly reported in January and February 1908,[476] with a strong hint that their endeavours were inter denominational. By March 1908 a branch had been opened at Penydarren, with the note that

> there is a future for Adult School work in and about Merthyr, which bids fair to become the centre of a great organisation in South Wales. The last winter demonstration took place previous Sunday.[477]

If there was a future it was not recorded in the FFDSA annual reports for 1908 and 1909, and it must be assumed that the school transferred out of the control of Friends. There were to be no further references to it in *The Friend*, and no references in the Quarterly Meeting or the Monthly Meeting minutes.

Any reading of FFDSA developments in Wales highlights the fact that the schools there were never large or dynamic. Several were established and in 1902 the reports on the restructuring of its committee and area structures highlights severe restrictions and weaknesses in its organisation.[478] There are periodic references to adult schools associated with Welsh meetings, but the records are sparse. The exception is Cardiff Adult School. Its register for

473. Annual Report, FFDSA, 1907.
474. *TF*, 11.10.1907, 682.
475. *TF*, 13.12.1907, 829.
476. *TF*, 17.1.1908, 46 and 14.2.1908, 110.
477. *TF*, 13.3.1908, 174.
478. FFDSA General Committee Minutes, M14, 3.10.1902.

1890–9 reflects a school of fluctuating fortunes,[479] thus in 1876 one of their committee members seems to have travelled from Bristol to assist in the organisation of the school there.[480] In 1883 it was recorded that Arthur Sessions had written 'conveying the information that the schools there had been discontinued owing to circumstances which seemed unavoidable.'[481] The school was reopened in 1886[482] but by 1889, at the FFDSA Annual Meeting, it was listed as an unassociated school, represented by S.G. Hobson. The school register from 1890-99 shows that in 1890, July-August, including teachers, there were seventy seven names on the register, with twelve leaving during the same period. The largest number on the register was 130, for the quarter January–March 1895. By 1899 there were only 18 scholars. In a 1915 report on First Day Schools to SWMM, covering 1908-1914 it was stated that Cardiff had closed in 1909. By 1912, Neath had 172 children and 11 teachers, and Swansea 22 children with 6 teachers associated with their schools. Neath meeting, for example, had had a school of long standing, still active in 1907, such that on September 26th, 1907 it held their annual social in connection with the Adult School, when a company of nearly fifty were welcomed.[483] By 1919, WQM would report to the YM that it recognised 'a lack of energy in the Schools as compared with former times.'[484]

Conclusion

Reliance on mission workers was naturally welcomed when it was available. WQM in its triennial report to the 1903 Yearly Meeting expressed thanks to the HMC for the assistance they had rendered, 'particularly in places where the Society has nearly died out.'[485] In 1911 of 26 meetings that had resident HMC Friends the highest number, seven,[486] were still within its compass, although there was only one Welsh venue, Llandrindod. Reliance entails

479. GRO, Cardiff FFDS Register, D/D SF 490.
480. FFDSA minutes.16.6.1876.
481. Ibid., 29.1.1883.
482. Ibid., M17, 16.4.1886.
483. *TF*, 11.10.1907, 673.
484. YMP, 1919, 136.
485. YMP 1903, 124.
486. Almeley, Evesham, Gloucester, Hereford, Llandrindod, Nailsworth and Swindon.

dependence. In its triennial report to Yearly Meeting in 1912 WQM felt that it was barely holding its own, hinting at the need for continued input. It rightly reflected that

> much of the growth of the past thirty years may be traced to the work carried
> on in many of the Meetings in connection with the Friends Home Mission
> and Extension Committee.[487]

In reality the HMEC did not have the resources to sustain its work nationally at the level that it wished, and had to develop a strategy, if such it was, that meetings should look to be self-sustaining, a sentiment as HMC, it had expressed, for example, in its annual report to the Yearly Meeting about Cardiff in 1899.[488]

Not all meetings sought the assistance of the HMC. Colwyn Bay was one such, since it primarily served retirees and holidaymakers in the area. It was attached to Lancashire and Cheshire Quarterly Meeting and an examination of the HMC minute books reveals that that Quarterly Meeting made little demand on it. The reasons for this may be partly explained by the tensional relationship that had existed over the years between the QM and LYM, around activity in Hardshaw East Monthly Meeting. Between 1861–72, there was controversy over the liberal views of David Duncan, followed, twelve years later in 1884 by the publication, *Reasonable Faith*, written by three Friends from the Quarterly Meeting, which challenged evangelical assumptions, and placed the QM within a broader liberal orientation.[498] The QM was not averse to mission work. Lancaster MM had sought help from the HMC concerning Wray Meeting[490] but in 1883 it 'declined to appoint' representatives onto the then newly formed YM committee but had complied by 1900.[491] It had a mission committee but its work was done 'By ordinary visits to Meetings' and through 'Public Meetings for Worship and for the exposition of Christian Truths'[492] relying on local Quakers, reflecting

---

487. YMP, Triennial Report 1912, 211.
488. YMP, 1899, 30.
489. See Kennedy, *British Quakerism*, 47–111
490. HMCEC, M8, 3.11.1882.
491. HMCEC, M7, 21.5.1883 and LCQM, M4, 19.4.1900.
492. LCQM, M3, 18/19.10.1899.

the broader arguments over a 'paid ministry.' When in 1903 this committee came to consider the needs of Hyde and Sawley meetings, this theme remerges. Their hope, was for the 'residence of well-connected Friends who might find business openings within their borders,'[493] thus avoiding any paid importation. There is a hint that the HMCEC might have tried and persuade the QM to change its approach. They requested that a deputation from them should visit in 1900, 'the purpose being to come into closer sympathy with the needs of the Quarterly Meeting, and to seek to stimulate efforts for the building up of the Society.'[494] In 1909 there is a revealing minute by the QM, which had been addressed by two members of the HMEC, 'We commend the work of the Committee to Friends and hope that some who have not hitherto supported it by their means may consider whether there is not something required of them in this direction.'[495] The caution of the QM about method and mission can be seen in a minute from 1906 concerning the gulf between Meetings and attendees of the adult schools and mission meetings. They were averse to openly evangelical approaches, hoping that the adult school and mission meeting might be invaded by the spirit of Quakerism,

> rather than by methods of those meetings invading our ordinary meetings,'
> and that 'periods of silence in Mission meetings gave the opportunity for
> spontaneous ministry, and that the singing of hymns should not be fixed into
> a routine.[496]

In 1900 there were no HMC workers within its area when there were 30 workers placed across the country, 8 within WQM. Neither did Lancashire and Cheshire Quarterly Meeting focus on Welsh matters. An examination of its minutes between 1880–1914 records no discussion on any matters pertaining to Wales.[497] Hardshaw West MM which covered north Wales, met for the first time in Colwyn Bay and in Wales in July 1913, when fifty Friends stayed in the locale over the weekend. It was not until 1982 that the Quarterly

---

493. LCQM, M2, 14/15.10.1903.
494. LCQM, M7, 19.4.1900.
495. LCQM, M6, 20/21.10.1909.
496. LCQM, M5, 18.1.1906.
497. LRO, FRL 1/1/1/41 and 42.

Meeting, in the guise of its successor Lancashire and Cheshire General Meeting, met for the first time in Wales.

Home missionary work to be successful in most of north and west Wales would have needed the use of Welsh, since here the language still dominated, but this was still true of the south Wales valleys at the turn of the century, an often overlooked factor in the demography of Wales. This never proved to be the case. Cardiff and Swansea, both of which had had Quaker presence since the seventeenth century, and Newport, were heavily Anglicised and therefore easier ground for the Quaker workers. Bishop and Sayce certainly had no Welsh, and as noted Radnorshire had lost its Welsh linguistic identity. All the missions were conducted in English, a barrier to greater extensive work across Wales, notwithstanding the rural and dispersed nature of the population, a lament that was heard from HRMM to WQM, in their report to Yearly Meeting in 1903:

> This Monthly Meeting extending from Aberystwyth on the west coast of Wales, to Bromyard, on the edge of Worcestershire, covers a large area, and as we look at the map out first thought must be how little we can do to influence the population in this wide district with the truth as held by Friends.[498]

They had expressed the same concerns in November 1893 when owing to a direction of Yearly Meeting, regarding the boundaries of Meetings in England and Wales, 'a considerable additional geographical area in Wales has been added to our Monthly Meeting far more than we feel at all competent to deal with.'[499]

It is not surprising that in Wales the HMC looked to those areas where Quakerism had once flourished. Radnorshire, with Pales and its thatched roof, must have caught the romantic Quaker imagination of people such as Newman, whilst the struggling meetings of Swansea and Cardiff offered immediate bases from whence mission workers could operate.

The story of activity by LYM in Wales from the 1870s to the First World War reflects very much the efforts and concerns of the HMC, a level of

---

498. YMP, 1903, 123.
499. HRMM, 23.11.1893.

activity that was possible because of the influence of such men as Henry Stanley Newman and Frederick Sessions, both influential members of WQM and of the HMC.

Despite the attention, by 1912 the condition of Friends in Wales was still a matter of concern. WQM expressed concern about the declining trend in its membership even though the Welsh statistics belied this. In 1881 HRMM had 177 members, by 1902 this had risen to 348, by 1912 stood at 335. Similarly, SWMM had 97 members in 1881, 181 by 1899 and, by 1912, it was 147. It bemoaned the fact that Cheltenham, despite having a new meeting house, was in imminent danger of closure, whilst Bewdley, Ross on Wye, Pales and Penybont had lost attenders heavily, 'by death and removals,' the latter's membership having dropped in twelve years from 62 to 32. Similarly Swansea had had a considerable 'falling off'. The Quarterly Meeting recognised that more of its members should respond to the demand of upholding its meetings, recognising that external assistance would not be forthcoming.[500]

HRMM would report to Yearly Meeting 1912, that there was 'little fresh work or service to notice in connection'[501] with their meetings. Llandrindod meeting, where it was felt the work was well maintained, expressed the view that they could feel 'the weakness due to lack of faithfulness in ministry on the part of the members generally, believed to be due to the deadening influence of the recurring 'seasons'[502] – a reference to their dependence on holidaymakers. There the use of associate membership had not proved to be the stepping-stone to full membership, even though such associate members were apparently faithful in their attendance and service. The Monthly Meeting was concerned about the heavy demands made upon their members, and the fact that everyone was perhaps not shouldering the burden as they should.[503]

The report for SWMM was not as bleak, but it was noted that the changes at Swansea had led to a 'considerable falling off'. The Quarterly Meeting itself noted that there were many openings for work but was hampered by

---

500. Ibid.
501. YMP, 1912, 213.
502. Ibid.
503. Minutes of HRMM – 1905 to 1923, are missing consequently a fuller picture of their concerns cannot be examined in detail. See Ch. 2, fn. 228.

the lack of workers, and 'by the wide area covered.'[504] It reflected on the general concern that was beginning to affect the whole Church across Britain that people were drifting away from the chapels and churches. In Wales the situation was felt more acutely, if only because people reflected on the impact of the 1904 Welsh Revival. SWMM's report to Yearly Meeting said that their Extension Committee had considered the position and had discussed

> the religious situation in South Wales … in view of the feeling of dissatisfaction and the longing for something higher and deeper among many of those who enter into the Christian faith during the great revival a few years ago; and on the other hand the drifting away from all church and religious influence of large masses of the people in South Wales.[505]

The pessimistic tenor of the WQM's report to Yearly Meeting may echo the concerns of an anxious minority, the comments in it concerning Llandrindod probably mirroring to a large extent, the views of Hercules Phillips. Yet, in January 1911 the annual public entertainment in connection with the Friends Sunday School had been held at the Victoria Hall, Llandrindod, which had been crowded, the entertainment apparently a great success. The president for the evening, Councillor Jeffrey Jones J.P, urging the young people present to study the history of the Society of Friends and to learn from the example of its leading men and women.[506] The pessimism of the Quarterly Meeting may partly explain mission developments within it in Wales in 1912, examined in the following chapter.

> In 1906 the HMC had added the word 'Extension' to its title so that it could be authorised to come into direct relation with Committees for Extension, Home Mission, or similar work formed by Quarterly or Monthly Meetings, so as to receive reports of their work and to give assistance in its power to providing Friends to act as Extension Secretaries or in other ways.[507]

504. YMP, 1912, 214.
505. Ibid.
506. *TF*, 10.2.1911, 63.
507. YMP, 1906, M24, 31.

Isichei comments that this change was symptomatic of the general change taking place within the Society, as attitudes imperceptibly changed.[508] What it meant was that inputs were becoming less focused on individual meetings, and the word 'mission' was starting to loose its attraction.

An examination of *The Friend* in the first decade of the twentieth century tells us of the constant activity at meetings in Llandrindod and Llanyre, which Newman as editor would have been delighted to report. Elsewhere Friends continued with their traditional concerns. Friends in Cardiff had been active in response to the famine in Russia in 1892. The Mayor of the city calling a meeting, with Francis W. Fox, who had been to Russia on behalf of LYM, describing his experiences (Fox was not a Cardiff Friend). A local group was established to raise funds with Arthur Sessions acting as treasurer, and S. G. Hobson, as secretary.[509] Again in January 1913 Cardiff Friends had taken the initiative in arranging a town meeting under the presidency of the Lord Mayor and 'representative of all shades of religious thought in the Welsh metropolis and surrounding districts.'[510] This resolved, on the instigation of the Bishop of Llandaff, seconded by Lleufer Thomas, stipendiary magistrate of Pontypridd, to open a collection for the relief of non-combatants in the Turkish-Balkan War; a further example of public, ecumenical and social outreach by Friends in Wales.

The overall picture of the way the HMC operated in Wales provides a chequered and uneven impression. Three large towns and the smallest rural county were the focus of its investment. The rest of Wales was largely ignored. Efforts in such places as Aberystwyth and Colwyn Bay were influenced by particular local circumstances, the existence of the University College at the former, and retirees and holidaymakers in the latter; a reminder of the largely unconscious and unrecognised class values pervading the Society's operations and expansion in those areas where it did not establish missions.

The numbers attracted into the membership of the Society in Wales remained small. This was an issue challenging the whole Yearly Meeting as it pondered why, despite the large numbers at their Adult Schools and

508. Isichei, *Victorian*, 1970, 101.
509. WM, 19.2.1892.
510. *TF*, 31.1.1913, 65.

Mission Meetings, there were not more convincements. Procedural amendments through the creation of associate membership made little difference with few from this group applying for full membership.

The answer as to why this should be may be found partly in comments made by Horridge in relation to the Salvation Army during the same period. It had 'by 1900 proved itself a lasting and effective working class movement in Wales,'[511] something that the Quakers could not claim, even though most members of their mission and school meetings would have been solidly working class. There was always ambivalence in the YM about attracting the working-classes to meetings amidst concerns that the Quaker approach to worship was something some might find difficult. The HMCs report to YM in 1901 is illustrative:

> One point is clear – that in many cases where a Mission Meeting is held, the attendance is largely increased by intelligent working people and sometimes by   the poorer classes ... There seems to be in Quakerism just what many want if we only knew how to put it.[512]

In Wales the Army for a time published the *War Cry* in Welsh, selling 10,000 copies in 1889, although it ceased publication in 1892 because it was deemed uneconomic. LYM never took on board this challenge and operated only in English.

The HMC would have seen no reason to deal differently with Wales compared to other areas of Britain, since their primary aim was to bring Quakerism to the people and to save souls. They were challenged by the situation in Scotland noting the 'absence of aggressive Christian work'[513] there, and that there was a great blank in Glasgow, adding somewhat paternalistically:

---

511. G. Horridge, 'The Salvation Army in Wales,' in *The Journal of Welsh Ecclesiastical History*, 6, 1989, 51–70.
512. YMP 1901, 34.
513. HMC, M5, 6.2.1902.

We earnestly desire that Friends in Scotland may be strengthened to carry forward the work that has before them as a Church. The value of further visits from English Friends has been spoken to.[514]

The activities of the HMC were not strikingly affected by any particular considerations unique to Wales other than the spread of truth. Despite this, it would be a mistake to believe that Wales was not conceived of as a different entity, affecting their perceptions and aspirations. There are indications of this in the way they saw and treated the Revival of 1904–05. The following chapter focuses on this and the reactions of Friends to it.

514. Ibid.

Chapter 4
The Welsh Revival, 1904–05

The attitudes and reactions of Friends to the Welsh Revival of 1904–05 is important given the centrality of the event if only to denominational development across Britain. It was a significant, albeit short-lived, event that left its mark on the evolution of Protestant thought, theology and Church organisation across the globe, some seeing it as Wales' lasting contribution to the world, 'One of the most intriguing aspects of the Welsh Revival of 1904 (was) its global spread.'[1] Quakers in Britain were never involved in any depth with it, and LYM was overall passive, despite some interesting, but largely hidden Quaker connections, which might have inspired or under-pinned some of the revivalists direction of travel. Some Friends were excited hoping that the revival might be a reawakening of the Quaker way, but were to be disappointed. It was an unrealised aspiration: new growth passed the Quakers by.

The cusp of change
The term *fin de siècle* conjures up visions of decadence and degeneration cultural malaise, death and ultimate disaster.[2] These themes were actively invoked at the end of the nineteenth century, when in 1895 Max Nordeau wrote an influential volume of that title. He saw the decline of society with its structures tottering and collapsing, 'suffered to reel and fall, because man is weary, and there is no faith that it is worth the effort to uphold them.'[3] This was a theme that challenged many in the Welsh churches as they perceived a weakening of faith, and retreat from church life.

---

1. See Noel Gibbard, *On the Wing of the Dove: The International Effects of the 1904–05 Revival*, 2002), 9.
2. Shearer West, *Fin de Siècle*, 1993.
3. Max Nordeau, 'Degeneration,' in the *Fin de Siècle: A Reader in Cultural History circa 1880–1900*, 2000, 13–17.

Britain on that cusp, permeated as it was with the self-conscious optimism of the creed of Empire as illustrated in Victoria's diamond jubilee of 1897, seemed triumphant. Yet by 1899 that confidence was being tarnished and eroded by the South African War. In December of that year Britain lost 3,000 men, and in May 1900, Mafeking had to be relieved.[4] LYM responded to the war in practical ways. In 1899 Sufferings established the Friends' South African War Victims Fund to assist non-combatants on a minute from HRMM,[5] who were concerned that the methods used to raise funds relied too much on 'martial instincts.'[6] In February 1900, the Monthly Meeting supported the views of the Dean of Durham, expressing opposition to troops being sent to South Africa.[7] The revelations of the ill-treatment of Boer women and children in concentration camps later added to Quaker concerns and efforts.[8] Kennedy comments that, despite this, the overall attitude of the YM to the war was a 'humiliating spiritual debacle,'[9] because they ignored its implications for their own peace testimony.

It was then a time of contradiction and complexity, characterised by a new search for a spiritual dimension to life and an increasing interest in mysticism, spiritualism and the occult.[10] As Tomalin sees it, this was partially a reaction against the stuffiness and hypocrisy of the Victorian period, reflected for example in the activities of the 'Bloomsbury' group, an influential group of writers, intellectuals, philosophers and artists who 'made up their minds that the twentieth century should be better than the nineteenth century.'[11] The American Quaker, Rufus Jones, and the Englishman, William C. Braithwaite, amongst others,[12] re-explored the history of the

---

4. Asa Briggs, 'Past, present and future in headlines: the 1890's,' in *Fins de Siècle: How Centuries End*, Asa Briggs and Daniel Snowman eds., 1996, 157.

5. MfS, M6, 1.12.1899.

6. Hewison, *Hedges of Wild*, 1989, 145.

7. HRMM, M13, 8.2.1900.

8. Hewison, *Hedges of Wild*, 1989, 187–224.

9. Kennedy, *British Quakerism*, 2001, 424.

10. See for example Alex Owen, "Occultism and the 'Modern' self in fin de siècle Britain," in *Meanings of Modernity: Britain from the Late-Victorian Era to World War Two*, Martin Daunton and Bernhard Reiger, eds., 2001, 71–96.

11. Claire Tomalin, 'Nothing matters, and everything matters,' in the *Guardian*, 16.09.06.

12. See Rufus M. Jones, *Studies in Mystical Religion*, 1909, and Braithwaite, *The Beginnings of Quakerism*, 1955, and The Second Period, 1961.

Society – 'The Renaissance of Quaker History'[13] looked again at its roots in Christian mysticism, challenging the evangelic inclinations in the YM. It was to be a period of reorientation, rediscovery and transformation, themes explored by Kennedy[14] looking at the life of LYM crossing the threshold into the new century. As he sees it, the YM was being transformed from an evangelical body into a more socially sensitive organisation, responding to themes of modernity and higher criticism in its theological outlook. He links this to the impact of the 'Manchester Conference' organised by the HMC in 1895, which opened the door to liberal modernity and the emergence of new leaders, not an occasion when Friends were all of one mind, but it did 'cede to the younger Friends who wanted the Society to embrace the critical methods of Biblical scholarship and experimental science,'[15] whilst ignoring anti-war testimony, social policy and the role of women.[16]

The conference sought to explore and dispel myths about the principles and practices of the Society, seeking to reinvigorate commitment from amongst the younger membership. Over 1,000 Friends attended, listening to over 39 papers. No decisions were made, and the YM did not formally follow up on the outcomes, but it sparked several important developments, such as the first Summer School at Scarborough in 1897 and the establishment of Woodbrooke Study Centre in 1902.

Some caution is needed with regard to any interpretation of evangelic dominance within the YM. Grubb, whilst acknowledging its influence and persistence, is at pains to establish the fact that it was 'moderate' in expression, arguing that it would be an over-simplification to see any sharp division between Quietist and evangelic positions.[17] Up to the 1870s most Friends wanted neither extreme,[18] and by the 1890s the movement away

13. Punshon, *Portrait*, 1999, 221–226.

14. Kennedy, *British Quakerism*, 2001.

15. David Blamires, 'The Context and Character of the 1895 Manchester Conference,' in *The Friends' Quarterly*, 30, 2, April 1996, 50–57.

16. Thomas Kennedy, '"What hath Manchester wrought?" Change in the Religious Society of Friends, 1895–1920,' in *Journal of the Friends' Historical Society*, 57, 1994–96, 277–301.

17. Mollie Grubb, 'The Beacon Separation,' in *Journal of the Friends' Historical Society*, 55, 6, 1988, 192.

from evangelic condemnatory language was already discernible in the YM epistles.[19]

The Manchester Conference paralleled undercurrents present across society. For the Church, these included the challenges of socialism and of theological disputation, as found in the preaching of R.J. Campbell, minister of the prestigious congregational City Temple, London and his 'New Theology,' which cut across fundamental Nonconformist theological positions, showing indifference to traditional viewpoints.[20] The industrial workers of Wales after 1880 were losing confidence in the ability of the churches to effect social improvements; they were turning to the trade unions and political action and were no longer impressed 'by the Nonconformist social pathology.'[21]

The religious revival of 1904 in Wales can therefore be seen as a response to a prevalent gloom and an attempt to recover lost moral values, amidst the decline perceived in religious life, and to re-kindle the fire of the 1859 Revival.[22] Turner sees the last decade of the nineteenth century in Wales as a period when, although denominations were consolidating themselves organisationally, it was against a background of clear decline in church life, and a membership calling for revival.[23] For Williams the 1904 revival was a conservative reaction to a changing social topography.[24]

Holmes believes social reform was one goal of revival, an opportunity for people to improve themselves, noting cynically that with regard to Wales

18. Mollie Grubb, 'Tensions in the Religious Society of Friends in England in the nineteenth century,' in *Journal of the Friends' Historical Society*, 56, 1, 1990, 4.

19. Ibid., 13–14.

20. See Horton Davies, *Worship and Theology in England 1900–196????* , 1965.

21. W. R. Lambert, 'Some Working-Class Attitudes towards organised religion in nineteenth-century Wales,' in *Llafur*, 2, 1, 1976, 14.

22. John Gwynfor Jones, ' "Ebychiad mawr olaf anghydffurfiaeth yng Nghymru": Diwygiad 1904–05' (' "Last mighty death gasp of nonconformity in Wales:" 1904–05 Revival') in the *Transactions of the Honourable Society of Cymmrodorion*, Vol.11, 2005, 105–143.

23. Christopher Ben Turner, 'Revivals and Popular Religion in Victorian and Edwardian Wales', unpublished PhD thesis, University of Wales, Aberystwyth, 1979, 107–108.

24. C.R. Williams, 'The Welsh Religious Revival' in *British Journal of Sociology*, 3, 1952, 242–259.

politicians recognised the power revival had as a symbol within Welsh society. They liked the fact that it improved morality and industrial relations and encouraged it as a way to win votes to promote their polices.[25]

Thus, Lloyd George tried, without success, to persuade the 'revivalist' Evan Roberts to share a political platform with him at Caernarfon in 1906.[26]

The Hegelian scholar Henry Jones of Glasgow University, addressing the Labour Festival of the north Wales quarrymen at Caernarfon in 1905, reflecting on the influence of its 1859 counterpart, perceived the revival as the 'spirit of the nation moving like the sea disturbed by the winds.'[27] It was again being tested, being raised up:

> one of the most beautiful and most precious images of our nation – that she can, from time to time, lose and forget herself in the best things of life; things above gold and silver, and far better than the pride which follows the shedding of blood.[28]

His was a peroration, linking the revival to national aspiration and social reform, comparing George Fox to Luther and Huss, and focussing on the vision that religious emotion should be channelled to 'the will', since proper religion 'creates ready and pure citizens prepared to suffer for others, and sacrifice for the sake of the broad principles of social life.'[29]

The Revival
The revival gripped the international imagination as the publication of two oft-quoted French books reveals,[30] and coverage in the national press was

---

25. Janice Holmes, *Religious Revivals in Britain and Ireland, 1859–1905*, 2000, 189.
26. Basil Hall, 'The Welsh Revival of 1904–05,' in *Popular Belief and Practice*, G.J. Cuming and Derek Baker eds., 1972, 294.
27. Henry Jones, Y Diwygiad: a'r hyn eill ddod o hono: Araeth gan yr Athraw Henry Jones ('The Revival: that which can come from it') 1905, 3. ('ysbryd cenedl yn ymsymmud fel y mor pan gynhyrfer ef gan y gwyntoedd.')
28. Ibid., 8. ('dyma un o ddelweddau prydferthaf a gwerthfawroccaf ein cenedl ni – y gall hi, o bryd i bryd, ymgolli, ac anghofio ei hun mewn pethau goreu bywyd; pethau uwch nac aur ac arian, ac annrhaethol well na'r bri sydd yn dilyn gollwng gwaed.')
29. Ibid., 14. ('creu dinesyddion pur a pharod i ddioddef dros eraill, ac i ymarberthu a ran egwyddorion eang bywyd cymdeithasol.')
30. Henri Bois, *Le Reveil au Pays de Galles* (Paris 1905) and J. Rogues de Fursac, *Un Mouvement Mystique Contemporain* (Paris 1905).

extensive. Jones, writing as a convinced evangelical and nationalist, saw it as a fruitful, exceptional blessing, one of the most stunning events in the history of modern Wales, but upon which Wales had turned its back.[31] E.T. Davies, an Anglican, was dubious who thought the revival unexpected since revivals, as phenomena, belonged to less sophisticated societies, the 1905 experience being an Indian summer for Welsh Nonconformity[32] – its last gasp.[33] Morgan locates the revival alongside many similar local outpourings, noting seven revival events worthy but locally based. He disabuses those who felt that the revival reflected a depressed, pessimistic country. Despite everything, 'Overall, Wales in 1905 was lively, optimistic, energetic, interesting and exciting'[34] and although people were inevitably worried that the world was changing, with too much emphasis on worldly and material issues, religion mattered and even the Labour movement used biblical rhetoric to spread its message.[35] Others reflect an older and widely-held view that the revival was 'an attempt to return the Welsh people to the Puritan certainties of an earlier age, and to the emotional sincerity and simplicity of eighteenth century enthusiasm.'[36]

The revival was for many, as Pope expounds, a powerful mass movement, and the emotionalism and mysticism which surrounded it were striking. He remarks that it was the failure of Welsh Nonconformity to provide a place for this very emotionalism which added to the chapels' unpopularity and contributed to their decline as the century progressed.[37] It was an outpouring of emotional fervour, where oral and narrative expression replaced doctrine.[38] Harvey sees it similarly, comparing the revivals of 1739 and 1859, where preaching had been central, to 1905 where music and

---

31. Jones, *Ffydd ac Argyfwng*, 1982, 222.
32. Davies, *Religion* etc, 1965, 168–173.
33. Jones, *Ebychiad*, 2005.
34. Densil Morgan, 'Diwygiad Crefyddol 1904–05,' in *Cof Cenedl XX: Ysgrifau ar Hanes Cymru*, Geraint H Jenkins, ed., 2005, 171. ('At ei gilydd, yr oedd Cymru yn 1905 yn wlad fywiog, optimistaidd, egniol, ddiddorol a chyffrous.')
35. Ibid., 174.
36. Prys Morgan and David Thomas, *Wales, the Shaping of a Nation*, 1984, 170.
37. Robert Pope, 'Evan Roberts in Theological Context,' in the *Transactions of the Honourable Society of Cymmrodorion*, 11, 2005, 144–169.
38. J.A. Owen, 'A Study of Orality and Conceptuality during the Welsh Religious Revival of 1904–06', unpublished PhD Thesis, University of Birmingham, 1997, 261,

paranormal phenomena, including visions, were more evident.[39] Jones comments that one reason for this was that the younger revivalists, often young women, displaced the ministers in their own pulpits. The sermon was replaced by spontaneous prayer and exultant hymn singing, which in turn affected the sustainability of the revival, because the scriptural and theological understanding of the converts was inadequate.[40] It was for many an enfranchisement, and in some measure liberation, that could not be ignored.[41]

Evan Roberts, the young ministerial candidate, became in the eyes of the public and mass media the figurehead for the revival. He was therefore, from a negative perspective, its product rather than its instigator, not its mainspring, indeed a 'man out of his depth.'[42] One leading Welsh Anglican critic of the period noted of him that he

> bore no traces of culture save that form of culture that one discovers in the peasant and the artisan… Those who came to hear a great sermon or even a sermon were disillusioned.[43]

Roberts could be seen to represent the ordinary believer, leading a movement that grew 'from below,' inherently a 'remarkable example of popular religion ... an excitement in Welsh national consciousness.'[44]

It is therefore perhaps not surprising that there was in the revival a tension between those who thought that religion should be presented as learning, with theological and scriptural reflection, and those who felt that being inspired by the Holy Spirit was sufficient. The Rev. Owen Evans, co-editor of *Y Dysgedydd*, commented that not everything that was being said or done by those involved in the revival could be supported. He was not

39. J. Harvey, 'Spiritual Emblems: The Visions of the 1904–05 Welsh Revival,' in *Llafur*, *Journal of Welsh Labour History*, 6, 2, 1993, 75–93.

40. Jones, *Ebychiad*, 2005, 126.

41. Owen, *A Study of Orality*, 1997, 306.

42. Geraint Tudur, 'Evan Roberts and the 1904–05 Revival' in *Journal of Welsh Religious History*, v4, 2004, 95.

43. J. Vyrnwy Morgan, *The Welsh Religious Revival, 1904–05: A Retrospect and a Criticism*, 1909, 55.

44. Hall, *The Welsh Revival*, 1972, 293, and fn 2 reference to J. Rogues de Fursac, *Un Mouvement Mystique Contemporain*, (Paris 1905)

surprised that mistakes had been made, considering that 'the mediums available to God's Spirit to work through, at the best of times, are fairly imperfect.'[45] He noted the sobriety of thousands of drunks, the closure of many taverns, and the fall in the level of crime and immorality as well as in swearing and blasphemy, but was concerned that there should be adequate preparation for those converted. Despite the imperfections the converts had to be nourished. As for the rest, the same author, commenting on the tragedy at Wattstown Colliery in the Rhondda when 119 men were killed on July 11th, 1905 desired that the unconverted survivors should take note of the Godly warning inherent in the tragedy, and that 'it was indeed a comfort to remember … that all is ruled and arranged by the infinite One wise and good.'[46]

The revival touched the whole of Wales, affecting both the rural and industrialised areas, but not everywhere was enthusiastic. Even parts of Ceredigion, where it was first made manifest, remained unmoved. Hence, for example, Pontarfynach remained aloof despite much evangelistic effort, with opposition to it from clerics such as the Calvinistic Methodist minister at Llangeitho. Some parts Flintshire and Montgomeryshire were relatively untouched, and overall the revival was stronger in South than in north Wales. Turner felt that in the industrialised areas many looked back to the values, especially their religious affinities, which they had carried with them when they had migrated from the rural areas, an affinity which was only undermined by non-Welsh in-migration at the end of the nineteenth century.[48] In this respect the revival might be construed, not only as the search for faith in the face of harsh conditions, but as another expression of national identity, with the chapels as cultural and linguistic oases. In the same way, in the seventeenth century, the Methodist Revival had 'given Wales for the first time in its modern history a national church – the

45. *Y Dysgedydd*, 28, March 1905, 136.
46. *Y Dysgedydd*, 28, August 1905, 385. ('y cysur yw cofio … fod y cwbl yn cael ei reoli a'i drefnu gan Un anfeidrol doeth a da.')
47. Huw Roderick, ' "A fire made of shavings": the 1904 Revival in Cardiganshire,' in *Ceredigion*, XV, 1, 2005, 107–138. See also Turner, *Revivals*, 1979, 353.
48. Christopher B. Turner, 'Revivalism and Welsh Society in the Nineteenth Century,' in *Disciplines of Faith: Studies in Religion, Politics and Patriarchy*, Jim Obelkevich, Lyndal Roper, Raphael Samuel, eds., 1987, 311–323.

Calvinistic Methodist Church of Wales'[49] which had helped shape the identity of a burgeoning Welsh society.

The political enthusiasm and fervour generated by the 'Welsh Revolt' around the 1902 Education Act should be seen as a component contributing to the revivalist fervour, since it articulated the promise of nonconformist success, albeit in the secular world. An article in *The Crusader* noted that opposition to the act in Wales was 'a great factor in awakening the spiritual life of the people.'[50] Munson's analysis of the passive resistance campaign, quoting John Clifford, was that it had revivalist overtones,[51] and similarly Turner relies on Clifford, 'You cannot touch men in their conscience without affecting their whole religious life.'[52]

The link between aggressive political agitation and religious fervour when the revival erupted in late 1904 cannot be discounted; 'the banner of educational and religious freedom and equality has been raised, and the greater majority of the Welsh nation enlisted under her.'[53] The defeat of godless secular activity was uppermost in the minds of many revivalists, and their delight at football and rugby matches being cancelled was proof that Wales was recovering her spiritual energy.[54] Nevertheless, the co-existence of sport and religion cannot be ignored. When Wales defeated New Zealand and won the Triple Crown in 1905, rugby became 'a leading factor in the definition of [the] nation's cultural – and perhaps spiritual – identity.'[55] Thus whilst the revival could be considered an example of 'introverted nationalism,' rugby was seen as being far more inclusive, a 'democratic pageant of the people.'[56]

The revival did not touch England to the same extent, and in that light its Welsh character becomes more pronounced. Although revival meetings in Wales were held in both English and Welsh, it was the Welsh-speaking communities that were most affected. When Evan Roberts visited Liverpool

49. Williams, *The Welsh Revival*, 1952, 243.

50. *TC*, 5.1.1905.

51. Munson, *A Study of Nonconformity*, 1973, 144.

52. Turner, 'Revivals and', 1979, 383, quoting Clifford from the Cardiff Times, 21.10.1905.

53. *Y Diwigiwr*, May 1904, 137.

54. Gareth Morgan, 'Rugby and Revivalism: Sport and Religion in Edwardian Wales,' in *International Journal of the History of Sport*, 22, 3, May 2005, 434–456.

55. Ibid., 448.

56. Ibid., 453.

in 1905 he only attended meetings in Welsh-language chapels. Indeed, Hall, relying on de Fursac, highlights the fact that Evan Roberts refused to go to Cardiff because he was unhappy to use English.[57] Not an unusual occurrence. At a meeting during the Llandrindod 'Keswick' Conference, Roberts only used Welsh, and when 'at the close several asked [him] to say a few words in English, he said he was willing, if God told him to speak in that language.'[58]

Pope is anxious that the revival's impact on England should not be ignored, especially given its international influence, arguing that it was something more than a Welsh affair.[59] Nevertheless, despite his inclination to argue thus, where the 'fire' of the revival was taken into England, it proved to be localised. In England, Quaker involvement regarding the revival was sparse. At its January 1905 meeting, Sufferings had been opened with an earnest prayer of hope

> that the revival of religious experience which is being known so extensively in Wales just now, may spread to England also, that we may contribute thereto by our prayers.[60]

John Owen Jenkins, the Radnorshire Quaker, evangelised around Almeley and Leominster. George Cadbury published a gold embossed New Year greeting to be left in every house in Selly Oak, Bournbrook and Stirchley, expressing the wish that the revival would soon reach those neighbourhoods.[61] At Bristol Friars Meeting, Howard and Louisa Nicholson, the HMC workers at Bethnal Green Mission, had ministered, a 'refreshing,' that had 'not been known at the Friars for many years.'[62] R. Hingston Fox, Charles Allen Fox's younger brother, noted that hundreds of ministers had met at F.B. Meyer's church in London in January where,

---

57. Hall, *The Welsh Revival*, 1972, 297.
58. *WM*, 11.8.1905.
59. Robert Pope, *Codi Muriau Duw: Anghydffurfiaeth ac Anghydffurfwyr Cymru'r Ugeinfed Ganrif*, 2005, 25.
60. *TF*, 06.01.05, 20.
61. *TF*, 27.1.1905, 61. Card is available in LSF, Vol. 1, 0–209 (184).
62. *TF*, 24.2.1905, 118.

Meyer stilled the meeting into silence and there followed a time of deep heart searching, when strong men, wont to be themselves teachers of large congregations, were bowed in silent humbling of soul.[63]

Fox saw others were now utilising the Quaker approach but he also, no doubt, knew that Meyer's maternal grandmother had been a Quaker. In Meyer's theology the priority was direct personal communion with God, and he 'commended the Quakers, despite their rejection of the sacraments, for their stress on God as Spirit, suggesting that this produced spiritual manifestations which were "mysteriously real."'[64] *The Friend* reported that the revival had reached the Free Churches in London, alongside the Torrey-Alexander Mission,[65] led by two American evangelists of those surnames, who would begin their labours at the Albert Hall the following month, and then for five months across Britain.

One aspect of the revival, which had particular relevance to Quaker theology, was that it could be seen as a natural extension of the 'Holiness Movement.' This sought the total rebirth of the Christian, the newborn being sanctified into perfection, as 'the culmination of growth in grace ... an inner communion with God, and not only a hope to be realised in heaven.'[66] Spencer sees the Quaker movement as being rooted in holiness since its inception. Throughout its history, Quakerism, in its traditions and witness has been infused with different interpretations of holiness, recovering in the process of its own development the 'experiential and transformational aspects of the Christian mystical tradition,'[67] whilst remaining grounded in orthodox Christianity. In this scenario the goal of perfection is at the centre of all spirituality, but reliant on the word and text. This would have resonated with the evangelical Quakers of the early twentieth century. Spencer demonstrated that it was closely allied to their understanding of

---

63. *TF*, 6.1.1905, 6.
64. Ian M. Randall, *Spirituality and Social Change: The Contribution of F. B. Meyer [1847–1929]*, 2003, 50.
65. *TF*, 6.1.1905, 5.
66. Carole D. Spencer, 'Quakerism as Holiness: An Historical Analysis of Holiness in the Quaker Tradition', unpublished PhD thesis, University of Birmingham, 2004, 330.
67. Carole D. Spencer, 'Holiness: the Quaker Way of Perfection,' in *The Creation of Quaker Theory: Insider Perspectives*, Pink Dandelion, ed., 2004, 151.

how George Fox and others saw their original mission, and the union that they sought with God through Christ, 'became the primary descriptor of the process of holiness:'[68] a restoration with God in an earthly glorification in the present and not merely in eternity.

The reliance on sanctification, as a second blessing through the baptism of the Holy Spirit into a higher Christian life, was a major element in revivalism. According to Irvin, this should be seen as part of the millennial quest for social and national redemption, with its expectation of the imminent kingdom and a reliance on personal and collective spiritual and moral discipline, so that each person becomes more Christ-like attaining perfection.[69] This was a step beyond conversion, since in the 'Higher Life' there was total victory over sin, an aspect that would cause difficulty for many evangelical Christians. The Keswick Convention was the most explicit expression of the Higher Life movement from the 1870s, and some saw it as not being revivalist, since it had merely substituted a vague vocabulary about the Christian chances of finding perfection within an evangelical sub-culture.[70] In a positive 1874 article *Y Faner* commented on the convention that it 'did not teach sinless perfection in the flesh, but taught that life should be lived in victory over sin, in communion with God.'[71] Some, however, considered it as a negation of the classic fundamental Protestant position; there was no continual sustained and gradual moral effort of sanctification through faith, merely instant conversion: 'No wonder ... this movement greatly priced silent mysticism.'[72] Put even more bluntly, 'Keswick theology's view of sanctification is theologically erroneous.'[73]

---

68. Spencer, 'Quakerism as Holiness,' 2004, 17.

69. Dale T. Irvin, 'Holiness Movement,' in *Encyclopaedia of Millennialism and Millennial Movements*, Richard A. Landes, ed., 2000, 179–181.

70. John Kent, *Holding the Fort: Studies in Victorian Revivalism*, 1978, 355.

71. YFAC, 9.9.1874. ('nad oeddynt hwy yn dysgu perffeithrwydd dibechod tra yn y cnawd, ond yr oeddynt yn dysgu y dylid byw bywyd o oruchafiaeth ar bechod, a chymundeb a Duw.')

72. Jones, *Ffydd ac Argyfwng* II, 79. ("Nid rhyfedd ... fod y mudiad hwn yn mawr brisio tawelyddiaeth gyfrinol.')

73. Andrew David Naselli, 'Keswick Theology: a survey and analysis of the doctrine of sanctification in the early Keswick Movement' in *Detroit Baptist Seminary Journal*, 13, 2008, 18.

Two of the primary influences on the Higher Life movement in Britain were the Americans Robert and Hannah Pearsall Smith. They attended the 1874 Oxford Conference for 'The Promotion of Scriptural Holiness of Life,' (which was sponsored by at least one Quaker, Charles Lloyd Braithwaite, reflecting its 'strong interdenominational flavour,')[74] and the follow up conference in Brighton in May–June 1875. This was an international gathering of some 1,000 people, with Robert Pearsall Smith presiding. Both Smiths were born into Quaker families, and they adhered to the sentiments and testimonies of their spiritual forefathers even though they had resigned their membership. A letter in the *British Friend*, from a Philadelphian Quaker, warned that this was because of their 'distinct ground of want of unity with the Society of Friends,'[75] presumably in an effort to discourage Friends in Britain from offering them support. Many within LYM nevertheless welcomed them. *The Friend* reported a meeting at Devonshire House on 2 July 1874 where, at the old meeting house, Hannah addressed a crowded meeting, as did Robert in the evening.[76] Their willingness to 'work with and indeed be part of interdenominational societies'[77] gave the holiness movement a wide following, as the character of the Keswick Convention demonstrated, given its Anglican and Quaker inspiration.

Quakers participated fully at both the Oxford and Brighton conferences. Robert Wilson of Broughton Grange, near Cockermouth, was one attendee at Brighton with Canon T.D. Harford-Battersby, vicar of St John's, Keswick. Both were inspired to organise the first Keswick Convention in 1876 and thereafter. Figgis, a historian of the convention, described Wilson as a 'massive figure' in its history, the person who selected its motto, 'All one in Christ Jesus' and was responsible for the three flags, 'Love-Joy-Peace' which flew over the convention tent. A man who loved prayer, 'it was hardly too much to say that without Mr Wilson's support and backing, there would have been no Keswick story at all.'[78] Wilson was an ecumenically-minded Quaker, liberal in his hospitality, an excellent organiser, who became

---

74. Melvin Easterday Dieter, *The Holiness Revival of the Nineteenth Century*, (London, Scarecrow Press, 1996), 8.

75. BF, 1st month 1875, 23.

76. TF, 7th month, 1874, 171–173.

77. Nigel Scotland, *Evangelical Anglicans in a Revolutionary Age, 1789–1901*, 2004, 399.

78. J.B. Figgis, *Keswick from Within*, 1914, 52.

chairman of the Convention in 1890. His sons were actively involved in the movement; William Henry Wilson (1853–1925) was a member of both the Home Mission and the Friends Foreign Mission committees,[79] and his third son became a trustee in 1906, acting as chairman in 1920. Also prominent at Keswick were Albert Head and his wife Caroline Hanbury, who was of Quaker stock, her parents being birthright Friends who became Anglicans.[80] This connection between Quakers in LYM and the Keswick Conventions is often overlooked, indeed ignored, but it witnesses to the way Quaker theology on perfection was intertwined into a broader movement, and that Robert Barclay's interpretation of the doctrine of perfection was

> adopted by a major part of English-speaking Protestantism – partly through Methodism, partly through the 'British Higher Life Movement' and the more or less parallel Keswick movement.[81]

It was the experience of Keswick that led a number of people in Wales to think about replicating the event in Wales. Foremost amongst them was Jessie Penn-Lewis, originally from Neath. As a child she had attended, with her two brothers, a school run by Quakers, most probably Christiana Abberley Price and her sister. At the age of fourteen she was proposed as Honorary Secretary of the Neath Adult Lodge of the temperance movement, of which Frederick J. Gibbins was undoubtedly a member. In her biography she describes a Quaker gentleman who gave private tuition to twelve boys, of whom three were her brothers, and who trained her in secretarial duties, so that she was re-elected regularly as secretary of the Temperance Lodge. She therefore had some familiarity with Quakers and an understanding of their practices; her description of an experience in Ireland in 1900 reflects this:

> They will be content to know that the Lord gave many tokens of His presence with us, and in many gatherings we had what an old Quaker used to describe as a 'heart tendering time,' the very best evidence of the brooding over hearts of the Holy Dove.[82]

79. DQB.
80. TF, 20.1.1905, 41.
81. Barclay, *Barclay's Apology*, 1969, xxv, Freiday's 'Introduction.'
82. Mary N. Garrard, *Mrs Penn-Lewis: A Memoir*, n.d, 202.

Indeed, she and her husband, a descendent of William Penn, were to be buried at Reigate Quaker burial ground.

In 1902 Jessie Penn-Lewis approached David Howells (known popularly by his bardic name Llawdden) the dean of St David's about the possibility of launching a convention in Wales,[83] an important reminder that the convention and the revival in Wales were not confined to nonconformists, an overlooked aspect in understanding the progress and activity of the revival.[84] Despite his allegiance to the Church of England, Howells was much admired by nonconformists across Wales, his evangelic fervour well known. In January 1903, a month before his death, he wrote in Y Diwigiwr, following on an earlier and similar appeal in December 1902,[85] that the great need in Wales was for a spiritual revival.[86] The outcome was the decision to organise a convention at Llandrindod in 1903 to replicate Keswick.

In May 1892 The Friend noted that a Holiness Convention was to be held at Llandrindod in July with William Haslam,[87] an Anglican priest and veteran Keswick speaker, expected to take part, invited there by the local Quaker John Owen Jenkins.[88] Phillips role as president of the local Free Church Council was important. They had invited F.B. Meyer to the town in 1902. It was in relation to this that the Rev. J. Rhys Davies wrote to Phillips in November asking for his help to act as organising local secretary for the 1903 convention.[89] It is then not surprising that both Jenkins and Phillips became part of the local arrangements committee, doing much of the groundwork, for what became the Keswick Movement in Wales,[90] Phillips serving as local secretary for 21 years.[91]

Like Keswick, the Llandrindod convention was an example of inter-church endeavour:

83. Roger Lee Brown, A Pool of Spirituality – A Life of David Howell (Llawdden), 1998, 305.
84. See Eluned E. Owen, The Later Life of Bishop Owen: A Son of Wales, 1961, 75–76.
85. Brown, A Pool, 1998, 305.
86. Y Diwigiwr, January 1903, 13–15.
87. TF, 20.5.1892, 330.
88. http://www.keswickinwales.org.uk/history , accessed 17.01.13.
89. Letter 11.11.1902, File 19, Brynmor P. Jones Research Papers, NLW 1895–1996.
90. Brynmor Pierce Jones, The Spiritual History of Keswick in Wales: 1903–08, 1989.
91. Who's Who in Wales, 1933, (London, A. Reynolds, 1933).

was it then a kind of ecumenical movement? The best answer is to say that for these people the 'IN CHRIST JESUS' was more vital than the 'ALL ONE,' but it was certainly possible for Anglicans and Welsh Quakers to work and worship alongside ardent chapel and mission hall people.[92]

Phillips ensured that reports about the convention appeared in the local press and *The Friend* was also interested, reporting that Mrs Penn-Lewis of Leicester had spoken at the Llandrindod meeting house during the 'Keswick of Wales' convention with 'great spiritual power.'[93]

The convention chairman at Llandrindod was the well-known Keswick advocate Albert Head. At this first convention many leading Welsh evangelical ministers attended, and in 1905 the multitudes came. Pierce Jones quotes Phillips:

the fruit of the yearly conventions cannot be told. We know a little, God knows all. From many parts of Wales I have heard of men and women whose lives have been transformed so much by the teaching that they have had that their names have been dear to all hearts and their lives prolific in fruit.[94]

If it is accepted that the 1903 Llandrindod Convention was instrumental in galvanising local endeavours across Wales, igniting the revival, then it would be appropriate to give some credit to Quakers, especially Radnorshire Friends, for their contribution in making the convention a success. *The Friend* in November 1904 would comment that 'The present awakening seems to have sprung in some measure from the Llandrindod Convention for the deepening of spiritual life.'[95] The *Radnor Express* took up the same theme, possibly written by Phillips, and thus reflective of personal pride in the local contribution:

The Spirit of God broke out in mighty power at the first Llandrindod Convention for the deepening of spiritual life, held in August 1903, and the blessing given has been one of many forces from which the present glorious

92. Jones, *The Spiritual History*, 1989, 4.
93. *TF*, 14.8.1903, 543.
94. Jones, *The Spiritual History*, 1989, 35.
95. *TF*, 25.11.1904, 775.

tidal wave of the Spirit has sprung ... Following the 1903 convention no less than seven local conventions were held in South and West Wales up to November 1904 – the first at Newquay on December 31, 1903.[96]

It is difficult then not to agree with Jones, that the foundations for the revival had been laid several years before, and that the 'Keswick' movement was an important causative element.[97] The Quaker thread cannot be overlooked even though, overall, the literature and studies concerning the Revival is sparse in its recognition of their contribution, probably because much of it is written by those whose theology and historical outlook falls into a more Calvinistically-inclined tradition.

Commenting on developments, *The Friend* referred to the pronounce-ment made by the Rev. Joseph Jenkins, the Calvinistic Minister at Newquay that a new kind of meeting was now required to demonstrate the life of the church to the people. Such meetings should have no set form, each demon-strating its own form of spontaneity, with all those present contributing in whatever way suited them[98] – in Quaker parlance, 'as they were led.' This reference to Jenkins indicates that his role in the genesis of the revival was known outside Wales. Jenkins and his nephew, the Rev. John Thickens of the same denomination, minister at Aberaeron, had been instrumental in setting up conventions for the higher life in Cardiganshire in 1903, following discussions with a man who had been at Keswick and who had stayed with Jenkins at his home. The theology of Keswick had not interested Jenkins, but he had reflected on its implications with the Rev. W.W. Lewis, Carmarthen, one of the few Welsh-speaking clergy who had attended the conventions.[99] Lewis had been influenced by the preaching of Reader Harris who established the Pentecostal Prayer League, another formative element in the complexity of revival and resurgence in the same period.[100] Jenkins in his earlier ministerial days had been influenced by the work and ministry of the

96. *RE*, 1.1.1905.

97. Jones, *Ffydd ac Argyfwng*, 1982, 122 –123.

98. *TF*, 25.11.1904, 776.

99. Eliseus Howells, 'Toriad y Wawr yn Ne Aberteifi,' in *Cyfrol Goffa Diwygiad 1904–1905*, eds., Parch Sidney Evans & Parch Gomer M Roberts, 1954, 29.

100. Nantlais Williams, 'Trem yn Ôl,' in *Cyfrol Goffa Diwygiad 1904–1905*, eds., Parch Sidney Evans & Parch Gomer M Roberts, 1954, 84–91.

Salvation Army and their holiness theology must have left its mark on him.[101]

The Keswick conventions had not permeated the life of the church in Wales to any degree, but Jenkins must have been impressed by their dynamism as to suggest to his Monthly Meeting that similar conventions should be organised within their area. Thickens, more of a mystic with a deep interest in spiritual experience,[102] then added another dimension influencing the imagination of their endeavours. The first signs that a broader revival was gripping Wales came in the autumn/winter of 1904. Evan Roberts was converted at Blaenannerch, Ceredigion, in September, at a convention organised by Jenkins and Thickens. R.B. Jones, a Baptist minister from South Wales held meetings during November in Rhosllannerchrugog, and in the Baptist churches of eastern Glamorganshire there were signs of agitation. In Cardiff during October, Torrey and Alexander had made a distinct impression. The fire had been lit but it was the activities of Roberts and his companions that caught the public imagination.

Jenkins' remarks to his Monthly Meeting and his ministry contrasted with the perception that Welsh nonconformity was formal and rigid. For Henry Stanley Newman, and many of his readers, Jenkins' approach described the essence of the Quaker experience, and, replicated by the revival, offered opportunities for Wales to get to know the Quaker way. Reported extravagances could be ignored for

> the evidence is strong that the Spirit of God is powerfully at work ... The revival is a fresh illustration of the fact that when men submit themselves tothe work of the Holy Spirit the result is power in other lives. We cannot measure the probable result of taking God at his word.[103]

This theme of the revival as offering an opening to the Quaker way was to be best expressed in the papers read at the Women's YM in 1905, when Elsie M. Cadbury, with others, addressed the gathering.[104]

---

101. Eliseus Howells, 'Parch. John Jenkins, 1859–1929' in *Deg o Enwogion (Ail Gyfres)* ed., William Morris, 1965, 19.

102. Gomer M. Roberts, 'Parch. John Thickens,1865–1952' in Morris, *Deg o*, 29.

103. *TF*, 25.11.1904, 777.

104. *TF*, 16.6.1905, 392.

Having attended at least two meetings, one in Cardiff mostly conducted in English, and the other in Llanelli, almost entirely in Welsh, she was keen to draw parallels between Quaker meetings and what was happening within the revival. Anyone was free to attend the revival meetings, which she saw as a gathering of people with one purpose, to wait on the Spirit and then to express its presence and power. At the Llanelli meeting there had been two impressive periods of silence, further reinforcing the parallels. Conscious however of the spontaneity of the congregation, she then questioned whether Friends were not overcautious, touching on the formality that silence and expectant waiting can bring

> restraint and self-control are valuable qualities; they are inherent parts of fine characteristics. Quakerism develops these qualities. Have we given them too great a prominence? ... There is no gathering so hard to stir as a Friends Meeting. Birthright members cannot be swept away, or carried out of themselves, except perhaps, on the rarest occasions.[105]

For her, Quaker spirituality relied on an experience of being carried out of oneself, and her comments are an obvious criticism of those Quakers who had never experienced conversion, relying instead on their birthright allegiance. The introduction of music was ever an issue, especially in the mission meetings. One Swansea Friend commented,

> As to the order of the services – without evolving any great tendency to ceremonial, due regard must be given, in the Principality especially, to the musical portion of worship. Such appeals to me as a convinced Friend.[106]

In this instance the Friend, Thomas Davies, was writing in response to an earlier communication by George Cadbury about how the Society grew and attracted new members; Cadbury favoured the use of singing. This touches on the paradoxes inherent in LYM between tradition and conviction. Elsie Cadbury urged Friends to recognise the power of song in worship, 'We must

---

105. Elsie M. Cadbury, 'Friends' Census and the Revival, I – The Revival,' in *Friends Quarterly Examiner*, 34, 1905, 317.

106. *TF*, 28.07.05, 494.

recognize the power of song,'[107] contrasting strongly with what the YM had said in 1854 about sacred music that it,

> not infrequently stimulates expressions and feelings which are far from being the genuine breathings of a renewed heart, and tends to delude the mind by producing an excitement often unhappily mistaken for devotion, and to withdraw the soul from that quiet, humble, and retired frame, in which prayer and praise may be truly offered with the spirit and the understanding also.[108]

The Welsh revival was to be seen as an opportunity for Friends, but one which implied that changes might be needed in their approach.

In its overview of events for 1904, *The Friend* commented on the revival as a spontaneous spreading of the Spirit, without benefit of clergy, and with the godless gathered into the net to the extent that the year should be seen 'as a year of great beginnings in the world's history.'[109] The editor was cautious but his sentiments clear: 'in many points the work now proceeding in Wales is similar to that carried out by George Fox and his early band of young men [sic] preachers.'[110] It was important, however, that allowances should be made for the Celtic temperament, since the brush of emotionalism and song could not taint Friends, departing somewhat from Cadbury's hopes. Newman was clear that a Pentecostal baptism had come to Wales, and his hope was that it should spread into England.

On 16 December 1904 *The Friend* had published an article, 'The Revival in Wales' under the *nom de plume* Siluriad, the Welsh form of Silurian, the name for a member of the Celtic tribe which inhabited south Wales at the time of the Roman invasion. The author must have been a Welsh speaker, in sympathy with things Welsh, since the article, unusually, included a Welsh quotation. The writer highlighted the fact that, although the revival was dominantly Welsh by language, it had not prevented non-Welsh speakers, of whom there were many, from attending and being affected by the

---

107. Ibid., 319.
108. *Epistles from the Yearly Meeting of Friends, 1681–1857*, Vol 2 (London, Edward Marsh, 1858), 378.
109. *TF*, 30.12.1904, 860.
110. Ibid.

meetings. The writer went on to reflect on the similarities between Quaker and revivalist meetings: 'in fact, it is to be noticed that the more the conduct of the meetings conforms to the original Quaker ideal, the more they seem to succeed.'[111] This reference to the Quaker ideal suggests that the writer was a conservative and traditionalist Friend.

The author was undoubtedly John Edward Southall, the Newport Quaker and publisher who was in membership with Fritchley General Meeting, the independent group of Quakers based in Derbyshire.[112] Siluriad was reluctant to draw any final conclusions about the revival, cautioning that 'What they are, and what they are not, I will not attempt to lay down here; my own views are not sufficiently formed.'[113] He had not by then attended any meetings. The writer noted that the ordained clergy played only a secondary role, the sermon was not pivotal, routine had been abandoned, there was reliance on individual testimony, and the role of women was noticeable. Up to then English congregations had not been much affected, 'except in some cases where the people are, through birth or association, in touch with Welsh Wales.'[114] This reference to the linguistic topography of Wales hints strongly at Southall as the author, given his writings on the language and his enthusiasm for its preservation and usage in education.

As a Fritchley Friend, Southall might have been suspicious of certain aspects of the revival, unlike Charles Linney of Weston-super-Mare, who in the same edition asked that 'God grant us as a Society a share of the present wonderful blessing.'[115] An editorial a week later highlighted the wondrous expressions of the fruits of the revival in temperance and better public behaviour, both individually and collectively, and the question was not where the revival would spread but would it ever stop. The editor was nevertheless anxious that the revival should not interfere with daily business, and that 'the liberties which have occasionally been taken with employers' time [should] pass away.'[116] From the witness of the revival in Radnorshire there was no question that, for one Friend, what was being seen

111. *TF*, 16.12.1904, 828.
112. For Southall see chapter 5.
113. *TF*, 16.12.1904, 828.
114. Ibid.
115. Ibid.
116. *TF*, 23.12.1904, 840.

and experienced was the 'revelation of the truth' made 'to our forefathers.'[117]

Many Friends took an active interest in developments in Wales, using it as experience from which they could learn. Individuals and parties of Friends visited the Principality, especially those linked with the HMC. J. Tylor Fox visited various places including the Rhondda, attending one meeting addressed by Evan Roberts whom he could not understand, but was aware of an earnest meeting and impressed by the fact that the worship did not rely on individual leaders. The meetings were 'much like our meetings for worship, except that congregational singing took the place of periods of silence' and was a restraining influence on what might otherwise have been emotional and discordant utterances. He was clear that song, allied to the 'rather emotional Celtic character,' were important elements in the success of the revival, aspects that need not hinder the spread of the movement into England, where it 'might possibly take on a rather different form.'[118]

William George Hall, the Home Mission worker in Swansea, was a close eyewitness. His articles reflect some understanding of what was being said at the meetings so he must have had help with translation. He described what he had seen of Evan Roberts at the Tabernacl, Morriston, a chapel which had seating for 2,000; it was full to overflowing. As nearly everything was in Welsh it sounded to Hall 'as if a fearful quarrel were proceeding' and when the youngish Evan Roberts arrived, condescendingly commented

> had I met him at Oxford I should have thought he might be an undergraduate. He is just the one to inspire the Welsh, and the danger to Evan Roberts and to the people is that of idolising him; for the Welsh are devoted to their leaders.[119]

A week later he described in greater detail what had happened at various meetings, anxious to highlight the Quaker aspects of what he had experienced; 'it is a Quaker meeting, the intervals of silence common to us being used in praise or singing.'[120] To emphasise the importance of the revival to

117. *TF*, 30.12.1904, 864.
118. *TF*, 06.01.1905, 6.
119. *TF*, 06.01.1905, 7.
120. *TF*, 13.01.1905, 27–28.

the reader he highlighted the fact that many leading names were in attendance, which if revealed would cause surprise. He had no compunction in naming the Rev. F.B. Meyer.

Hall reported to the February meeting of the HMC, alongside others from the committee who had visited Wales: Henry Lloyd Wilson, Edith Morland of Birmingham, Richard Beck from Southampton and Henry Stanley. Newman. Hall gave an overview of previous revivals in Wales, reiterating boldly that in his opinion

> and that of unbiased Christian people in South Wales, the revival was a striking testimony to the principles of Quakerism; in fact, he suggested that there might be more real Quakers in South Wales at the present time than in all the rest of the world.[121]

Henry Lloyd Wilson reported that he had gone underground with a group of miners where they had had a revival meeting. Reference to children as instruments of revival was considered telling. For the whole of the committee it was evident that the Holy Spirit was at work, the focus was on present needs not future reward, and God was waiting for his people.[122]

In its annual report to the 1905 YM, the HMC was clear that the revival challenged Friends to set aside their preconceived ideas. It was the greatest exemplification of Quaker principles since the days of George Fox, and acknowledged as so by many religious leaders, such as the Congregationalist minister Sylvester Horne, who was to be elected M.P for Ipswich in 1910:

> to a great extent the Revival in Wales is a triumph of Quakerism. The people are rejoicing in recovered liberty. The one-man ministry is suspended. Testimony and witness are discovered to be the privilege of all. Men and women testify and pray, and all are edified.[123]

Newman would take up these themes in his editorials in *The Friend*. In February 1905 he quoted the assertion of one anonymous London minister, most probably Rev. John Clifford the Baptist leader and minister of

121. *TF*, 10.02.1905, 85.
122. Ibid., 86.
123. *YMP*, 1905, 26.

Westbourne Park Church that the revival was a triumph of Quakerism because it was free of human arrangements. As editor he recognised that this was not directly because of Friends, rather that the discovery of the Spirit was 'being reasserted in vast assemblies entirely outside our borders.'[124] The revival for him, following upon W.T. Stead, journalist, evangelist and social reformer who wrote several prominent articles and a book on the Revival, was its own organ, reliant only on God. The revival meetings controlled themselves and the Religious Society of Friends could rejoice provided individuals were willing to unbend.[125]

The minutes of the HMC itself are cautious and sparse. By April 1905, Sophia M. Fry and George S. Davidson, respectively their secretary and assistant secretary, had visited south Wales. The committee decided to print 500 copies of Davidson's report for internal circulation to members of the committee and the FFDSA council[126] but then this was rescinded.[127] Indeed, their deliberations were overshadowed by doubt as to what they might, or could do, with respect to the revival in conjunction with the FFDSA, echoing not so much indifference but an element of respect and caution. The YM Library Committee had also considered the revival, and had decided against publishing any special tracts in Welsh at that time, because 'the movement in Wales is largely free from anything of a "denominational" character and we should aid it to remain so.'[128] This caution was possibly edged with realism, that any specific literature aimed at interesting converts to Quakerism would have had limited appeal, and might have been construed as aggressive interference. The HMC did however agree to publish two tracts in Welsh, 'explaining our views of spiritual truth,'[129] one on the doctrine of Friends, the other 'To Seekers of the Truth.' Their focus, with the FFDSA, was much more on expanding the adult schools, presumably as a means of ensuring ongoing support to converts. For this reason they decided, in conjunction with the FFDSA, 'to send copies of the booklet *How to Start an*

---

124. *TF*, 3.02.05, 65–66.
125. *TF*, 27.01.05, 60.
126. *HMEC*, M2, 6.4.1905.
127. *HMEC*, M3, 6.7.1905.
128. *TF*, 12.05.05, 322.
129. *HMEC*, M3, 06.04.05.

Adult School with an offer of help in organisation to the ministers and all denominations in the Revival District.'[130]

By 1905 the committee had only the worker left in south Wales, Hall in Swansea, but during the early part of that year were challenged as to what assistance they could give to Cardiff. They felt that a volunteer might be recruited, but made no specific arrangements.[131] The executive committee meeting during the 1905 YM agreed, with regard to the revival, 'that no definite action could be taken at the time.'[132] Perhaps the call of Mabel Thompson to the meeting on ministry and oversight had had some impact, when she urged 'that instead of preaching ourselves, we must let Christ be the theme of our ministry. There was a danger lest we preach "Wales" and not Christ.'[133] After July 1905 there is no record of discussion relevant to the revival until 1912.

Some Quarterly Meetings considered the revival. In April 1905, Lancashire and Cheshire Quarterly Meeting, in their women's meeting, listened to Frances Thompson, with another unnamed Friend, give an enthusiastic account of her visit to Wales.[134] The role and prominence of women in the revival gave, no doubt, an added edge to her contribution. As Newman had said, 'many are startled at the freedom with which women are taking part in these gatherings.'[135] When Warwick, Leicester and Stafford Quarterly Meeting discussed the event at its January 1905 meeting, all were agreed as to the depth and reality of the work and the 'truly Quaker lines of much of the proceedings,'[136] listing those features with which Friends could identify. London and Middlesex Quarterly Meeting were similarly attuned to the awakening.[137]

The responsibility falling on WQM was more immediate given that the revival was affecting its area. Gathering in Worcester in April, many present had had first-hand experience, Hall, Newman, Elsmere amongst them.

130. *HMEC*, M4, 06.04.05.
131. *HMEC*, M3, 06.07.05.
132. *HMECEC*, M9, 09.06.05.
133. *TF*, 02.06.05, 339.
134. *TF*, 05.05.05, 282.
135. *TF*, 03.02.05, 65.
136. *TF*, 03.02.05, 72.
137. *TF*, 17.2.05, 106.

Friends from Cardiff had visited revival meetings; Arthur Sessions had been to Cwmafon. They had shared their experiences and held a series of meetings, where 'Among those who took part … was an American cowboy, who was formerly in Buffalo Bill's "Wild West" show, and who has accompanied John O. Jenkins to his farm at Penybont.'[138] WQM listened to George Davidson give an account of his experiences, suggesting how the churches might seek to ensure that the work of the revival was made permanent. It encouraged its satellite meetings, especially those where adult work flourished, to take their share in providing for the social and spiritual needs of converts. It also reminded everyone that they should first receive the Spirit into their own hearts and be willing to surrender, on the basis that the 'question is largely a personal one,' an indicator perhaps that some were suspicious and resistant to the Pentecostal experience to which the minute alluded. They sent their minute to the YM:

> The Revival has touched us, or will touch us, only as we as individuals (or even as Meetings) have been or are willing to place ourselves in the same attitude as that expressed in the prayer 'Bend Me.'[139]

Some weighty Friends from Leeds wished the YM to take advantage of the revival during its sessions and wrote accordingly, 'the approaching Yearly Meeting may be a time of refreshment and a starting point for new service for our Society.'[140]

If there had been any hesitations in February, by July 1905, WQM was more certain about its understanding of the revival. It agreed to send a message to Evan Roberts, which was cordially adopted.

> This meeting representative of the Society of Friends in South and Central Wales and the bordering English counties, in assembling at this time at Llandrindod Wells desire to convey an expression of its hearty thankfulness and gratitude to our Father in Heaven for the way in which he has used Evan Roberts and those associated with him in reviving the spiritual life in Wales,

138. *TF*, 03.03.05, 139.
139. *WQM*, M16, 27.04.1905.
140. *TF*, 21.4.1905, 243.

and for the renewed testimony for the Baptism of the Holy Spirit, and to personal allegiance for His direction in congregational and individual life.[141]

Frederick J. Gibbins delivered the message to the revivalist's home in Loughor, but not seeing him, gave the message instead to his brother Dan.[142]

In their triennial report to YM in 1906, WQM looked at the way the revival had impacted upon them, but by May the exuberance of the revival was already receding. They referred to what had gone on in Cardiff, Leominster and Radnorshire. No reference was specifically made to Swansea, which in March 1905 had conducted two weeks of meetings, some lasting two to three hours, where 'the Welsh *hwyl* and *tân* (flame) seemed to set all on fire. Many of the hymns were sung to the Welsh minors.'[143] The Quarterly Meeting concluded their report using the words of what had come to them from SWMM that the

> Welsh revival has had our heartiest sympathy, but it has shown us our weakness and we have been humbled while the great work has been going on around us. As a Society we have maintained theoretically our dependence on the work of the Holy Spirit, yet practically we have to learn of others outside our borders what a Pentecostal baptism in all its fullness truly means.[144]

The statement bears admission of a collective failure that they had not done more. Interestingly, there are no minutes for the Evangelistic Committee of WQM recorded after November 1904 until November 1907. The absence of records may indicate that the committee felt that the revival was so powerful by the winter of 1904, that its work could be left to its own leadings. Once the revival fire had weakened the group reconvened in 1907, responding to the needs of the Quarterly Meeting.

The FFSDA had also considered the impact of the revival. At their annual conference in spring 1905 they listened to Richard Westrope, who had visited Wales with F.W. Meyer, staying at Merthyr for four nights,[145] declare

141. *WQM*, M6, 13.07.1905.
142. *TF*, 21.07.05, 469.
143. *TF*, 10.03.05, 157.
144. *YMP*, 1906, 128.
145. *TF*, 3.2.05, 69.

that as a movement they did not 'go deep enough' in their attempts to bring members to God. Wales was teaching the world, whilst the teaching of Evan Roberts was 'exactly that of the early Quakers … what we have seen in Wales is Quakerism re-baptised.'[146]

One Friend, conscious of the need for a renewal of spiritual life in the YM, was anxious that wider social issues should not be ignored. Revival was not merely an individual matter; the foundations of the kingdom were to be found 'in the very midst of the community, where brotherhood ought to reign.'[147] If this was a call to consider the wider needs of a new social order it was an aspect of the revival that was overlooked by Friends at that time even though the Friends Social Union had been formed in 1903.

Interest amongst Friends abroad was evident. J.J. Armistead, writing from Stavanger, rejoiced at what was happening in Wales, seeking to draw parallels with his missionary efforts in Norway, and his discovery of a group of seekers in a remote fjord, who, to his mind, were earnest for truth, this being the key to revival.[148] Warburton Davidson writing from China drew inspiration from what was happening in Wales, and hoped that the same manifestations could be shared amongst Chinese Christians. He felt that the missions could be uplifted and inspired anew, since many of the nominal Christians now connected with the four missions were cold and indifferent:

> the Monthly Meetings have been poorly attended, and they have been markedby an absence of life and power, and of that true unity which should exist in such a community of believers in the Lord Jesus Christ.[149]

Overall Sufferings took but a muted interest in the revival; this can be explained by several factors. In the first place there was an expectation that the HMC would have provided the most suitable setting for oversight and discussion. Second, the nature of their activities meant that they sought a broader view of the affairs of the YM. During 1905, for example, their principal focus was with foreign matters such as the Congo and lynchings in

---

146. *TF*, 07.04.05, 211.
147. *TF*, 20.01.05, 38.
148. *TF*, 06.01.04, 5.
149. *TF*, 30.06.05, 425.

the United States, as well as internal domestic matters. The third factor was possibly a reluctance to engage overmuch with the phenomenon of the Revival given that Sufferings was a microcosm of the YM at large, and not everyone would have been enthusiastic about the outpouring. In this context the tension between liberal and evangelic Friends may have some bearing at a time when the spread of liberal theology amongst Friends was rapid.[150] By 1905 the matter of evangelic or Pentecostal expression was best left to the HMC.

Bringing Quakerism to the beneficiaries of the revival was the reason that John Edward Southall asked Sufferings for permission to borrow and republish the Welsh translation of John Crook's *True Principles*, originally translated in 1703 by Thomas Cadwalader, but they declined 'on account of the rarity of the tract.'[151] Southall went ahead with his project and published.[152] In April 1905 Sufferings asked the Library and Printing Committee to consider issuing tracts in Welsh 'for gratuitous distribution.'[153] The committee reported that the HMC were preparing to print tracts in Welsh, and had no recommendation of their own to make, but referred to some tracts worthy of translation if Sufferings felt so inclined. They had consulted Frederick J. Gibbins as to what might be done. Gibbins' reply was rather ambivalent and cautious. He informed the committee that, although in sympathy with the Revival, he had not personally attended any meetings and so could only express an opinion. He emphasised the unsectarian character of the outpouring, and that introducing the 'distinctive views of any sect' would be unwise. He had a preference as to what might take priority for translation, favouring a tract by John Dorland. If the committee was to proceed then he suggested that Tobit Evans be asked to prepare the translation. Gibbins was concerned about distribution, realising that many Friends in South Wales would object to such an undertaking, and to the distribution of any sectarian tracts, including those that came out of such

---

150. Isichei, *Victorian*, 1970, 39.
151. *MfS*, M17, 3.3.1905.
152. Egwyddorion y Gwirionedd, neu y pethau hynny ynghylch athrawiaeth ac addoliad a sicr gredir ac a dderbynir gan y bobl a elwir CRYNWYR (Quakers) sef yn mherthynas i Grist ei ddioddefaint, marwolaeth, adgyfodiad, ffydd yn ei waed ef, y cyfri o'i gyfiawnder ef a'i sancteiddrwydd etc.
153. *MfS*, M41, 7.4.1905.

events as the Keswick Convention; another reminder of the differences of theology amongst Friends. In the event Sufferings decided, no doubt heeding Gibbins' hesitations, to take 'no present action in the matter.'[154]

The last word on the revival and attitudes within LYM can go to John Edward Southall. If he was 'Siluriad,' writing in December 1904, then by January 1905 his views had crystallised true to his own Quaker conservative leanings. In a letter to *The British Friend*, he outlined his understanding of what was happening in Wales. He made it clear that in no way was Evan Roberts to be compared to the old powerful Welsh preachers. This was not a person who monopolised meetings; he did not even have the physical presence to do so. Southall attended the same meeting in Morriston as had W.G. Hall and was wary writing in a letter to the British Friend:

> Many people speak of this revival as if it were a form of Quakerism, butthat is not my experience. It is a movement tending to break down some of the conventionalities of religion as to grant to congregations a greater measure of liberty than they have hitherto enjoyed. A real spiritual influence has been felt; the facts of life and death and judgement have come before the careless in such a manner as to cause them to feel the existence of God, and of His claims on their lives; but it is not that simple gathering to and centering in this influence which characterised the Quaker revival of the seventeenth century; it is a long way behind that.[155]

This reveals his understanding of Quaker spirituality, embedded for him in quiet waiting in the silence. BYM issues a powerful leaflet as an introductory pamphlet to those new and unfamiliar with silent meetings, which is supposedly based on a passage from a book entitled *The Power of Stillness* whose authorship is attributed to Southall. A report to WQM, however, includes a passage saying that 'two tracts have been translated into Welsh and printed – viz. *The Power of Stillness* and *Pardon, Purity and Peace,*'[156] indicating that the leaflet was never taken from a book, but written as an original and complete tract in itself. Sadly the report does not indicate

---

154. *MfS*, M19, 5.5.1905.
155. *BF*, January 1905, 19.
156. *WQM*, 25.9.1912.

authorship; it probably was Southall, but there never was a book. As for the revival and the use of silence, for Southall its authority was not yet; 'the time may come in which silent waiting on God will be valued'[157] more so than the congregational singing considered to be indispensable.

Southall in his letter of January 1905 indirectly makes clear his dissatisfaction with the abrasive evangelical wing within LYM. As for the revival and its outcome, he was hopeful that the periods of silence used by Evans Roberts would eventually be valued. The outcomes could not be predicted, except that he was optimistic that it would make a difference, and Wales would not sink back into what he conceived of as being an inferior form of routine in worship. The hand of the 'Wonderful Counsellor' was over all; the Divine Spirit through its restraint and influence would rule and reign.

Southall's language and imagery was unmistakably that of the conservative Quaker. He was no doubt disappointed at the revival's outcome: by the end of 1905 its energies were being dissipated, unable to sustain its own momentum. Evan Roberts withdrew from the field, going to live with Jessie Penn-Lewis and her husband in Leicester, never again to impact in any major way on Welsh religious life. In many ways he became a romantic memory and something of a recluse. Roberts was in Llandrindod in August 1906, sharing a platform in a tented meeting organised by the Free Church Council. Both languages were in use at the meeting, and according to a correspondent, probably Hercules Phillips, this 'made the whole meeting seem more cosmopolitan, and we were lifted above the boundaries of denominationalism and nationality.'[158] The author could not resist the temptation to return to some of the earlier themes about the close linkages between Quakerism and the character of the revival. Evan Roberts, in the way he controlled the meeting, demonstrated the combined qualities of a true Quaker minister and elder, exercising prompt oversight when he felt silence was needed, and that in Quaker meetings extreme individualism could become a hindrance, control essential. By his actions Evan Roberts was showing that he was 'essentially a Quaker without being in bondage to preconceptions as to correctness or custom.'[159]

157. *BF*, January 1905, 19.
158. *TF*, 24.08.06, 562.
159. Ibid.

For Welsh Nonconformity the challenge of the revival was how to hold on to the new adherents. What they actually faced was the challenge of increasing secularisation, empty pews and the call of modernity.[160] With the sweeping victory of the Liberal party (nine Quakers were elected across Britain) in the 1906 General Election, taking every Welsh seat, Welsh expectations for action on education and disestablishment now took precedence as the revival waned. These were themes that *The Friend* fully supported, in one editorial espousing strongly the claims for educational devolution to Wales,[161] and making clear its support, yet again, for religious equality.[162] As for the 'modernity' of Friends across Britain, the Woodbrooke Settlement's spring term programme for 1905 reflected the growing challenges and broader interest in religious matters, whilst in Llandrindod in the summer of 1906 a Quaker school of an 'experimental' nature was organised. It was 'experimental' in the sense of being a new departure, allowing for exploration of more modern subjects by scholarly Friends, leaning heavily on developments at Woodbrooke. The following lectures were listed: W.C. Braithwaite (Principal Lecturer): The Land and the Book: How we got our New Testament; Christ the need of To-day; Theodore Neild: The Prose Writing of Whittier and Frances Thompson on Francis of Assisi; The Authority of Conscience; The Old Testament and War.[163]

For Thomas Davies of Swansea the challenge facing Friends was simple. He asked why it was that, whereas all the other denominations in Wales were increasing in numbers, the same could not be said of Friends?[164] He had read Thomas Rees's *History of Nonconformity in Wales*, which claimed that in 1715 there were at least 3,000 people in attendance at Friends' meetings across Wales. Rees' figure seems a gross exaggeration given the few meetings in Wales at the time. He had relied on the work of Dr John Evans, who 'about the year 1715 ... collected, with remarkable care and industry, the statistics of the Nonconformist congregations throughout

---

160. See Dewi Eurig Davies, *Diwinyddiaeth yng Nghymru 1927–1977*, 1984, especially Ch.1.
161. *TF*, 30.3.1906, 198.
162. *TF*, 14.09.1906, 621.
163. *TF*, 07.09.1906, 606.
164. *TF*, 23.02.1906, 127.

England and Wales,'[165] but what Davies highlighted, unwittingly from his perspective, was that Friends had not benefited from the revival in terms of new adherents. In Swansea the work continued, W.G. Hall reporting on their temperance efforts:

> there is much drinking here amongst men and women. Women are often seen staggering drunk with infants in their arms … our Band of Hope numbers about 140 and the children are largely of these drinking parents.[166]

In all other respects the meetings across Wales maintained their own quiet profiles. In January 1907, at the prize giving for the Children and Adult Schools in Swansea, 190 took tea and the Mayoress distributed a hundred prizes, whilst in Colwyn Bay, William Edward Turner of Birkenhead gave a public lecture on 'The Message of Quakerism,' and Friends there felt encouraged to further the Quaker message in north Wales.[167] In March, again at Swansea, an 'at home' was given for 70 at the meeting house, the guests of Richard Watkins, where after tea all 'the Christian work came under review.'[168] At Llandrindod the needs of the visitors still had to be catered for.

The Children of the Revival

The outcome of the revival saw some leave their denominations to establish what became part of the Pentecostal movement because, in their eyes, their denominations failed to capitalise on the gifts of the revival: 'the converts have extensively been obliged to band together … the older Christian communities having in such cases shut out their fresh glorious flow of Revival grace and power.'[169] In 1911 David Powell Williams separated from his Congregational church in the Amman Valley to establish at Penygroes,

---

165. Thomas Rees, *History of Protestant Nonconformity in Wales from its Rise to the Present Time*, 1861, 286.
166. *TF*, 30.3.1906, 209.
167. *TF*, 25.01.07, 61.
168. *TF*, 29.3.1907, 205–06.
169. Eifion Evans, *The Welsh Revival of 1904*, 1987, quoting T. B. Barratt, one of the most important of European Pentecostalists, 196.

Carmarthenshire, what evolved into the Apostolic Church.[170] In 1915 another Welsh Congregationalist convert, George Jeffreys of Maesteg, with others in Northern Ireland, established what became the Elim Four Square Gospel Alliance. These 'outcasts,' for there were many, became known by some as the 'children of the revival.' This is a term which is used in at least three different ways in the literature. First, those who were converted by the revival, in effect all converts, across all the denominations. Second, only those who felt that they had been forced out of their denominations, becoming almost children/orphans in need of new parentage, the 'outcasts.' The third usage are those who, after the Revival, became the backbone of the Welsh evangelic church in the next decades, such notable figures as the Rev. Nantlais Williams, Ammanford, who struggled to ensure his denomination, the Presbyterian Church of Wales, adhered to its founding articles. It was to be the needs of the outcasts that exercised the HMEC.

The Llandrindod 'Keswick' Convention of August 1911 seems to have been successful, with many Friends in attendance,[171] and the success of the proceedings may have galvanised Hercules Phillips. In October 1911 the HMEC considered a letter from him 'concerning the religious outlook in South Wales.'[172] They decided that three of their number, J. Bevan Braithwaite Jnr, George B. Wetherall and Richard Beck, should consult with their secretary as to what action might be possible, and confer with WQM's Extension and Evangelistic Committee, of which Phillips was convenor. Phillips must have anticipated the deliberations of his own committee, since his letter was sent prior to their December sitting. The committee considered the matter further in December when the Quarterly Meeting was in Gloucester, with the delegation from the HMEC. They reflected on the religious position in South Wales:

> At the present time ... there are many 'children of the Revival' scattered in groups in different parts of the Principality, seeking further light, and not finding satisfaction in any of the Church organisations. It was felt that to some

---

170. See Henry Byron Llywellyn, 'A Study of the Apostolic Church in Wales in the context of Pentecostalism,' unpublished M.Phil thesis, University of Wales, Cardiff, 1997.
171. *TF*, 25.8.1911 lists five Quaker visitors.
172. *HMEC*, M7, 5.10.1911.

of these, Friends might have a message, provided that the right exponents of it were to visit these districts.[173]

The committee recognised that there might be an opening for service in certain districts of south Wales, and asked the sister and brother, Rachel B. and J. B. Braithwaite Jun. to 'lay the whole subject before Max I. Reich,'[174] who had felt a call to give service amongst the 'children of the revival.' To expedite matters, should Reich be released for service, a small sub-committee was appointed consisting of Caroline E. Gibbins (Neath), Hercules D. Phillips (Llandrindod), W. H. Nicholls and Richard Watkins (Swansea). They also considered a letter from John Edward Southall, writing about the religious outlook in Wales, but sadly no details are given of its contents.[175] Reich had attended the Llandrindod Convention and was certainly there in 1905;[176] he would therefore have known Phillips and no doubt they must have talked about the possibilities in Wales at that time. Reich had been to Swansea Meeting in November 1910 as part of the HMECs efforts to support them following the difficulties surrounding the departure of W. G. Hall. No doubt that visit, and what he learnt, must have wetted his desire to return.

Reich[177] was a German Jew who came to Quakers via the Plymouth Brethren and was accepted into membership by Westminster and Longford Monthly Meeting in 1904.[178] One of his visitors was Herbert Sefton Jones, the son of William Jones, the Ruthun Quaker. His enthusiasm for evangelistic service was well known. In September/October 1910 he had been released by his Monthly Meeting for service in Scotland, staying there until February of 1911.[179] In December 1911, with a minute from Sufferings, initially alone and then accompanied by Charles E. Gillett, another Home Service worker, he had given service in Denmark and Germany. Reich reported to Sufferings on his experiences at their January 1912 meeting.[180] John Edward Southall was

173. *TF*, 15.12.1911, 820.
174. Evangelistic Committee WQM, M3 6.12.1911. (ECWQM).
175. Ibid. M9, 6.12.1911.
176. *TF*, 11.8.1905, 524.
177. See *TF*, 31.8.1945, *The Friend* (Philadelphia), 8th month 30, 1945.
178. *TF*, 13.10.1911, 646.
179. *BF*, October 1910.

with them for part of the journey and his concern for the religious outlook in Wales must surely have been an item that they would have shared.[181]

The HMEC discussed the outcome of discussions with WQM at their January meeting and agreed to support work in Wales. Reich was available for service in South Wales, restating his concern for 'work among those ... reached by the Welsh Revival ... but who are not finding special help in any of the places of worship ... at present available to them.'[12] During March, Reich, with Richard Beck, had begun his contacts in Wales, the first visit being to Llanofer, then moving westwards to Tenby and Brynaman.[183] Rachel Braithwaite co-ordinated their visits and activities. In April 1912, ECWQM considered what progress had been made, noting that to date costs amounted to £97. This meeting was augmented by the presence of Max Reich, Thomas Richards, Arthur Dickinson, 'who had been engaged in religious service in South Wales,' and G. B. Wetherall, on behalf of the HMEC, along with four others. Rachel B. Braithwaite was unable to be present having 'missed the railway connection at Bristol.'[184]

By the end of April twenty-eight visits had been made within Monmouthshire, Glamorganshire and Pembrokeshire, where groups were found in much fluidity, and whose members had not yet 'reached the end of their spiritual journeys' but there was considerable optimism:

> The feeling of all the visitors was that there was no doubt of there being an open-door for truth as they had learned it, especially amongst those who were known as the Children of the Revival ... there was great work before Friends in South Wales, and an open door ... had been opened to them.[185]

Each of the Monthly Meetings within the Quarterly Meeting had been asked to make a collection to support the work, hoping to make a

180. *TF*, 12.1.1912, 18.
181. *BF*, January 1912, 25.
182. *HMEC*, M8 1.2.1912.
183. Uncatalogued *HMEC* correspondence, FHL.
184. ECWQM, Report 24.4.1912.
185. ECWQM, 24/25.4.1912.

contribution of £25,[186] the rest coming from the HMEC. The question of collection seems to have been an issue amongst some meetings. Cardiff PM agreed to collect in June 1912, minuting later that they had collected 7/6, noting somewhat sourly 'It was felt that more interest would have been taken in this movement if our Preparative Meeting had been consulted in this matter.'[187] Similarly in June, SWMM had collected 7/6, having listened to Richard Watkins describe his experiences of being with Reich.[188]

The Quarterly Meeting itself considered four full reports on the mission, and these in many ways provide possibly one of the most detailed records of a specific home mission effort. The first report covered activity from February to April, during which, at various times, Rachel Braithwaite, John O. Jenkins, John Edward Southall, Richard Beck and Arthur Dickinson had assisted Reich. Significantly their contacts had been provided 'mostly by John Edward Southall of Newport.'[189] Eight groups had been identified from across the Principality who were seeking after a deeper spiritual life with greater freedom from ritual, but the Quaker group had no wish to approach them in a spirit of proselytising, attracting them to Friends,[190] but rather to bring them

> a clear message concerning the work and place of the Holy Spirit, leaving them to the Lord for further guidance as to what branch of the Christian Church they shall settle into as their spiritual home.[191]

Nevertheless, the group no doubt must have hoped that they would find a haven with Friends. In an anonymous article, one of a series entitled, 'The Churches of Wales, Missions and Ministers No. 15: The Story of Quakerism,'[192] reference was made to Reich's mission, and that 'the ministry of the visiting

---

186. *WQM* M14, 24/25.4.1912.

187. *CPM*, M4, 3.8.1912.

188. SWMM, M17, 13.6.1912.

189. *WQM*, 'Report of Visits in South Wales,' n.d. Covers the period 2nd month to 4th month, 1912.

190. *The Christian*, 6.3.1913.

191. *WQM*, 'Report of Visits in South Wales,' n.d. Covers the period 2nd month to 4th month, 1912.

192. *South Wales Daily News* (*SWDN*), 10.10.1921.

Friends was much valued, but the ground did not appear to be ripe for establishing Friends' meetings for worship.'[193] The author was Hercules Phillips.[194]

The group visited and talked to Dan Roberts, Evan Roberts' brother; he was to stay within the Presbyterian fold but had felt drawn to Friends, and had corresponded with Southall. This may be behind the earlier reference to Southall having communicated with the Evangelistic Committee in December 1912. Roberts was pleased that Friends were interested in the plight of the scattered groups. Their discussions with the Congregationalist, Rev. Prof. Keri Evans of Carmarthen, a regular contributor to the Llandrindod Conventions, elicited expressions of satisfaction with what Reich had said in the town. Dan Roberts and Southall paid a visit together to Carmarthen sometime between May and July 1912, with efforts made to engage with known revivalists.[195]

The second set of visits came during the summer of 1912, and the committee was encouraged to maintain their efforts. At Tenby and Carmarthen groups were meeting regularly as Friends, and although no one as yet had applied 'for membership in our Religious Society,' they revealed their hopes by adding that, 'They and we are anxious to wait until the way is made quite plain if they are to take this step.'[196] At Waunllwyd one of their contacts had been Pastor T. M. Jeffreys, but not one of the two Jeffreys associated with Elim Church, who wrote warmly of the service offered by Friends.[197] By this time two leaflets had been translated into Welsh for enquirers, one being Max Reich's, 'Pardon, Purity and Peace.'[198]

In October 1912 the Quarterly Meeting decided to continue their efforts. Reich was again joined by Richard Beck, along with Alexander Dunlap of Cockermouth, Charles R. Gillett, with a minute of service from Worcester and Salop Monthly Meeting, and Herbert D. Headley. Dunlap apparently 'came into Wales on his own concern and with the approval of the South

193. Ibid.
194. *TF*, 21.10.1921, 698.
195. *WQM*, 'Report of visits amongst the Children of the Revival in South Wales,' 25.9.1912.
    Dates are deduced from comparing various texts.
196. Ibid.
197. Ibid.
198. 'Maddeuant, Purdeb a Heddwch,' Newport, J. E. Southall, 1912.

Wales united sub-committees'[199] and for part of the time conducted his own efforts before uniting with Reich and his companions. They were thankful for the kindly welcome they received, and 'when the nature of our work became known … they have wished us God speed' and were convinced that they were a

> means of bringing a steadying influence into the churches of Wales in this time of unrest which will be of much more permanent value to the cause of truth and righteousness than if we were to obtain a few additions to themembership of the Society of Friends.[200]

SWMM minuted that there had been some opposition to the messages and that 'there had been difficulties on the way,'[201] but was pleased that the group wished to persevere and that they wished to give the children of the revival 'the message which they believe Friends have to deliver.'[202]

WQM received a final report on the outreach work to the 'Children' in September 1913. It noted that Reich had again visited Wales for seventeen days in February with a twofold purpose, to visit some of the 'Children' and to assist meetings. This time he was accompanied by Charles E. Gillett, Herbert D. Headley and Richard Watkins. The report is descriptive, emphasising the welcome shown and Rachel Braithwaite's service, especially her contact with more isolated Quakers in west Wales.[203] The meeting reflected on what they had heard and noted that there was 'hunger among many seekers in Wales, including ministers of religion, for a truly spiritual religion,'[204] by which they obviously meant Quakerism. Interestingly, the HMEC had received and considered a report on the mission's endeavours in February 1913, listening to Reich, Braithwaite and Beck give accounts of

---

199. *WQM.* 'Further Report of Visits to Children of the Revival,' dated 10.11.1912. Difficult to identity the precise makeup of this committee, and may be reference to the joint HMEC and WQMEC.

200. Ibid.

201. SWMM, M22, 30.10.1912.

202. Ibid.

203. *WQM,* "Further Report of work amongst the 'Children of the Revival' and Friends in South Wales," 25.9.1913.

204. *TF*, 3.10.1913, 643.

activities still in progress. Rather patronisingly, their minute highlighted the ill-balanced fervour and fracture existing amongst groups, and the deplorable 'low standards in everyday life and conversation'[205] amongst professing Christians and office holders. They recognised that this had not been a proselytising campaign, but rather that Friends had sought to bring a steadying influence amongst the 'unstable and flighty.'

The furthest north that any of these visitors reached was Aberystwyth. The language of their meetings was English, although in Brynaman they found that people expressed themselves better in Welsh. What was the outcome? Seemingly little. *The Friend*, interpreting discussion at the February 1913 HMEC meeting, felt that what Friends had brought to the Welsh, presumably because it sensed unresolved turmoil within Welsh nonconformity, was a 'steadying influence and the emphasis upon reality in life which ... seem(s) to be needed by Wales just now;'[206] another somewhat paternalistic and patronising analysis, redolent of a belief in Quaker superiority.

One lesser outcome was the fact that the fledgling Pentecostalists Geoffrey and Stanley Jeffreys, who were preaching mainly in the Upper Swansea valley in what was described by one newspaper as 'another Welsh Revival,'[207] were invited in February 1913 to accompany John Owen Jenkins, of Penybont, to conduct revivalist meetings in Radnorshire.[208] Jenkins had visited and given service with the brothers in Cwmtwrch and had been impressed by their efforts, although when they had addressed the Quaker meeting at Penybont there was some criticism of their faith healing and speaking in tongues.[209]

WQM at its October 1913 gathering listened to Rachel Braithwaite share her experience of the work, her narrative convincing the meeting that there was much hunger among seekers in Wales, including ministers, 'for a truly spiritual religion,'[210] a hunger which obviously Friends should fill – they tried and failed.

205. HMEC, M6, 6.2.1913.
206. *TF*, 21.2.1913, 117.
207. *The Christian*, 5.3.1913
208. *TF*, 28.02.13, 139.
209. *RE*, 6.3.1913.
210. *TF*, 3.10.1913, 643.

The mission to the 'Children of the Revival' is unusual in that Friends, having had peripheral involvement in the revival, five years later felt that they had a particular offering to make what was in effect a 'schismatic' remnant of the original upheaval. The endeavour provides limited insight into an unexplored relationship between Friends and the growth of Pentecostalism, at least in Wales.

It was possibly the last important collective mission effort by the HMEC, whose focus was changing as it responded to different demands within the YM, changes that were not welcomed by everyone. When in 1918 the YM took to considering a revision of the Book of Discipline, a group of twenty-six, dominated by Friends from WQM, wrote that the proposed revisions would weaken the long-held theological position of the YM, and the well-considered statements drawn up over the years by 'properly authorised Friends,' reiterating the evangelic orientation of Friends in the Quarterly Meeting. They felt that 'Holy Scripture' was under attack, and stressing what for them was the core of their faith and the position of the YM:

> we believe that our redemption has been accomplished for us upon the Cross by our Lord Jesus Christ, who by the power of the Holy Spirit was born of the Virgin Mary, and was made an offering for sin.[211]

In May of the same year, by contrast, Horace Fleming reflected the demands of the change that was slowly taking place, asking for a new home mission campaign to evangelise and educate, with workers that

> appeal to the trade unionist on the one hand and to the teacher and public school man on the other … to help them qualify themselves for the playing of a larger part in the making of a new social order.[212]

In January 1914 *The Friend* welcomed the publication of a new periodical dedicated to national social progress in Wales. *The Welsh Outlook*, with its uplifting motto 'Where there is no vision the people perish,' was a fine

---

211. *TF*, 20.9.1918, 574. Amongst the 26 names were William J. Fearnside, Clara R. Fearnside, Caroline E. Gibbins, W. B. Gibbins, and Frederick Sessions.
212. *TF*, 3.5.1918, 277.

example of the blossoming of the 'nationalist' spirit and was commended to Friends, not only in Wales but also in the west of England.[213] This progressive development was complemented by the inauguration of the first Welsh Summer School on Social Service held at Llandrindod Wells, with which Friends were associated. Pope notes that some of those associated with the school, the first of its kind in Britain, realised that it marked the beginning of the end for the old Liberal Nonconformist hegemony.[214]

The periodical and the school of social services serve as signposts to the changing character of religion in Britain and in Wales. The needs of those such as the 'Children of the Revival' were marginal, as they ploughed their own furrows.

Conclusion

The revival was understood as a Welsh event having broad implications across Christendom. For many Quakers it was initially a sign of reawakening which, despite the hopes of some, did not impact significantly on their denomination. Later, and for some reason that is not entirely clear, they thought that they had a role amongst the embryonic Welsh Pentecostalists but inevitably, given LYMs gradual shift to a more liberal, less fundamentalist and less emotional understanding of religious expression, this was a forlorn hope which led to nothing.

According to one historian, what the Revival did was 'provide for countless men and women … new hope and comfort in the face of brutalising material conditions,'[215] Williams loosely suggesting that it was a watershed moment for popular religion.[216] It was an outpouring that brought much needed hope to the future of religion across Britain, a counterbalance to *fin de siècle* pessimism.[217] It was to be a disappointment. The recall to tradition was short lived and the Revival was unable to hold the allegiance of its converts, although the sentiment of religion persisted and Nonconformist traditions held their grip on even the most industrialised

---

213. *TF*, 16.1.1914, 44.
214. Pope, *Building Jerusalem*, 1998, 133–136.
215. Morgan, *Rebirth*, 1981, 135.
216. Williams, *When Was Wales*, 1985, 240.
217. Morgan, *Diwigiad Crefyddol*.

areas, such that 'workmen sang hymns in the Tonypandy riots in 1910.'[218] For those touched by Pentecostal fervour, it was a new beginning, as the Quakers realised.

Turner analyses, as important factors in the making of the Revival, the importance of social tensions, the natural disasters of the time such as the cholera outbreak in Aberdare, typhoid in Trealaw and the crash of the Paddington-Llanelli Express, all in 1904,[219] which encouraged the outpouring and media reports that accentuated the understanding people had of their effects and potential. In this sense Evan Roberts was as much a product of the media[220] as he was an instrument of the Holy Spirit. The moral lessons derived from the Revival were those of which Samuel Smiles would have been most proud, 'largely those of self-help.'[221] Jones questions whether the Revival was not the last attempt

> by ordinary Welshmen to make of religion what it had once been – popular, non-clerical, unlearned, unsophisticated, enthusiastic in the community and Welsh in language.[222]

If so, then Quaker expectations were partially fulfilled, reinforcing the optimism that they nourished about the possibilities for the Society from the Revival in Wales. As Newman expressed it in his address to the YM on the state of the Society, 'What we wanted to come to realise in our own meetings here in England was the very same power that was felt in the meetings in South Wales.'[223] He and his fellow Quakers would have seen the popular tendencies identified within the Revival, given their understanding of Welsh nonconformist traditions, as signs of Quaker renewal. This must be a partial explanation for the mission by Reich and others in 1912. Throughout it was

218. Carol Anne Dobbs, 'The Welsh Religious Revival of 1904', unpublished B.A dissertation, University of Birmingham, 1974, 48.
219. Turner, *Revivals* etc, 1979, 378.
220. Pope, *Codi Muriau*, 2005, 17.
221. Turner, *Revivals* etc, 1979, 383.
222. Ieuan Gwynedd Jones, 'Language and Community in Nineteenth Century Wales,' in *Mid-Victorian Wales: The Observers and the Observed*, 1992, 78.
223. *TF*, 2.6.1905, 350.

clear that 'when they saw how the power of the Lord was taking possession of these people it was clear that south Wales was preaching Quakerism to them.'[224] They were lulled into false expectations from direct witness, from media coverage, if not indeed because of their own smugness, influenced by what they perceived as the way Quaker contribution to the holiness movement had touched Wales.

If the Revival was the 'final flourish of piety and social conservatism,'[225] then this would have resonated with those in LYM adhering to an evangelic agenda. Reich's mission could then be conceived as one of the final expressions of evangelic fervour by the HMEC, and interestingly, to parts of Wales where they had not ventured previously.

For those such as John Edward Southall, concerned as he was for the future of Wales, the Revival must have been an event that could presage a rekindling of linguistic and national pride, whilst recovering those truths to which he remained loyal, outside the confines of LYM. He would have detected, as he did in his writings, that the Revival offered 'ministry as a gift from above ... dependent on divine openings,'[226] but was hesitant about its outward forms such as singing, looking upon them not 'as a part of Divine worship so much as a means of drawing the multitude.'[227] In that sense he did not identify totally with what was for many the joy of the Revival, confirming what some saw as the failure of Quakerism in Wales, that it had not been able to sublimate aspects of the *noson lawen*[228] into its proceedings as the Methodists had been able to do.[229] In that, the joylessness of Quakers was confirmed, as Dewi Mon had sought to demonstrate in a reply to an article by Southall.[230]

For many in LYM the Revival confirmed that in Wales things were

224. Ibid.
225. Tim Williams, 'Language, Culture, Religion,' in *Wales 1880–1914*, Trevor Herbert and Gareth Elwyn Jones eds., 1988, 82.
226. J. E. Southall, *Paid Ministry*, 1897, 2.
227. Ibid., 8.
228. 'Merry night' – an opportunity for people to gather to celebrate. Music was central, the Methodists adapting folk songs as hymn tunes.
229. Jones, 'John Kelsall', 1938, 133.
230. Dewi Môn. 'Paham nad wyf yn Grynwr' in *Y Genninen*, No 4, Vol XIX, October, 1901, 281–285.

different, bearing their own characteristics and behaviours. As an event it signified potential, an excitement, but the Quaker response was limited. It was restricted because they did not have the wherewithal to respond, and because of reluctance to be seen to be taking denominational advantage of an excitement where the will of the Holy Spirit was supreme.

Chapter 5
Three Quaker Men

The contribution that any organisation makes relies, in part, on the activities, pronouncements and presence of individuals within it. They will often be recognised as celebrities, public figures either much admired or loathed, whose contributions have an impact on those around them. The rest, the 'quiet' and unseen will ensure, through their less visible contributions, that the organisation functions effectively maintaining its role, witness and endeavours These 'quiet' contributors, in general, seek no publicity or recognition and will remain relatively unknown. The visibility of the organisation will rely on its public elite, those individuals whose influence touches the public sphere.

Light, examining local politics in small towns in Victorian Wales, highlights the importance of personalities in their locales, individuals who contribute to civic life and its well-being.[1] Her analysis is as relevant to the life of rural and county Wales. These are people whose national impact was not perhaps as visible or recognised, except as part of the collective. They were prominent individuals, wherever they were, who who had 'a decisive influence over a multitude and ... altered part of the stream of history.'[2] Similarly those who remained quiet and on the margins, except when they become fleetingly prominent, also contributed to the culture and 'history of everyday life' reflecting conditions, interests as experienced by the ordinary people, providing a human face to the events around them. Neglected figures, but not mundane, who supplement the broader social contexts of which they were part[3] but then brushed aside by time and the historians pen. History is then a 'multifaceted flow with many individual centres'

1. Julie Light, '...mere seekers of fame'?.., 2005, 88–99.
2. Dom David Knowles, 'The Historian and Character' in *The Historian and Character and other Essays*,1963, 15.
3. See Georg G. Iggers, *Historiography in the Twentieth Century: From Scientific Objectivity to the Postmodern Challenge*, 1997, Chp., 9.

where people live and 'establish their identities apart from the larger, traditional, national wholes'[4] carrying on with their lives without particular reference to any leaders. They are nevertheless caught within the currents of social transformation over which they have little control. Here leadership, authority and power complement each other but their impact is not necessarily computable, and will be affected by the contributions of individuals and the many, 'not as a negation of history of broader social contexts but as supplement to it.'[5] Ginzburg defines it thus:

> In a modest individual who is himself lacking in significance and for this very reason representative, it is still possible to trace, as in a microcosm, the characteristics of an entire social stratum in a specific historical period.[6]

No Quakers in Wales during the Victorian and Edwardian periods achieved any real public prominence or notoriety. Their voices were overall generally subdued or hidden. F. W. Gibbins, Neath, as noted, was peripherally involved as a Member of Parliament but only for a few months, but making a contribution to the alleviation of social conditions in Wales, vice-President and treasurer for many years to the Welsh National Memorial Fund, which campaigned to eradicate and treat tuberculosis.[7] His work as a prominent industrialist in the tin-plate industry remained his principal legacy although sadly overlooked by Milligan.[8]

Samuel G. Hobson was briefly connected with Cardiff after his father moved there in 1885, but in 1887 as 'a youth of 17, I mounted a chair at a street corner in Cardiff and gave ingenuous and halting support to the Socialist faith.'[9] In 1891, still living in Cardiff, his Quaker orthodoxy was clear, 'It may ... interest your readers to know that the Quakers are again making headway; indeed they seem inspired with the old evangelical spirit

4. Ibid., 8.

5. Ibid., 117.

6. Carlo Ginzburg, *The Cheese and the Worms: The Cosmos of a Sixteenth Century Miller*, 1992, xx.

7. Pyrs Gruffydd, 'A Crusade against Consumption: environment, health and social reform in Wales, 1900–1939,' in *Journal of Historical Geography*, 21, 1995, 39–54.

8. Edward H. Milligan, *The Biographical Dictionary of British Quakers in Commerce and Industry 1775–1920*, 2007.

9. S.G. Hobson, *Functional Socialism*, 1936, 13.

of two centuries ago,'[10] but his adherence to socialism was to prove much stronger. He remained a Friend until about 1900, remaining attached to some Quaker principles, being 'a vague pantheist touched by mysticism, [his] belief in spiritual evolution was a foundation of his political thought.'[11] Recognised as the father of guild socialism his influence was to be overshadowed by the endeavours of those such as G.D.H. Cole, and he never achieved any prominence politically. Indeed he had a somewhat chequered career with a reputation for financial recklessness.[12] He was not visible in Welsh public life but served as personal secretary to Keir Hardie, and from 1892–4 was chairman of the small Independent Labour Party in Wales.

The lives of three Quakers touched upon in the preceding chapters are now examined in greater detail. Their contribution to Welsh life cannot be overlooked; it was substantial but is now inevitably sidelined by the ebb of historical significance, both denominationally and nationally. They are worthy of closer examination. It is sad that there are no women to be included alongside them. As O'Donnell argues, Quaker women were largely conservative during the nineteenth century[13] and in Wales not particularly visible or their exploits well documented. Emma Bishop worked briefly in Cardiff for the HMC and Caroline Gibbins would have been well known in Neath, but neither can be observed to have served the wider society, being confined largely to their neighbourhoods. The names of no other Quaker women impact when reading primary material, but it is often forgotten that women were not allowed to serve on Meeting for Sufferings until 1896, and the first united Yearly Meeting of men and women did not meet until 1909.

Henry Tobit Evans (1844–1908)

The preceding sections have highlighted that Friends were not embedded in the politics of Wales. Reading relevant articles in *The Friend* Welsh issues were only seemingly for the Welsh, which Friends could look at with

10. *WM*, 21.1.1891.
11. Joseph O. Baylen and Norbert J. Gossman, eds., *Biographical Dictionary of Modern British Radicals*, Vol 3, 1870–1914, A–K, 1988, 444.
12. Margaret Cole, *The Life of G.D.H. Cole*, 1971, 103.
13. Elizabeth A. O'Donnell, 'Woman's Rights and Woman's Duties: Quaker Women in the Nineteenth Century, with Special Reference to Newcastle Monthly Meeting of Women Friends,' unpublished PhD thesis, University of Sunderland, 1999.

supportive detachment. The numbers of Welsh Quakers involved in politics were few. One exception was Henry Tobit Evans who fits in well with Light's analysis of Victorian and Edwardian politicians, a newsworthy celebrity, whose 'activities [were] discussed both in the pages of local newspapers, and through local gossip.'[14]

Some might argue that he was a curiosity given his background, his progression in public life, and his membership of the Religious Society of Friends. Morgan describes him as 'a lone wolf.'[15] By nature he was probably something of a rebel, his transformation from Radical Liberal to Liberal Unionist reflecting this. In this change of allegiance he might have been influenced, through and because of his Quaker connections. Similarly his membership of the society, and his apparent use of plain speech, at least in English, adds to a portrait of him as a person who challenged convention, 'An able, determined man (who) could not be turned from the path that he considered to be the right one.'[16] The fact that he joined a Society in an area which had had no Quaker presence since the 1780s, to be a lonely representative, demonstrates a person with a resolute streak of independence within him.

Tobit was born in 1844 at Fronfelen Ganol, Penybryn, Ceredigion, the second son of four children to David and Elinor Evans. His father was described as a poor smallholder/farmer and a Congregationalist. As a child he was taught the rudiments of Welsh grammar by the local blacksmith, 'Evans y Gof,'.[17] He had apparently a thirst for knowledge, becoming later in life something of an expert on the use of Welsh in place names. He took an interest in all matters Celtic, studying the Cornish language, corresponding with F.W.P. Jago, the Cornish antiquarian and lexicographer,[18] visiting and writing about Cornwall, publishing in 1901 his 'Holiday Rambles in Cornwall' which were translations from the Welsh of articles

---

14. Light, '... mere seekers of fame,'?... 2005, 92.
15. Morgan, 'The Liberal Unionists in Wales,' in *Modern Wales*, 1995, 40.
16. D.J. Davies, *Hanes Hynafiaethau ac Achyddiaeth Llanarth, Henfynyw, Llanllwchaiarn a Llandyssilio Gogo*, 1930, 2nd ed., 109. ('*Dyn galluog, ... penderfynol oedd, ac nis gellid ei droi oddiar y llwybr a farnai ef oedd y llwybr iawn.*').
17. Taken from an unpublished handwritten manuscript at Ceredigion Library Service (CLS), at the Aberystwyth branch, catalogue reference C82.
18. NLW, MS 18618C, letter 6.1.1901.

originally written for his newspaper. Similarly, he was to visit the Isle of Man in pursuit of his interests.[19]

At the age of 14 was apprenticed to a grocer in Brynmawr.[20] In 1866 he may have still been in south Wales, since he won a prize for his strict metre poetry at the Hirwaen Cymmrodorion Eisteddfod in that year.[21] According to one obituary he eventually moved to Liverpool to follow a career in commerce,[22] although in 1865 by his own testimony he was living in Oswestry.[23] In 1870 he became a student at the Bangor Normal College, leaving in 1871,[24] returning to his home county as principal teacher at the British School at Llechryd in the Teifi valley. The school log book for February 12th 1872 records that he took charge of the school on that day, and 'examined most of the classes in Reading and Arithmetic; found the children backward in both subjects.'[25] The inspector's annual report for that year noted that the school was under fair discipline, and that in 1873 Evans had received his teaching certificate.

During his time at the school he become embroiled in what the *Western Mail* described as a 'Political Scandal,' when names were illegally added to the Llechryd rate-book in order to promote the interests of Nonconformity.[26] He had already come to the attention of the same paper in 1870 for his political views, being dismissed as someone of whom, 'We have never heard … nor do we wish to hear of him again.'[27]

By 1878 the school had 59 pupils, and he stayed there until September of that year, when he then married a young widow from London, Elizabeth Thomas, originally from Llanrhaeadr, Montgomeryshire, whose first husband had apparently been a prominent and well-to-do London-Welsh Baptist. Through marriage he acquired a stepson, and there were to be two daughters from the union. As a headmaster he would not be well paid, and

19. NLW, MS 18114C, letter A. Moore, *Woodbourne House*, Douglas, 6.7.1897.

20. CLS, C82.

21. *YFAC*, 13.1.1866.

22. *YFAC*, 20.05.1908.

23. *Royal Commission on Land in Wales and Monmouthshire: Minutes of Evidence*, 1895, Cmd. 7661, Vol. III, 46,598, p 562. (RCLW)

24. E-mail communication with Archivist, University of Wales, Bangor, 25.7.2006.

25. Ceredigion Archives (CA), 63a. Log Book, Llechryd British School.

26. *WM* 29.8.1874.

27. *WM* 1.2.1870.

the assumption is that his new wife, as a young widow, was financially well endowed, such that he could give up his teaching, move to Aberystwyth to work as a journalist, and then take up farming and publishing. In 1880 the family moved to live and farm at Llanarth, to the south of Aberaeron, until 1904 when he moved to a new house that he built for himself at Sarnau, thus staying in south Ceredigion until his death in 1908.

Tobit was brought up a Congregationalist, but his maternal grandmother, a strict Calvinistic Methodist, had greatly influenced him.[28] He had however been convinced by the theology of the Quakers having read Robert Barclay,[29] and applied for membership amongst them whilst living in London, before and after his marriage, applying to Westminster and Longford Monthly Meeting in March 1879. In his letter of application he explained that he had been a regular attender at Westminster Meeting for the previous two months, and before that for two months at Devonshire House. He outlined that he had

> been a member with the Independents ... for nearly twenty years but during the last year or two have felt a great desire to join the Society of Friends. In that part of Wales ... where I resided this was impossible but as soon as I came to London (four months ago) I determined to do so.[30]

There was however some haste, as he was about to leave London in twelve to fourteen days. He apologised that he had not written earlier; this was because of his wife's illness. Two Friends were appointed to visit him, one of whom was Joseph Bevan Braithwaite, probably the most prominent evangelic in LYM at that time. On April 17th the Monthly Meeting considered their report, which concluded that he 'was one who had largely adopted the views of our Society.'[31] The Monthly Meeting was exercised by the fact that he would be isolated from them in his home area, and asked that his visitors keep in touch with him, to report back at a later time when they felt ready concerning a final decision. One of the visitors corresponded with him, and also with Josiah Newman of Leominster who had been

28. NLW, MS 3191C III, Daniel Davies, Ton Pentre, Letters, 287i, 14.2.1902.
29. Ibid. letter 7.7.1902.
30. LSF, Westminster and Longford Monthly Meeting (WLMM) Minute Book, M11, 13.3.1879.
31. WLMM, M6, 17.4.1879.

staying at Aberystwyth, and who visited Tobit and was supportive of his case.

In September 1879 the Monthly Meeting approved his membership, noting that he 'was one who has been through living faith brought to the saving knowledge of the Lord Jesus Christ; and to the full conviction of the Christian Truth which distinguish our religious Society'[32] but transferred him into the care of HRMM. There is no minute of transfer recorded by them, and he was assigned to Pales Meeting, then the nearest meeting to Aberystwyth, and he was still listed under the Pales for 1897 even though by then there was a meeting at Aberystwyth.[33]

The Quaker meeting in Ceredigion was established in 1894, but it is unlikely that he was ever a frequent attender since he lived a fair distance from the town. Interested in Welsh Quaker history Tobit had seemingly hoped to write their history.[34] Attendance at his Monthly Meeting or Yearly Meeting was not part of his routine, and it is doubtful that he frequented regularly, if at all, and so survived as a fairly lonely Quaker on the Western reaches of his Monthly Meeting.

Following acceptance into membership he indicated that he had cut off contact with the Congregationalists, 'the most difficult task that he ever undertook'[35] drawing opprobrium upon himself: 'I am an old tomcat in the eyes of the Congregationalists.'[36] Interestingly, having transferred his denominational allegiance he continued to be involved in the controversy surrounding the future of the Congregational College at Bala, which raged from 1879 until 1892 and split the denomination.[37] He was still involved in the argument in February 1880, when he was attacked as an 'agitator' ('terfysgwr') by a supporter of the camp which wanted to move the college from Bala, and who rightly accused him of double standards because of his changed denominational affiliation:

32. WLMM, M5, 18.9.1879.
33. HRO, BG 63/1, 'WQM, List of Members 1897.'
34. *Carmarthen Journal*, 22.5.1908.
35. NLW, MS 3191C III, Daniel Davies, Ton, Letters, 287i, 7.7.1902. ('... *y gwaith caletaf a wnaethum erioed.*').
36. Ibid. *YFAC*, 11.2.1880.
37. See *YFAC*, 23.7.1879.

Does he not claim to be a Quaker? This sect does not believe in the 'ministry,' or the 'sacraments.' That is why probably Tobit writes so scathingly about Congregational ministers. But if he is a Quaker, who rejects the necessity for a ministry, why is he concerned with issues of governance of an institution created to educate men for the people? [38]

Despite this, in April 1882, he still presented a notice of motion at a meeting of the general committee of the College in Bala regarding the future of the college.[39]

One of his obituaries notes that 'a quarter of a century ago he was an extreme radical.'[40] His activities at Llechryd reflected this, as did his connection with Michael D. Jones, the leading Welsh political nationalist of the time, who was to inspire the establishment of the Welsh colony in Patagonia. Jones was also the principal of the Congregationalist College at Bala, and this explains why Tobit fervently immersed himself in that controversy, supporting Jones remaining as Principal of the College at Bala.

His admiration of Michael D. Jones, and his radical position, is reflected in the fact that in 1879 he was for a time joint secretary of Jones' 'Testimonial Committee,' and writing to another distinguished nationalist, pacifist and Congregational minister, Samuel Roberts, (commonly known as 'SR') was hopeful that they could raise £300 in Wales for the testimonial, especially since they had received £30 from the friends of the Welsh settlement in Patagonia.[41] Even after he had abandoned the Liberal Gladstonian cause, his admiration for Jones never waned, describing Jones as, 'a giant of a Welshman and a proper Christian.'[42]

He maintained close connection with 'SR' who advised him about his ventures as a publisher, telling him to be careful given his own experiences

---

38. *YFAC*, 11.2.1880. (*'Onid a'r Crynwyr yr hona ef berthynas? Nid yw yr enwad hwnw yn credu yn y 'weinidogaeth,' na'r 'sacramentau.' Dyna yr achos, mae'n debyg, yr ysgrifenna Tobit mor ddirmygus am weinidogion yr Annibynnwyr. Ond os Quaker yw, yn gwadu yr angenrheidrwydd am y weinidogaeth, beth sydd a fyno efe a llywodraethiad sefydliad i addysgu dynion gogyfer y werin?'*).
39. *WM*, 12.4.1882.
40. *WG*, Obituary, 14.5.1908.
41. NLW, MS 9511D, SR and JR, Letter 1881.
42. NLW, Papers of O.M. Edwards, AG 1/12, 84, letter 27.8.1887. (*'Cawr o Gymro a hên Gristion cywir'*).

which had proved costly 'because of carelessness and lack of experience.'[43] He was to attend SRs funeral in 1885.[44]

Tobit's radicalism becomes more apparent when in October 1878 he corresponded with Charles S. Parnell, the Irish Nationalist leader, who writing back to him was anxious that they should meet as soon as possible to discuss their common interests. Parnell gave the address in London at which he would be soon staying, in the hope that Tobit might be able to visit.[45] In that year the Irish Land League had been founded with Parnell as its President, and Evans had written articles for *Y Faner* about the evictions that had occurred in Wales following the 1859 and 1868 elections, entitled 'The Political Martyrs of Cardiganshire.'[46] He identified with the League's ambitions of fair rent, fixed tenure and free sale of land, seeking the establishment of a Welsh equivalent. It is unclear whether they met but a newspaper report several years later noted that 'Mr Tobit Evans was at one time such an extreme Home Ruler that Mr Parnell was reported to have offered him a seat in Parliament as one of his personal adherents,'[47] indicating that they did perhaps meet.

In August 1882, Tobit was at Sarnau, Ceredigion, explaining to a meeting of farmers, the objectives of the League, supporting the establishment of a similar organisation in the county.[48] In February 1886, he was expected to chair a public meeting in Blaenau Ffestiniog addressed by Michael Davitt, founder of the Irish Land League, as part of what was a national tour across Britain, but pulled out because of personal and family illness.[49] This was undoubtedly an excuse since by then he was supporting the Unionist candidate[50] in Cardiganshire and Davitt was to address Liberal election meetings at Lampeter and Aberystwyth, and advocating Irish Home Rule.[51]

Nevertheless, Tobit continued to support land reform and to protest against the unfair treatment of tenant farmers, highlighted by the fact that

43. NLW Papers 18618C.
44. *YFAC*, 3.10.1885
45. NLW, MS 18114C, Letter 16.10.1878.
46. *WG*, 14,5,1908.
47. *WM*, 19.12.1891.
48. *YFAC*, 9.8.1882.
49. *YFAC*, 17.2.1886.
50. Morgan, 'Cardiganshire Politics, the Liberal,'1967, 325.
51. *Daily News*, 6.2.1886 report of meetings in London.

he gave evidence four times to the Welsh Land Commission in 1894. In 1893 he explained that he had been part of a local effort to collect evidence amongst farmers concerning their grievances, and appeared for the first time[52] before the commission giving evidence on his own behalf and on behalf of John Morgan, an elderly and profoundly deaf monoglot who accompanied him, but who did not give direct evidence, and with whom communication was difficult. Morgan's complaint was that having been a tenant to the Liberal politician Lord Carrington, (chairman of the commission, but not on the day evidence was given), he had not been compensated when he gave up his tenancy for improvements worth £200 he had made to the mill. Despite approaches to the land agent nothing had happened and as a result his health was affected, and he and his wife were now paupers dependent on the Parish. Highlighting the insecurity that existed amongst farmers Tobit argued for compensation to tenants for 'unexhausted improvements.'[53] Reading the evidence there was a sub-text that he was thought to be attacking the chairman for his politics, highlighted by disputation over the evidence he presented as to whether Morgan had spent the £200 or not. The implication was that Tobit was happy to pursue the case because of his Liberal Unionist affiliation. Indeed, *Y Faner* commented that his appearance before the Commission was not something of which he should be proud.[54] The fact that one commissioner who was present, Frederic Seebohm, was a Quaker and Liberal Unionist was of no assistance.

The Commission felt that further evidence was needed and so Tobit promised to pursue this. The next day he reappeared before them at Tregaron, explaining that the receipt for £200, on which the evidence was based, was in fact a copy. He was challenged that he had misled the commission because the incident on compensation was not the great scandal in the area that he claimed.[55] He therefore reappeared for the third time at Aberystwyth, where he was again unable to prove the expenditure. The chairman then accused him of having 'brought a very serious charge against the Chairman of this Commission, and you have not tred to substantiate the

52. RCLW, Vol. III, para.45, 580 at Lampeter 25.4.1894.
53. RCLW, Vol. III, para.45,615, 518.
54. YFAC, 2.5.1894. ('... *ddim yn rhywbeth iddo ymfalchio ynddo.*').
55. RCLW, Vol. III, para.46,598, 562.

case at all.'[56] He refuted the charge, stating that it was for Carrington to challenge the evidence; he had relied on his witness.

Tobit reappeared before the commission again in October 1894, at Carmarthen, where three commissioners who had heard his original testimony were present. He had been tenacious in his support of Morgan's case, but then his own probity was being questioned. He now wished to substantiate what he had previously told the commission, relying on the evidence of two local men. There was some disputation as to whether the commission could hear him, since he had failed, to appear before them when they had met at Machynlleth, despite being invited. The nature of that invitation was argued over, but eventually he 'was to be called as a matter of courtesy.'[57] Perhaps this is a sign that he was no minor figure whose pronouncements were to be simply ignored. His tenacity is another sign that he remained attached to his radical roots despite the political sensitivities.

During his time in London he had come into contact with John Bright. In the *Yr Undebwr Cymreig*, 'The Welsh Unionist', a monthly which he published and printed beginning January 1890 from his home in Llanarth, and which ran into twelve issues, he referred to the fact that he had had the privilege of co-sitting and co-worshipping with Bright at Westminster Meeting House, St Martin's Lane, several times, and had listened to Bright speaking at the House of Commons in 1878.[58] His connection with Bright was not in any way personal. Bright, writing to him in May 1887, responding to a request for a copy of his speech to the Commons on Home Rule in July 1886, addressed Evans as 'Dear Sir' an unusual appellation from a fellow Quaker: probably Bright was unaware of Evans' adherence. He was told curtly to look at a book on the subject and that the speech was printed in *The Times*.[59] This general connection and admiration for Bright possibly proved to be crucial as to why Evans turned to the Liberal-Unionist cause, and remained loyal to it. His admiration for Bright is apparent from his praise of him.

---

56. RCLW, Vol. III, para.48,674, 691.
57. RCLW, Vol. V, para.73,854, 115.
58. *Yr Undebwr Cymreig*, (*YUC*) No. 1, January 1890.
59. NLW, MS 18114C, letter 5.5.1887.

Fairness, justice and conscience led him at all times, and neither the smiles of his fellow ministers and their leaders, nor the acclamation and praise of the people and journalists affected him … [his] untainted personality, his obvious talents, his pure language, his enchanting voice, his grave seriousness … all had an impact on those who listened to him.[60]

Bright was esteemed and almost idolised by his co-religionists, as 'the great exemplar of a Christian politician.'[61] His example would have been an important influence on Evans as he followed Bright away from his own political roots, and also into Bright's denomination.[62] In 1886, Bright had made clear his objections to Irish Home Rule,

> to hand over a million and a half of Protestant and loyal people of the north of Ireland tothe tender mercies of the ruffians and rebels who sat opposite us in the late Parliament is more than I can consent to.[63]

Bright had an almost pathological hatred of Parnell, did not trust him, and regarded him and his party as nothing more than scoundrels and ruffians.[64] These were the themes that underpinned much of Evans' efforts and journalism in the Liberal Unionist cause.

Bright had fully supported disestablishment in Ireland largely because he could see that the position of the Church there was untenable, adding to the Irish sense of injustice. Many in Wales, with Liberal Unionist sympathies and retaining their radical sentiments, were confronted by a paradox. They were now allied with the Tories but were placed in an awkward position with regard to Welsh disestablishment, which they supported. The element of dissonance that this must have generated would no doubt have been

60. *YUC*, January 1890. ('… *taws, cyfiawnder a chydwybod oeddynt yn ei arwain ef bob amser, ac nid oedd gwenau ei gydweinidogion a'r phendefigion, na bloddest a moliant y bobl a'r newyddiaduron yn effeithio dim arno … [ei] gymeriad dilychwin, ei dalentau disglaer, ei iaith bur, ei lais swynol, ei ddifrifoldeb dwys … yn cael dylanwad mawr ar* bawb a'i gwrandawant').
61. J. Travis Mills, *John Bright and the Quakers* (London, Methuen and Co., 1935), 40.
62. Searle, *The Liberal Party*, 1992, 16, sees Joseph Chamberlain and Lloyd George as 'lineal descendents' of John Bright, a description for Chamberlain with which Evans would have agreed.
63. Quoted in Keith Robbins, *John Bright*, 1979, 256.
64. Ausubel, *John Bright*, 1966, 236 & 227

significant, but unspoken. On Welsh disestablishment Bright was silent, refusing to advocate an attack on the Church of England, 'believing that the Church itself must wish for disestablishment before it was undertaken.'[65] This was not a position most in LYM could have countenanced, but Bright was never a prominent religious radical and did not give a lead to political nonconformity.

Sturgis is of the opinion that Bright's stand against Home Rule was consistent with his entire political career; Ireland should be content with her connection with Britain; Scotland was the example to follow. There was a need for resolute government, and as a Quaker and free trader this left him ill-equipped to comprehend and understand the forces of nationalism. Bright regarded 'boundaries as political and economic conveniences, not demarcations of sentiment.'[66]

Tobit supported such views but many of his endeavours also point towards a sympathetic and emotional understanding of his own Welshness and national identity – one obituary proclaiming he was a 'Welshman of Sterling Patriotism'[67] referring not only to his support of all matters Welsh, but also to his allegiance to the crown. He was a fervent cultural nationalist but within the confines of his Britishness.

Bebbington highlights that the majority of Nonconformists continued to support Gladstone, and those who did not fell into one of four camps: those who followed Chamberlain in the cause of British patriotism and against Home Rule for Ireland; those who were fearful of breaches in Liberal principles such as Bright; those fearful of Catholicism, such as the Rev. C. H. Spurgeon, and finally, those who wished to relinquish their radicalism – 'the social conservatives.'[68] Evans' writings touched upon all four. He and Thomas Gee had much in common. Gee described Irish Home Rule as, 'Home Rule as Rome Rule.'[69] Yet Gee remained loyal to Gladstone even though he was supporting Cornwallis-West,[70] the M.P. elected for the Liberal

---

65. J.P. Parry, *Democracy and Religion: Gladstone and the Liberal Party, 1867–1875*, 1986, 227.

66. James L. Sturgis, *John Bright and the Empire*, 1969, 186.

67. *WM*, 12.5.1908.

68. Bebbington, *The Nonconformist*, 1982, Ch 5, 84–105.

69. Morgan, *Modern Wales*, 1995, 37.

70. Morgan, *Wales in British*, 1991, 71.

Unionists in West Denbighshire in the 1886 election. Gee originally supported Chamberlain, possibly because his paper's circulation was falling, but by
July 1886 this had changed and the older allegiance rekindled.[71]

Prior to the 1886 election the *Cambrian News*, strongly Gladstonian, was
already critical of Tobit, despite his prominence in the County Liberal
Association.[72] He was elected as a Liberal to the Llanarth School Board in
1883.[73] By 1884 he was a justice of the peace for the county,[74] reflecting his
obvious standing within the Liberal establishment on a bench dominated by
the gentry and Anglicans.

The criticism stemmed from a little-reported event in Welsh political life,
but one reflective of Tobits' sentiment and loyalty. In October 1885 Michael
D. Jones wrote to him and others, asking his opinion about forming a society
to promote

> understanding, union and co-operation throughout the Principality, and in
> Parliament, in the choice and support of representatives of the people in the
> House of Commons to ensure measures for Wales from the hand of the British
> government in relation to the following which from time to time are of
> concern ...[75]

listing such matters as land law, local government, disestablishment and
disendownment of the Church, the language in elementary schools,
Intermediate and Higher Education, and the appointment of the native
Welsh to posts in Wales, causes dear to Welsh radicals.

In January 1886 the *Cambrian News* sharply attacked Tobit because he had
been organising a society in Ceredigion in response, as he said, to the
invitation from Michael D. Jones.[76] In December 1885 he arranged a public

---

71. Jones, 'Rhyfel' in *Radicaliaeth*, 1975, 95.
72. *YFAC*, 13.11.1880.
73. *YFAC*, 27.6.1883.
74. *YFAC*, 9.7.1884.
75. NLW, MS 18438B, Letter dated 17.10.1885. (*'sefydlu cyd-ddealltwriaeth, undeb a
    chydweithrediad drwy y Dywysogaeth, ac yn y Senedd, mewn dewis a chynorthwyo
    cynrychiolwyr i Gymru yn Nhy y Bobl i hawlio sylw a mesurau i Gymru o ddiau llaw y
    llywodraeth Brydeinig mewn cysylltiad a materion canlynol ac eraill a fyddont o dro i dro
    yn galw am y cyfryw.'*)
76. *YFAC*, 30.12.1885.

meeting in Aberystwyth to promote what the paper described as an 'Alleged Welsh Political Union,'[77] or 'Bogus Political Union'[78] as they later labelled it. Evans' intention, as he said, was 'to form a Welsh Political Union'[79] but not a new political party. Jones in his communication used the word *cynghrair* to be translated as 'league' or 'union', reflective of such pressure groups as the former National Reform Union of 1864, or the Land Leagues. The newspaper gave no description of what was said at the December meeting, only that it was poorly supported. Its ire towards Evans was clear, claiming he was insignificant, of trifling influence

> we admit that he might under some extraordinary circumstances which do not now exist, be chosen to represent the discontented farmers of Wales. We need not on this occasion set forth the attributes of a popular leader, but everybody who knows Mr Tobit Evans will admit that he not only does not possess these, but could not readily acquire them.[80]

Tobit defended himself, describing the newspaper as a 'pro-English private pamphlet.'[81] Behind the invective, there was an element of personal professional jealousy, being an attack on John Gibson, the Lancastrian monoglot English editor of the paper, commenting sarcastically, that in order to qualify for the office of leader you would have to be 'a monoglot Englishman unacquainted with the habits and customs of the Welsh people.'[82]

At the end of December a meeting was held in Llanon to the south of Aberystwyth, under the chairmanship of the vicar, to consider the establishment a branch of the 'Welsh Party' with the intention of inviting Evans to address their next meeting.[83] Several such meetings were arranged across the south of Ceredigion and north Pembrokeshire. On January 12th at Troedyraur it was reported that Tobit felt there was a strong need for a Welsh political society similar to the Irish parliamentary grouping.[84] On the

77. *CN*, 8.1.1886.
78. *CN*, 22.1.1886.
79. *CN*, letter 15.1.1886.
80. *CN*, Editorial 8.1.1886
81. *CN*, Letter 15.1.1886.
82. ditto.
83. *YFAC*, 2.1.1886.
84. *YFAC* 20.1.1886.

thirteenth at a meeting at Tan y Groes,[85] he emphasised the need for unity amongst the Welsh, the need for education through the medium of Welsh and the right of the Welsh as a nation for specific laws. By mid-February, he was writing strongly to defend the 'Union.' It was intended to counter the fact that too many societies in Wales were English, working to an English agenda and spirit 'forced on the Welsh speaking people to Anglicise them.'[86] He suggested that the Welsh were by nature warm, loving, tending towards the religious, whilst the English were cold, without feeling, commercial, and looked at everything in the light of the pound, and that this was their religion. For this reason he rejected any dependency on the English dominated towns of Wales:

> I believe that it is in Welsh Wales that we should develop any national Welsh movement; because the traditions, needs, language and feelings of the Welsh-speaking Welsh, are totally different to the English speaking Welsh. [87]

He listed six specific objectives for the new movement, as agreed at the Aberystwyth meeting. His broader political 'nationalist' viewpoint would have adhered to Michael D. Jones' views: not arguing for political independence, but calling for a Welsh parliament, envisaging a federal model similar to 'the different States of America.'[88]

Jones' efforts for a national body were to be largely stillborn, his biographer noting that, despite this, the effort proved 'an inspiration to the formation of a Liberal Union in the principality, and the Welsh Party in parliament.'[89]

Tobit's embryonic movement did not flourish and disappeared as suddenly as it appeared, as the 1886 election and the broader Unionist/Liberal divisions engulfed it, and also, possibly, because of the parallel efforts to establish the Welsh Land League. The evaluation of one disgruntled cynical attendee at one of the meetings, provides insight into local and

85. *YFAC*, 27.1.1886.
86. YFAC, 17.2.1886 ('... *gweithio yn ol cynlluniau Seisnig, ac mewn ysbryd Saesneg, a cheisir eu gwthio ar Gymry Cymreig er mwyn eu Seisnegeiddio.*').
87. Ibid.
88. Jones, E. *Pan. Oes a Gwaith y Prif Athraw y Parch Michael Daniel Jones*, 1903, 240.
89. Ibid., 261. ('... *symbyliad mawr i ffurfio y Cynghrair Rhyddfrydig yn y Dywysogaeth, a'r Blaid Gymreig yn y Senedd.*').

partisan reactions to the endeavour; Tobit had merely talked

> about his own life, what he had done and is doing, his advent as ex-officio to the Board of Guardian at Aberayron, his unparalleled condescension by sitting among the illiterate farmer guardians ... and not in the circle of his own equals.[90]

The county Liberal establishment, no doubt anxious, would be helped by such criticism.

The parliamentary election of 1886 was the turning point for Tobit politically. His disgruntlement about Irish Home Rule was solidified as he gave his support to David Davies, Llandinam, who had been M.P. for the disbanded Cardigan Boroughs, and now stood for the new county seat, opposing Home Rule. Davies must have vacillated about standing for the Liberals and efforts for him to do so were thwarted, when in June 1886 only Evans and two others supported his candidature. Tobit was obviously keen for Davies to stand and in January had written to Edward Davies, Davies's son, urging that his father should not resign his candidature, but that caution was necessary as to what the older Davies wrote. He said that he would use the forthcoming meetings of the 'Welsh Political Union' to put down any opposition to David Davies.[91] Tobit's support saw him acting as the organiser in the Aberaeron area for Davies, who lost by nine votes to the Gladstonian Liberal, Bowen Rowlands. Davies' defeat embittered him of politics, and writing to Evans in January 1890, Davies pointedly said that he 'would give no more money for political purposes ... on this I will keep my word,'[92] suggesting that they had had prior discussion on the topic. Morgan suggests that Davies harboured ill-feeling towards Evans, that he was an, 'arch traitor' and friend to many foes,[93] basing this judgement on several letters from D.J. Jones, The Priory, Lampeter, during and following the election, who cast doubt on Tobit's integrity. These letters are tinged with elements of personal animosity:

---

90. *CN*, letter 'Still Born Political Union' 5. 2.1886.
91. NLW, Llandinam Papers, 301, letter 29.1.1886
92. NLW, MS 1882B, letter 21.1.1890, from David Davies, Llandinam.
93. Morgan, *Modern Wales*, 1995, 40.

Believe me that the fact of Tobit having been allowed to play such a prominent part of your father's side did not do any good to him. Several went against him to spite Tobit. This is an undeniable fact. He has more personal enemies in this county than any man living here. He is a dangerous man. He cares not what he does or says.[94]

This harshness probably arose from the efforts to establish the 'Welsh Political Union.' Tobit's rabid anti-Toryism, evident in the earlier 1885 election, would not save him when he had commented on one area of the county which was 'rotten – nearly half of the people are pronounced Tories.'[95]

The 1886 election was a disappointment to the Welsh Liberal Unionists because twenty five Liberals were returned compared to their two candidates. Tobit's political trajectory had, however, been settled, as he entered into correspondence with Joseph Chamberlain. Chamberlain was anxious to retain Welsh support for his programme, 'strongly radical and nonconformist,' hoping that the people of Wales would see 'that their interest does not lie in establishing a separate Irish parliament.'[96] At this juncture Tobit sought Chamberlain's support and finance for a paper in Welsh to advertise their cause. Chamberlain endorsed such a venture but as for funding Tobit was encouraged to write to the Liberal Unionist Committee in London.[97]

It was three years later in January 1889 that Tobit launched his monthly, *Yr Undebwr Cymreig*. Publication ceased in December, and it is unclear whether or not he received any financial backing from London. One political adversary commented that Tobit and another had been authorised to travel up to London by the Ceredigion Unionists to seek funds,[98] this was denied.[99] By the time of its demise Tobit felt that the paper's objectives had been realised, especially since Parnell's extra-marital affair, made public in December 1889, had killed his career and with it the aims of the Irish nationalists.[100]

---

94. NLW, Llandinam Papers, 302, letter 22.8.1886 to Edward Davies.)
95. NLW MS 19463B, 31, letter to H. C. Fryer,
96. NLW, MS 1882B, letter 4.1.1887.
97. NLW, MS 1882B, letter 9.3.1887.
98. *YFAC*, 4.6.1887.
99. *YFAC*, 6.7.1887.
100. *YUC*, December 1890.

In the first edition of *Yr Undebwr Cymreig*, Evans threw scorn on the idea of Home Rule for Wales, as expounded by W. J. Parry, the M.P. for Arfon, and especially his thoughts about making Aberystwyth the capital city.[101] In the February edition he had elaborated satirically on the same ideal, by writing about who would rule in the Free State of Bardsey – attacking those whom he also admired; the Governor was to be Michael D. Jones, the Prime Minister, T. E. Ellis, M.P. for Merioneth (who became Liberal Chief Whip in 1892), and as Chancellor, David Randell, the M.P. for Gower.[102]

Morgan notes that Tobit was appointed as agent for the Welsh Liberal Unionists in October 1889,[103] but in this he may be mistaken. He had been active in their organisational attempts, and in July 1887 had placed an advert in *Y Faner* asking for the addresses of 'every Unionist in North Wales.'[104] The infamous Leigh Maclachlan was Liberal Unionist agent in south Wales for part of 1889,[105] and Tobit was probably only appointed as agent for north Wales, a position which he resigned in 1891, being replaced by MacLachlan.[106] His service must have been valued because Joseph Chamberlain wrote to him in October 1891, thanking him for his service, and indicating that there was the possibility that a 'limited agency confined to the three counties might be worked out for £6 or £7 a month.'[107] This seems not to have happened.

Interestingly Tobit, given the previous critical letter from D. J. Jones, Lampeter, must have been a person who attracted the personal ire and jealousy of his acquaintances. Maclachlan wrote to him of W. Thomas, the Liberal Unionist Manchester secretary,

> For some reason he dislikes you and I feel sure he would do you a mischief if he could. I believe him to one of the d- – st liars in the country … Every time I go up to his office he tries to pump me about you. I think he would like to have got your post.[108]

As agent Tobit worked and campaigned for H.J. Ellis Nanney, the Tory

101. *YUC*, January 1890.
102. *YUC*, February 1890.
103. Morgan, *Modern Wales*, 1995, 42.
104. *YFAC*, 20.7.1887.
105. NLW, MS 21989C.
106. *YFAC*, 11.3.1891.
107. NLW MS 18618C.
108. NLW, MS 18882B, letter 18.4.1890.

candidate against Lloyd George, when he was first returned to parliament by a margin of 18 votes, in the Caernarfon Boroughs by-election of 1890. Tobit describes meeting Lloyd George on the day of the election at Afonwen Station, Caernarfonshire, and he ascribed his success to the fact that the sailors of Nefyn had been prevented by the weather from returning to port and thus were unable to vote; they were Unionists – 'They know the Irish too well to be able to trust them.'[109]

One result of Tobit's Unionist allegiance were physical attacks upon him and his property; *Y Faner* reporting a mob attack on his home in the summer of 1886.[110] There was also an incident in the summer of 1895 when it was suggested that Evans was an intended victim.[111]

Tobit's own political career was modest. In 1889 he stood for the County Council at Llangranog where he sought to distance himself from the denominational character of the elections, anxious to show that he was a 'Friend' owing no allegiance to the mainstream denominations, who overall dominated how people voted. He polled 47 votes to the 106 gained by Job T. Davies, described as a Calvinistic Methodist.[112] He stood again for Llantysilio-Gogo in February 1892, calling in his manifesto for a craft school in the county, particularly to teach agriculture and navigation, and for the publication of the council's accounts in Welsh. His manifesto went on to say that he was opposed to choosing candidates on the basis of their denomination, a marker that was important in attracting votes[113] but due to pressure of work he withdrew his candidature.[114] He obviously believed that being a Quaker took him above the usual denominational posturing, that he was not interested in inter-denominational rivalry that, to his mind, overshadowed local politics, 'I am a Quaker by religious conviction, and I do not have any position to frighten any denomination at the cost of belittling another.'[115] Nevertheless his Quakerism and its peculiarities were used to mock him, as one letter in the press illustrates.

'Haitch' attacked him with regards his political ambitions, and the way he

109. *YUC*, April 1890.
110. *YFAC*, 21.8.1886.
111. *YFAC* 12,6,1895.
112. *Ye Brython Cymreig (YBC,)* 12.02.1892.
113. *YBC*, 19.02.1892.
114. *YBC*, 26.02.1892.
115. NLW, Papers of Daniel Davies, Ton, MS 3191C III, 287i, letter 14.2.1901.

addressed letters to the editor of the *Cambrian News*, 'Why did he not 'thee'
and 'thou' you, as he 'thees' and 'thous' other people.'[116] Evans responded
reflecting the Quaker stance on plain speech, whilst also taking a swipe at
John Gibson the editor:

> One of your nameless, silly correspondents asks, why I did not 'thee' and
> 'thou' you. Is he so very dull that he cannot see? I do not know whether it is
> a part of my duty to teach such a deadhead, but if it is so, tell him that as
> editors style themselves 'we'I do not like to mix up my numbers and persons
> in the clumsy way some correspondents do. The sovereign of the realm and
> editors are the only personages who have this privilege to use 'we' in the
> singular, and I should deem it the next thing to high treason to 'thou' and
> 'thee' an individual who calls himself 'we' and is big enough to think he can
> settle the destinies of the empire.[117]

In March 1895 he again stood again for the County Council, without
success,[118] but later in the same year was elected as a Unionist onto Lampeter
Borough Council.[119] Some encouragement was given to Evans to stand as a
parliamentary candidate; *Y Faner* felt that the Tories should select him to
fight Ceredigion,[120] but in 1893 he stated that he would not be contesting any
parliamentary election.[121]

During 1889 he published his pamphlet on the *Y Berw Gwyddelig* ('The
Irish Ferment'), being an historical examination of the state of Ireland, based
on information gathered on a month-long visit there in October 1888. He
had stayed with, and interviewed, prominent Irish Quakers, people who in
his opinion and in his introduction, none could possibly mistrust given their
history and provenance, drawing on a common representation of the
Quakers as an honest, upright people. This tract was to be one of ten such
leaflets, principally on the Irish question, that he published under the name
of the Society of the Welsh Unionist Press. One such was *Goleuni ar Gyflwr
yr Iwerddon* ('Light on the Condition of Ireland') by the Rev. D. Lloyd Jones,

---

116. *CN*, 22.1.1886.
117. *CN*, 29.1.1886.
118. *WM*, 11.3.1895.
119. *WM*, 2.11.1895.
120. *YFAC*, 8.2.1890.
121. *WM*, 5.7.1893.

the Calvinistic Methodist minister at Llandinam,[122] amongst whose members was the former M.P., David Davies.

This 1888 visit had not apparently been Tobit's first to Ireland, he had seemingly visited in 1885 possibly to see and hear for himself what lay behind the debate for Home Rule. As a result of his investigations he was persuaded by 'Friends and other Protestants that the task of legislating could never be trusted to the Papists of the Green Isle.'[123] Listening to the voice of the Protestant in Ireland was crucial to his understanding and attitude, as indeed it was for all the Quakers who supported the Liberal Unionist cause. Thomas Hodgkin commented on the perils facing Irish Quakers, and of 'the danger in which these poor Friends' earthly citizenship is threatened.'[124]

In December 1891Tobit wrote to one prominent Welshman challenging statements made by Alfred Webb, the Irish M.P. whom he said was not representative of Irish Protestants, with no more right to that label than John Gibson or Charles Bradlaugh, who were hypocritical in relation to religious matters. He was anxious to point out that Webb was no longer a member of the Religious Society of Friends; 'his connection ended a quarter of a century ago.'[125] This was obviously an attempt on his part to defend Friends whilst also denigrating Gibson.

It 1892 he launched his weekly *Ye Brython Cymreig*, intending to serve the whole county of Ceredigion, but in reality concentrated on its southern and middle parts – the northern part of the county was served by the Tory-inclined *Aberystwyth Observer* and by the Liberal *Cambrian News*. Idiosyncratically, he did not use the Welsh form of the definite article 'y' in his title,' but used the quaint definite article 'ye', because, he said, he wished to ensure that he did not transgress copyright law given the former *Y Brython* publication. He felt the new title would highlight the fact that the Welsh were not the only Britons, but stood alongside other Celts. The *Western Mail* reported that 'the Welsh patriot, Michael D. Jones' had suggested the name for the paper.[126]

---

122. D. Lloyd Jones, *Goleuni ar Gyflwr Iwerddon*, n.d.
123. NLW, MS 3191C III, Daniel Davies, Ton, letter 7.7.1902.
124. Creighton, *Life and Letters*, 1917, 162.
125. NLW, D.R. Daniel Collection, 1078, Letter 24.12.1891. ('*mae ei gysylltiad wedi darfod agos chwarter canrif.*').
126. *WM*, 7.7.1893.

In his first editorial Tobit made clear the attitude and policies to be adopted. The editor, he said, was a Liberal Unionist but the paper would be guided by free, independent and perfect principles. Some forms of advertising would not be accepted, primarily those related to gambling, the black arts, fortune telling, money lending and fraudulent medics.[127] He made plain his distaste, given his opposition to Irish Home Rule, for the Liberal Party and W.E. Gladstone, whom he often described as that 'Old Man from Hawarden.' His admiration for Joseph Chamberlain, who had just visited Ceredigion the previous year, was plain. During his visit to 'Highmead,' Llanybydder, Chamberlain had given 'an able and eloquent address to some twelve or fifteen hundred people from the progeny of the Old Welsh Britons.'[128]

The newspaper's unionist credentials are evident throughout, and he was clear that Home Rule was nothing more than an attempt by the Papist clergy to keep the Irish Protestants in their place, being particularly bitter about the way some Welsh nonconformist ministers treated their Irish protestant brethren. Writing in May 1898, concerning the three hundredth anniversary of Oliver Cromwell's birth, he referred to Cromwell's distrust of Catholics, a situation that was totally different from that taken by

> Welsh nonconformists, or at least most of them. In the year 1886 almost all of the nonconformist ministers in Wales followed the old PAPIST FROM HAWARDEN, supporting him with all of their might so as to hand over their brethren in Ireland bound hand and foot, to the Catholic Priests of that unhappy island. They scorned and cursed every conscientious Nonconformist such as John Bright and Joseph Chamberlain for daring to challenge Mr Gladstone ... the Editor of *Ye Brython Cymreig* was also much persecuted.[129]

127. *YBC*, 1.1.1892.
128. *YBC*, 1.1.1892. ('*Traddododd anerchiad galluog a hyawdl iawn i ryw ddeuddeg neu bymtheg cant o epil yr Hen Frythoniaid Cymreig.*').
129. *YBC*, 5.5.1898. ('*Yr hyn oedd wahanol i Anghydffurfwyr Cymru, neu o leiaf y mwyafrif ohonynt. Yn y flwyddyn 1886 aeth agos holl weinidogion Anghydffurfiol Cymru ar ôl yr hen BABYDD O BENARLAG, gan ei gynorthwyo a'u holl allu, i drosglwyddo eu brodyr yn yr Iwerddon yn rhwym, draed a dwylaw, i offeiriad Pabyddol yr Ynys annedwydd honno. Dirmygent a melldithient bob Anghydffurfiwr cydwybodol fel John Bright a Joseph Chamberlain am feiddio gwrthdystio yn erbyn gwaith Mr Gladstone ... erlidwyd llawer ar Olygydd Ye Brython.*').

In the context of the ongoing argument over Home Rule he consistently expressed strong anti-Catholic sentiments, which permeated much of his writing on the subject.

In 1889 came his pamphlet *Gwyddeleiddio Cymru* ('The Irishing of Wales') stridently summarising his views, in what would now be considered racist tone, accusing many of the Welsh of having swallowed Irish and Catholic doctrines, using the term *'gwyddeleiddio'* to convey general disorder and unseemly or unacceptable behaviour, especially amongst members of the establishment; they no longer behaved in an acceptable and civilised manner.[130] In June 1895, he defined *Gwyddeliaeth* ('Irishism') as those Irish practices and acts that had crept into politics in Wales,[131] reflecting acts of lawlessness identified with Irish politics in the struggle for Home Rule.

In January 1892 he attacked the Ceredigion Joint Watch Committee, which he served on in his role as a Justice of the Peace, for supporting the police who had enticed or entrapped a local publican into selling beer on a Sunday. He attributed such acts to the 'Irish' influence, stating that it was not acceptable to derive good from anything that was bad.[132] Reporting on an attack in Llanidloes in July 1892 during the general election upon the Tory candidate in Montgomeryshire Sir Pryce Pryce-Jones, and his wife, he accused the 'Irish Welsh' – *y Gwyddeliaid Cymreig* – of fermenting violence.[133]

Since he had left the Liberal Party he was at pains to express his own liberalism on many issues, but felt that he had to criticise those who in his estimation had betrayed that cause, including nonconformist ministers and the Welsh Liberal Members of Parliament, especially the member for his own county. In 1892 this was Bowen Rowlands, Q.C., a non-Welsh speaker, a characteristic of which he did not approve. This reflected as he had said on many occasions, 'the Anglicisation of our country (as) one of the principal objectives of many 'leaders' of the Liberal Party in Wales, and injuring things Welsh.[134] This seems an awkward statement coming from a Liberal Unionist,

---

130. Henry Tobit Evans, *Gwyddeleiddio Cymru* (Llanarth, Cymdeithas y Wasg Undebol Gymreig, 1889).
131. *YBC*, 7.6.1895.
132. *YBC*, 22.1.1892.
133. *YBC*, 22.07.1892.
134 *YBC*, 26.4.1895. (*'Fel y dywedasom lawer gwaith, Seisnigio ein gwlad ydyw un o brif*

especially since they supported the Conservatives who were unsympathetic to a Welsh agenda. Bowen Rowlands did not seek re-election for Ceredigion in 1895, and all Evans' prejudices about him were no doubt confirmed when he reported in June 1896 that Rowlands had been received into the Roman Catholic Church.[135]

The new Liberal member for Ceredigion was Mathew Lewis Vaughan Davies, of Tanybwlch, Aberystwyth, also a non-Welsh speaker, who defeated his Unionist opponent, John C. Harford, the owner of the Falcondale estate in Lampeter. Harford was similarly non-Welsh speaking and from a Bristol banking family but descended from 'an old family belonging to the Quakers.'[136] His election address was anti-disestablishment, and no reference to this, or the fact that Harford was unable to speak Welsh, appeared in *Ye Brython*, a selective but not perhaps surprising omission.

Tobit's general feelings about his fellow countrymen reflects a certain exasperation on his part, 'we the innocent Welsh are led in every subject by English leaders. It is entirely from there that they receive their instructions, or rather the way they are to act,'[137] adding that the Irish were far more cunning. His often strident comments as to the state of the Welsh language and of the Welsh nation would, by today's standards, mark him as a rampant, if not xenophobic nationalist, which was far from being the case. He was a fervent royalist, noting at the time of Victoria's Jubilee, that 'without hesitation you can say that the Welsh are as loyal to the crown as any British nation.'[138] He was nevertheless unhappy that the Union Jack did not have on it something to represent Wales, such that 'no self-respecting Welshman can look at her flying in Wales with any pleasure or enthusiasm.'[139]

---

amcanion lliaws o 'arweinwyr' y 'Blaid Ryddfrydol yng Nghymru' a sarhau pethau Cymreig.').

135. *YBC*, 12.6.1896.

136. *YBC*, 21.9.1895.

137. *YBC*, 15.1.1892. ('*Cymeryd eu cyfarwyddo ym mhob pwnc gan yr arweinwyr Seisnig y mae pobl ddiniwed Cymru. Oddiyno yn gyfangwbl y derbyniant eu cyfarwyddo, neu yn hytrach y gorchymynion sut y meant i weithredu.*').

138. *YBC*, 07.1.1898. ('*Gellir dywedyd yn ddibetrus fod y Cymry mor deyrngarol i'r Goron ag unrhyw genedl Brydeinig.*').

139. *YBC*, 03.7.1896. ('*... ac am hynny nis gall unrhyw wir Gymro edrych arni yn chwifio yng Nghymru gydag unrhyw bleser na brwdfrydedd.*').

He was passionate about the language and very conscious that many Welsh speakers and his readers were monoglot, so that the presence and availability of Welsh-speaking officials was an important consideration. Time and again he took up the issue of non-Welsh speakers being appointed to influential positions. He condemned English-speaking officials holding public office and found it distasteful that H.C. Fryer, the Clerk to Ceredigion County Council, had no Welsh 'Kill the pig in English; 'a translation of a Welsh idiom – *Lladd y mochyn yn Saesneg* – not as a personal insult, but indicating that activities were being conducted by the council through the medium of English. Fryer, a solicitor by profession, had been a leading Liberal in the county and at one time their registration agent.

In February 1892 Tobit fully supported the Welsh M.Ps in their condemnation of the appointment of Judge Beresford, who had been appointed to the Welsh circuit despite having no Welsh. This accentuated problems of communication in trials; some judges refused to hear any testimony in Welsh, even when a witness had no English! This opposition by the Members of Parliament gave Tobit cause for optimism that the Welsh were gaining in maturity and

> that the time was not far off that every candidate for a post under the Government in Wales would have to be able to speak Welsh ... and it would be a proper thing for parents who seek to bring up their children without knowledge of Welsh to remember that.[140]

When reporting the fact that Limerick County Council in Ireland had decided that within twelve months preference in appointments would be given to those proficient in Gaelic, he congratulated them, seeing this as a reasonable step, and something that should be done in Wales, 'but which County Council will take up the challenge?'[141]

He noted in January 1894 the appointment of L. J. Roberts, a native of Aberaeron, as one of Her Majesty's Inspectors of Schools, as someone he knew who was fervent for the teaching and use of Welsh, but was fearful that Roberts would send his reports to the Chief Inspector in Welsh, 'given

140. *YBC*, 26.02.1892. ('... *ac yw'r amser ymhell cyn y bydd yn rhaid i unrhyw ymgeisydd am swydd yng Nghymru fod yn medru deall a siarad Cymraeg ... da fyddai i rieni plant ydynt yn ceisio dwyn i fyny mewn anwybodaeth o'r Gymraeg gofio hynny.'*).

141. *YBC*, 27.07.1900. ('... *ond pa Gyngor Sirol gymer y pwnc mewn llaw?*').

his extreme views in this direction,'[142] thus alienating those with influence. For Tobit the emphasis on the use of Welsh was on ensuring that monoglot Welsh speakers were not disadvantaged. He did not campaign for equality and status for the language. He was concerned primarily to ensure that Welsh was spoken and used as a language of instruction in the schools. When the English-born Quaker, John Edward Southall of Newport, heard of Roberts' appointment, he wrote to T. E. Ellis, M.P., seeing it as an important appointment, that – alongside the impending retirement of Inspector Watts, someone who had no love for the language – was likely to do much to forward the objective that within 'two or three years ... Welsh will ... be taught in most of the elementary schools of Monmouthshire and Wales.'[143] Southall noted with pleasure that he had in fact shaken Roberts' hand at the station of Aberystwyth, from where he had written his letter. Evans and Southall would have known each other given their connection with, and support for, the Welsh Language Society, but also as Quakers and as journalists and publishers.

The Society for the Utilisation of the Welsh Language (SUWL) was founded in 1885, to promote Welsh as a subject in schools, but more importantly to ensure that children in Wales became bilingual, using Welsh as a medium of instruction. Dan Isaac Davies, a schools' sub-inspector at Merthyr, is credited as the founder of the society, but he acknowledged that it was Tobit Evans, who suggested the formation of such a society, an attribution that demonstrated Tobit's allegiance and dedication[144] but despite this Tobit failed to be elected onto the first Council of the new Society.[145]

In his paper Tobit argued that the Anglican Church in Wales was failing because of her Englishness and her tendency to 'attempt to anglicise our nation.'[146] One of the curses of Wales to his mind were the 'English causes', the efforts of the Welsh denominations to establish English-speaking congregations. The fact that he himself belonged to a denomination that made no use of Welsh seems not to have bothered him. His biting comments on preachers using English to Welsh-speaking congregations are worth

142. *YBC*, 26.01.1894.('... *gan mor eithafol yw ei olygiadau yn y cyfeiriad yma.*').
143. NLW, T.E. Ellis 2, 3784, letter 14.4.1894.
144. J. Elwyn Hughes, *Arloeswr Dwyieithedd: Daniel Isaac Davies 1839–1887*, 1984, 61.
145. Ibid. 92.
146. *YBC*, 20.11.1898.

noting. He was exasperated by the whole notion. In January 1900, for example, he attacked the Rev. Hugh Price Hughes, probably the most prominent Wesleyan Methodist in Britain, and Carmarthen born, who in the first assembly of Welsh-speaking Wesleyans in Machynlleth, had dared to 'oppress the monoglot Welsh. The Pope if he came would insist on speaking Latin, Hughes insisted on speaking English, and forcing others to do the same thing.'[147] The fact that Ceredigion County Council only advertised in the English-language press and did not use *Ye Brython* pained him, adding to his feelings about that Liberal-dominated body. In this instance he was being commercially minded.

Around December 1897 he became editor of the Tory supporting *Carmarthen Journal* but continued to publish *Ye Brython Cymreig*. Reading both papers it is not surprising that the content of the one reflects the other. In September 1901 he gave up on *Ye Brython*, 'temporarily' because of ill-health, but from his correspondence his health from around 1902 was deteriorating and the paper was never revived. In December 1902 he spent three months in London and Bath having medical treatment.[148] By 1907 he was apparently in too much pain to write, his daughter doing this for him.[149]

His parting editorial barb in *Ye Brython* was directed at the Welsh denominational colleges because Welsh did not figure on their curricula. He had done his best 'to resist the English-Welsh who seek to govern our dear little country, and defeat those who support that.'[150]

Tobit's Unionist and imperial sympathies as editor are plain, noting that 'our gracious Queen is a zealous advocate of preserving the Welsh language'[151] (even though she only spent a total of seven nights in Wales during the whole of her reign[152]), and commenting in May 1900, on the occasion of her birthday, that it was the heartfelt wish of every true born

---

147. CJ, 21.1.1900. See Ch. 3, fn.12.
148. NLW, 15685E, 84.
149. NLW, 15685E, 78
150. *YBC*, 27.9.1901. ('*... i ymladd yn erbyn y Sais-Cymry sydd yn ceisio llywodraethu ein gwlad fechan annwyl, ac yn erbyn y rhai hynny sydd yn gwarogi hynny.*').
151. *CJ*, 18.5.1900.
152. John S. Ellis, 'Reconciling the Celt: British National Identity, Empire, and the 1911 Investiture of the Prince of Wales,' in *The Journal of British Studies*, 37, 4, Oct., 1998, 390.

Briton that she be given a long life and good health.[153] In both newspapers he defended the actions of the government in the South African war, giving short shrift to the pleas of Emily Hobhouse, who had been deported from there for revealing the condition of Boer women and children in the concentration camps. Relying on a military source he expounded that these were 'absolutely without foundation.'[154] Latterly he quoted from a copy of a letter from Lance Corporal David Thomas of the 2nd Battalion South Wales Borderers denying reports of the ill treatment of the Boers. Thomas had 'never heard of any outrage,' and defended the conditions under which the Boers were held. Yet 25–28,000 people died in these encampments; they 'outnumbered combatant deaths on both sides during the war, and amounted to 10% of the Boer population' whilst 15,000 indigenous Africans also died in separate camps.[155]

Despite such imperial sentiment he had no time for the fact that in 1900, the then Chief Constable of Caernarfonshire, 'some Englishman by the name of Colonel Ruck,'[156] had sent in troops to Bethesda to control the striking quarrymen there.

He fulminated against Welsh Nonconformist opposition to the 1902 Education Bill, seeing in it a 'storm of malice and misrepresentation'[157] to legislation that to his mind consolidated and unified education across Britain, removing rather than accentuating religious differences: 'We hear mutterings of a stubborn Radical opposition ... fractious and partisan, and it is not in the true interest of education.'[158] Support for the government was important and he would no doubt have shared Balfour's puzzlement at the anger shown about the proposals for rate aid to church schools, especially since central government had already been paying such grants for a number of years.[159] But since 1892, when he began publishing *Ye Brython*, his commentaries about the government attest to his ongoing support for their

---

153. *YBC*, 18.5.1900. ('*Dydd Iau nesaf fydd dydd pen blwydd y Frenhines. Gwyddom mai dymuniad calon pob gwir Frython yw Hir oes ac iechyd i'r Frenhines Victoria.*').
154. *CJ*, 10 and 31.01.1902. He made no reference to Quaker relief work in South Africa.
155. Iain R. Smith, *The Origins of the South African War 1899–1902* (London, Longman, 1996), 5
156. *YBC*, 16.11.1900.
157. *CJ*, 10.10.1902.
158. *CJ*, 4.4.1902
159. G.R. Steere, *A New England? Peace and War, 1886–1918*, 2004, 332.

endeavours whilst maintaining allegiance to his radical leanings. Thus he continued to refuse to pay his tithes. *Y Faner* portrayed him as a hero in this respect.[160] The *Western Mail* was critical, highlighting the fact that as a J.P., Tobit had responsibility to uphold the law.[161] In a lecture given before the Cymmrodorion Society in London, the lecturer, W. Jenkyn Thomas referred to Tobit's tithe protest as being, 'true to the principles of the Quakers in refusing to pay tithes ... and had just received the fourth or fifth summons for his refusal.'[162] In truth however, as one author demonstrates,[163] tithes were no longer by then a vital concern within LYM, but continued resistance no doubt suited Evans' public persona.

It cannot be said, from the available evidence, that Tobit wore his Quakerism overtly. He was not a 'public Friend' giving visible support to the witness of the Society, and his attempt to distinguish himself from other nonconformists in the County Council election of 1889 was a failed bid to rise above petty denominationalism. Certainly his journalism shows no denominational bias but his infrequent Quaker references do hint at an element of denominational pride. His publications bore no denominational bias, they were, as far as he was concerned, 'undenominational,'[164] but they were strong in their defence of Protestantism, especially in Ireland, and pointedly unkind to Roman Catholicism – 'the Papist will not be satisfied with equality if he can gain the upper hand.'[165]

In May 1898 he published and edited *Y Gloch*, an independent weekly for the services of the Anglican Church, but this was abandoned in June of the same year, probably because it was not financially viable. He noted its inevitable end given that *Y Llan*, another Anglican publication, was going to be published weekly; instead he said he would publish a free quarterly, which never appeared.

As editor of the *Carmarthen Journal* he used the witness and writings of John Bellows, the Gloucester printer and Quaker, twice in support of the

160. *YFAC*, 11.7.1899
161. *WM*, 17.6.1895.
162. *Liverpool Mercury*, 5.4.1894.
163. See Eric J. Evans, *The Contentious Tithe: The Tithe Problem and English Agriculture 1750–1850*, 1976, 58–60.
164. *YBC*, 24.8.1900. ('anenwadol')
165. Evans, 1889, *Gwyddeleiddio Cymru*, 3.

South African War to justify his own position, relying on Bellows' Quaker allegiance to partly validate his own stance,

> it will be borne in mind that Mr Bellows is a member of the Society of Friends, whose creed discountenance war under any circumstances, andthat, therefore his testimony is all the more valuable.[166]

He and Bellows maintained a personal friendship. Bellows' wife notes in her husband's biography a letter dated March 3rd 1892 in 'reply to his friend Henry T. Evans a Quaker magistrate in Ceredigion – who had sought his opinion and advice during the Welsh anti-tithe agitation.'[167] Both were fellow travellers politically, and Tobit could proudly note that this fellow Quaker had been one of the first to speak out against Irish Home Rule, having published at his own cost pamphlets in English, Welsh and Gaelic 'against this wild scheme,' attesting that Gladstone's defeat in1886 was 'largely due to the pen and press of John Bellows.'[168] Bellows was a prominent Liberal Unionist allied, as were his family, for a long time with that cause, and a member of the Nonconformist Unionist Association formed in 1888.[169]

Both the *Carmarthen Journal* and *Ye Brython* carried in May 1900 the statement issued by HRMM, on 'The Society of Friends and the Military Spirit of the Day' in the form of an advert, presumably published on a commercial basis. *Ye Brython* in 1893 reported the death of L.Ll. Dillwyn, the radical member of parliament for Swansea, noting his Quaker ancestry.[170] In 1892, three years after the death of John Bright, Evans wrote an article in his praise. In January 1899 he reported on the opening of the new meeting house at Llandrindod, commenting that at one time the Friends had been numerous and strong, especially in the north, and that this opening was the first time in many a year that they had opened a new 'chapel' in Wales.[171]

He was aware and proud of the endeavours of his fellow Quaker, John Edward Southall, in support of the Welsh language, commenting that Southall had just published a small but valuable booklet on the 'Future of

166. *CJ*, 31.8.1900.
167. Elizabeth Bellows, *John Bellows: Letters and Memoirs edited by his wife*, 1904, 92.
168. *CJ*, 23.3.1900.
169. *TT*, 13.5.1901.
170. *YBC*, 24.6.1892.
171. *YBC*, 6.1.1898.

Welsh Education,' noting that Southall reasoned with skill and great ability that Welsh 'should be given a far more prominent place in our schools than given at present in order to ensure the best and most satisfactory results.'[172]

It was almost in the last issue of the paper that Tobit allowed any element of Quaker evangelising to creep in. Many Welsh language newspapers would give space to religious reportage, denominational news or comments on sermons, and in this context he published part of J, E. Southall's 'Why I am a Quaker,' which had first appeared in the monthly magazine *Y Genninen*. Its inclusion would not have surprised the readership, but the subject was unusual. In *Yr Undebwr*, January 1890, in his praise of John Bright, he had described in some detail procedures in a Quaker wedding, and this might have attracted whimsical interest amongst readers.

Once retired and in failing health, Tobit spent his time on antiquarian activities. In 1896 he was in correspondence with David Samuel about the Cambrian Archaeological Association's gathering at Aberystwyth, inviting them to tea when they visited his home area.[173] In 1901 he was writing to leading Quakers such as Norman Penney, the Librarian at Devonshire House, London, the head office of the Friends at that time, regarding Quaker history. Penney writing to him, asked him, 'Dost thou know John E. Southall of Newport? He hath written on Quaker subjects in Wales.'[174] Similarly he corresponded with Frederick Gibbins of Neath who was willing to lend him some of his books 'with the same limitations,'[175] suggesting that there had been previous exchanges between them. In 1902 he communicated with J. H. Davies, then a barrister in London and a well-known antiquarian, concerning amongst other things the Quakers of Ceredigion. Davies went on to publish a small pamphlet on *Y Crynwyr yng Nghymru*[176] and assisted Norman Penney in his historical researches especially with regard to Fox's journeys in Wales.[177] As editor of *The Journal of the Welsh Bibliographical*

---

172. *YBC*, 17.8.1900. ('*Mr Southall yn ymresymu gyda medusrwydd a gallu mawr y dylai yr iaith Gymraeg gael lle llawer mwy amlwg yn ein hysgolion nag a gaiff yn bresenol mewn trefn i gael canlyniadau goreu a mwyaf boddhaol.*').

173. NLW, MS 2819C, David Samuel Collection, letter 07.09.1896.

174. NLW, MS 18438B, Letter 12.8.1901

175. NLW, MS 18438B, Letter 8.2.1901

176. *Y Crynwyr yng Nghymru*, (Merthyr, Pwyllgor Canolog Cynghrair Eglwysi Rhydd ac Efengylaidd Cymru, n.d.)

177. NLW, MS Cwrtmawr 4 770B: 'Notes on the Quakers,' January 11.1913.

Society Davies was undoubtedly the author of the *Bibliography of Quaker Literature in the English Language relating to Wales*.[178] His father and Tobit were close friends since he was another prominent Liberal Unionist who was also not elected in the 1889 Cardiganshire County Council elections.

If Tobit did not write the history of the Quakers, in 1910, his daughter Gwladys published posthumously his history of the 'War of Rebecca,' describing the happenings in language reflecting her father's original radicalism:

> open revolt against their oppressors ... the embodiment of the peasants' anger
> and righteous indignation at the trampling underfoot of his rights and his
> feelings. Rebecca was the spirit of a nation asserting itself against the
> wrongdoings and evil actions of the few ...[179]

His treatment of the subject is far less sympathetic than implied by his daughter, reflecting much more his position as a Justice of the Peace and establishment figure, especially his treatment of the rioters, when, in the later stages of the disturbances they began to destroy private property and endangered human life. In the book he uses far harsher language, describing the agitators as a 'mob of Rebeccaites,' 'riotous mob' and warning 'the evil spreads,' giving no indication of any higher ideals.

Primarily between 1901 and 1902 Tobit corresponded with Daniel Davies, Ton Pentre, (Davies was an avid book collector, antiquarian interested in the history of Methodism in Wales) concerning his interest in religion and about his intention to write historic volumes. This correspondence reflects a continuing bitterness Tobit felt towards some leading Welsh Liberals, such as Beriah Gwynfe Evans, former secretary of the Society for the Utilizing of the Welsh Language and of Cymru Fydd, a journalist, editor and author of a volume on Welsh dissent. He pointedly told Davies that he had not bought this book, nor a volume by another leading Liberal, John Morgan Jones, because as far as he was concerned he had 'no faith in either of these 'able' (if you will) men as unbiased historians,'[180] adding sardonically that he could

---

178. *Journal of the Welsh Bibliographical Society*, Vol 1, 7, August 1914, 203–225.
179. Henry Tobit Evans, *Rebecca and her daughters: Being a history of the Agrarian Disturbances in Wales known as 'The Rebecca Riots*, 1910, 27.
180. NLW, Daniel Davies, Ton, MS 3191C III, 287i, letter 14.2.1901.

not remember if he had thanked a friend for the privilege of having borrowed them, accusing Beriah Evans of being interested in him only when it came to collecting his annual subscription to the Welsh Language Society, otherwise showing him only disrespect because he was a Unionist. Had he known of Lloyd George's private comment about Beriah, that he was 'abominably defective'[181] he would no doubt have been delighted. Beriah was by all accounts an incompetent, inept and somewhat quixotic organiser, whose approach partly contributed to the failure of Cymru Fydd. By May 1901 Tobit had relented and bought both books.[182]

Some of Evans' phrasing in his letters, in its sarcasm if not bitterness, might not be what would be expected of a Quaker, but he saw himself as a plain speaker who to use a Welsh idiom, spoke out *heb flewyn ar ei dafod* (without a hair on his tongue). There was perhaps a streak of vindictiveness in him, or perhaps it was just that stubbornness which had carried him through to support the Unionists, and ally him with the Tories. Hence, despite the expectation in the discipline of the Yearly Meeting that Quakers should avoid litigation, he was involved in at least two cases brought before the courts. He was perhaps just litigious. One civil case he won,[183] the other, a criminal case, was a charge of poaching he brought against a local man. He tried in court, unsuccessfully, to have the charges dropped, and then stood down from the bench to give evidence – the *Cambrian News* gloatingly reported that the case was lost, and that he had had to pay the costs of two witnesses.[184]

Contact with leading Welsh Liberals was never curtailed. When in 1897 O.M. Edwards, lost his youngest son, Tobit wrote to him to sympathise. Insensitively in the same letter he sought the grieved parents' help in finding a book on Cornish literature, which he had been unable to find. He was especially grateful for all Edwards was doing:

> his labour and great faithfulness to the old country, and to the old languageof our fathers ... I am also trying to do my best for the same cause ... and the worshippers of the English here feel angrier with me than with the devil.[185]

181. Quoted in Price: *David Lloyd*, 2006, 170.
182. NLW, Daniel Davies, Ton, MS 3191c III, 295, letter 7.7.1902.
183. NLW MS, 15685E 97.
184. *CN* 29.1.1886.
185. NLW, O.M. Edwards Papers, AG1/11, Jan–March 1897, letter 17.3.1897. ('... *yn mawr*

Edwards

Edwards in reply[186] referred to his continued struggle with the family's loss and sought an article from Evans on Cornish literature for his magazine *Cymru*. Tobit was still corresponding with Edwards in 1899, describing him as 'gentle friend' but was not free of sarcasm when, following Edwards' victory at the Merioneth by-election he commented, 'that he has published his thanks to his electors in English.'[187]

Tobit died at his home in Sarnau in May 1908. The obituary in the Tory *Welsh Gazette* describing him as a man of strong views, uncompromising in his beliefs, and for 'many years a member of the Society of Friends and his views on all religious questions were characterised by great breadth and liberality.'[188] He had been a great influence in his county, a sterling patriot with no patience for those who ignored their Welsh nationality and language; his death was a loss to Wales. The *Carmarthen Journal* was similarly laudatory. *The Friend* did not report his death, but reviewing his posthumous book on the Rebecca Riots, noted that he had been 'a Welsh-speaking Friend of considerable literary talent.'[189] His funeral was not Quaker, there were no Quakers in his locale and he lived quite a distance from any Quaker meeting, and so he was buried at his local parish church, with Anglican clergy much in evidence; according to the report on his funeral, there were at least three Anglican clergy present if not six![190] A hint perhaps that he frequented Anglican services.

Given his relative isolation from the general life of the Society it is difficult to gauge how he saw his Quakerism in relation to his background. He did not write to the Quaker press, but from 1883 to 1894 was listed as a correspondent to the Friends Tract Association. He translated into Welsh, and had published in 1884, two of their tracts.[191] He was present at the

---

edmygu eich Llafur ach ffyddlondeb mawr i'r hen wlad, ac i hen iaith ein tadau ... yr wyf finnau yn ceisio gwneud fy ngorau dros yr un achos ... ac y mae y Sais addolwyr yma yn teimlo mwy dig wrthyf nag ydynt wrth y diafol.').

186. NLW, MS 18681C, letter 20.8.1897.
187. *YBC*, 12.5.1898.
188. *WG*, 14.04.1908.
189. *TF*, 15. 9.1911, 604.
190. CJ, 22.5.1908.
191. LSF, Minutes Friends Tract Association (FTA), 5.5.1884. In 1884, '*Cymdeithas y Cyfeillion a enwir yn gyffredin, 'Crynwyr'* ('Society of Friends commonly known as Quakers') and one other *Llwon* ('Oaths').

ceremony in Llandrindod Wells in July 1897, when the foundation stone for the new meeting house was laid, addressing the gathering in Welsh. This visibility provides some indication of his position as a man of some social standing. In his address, he reflected on the historical roots of Quakerism in Wales, and his own personal knowledge of it. He exalted the presence of Friends in Radnorshire that 'we have already been here very long – as early if not earlier than most of the other denominations' and 'the story of the sufferings of Friends … in this and other counties of Wales is a long one.'[192] He went on to talk about the endeavours of Howel Harris, one of the founders of Calvinistic Methodism in Wales, addressing the crowd saying,

> You, the Methodists of Wales, are greatly indebted to him. But did you know that he was a Quaker … Of course I do not mean to say that Harris was a member of the Society of Friends. He was a nominal member of the Church of England, but a Quaker in reality.[193]

How and why? Because Harris' preaching, drawing on the power of the Holy Spirit, was not scripted; he prophesied like the Apostles of old as did the Quakers who were moved by the Spirit, arguing this was something that was still needed, since there was too much paper preaching and reliance on scholarly education amongst ministers. He saw Llandrindod as an important Welsh centre for Quaker growth and regarded it as right that Friends were settled there. His allusions to Harris' Quakerism is misplaced, given that Harris was an ardent Calvinist, but by linking his name to the endeavours of the Quakers, he was legitimising and re-establishing their Welsh credentials and future hopes for growth across the country.

As a leading journalist and political writer, writing primarily in Welsh, and a minor public figure in Wales, Tobit was probably not so well known amongst Friends, and his circle of influence and primary interest was restricted to his country.

As a political figure in a county dominated by the Liberals, producing no major Welsh political figure until the 1920s,[194] it is not surprising that Evans

---

192. *TF*, 6.8.1897, 517.

193. *TF*, 6.8.1897, 517–518.

194. K.O. Morgan, 'Cardiganshire Politics: The Liberal Ascendancy, 1885–1923,' in *Ceredigion*, V, 1964–67, 311–339.

remained largely on the fringe of Welsh national political life. Yet some had seen it differently:

> Tobit wields a greater influence over her Majesty's Ministers than any living Welshman, indeed, very few are aware that Tobit Evans acts as a kind of fingerpost to the Government as regards appointments and matters essentially Welsh.[195]

This is an exaggeration, and the failure of the Liberal Unionist cause to find favour in Wales was in many ways his epitaph.

Very few Friends would have been able to read the poems published in his honour in *Y Genninen*, written by a country poet, Cledlyn, Cwrtnewydd, in the strict metre style of the *englyn*, which some regard as the Welsh *haiku*, and which are very often used for panegyric purpose,

> *Noswyliodd, hynaws Walia – gawr arall,*
> *Gwir wrol ei yrfa;*
> *A than dy gwys gorphwysa*
> *Car calon it, Tobit da.*

> *Llenor llawn o ruddin – brwd Frython,*
> *Brad frathai yn gethin;*
> *Iddo ef ein iaith oedd win,*
> *Wron garai ein gwerin.*[196]

195. WM, 19.12.1891, quotes from *The Christian Commonwealth*.
196. *Y Genninen*, XXVI, 1908, 187. The englyn has four lines of ten, six, seven, and seven syllables, all using the same rhyme – though not as end rhyme in the first line; what follows is a loose and free translation.

> Gentle Wales says goodnight – another giant,
> Truly brave his endeavour;
> Under your grave rest,
> Dear heart, good Tobit.

> Author full of bravery – fervent Briton,
> Treachery bites severely;
> To him, the language was wine,
> Brave man loved our people.

Hercules Davies Phillips (1869–1945)

Radnorshire is the smallest of the Welsh counties, from whence the Welsh language was to retreat earliest; not the most prominent of counties in terms of its contribution to the national life of Wales. It was no centre of magisterial activity, some seeing it unkindly as a backwater. W. Llywelyn Williams, journalist, leading member of Cymru Fydd, referring to the potential of a bilingual, vibrant, intellectual Wales, contrasts this to the danger of the country becoming 'as stagnant as Radnorshire.'[197] Yet, the county saw itself as definitively Welsh, and any reading of the *Radnor Express*, from its first publication in 1898, for example, dispels any other interpretation reflecting as it did the views of many of its readers. The editorial for the New Year edition, commenting on the 1916 New Year Honours list, is a good example of this orientation, praising as it did the contribution of the newly-knighted Owen M. Edwards to the life of Wales:

> Few Welshmen are more deserving of honour than Sir Owen. Through his abilities and energies the standards of the schools has [sic] been raised, and the Welsh scholar given a broader outlook ... His powerful and facile pen has been, and is, freely used for the betterment and uplifting of Welsh nationality by his *Story of Wales* he had told our English neighbours the thrilling tale of his country.[198]

Its editorials and articles lent heavily towards support for the Liberal Party and nonconformity, as coverage of the 1902 Education Act reveals.

Radnorshire clung proudly to its Quakerism, a prominent centre in the last decade of the nineteenth and early part of the twentieth centuries, because of the endeavours of people such as Hercules Phillips, who was, according to his Quarterly Meeting, not only one of the best-known Friends in Mid Wales, but across Wales, 'a man for whose life and service Welsh Friends can be very thankful.'[199] He served well beyond his home area, although reading his very short autobiographical notes it becomes clear that his service and devotion to Radnorshire and the Llandrindod area was primary. He was a tenacious, hard worker committed to the witness of

---

197. *Young Wales*, 1, 1895,176.
198. *RE*, 6.1.1916.
199. WQM, Testimony to the Life of Hercules Phillips, M1, 4.4.1945.

Quakers, and it was largely through his efforts that LYM met for the first time in Wales in Llandrindod Wells in 1924.

His biographical notes and accounts of the life of Llandrindod Meeting are an unusual contribution by a Welsh Friend; there are no personal papers of significance preserved relating to the life of individual Quakers, reflecting on the activity of the Society in Wales in the period of this study. Phillips' writings offer a useful insight into the work at Llandrindod and environs, of the ebb and flow of evangelical mission, offering a glimpse of the ecumenical links that Friends had developed there, and of the fact that Quaker activity mirrored that of the other nonconformist denominations.

Phillips served for a time alongside Elsmere at Llandrindod, the HMC appointing him as Elsmere's successor. Phillips comments that

> for a few months I was a whole-time worker under the Home Mission Committee, but I did not like the position and when an offer of local correspondent for a weekly newspaper was offered to me I accepted it and from that time combined the positions of Home Mission Worker and Journalist.[200]

That jarring phrase that he 'did not like the position' is somewhat surprising given his subsequent activities and lifetime commitment to the Society. It may well have been that the level of remuneration offered by the HMC was inadequate, and that by taking a job that fitted in with his mission work, he was strengthening his personal position. In another paper written in 1934, at the time of his retirement from journalism, this seems to have been his rationale. He explained that his service, for what was by then the Home Service and Extension Committee, from the start was part time and that his acceptance of a post of journalist was taken because in his 'judgement it was more Quakerly and more spiritually healthy for myself and the Meetings.'[201] The Home Mission Committee in July 1897 had indeed encouraged Phillips 'to take up work as a reporter that this will not interfere with his Home Mission Committee work.'[202]

200. Phillips, *Personal Story*, 1941, 3.
201. Phillips, *The Growth of Llandrindod*, 1934, 7.
202. HMC, M8, 1.7.1897.

Phillips was born in Knighton in 1869, one of three children, his father a gardener and groom, and an Anglican. He was educated locally, and served at Knighton for a short time as a pupil teacher. When aged 12 or 13, whilst on holiday in Leominster, he was converted and according to him made his first contact with Quakers. When he moved to Llandrindod he joined actively with the Calvinistic Methodists. Indeed, and for a time, he was considering ministerial training with them at Trefeca, their college based on the former home of Hywel Harris in Breconshire but such a proposal troubled him because his 'religious convictions ... were not wholly in accord with those of the denomination.'[203] He conferred with Elsmere about his uncertainties and 'also my reasons why I could not join the Society of Friends' upon which regrettably he does not enlarge. He was one of a group of young men at the time taken under Elsmere's wing. All his doubts about the Quakers were eventually dispelled, and HRMM accepted him into membership in May 1893. His application read:

> Being desirous of becoming a member of the Society of Friends I herewith make application for membership. I have had the joy of knowing Jesus as my Saviour now for a little over 7 years, but have hitherto been connected with another section of the Church. Owing, however to changes, or as I am inclined to think advancement in my religious views I have severed my membership with that body and I believe I am true to my convictions in making this application. Needless to add I have looked above for guidance, and it is my belief that this step is in accordance with our Father's will. I remain your sincere friend and brother. [204]

In 1886 he was apprenticed to a printer and newspaper proprietor in Llandrindod as a compositor, so it is not surprising that in 1896 he took up journalism. His career as a reporter explains why news of Friends and their activities featured so regularly in the *Radnor Express*, although the paper, like many at the time, devoted considerable space to reporting denominational activities. This exposure, in such a small geographical area, reflects the importance of Friends as a denomination in the locale. Phillips no doubt recognised the potential reportage had for outreach. This must be one reason why he reported in the edition for July 21st 1898 that the Rev. John Jones,

203. Phillips, *Personal Story*, 1941, 2.
204. HRMM, M18, 9.3.1893.

the Baptist Minister at Llandrindod Wells had paid a visit to the Pales, attending his first Quaker meeting, something that he had apparently always wanted to do; a development that was seen as an opportunity to extend the invitation to others in the area who were similarly interested. Mr Jones 'gave an address on the raising of Lazarus, and also preached in the afternoon.'[205] This visit should be seen in the light of a minute by Llandrindod Meeting from February 1896, when it was recorded that

> Attention having been called to a certain statement in a book written by John Jones, Baptist Minister, of Llandrindod Wells, which we feel misrepresents us as a Society in the County of Radnorshire. We decide to call the attention of the Monthly Meeting to the same.[206]

There is no record of the Monthly Meeting responding to this. By 1898 Jones must obviously have satisfied Friends that he was now sympathetic to their endeavours, and been persuaded of any errors that he harboured. Thus in December 1904 Llandrindod Wells Preparative Meeting minuted that they had received a request from Jones that he would like to speak at the meeting house on a Sunday evening. Indeed, reading accounts of denominational and ecumenical activities in Llandrindod, Jones and Phillips were closely allied in several endeavours. Both shared much in common. At a meeting of the Central Wales Free Church Council in May 1917 for example, Phillips had proposed a 'special conference of ministers ... to consider what the Free Churches could do to promote the speedy coming of the Kingdom of God.' He was concerned to shape a policy for the future, especially to help soldiers hold on to their faith. The Council agreed to this and Jones and Phillips were asked to arrange it.[207]

To prepare for his work with the HMC, Phillips was sent by them in 1896 to Northfield, Birmingham.[208] On his return to Llandrindod on the 1 October 1896, he became, for the second time, Clerk to Llandrindod Meeting,[209] serving in that capacity until January 1918. He was originally made Clerk in

---

205. *RE*, 21.7.1898.
206. LlWPM, M11, 20.2.1896.
207. *RE*, 10.05.1917.
208. HMCEC, 1.5.1896,
209. LlWPM, M7, 1.10.1896.

September 1893, following the Monthly Meeting decision to give the meeting status as a Preparative Meeting, resigning as Clerk when he moved to Birmingham. In 1902 he was recorded as a minister by the Monthly Meeting,[210] which he was to serve for twelve years as Clerk, also becoming secretary to WQMs Evangelistic and Extension Committee. In 1904 he became Assistant Clerk to WQM, eventually serving as its Clerk. He retired from Home Mission work in 1934.

The activities of Llandrindod Meeting were commonplace but the centrality of the town meant that it attracted many national Welsh conventions to which the meeting contributed. A reading of their minutes provides insight that its orientation was less traditional than most and Phillips must have been instrumental in encouraging the meeting. In 1893 they purchased Sankey's hymn books[211] and in 1909 felt the need for singing practice 'with a view to the helping of congregational singing.'[212] Their adherence to the Quaker disciplines was looser than other meetings, their appointment of a caretaker in 1911 being decided 'on a vote by ballot.'[213] Despite the traditional understanding that Quakers did not rely on voting, there is some evidence that some meetings especially of allied bodies in this period did vote. For example the Friends Tract Association recorded, 'That it was proposed by J. Hingston Fox and seconded by Mary P. Hack, that the Council, officers and Executive … be reappointed for another year (Carried unanimously).'[214] They enthusiastically used the associate membership scheme, in 1902, twenty-two being so admitted.[215] In addition to his Sunday responsibilities at Llandrindod Phillips would visit and conduct meetings at Llanyre most Sundays.

An examination of *The Friend* especially from 1896 to 1912 reveals regular details of those small activities that gave life to Llandrindod and Llanyre meetings – the trips, the children's parties, the concerts, etc. Such reports must have depended on Phillips the journalist, and marked him as a person who knew how important it was to the meeting that its activities were known and communicated widely.

210. HRMM, 9.1.1902.
211. LlWPM, M10, 3.10.1893.
212. LlWPM, M16, 2.9.1909.
213. LlWPM, M10, 1.6.1911.
214. LSF, FTA, M4, 14.6.1897.
215. LlWPM, M2, 6.2.1902.

He was active locally. The list of organisations to which he was attached, religious and otherwise, is impressive. He was particularly enthusiastic about the ecumenical movement, and was one of the founders and first honorary secretary of the Llandrindod Wells Free Church Council. He was at the 1904 inaugural meeting of the Central Wales Free Church Federation, being elected onto its executive committee[216] and served as their President for some time. Elected onto the Executive Committee of the National Free Church Council of Wales, he was appointed as its English language press represent-ative in 1917.[217] He was still serving on it when the British National Church Council visited Llandrindod in 1923. His active involvement in the passive resistance movement, already discussed, was undoubtedly strengthened by his ecumenical connections.

Phillips was a co-opted member of the Radnorshire Education Committee, and was the first Probation Officer for the Children's Court at Llandrindod, active in the Scout movement, and for a year (1923) served as President of the South Wales branch of the National Union of Journalists, which he had joined in 1909 when it was established.[218] He had he said been active in the Radnorshire Liberal Association 'until [the] war of 1914–18 when I resigned my membership and never again felt free to be associated with any political party.'[219] Despite his pacifism, or possibly because he saw beyond it, he records that he was made an honorary member of the local branch of the British Legion, a position telling us something of his stature in his adopted home town. In February 1918, at a meeting of the Llandrindod War Relief Committee, he had expressed the view that it was time that a temporary roll of honour to local men who had fallen in the war should be in a public place.[220] It was pointed out to the meeting that both the Urban District Council and the War Relief Committee had discussed this issue previously but made no decision. This time the paper recorded that the matter was to be pursued.

This attention to the importance of remembrance reflects that Phillips was not rigid in his approach. He committed himself to the Quaker peace

216. *RE*, 21.10.1904.
217. *RE*, 5.4.1917.
218. E-mail communication, Keith Robinson, General Secretary, NUJ, 18.10.06.
219. Phillips, 'Personal', 1941, 4.
220. *RE*, 14.2.1918.

testimony ensuring that that message was understood locally, but he was also sensitive to the sacrifice of those who fought and thus reflecting an element of communal solidarity, whilst being consistent with his denominational position. This was not someone abandoning his principles. His peace advocacy had been transparent and educative. On January 27th 1916, the *Radnor Express* outlined a speech by him, probably self-reported, at the Friends Meeting house entitled, 'Quaker Soldiers: What they are doing.'[221] In his address he thanked the Prime Minister for having ensured that the new legislation on conscription contained exemption clauses for conscientious objectors on grounds of religion. He went on to explain that amongst the twenty thousand Quaker community in Britain, with its 2,000 men of military age, over 300 had already volunteered, 'many in the RAMC' and that the Society had not judged them for this. From those associated with the Llandrindod Meeting 20 had already volunteered. To ensure that conscientious objection was understood and not seen as an easy option, he highlighted the fact that there were 500 Friends in the FAU, three of whom had been killed. In addition he explained that the Society was actively engaged in relief work in Northern France and Serbia, having raised over £100,000 in twelve months towards such work. It was no doubt with great sadness that in the week following this speech he became aware of the death of Private Gilbert Oliver, aged 24, who had joined the Banker's Battalion two months previously, alongside his four other brothers. Another brother, William Oliver, was killed in October 1918, in Salonika. 'Gus' Oliver, was seriously wounded, and Stuart Oliver was held as a prisoner of war.[222] Their mother was a member of Llandrindod meeting. Under such circumstances it is perhaps not surprising that Phillips was interested in honouring the dead.

In November of the same year, and under the same banner headline, another article gave details of twenty-one names of those associated with the meeting, past or present 'who were serving their country, noted the death of four,'[223] and three names of members associated with the FAU.

During 1916 the Quakers sought to ensure that the issue of conscience

221. *RE*, 16.1.1916.
222. *RE*, 10.10.1918.
223. *RE*, 9.11.1916.

was not lost from public view and was reported in the local paper. In March, the Monthly Meeting at its gathering in Llandrindod arranged a public meeting on the subject of the war and the social order. In April, Phillips gave a public address on 'What is Conscience?' whilst in association with the holding of WQM at Llandrindod in September, J.W. Graham and others, had addressed public meetings on the theme of 'Conscience and War;'[224] this at a time when it was reported that two members of the meeting were seeking exemption as conscientious objectors, namely Bernard Bentley in March and John Davies in August 1916.[225]

In September 1917, during a three-day meeting arranged in Llandrindod by the Fellowship of Reconciliation in Wales, a public meeting at the Baptist Church was abandoned because of public protest.[226] The meeting house was then used for further sessions with no agitation. Phillips' role in the arrangements was acknowledged.

The protests against the Fellowship of Reconciliation should best be seen more as local reaction against outsiders, rather than hostility to the principles being espoused. There is no record that the stand taken by Friends in the area attracted any hostility, but no doubt local people would have been familiar with those associated with the meeting who had taken up arms and would then have been more sensitive to their position. In this regard the witness of men such a Phillips must have had some impact. When C.M. Binyon, Clerk to Hereford and Radnor Monthly Meeting at the time, and a member of Llandrindod Meeting, addressed the Military Appeal Tribunal in March 1916 in support of Bernard Bentley's exemption from military service, the chairman, seeking to ascertain whether Bentley would serve with the FAU, could sympathetically refer to the fact that many from the Society were already in the FAU, including Binyon's son.[227]

Phillips was to prove to be a tireless worker for the Yearly Meeting and his efforts and achievement in bringing the Yearly Meeting to his home town reflects his stature within the Society. This was the first time that LYM had ever met in Wales. He was a loyal Friend, and not so doctrinaire as his evangelical background might lead some to believe. In July 1901 he wrote of

224. *RE*, 16.3, 6.4 and 28.9.1916.
225. *RE*, 16.3 and 24.8.1916.
226. *RE*, 13.9.1917.
227. *RE*, 16.3.1916.

his experience of having attended a Free Church Council Conference at Cardiff the previous month, comparing this to his attendance at Yearly Meeting that year. He was critical of the way some of the conference sessions had been conducted, but was clear that Friends had something to learn from how things were organised, indicating that he was not an innate conservative but astute as to the way of Friends:

> One thing we may learn from the Cardiff meetings is the need of organisation and good arrangements being made for Yearly Meeting. Perhaps the Cardiff meetings were over-organised, focussed, and concentrated, to such an extent that individual liberty, and – what is more important – the work of the Holy Spirit were seriously restricted. Still there is a happy medium between the two, and it would be well for us to seek after this. Many of our Yearly Meeting sessions were burdened with long reports, which took up much valuable time, and I could not help thinking how much better it would have been if as at Cardiff these reports had been printed and handed to delegates and representatives, and then taken as read. All friends who are interested will doubtless take the trouble to find out what a report contains.[228]

When the Yearly Meeting at its session in Llandrindod decided to dispense with the role of recorded ministers, he informed his Preparative Meeting that he had resigned his position as same 'believing that it is the wish of the Society this should be done and he unites with the decision arrived at.'[229] This is in marked contrast to the actions of his colleague B. J. Elsmere who clung fervently to his appointment.

Phillips' rejection of a more dogmatic understanding of faith is reflected in the support he was later to give to the excommunicated Presbyterians in Tymbl, south Wales in 1928. He was notable in his vocal and practical concern for their welfare and of their excluded minister the Rev. Tom Nefyn Williams, whose theological pronouncements were distinctly Unitarian and pantheistic.[230] There was considerable excitement that this group at Tymbl might all become Quakers, which Phillips supported, until South Wales Monthly Meeting decided that this was not possible because of the

---

228. *BF*, 7th month 1901, 204–205.
229. LlWPM, M7, 5.6.1924.
230. See O.G. Evans, 'Llain y Delyn, Fellowship House, Tymbl and its relation to the Quakers in Britain', unpublished M.Phil Thesis, University of Birmingham, 2001.

expectations of the Yearly Meeting with regard to the way applications for membership should be handled.[231] This connection with Tymbl illustrates the fact that Phillips saw beyond his own denomination, and was alive to movements affecting the church across Wales. In part no doubt, his ecumenical connections strengthened this interest. His contribution and interest in 'Keswick in Wales' and his responsibility as its local secretary, as previously noted, should be understood in the light of this.

His membership of the Federation of Education Committees for Wales, the Central Welsh Educational Board and of the Court of Governors of the University of Wales points further to interests and national connections, socialising with the Welsh great and the good. He became local secretary to the Welsh School of Social Service, a body that gathered together those in Wales who were interested in and concerned for social conditions and their analysis, encouraging the Welsh churches to take more interest in social affairs, taking them away from their aloof theological and Calvinistic stance where, 'In practice a man could, on his way home from a fervent prayer meeting, walk through a bad slum and feel nothing of its horror.'[232] The school predated its English equivalent, and at its first poorly attended conference in Llandrindod in September 1911, all the speakers were Congregationalists or Baptists. But the following year programme could announce that it was now under the auspices of the Church of England with the support of the Nonconformist denominations, the Quaker input, no doubt, being well-represented by Phillips.[233] The meeting house at Llandrindod was a principal venue for the school's meetings, and although there is no record that Phillips was ever a member of their national committee, he loyally served as organiser for the school's annual gathering in Llandrindod. Pope indicates that after the school held a conference in Cardiff in December 1911 Phillips was added to its committee, but if so his membership was short lived.[234]

One consequence of being associated with the school would have been Phillips' connection with its leading supporters, many of whom were prominent in Welsh public life, people such as Daniel Lleufer Thomas,

---

231. *SWMM*, M6, 10.9.1932.
231. Gwilym Davies, *Welsh School of Social Service 1911–1925*, 1926, 4.
233. Ibid. 17.
234. Pope, *Building Jerusalem*, 1998, fn. 29, 134.

stipendiary magistrate for the Rhondda; Miall Edwards, professor of Christian Doctrine at the Congregational Memorial College in Brecon; Percy E. Watkins, in 1911 registrar of the University College of South Wales, Cardiff; and the sisters Davies of Llandinam and Gregynog, benefactors of many Welsh national institutions. This connection with the school meant that Phillips, and no doubt others in his meeting, were drawn into the increasing debate about the role of the Church in the world, and its responsibilities for the social order; a debate that was to dominate much of the Yearly Meeting before, during and after the war years. The school's programme shows that Friends contributed to it: 1921, Sir George Newman on public health; 1922, Margery Fry as honorary secretary of the Howard League; 1924, Sidney Herbert on International Relations; 1933, John Macmurray – although not at that time a member of LYM – speaking on Voluntary Effort in the Social Crisis.

In October 1916 the Yearly Meeting War and Social Order Committee called a four-day conference to establish whether the Yearly Meeting could define a fresh understanding of its contribution to social action.[235] This was a subject that was to challenge many within the Yearly Meeting, seeking to reorientate itself to the pressing social conditions after the war. When in November 1927, Llandrindod Meeting came to consider this the meeting approved a statement, which in part said that

> the function of the Church is to apply the principles of the teaching of its founder to every relationship of life and in all things to seek first the Kingdom of God … It is not the function of the church – unless there is a united desire that such should be done – to pronounce upon economic theories or systems. [236]

This reflects the innate conservatism of the meeting, but with a hint that some were prepared to take a more strident position, reflecting change in attitude within the meeting since 1909, when it was asked to deal with a circular on 'social questions' and decided to take no action.[237] All this reflects the fact that Quakers such as Phillips were able to move on and adjust to changing social demands.

---

235. See Kennedy, *British Quakerism*, 2001 in particular Ch. 10, 357– 387.
236. LlWPM, M3, 13.11.1927.
237. LlWPM, M10, 2.9.1909.

Phillips's outlook then was broad with sensitivity to wider issues. In 1925, he was appointed to the executive committee of the Welsh National Council of the League of Nations Union,[238] serving until 1927, not seeking re-election in that year. A close examination of the minutes shows that he was not as diligent in attendance as he probably would have wished.[239] The League in Wales, established and encouraged largely through the largesse of Lord Davies of Llandinam, became an important focal point for Welsh peace activists, testifying to the sorts of networks to which Phillips was attached. One of his fellow members on the Executive was the Rev. George M. Ll. Davies, Presbyterian minister, former Christian Pacifist M.P, secretary of the Fellowship of Reconciliation, imprisoned conscientious objector who was to become closely involved with the schismatics of Tymbl, and prominent with Friends in the south Wales valleys during the Depression.[240] Davies' wife became a Friend, but he, despite his deep connections, did not.

In these national Welsh connections Phillips is exceptional amongst Welsh Quakers, although some of this service extends beyond the timeline of this book. Such connections would have undoubtedly meant, from the viewpoint of others, that the Religious Society of Friends could be relied on for its support and interest. Phillips seems to have been a contented all-rounder.

Undoubtedly, and because of his influence, Llandrindod meeting was responsible for nurturing two workers for the HMC. In February 1903, it had a second interview with Harry Frizzell, who had been helping at the Friends Mission at Sherborne Street, Gloucester, sanctioning his stay there. His original interview had been in April 1902, when he was described as superintendent of the First Day School at Llandrindod. At that same meeting William Morgan had his second interview, and, having offered his services, was permitted to extend his visit at Elsenham and New Sheldon.[241] Frizzell at his first interview in April 1902 had indicated that he felt that his work 'will be in meetings of working class membership.'[242] From Gloucester he eventually moved to Rochester, and in 1913 in an interesting comment on

238. NLW, League of Nations Union Papers, A2/3.
239. NLW, League of Nations Union Papers, A1/1.
240. See E.H. Griffiths, *Heddychwr Mawr Cymru*, Vol.1, 1967 and *Seraff yr Efengyl Seml*, Vol. 2, 1968.
241. *TF*, 11.4.1902, 228.
242. HMC, 3.4.1902.

the way the committee treated its workers, the HMEC agreed to make contributions towards the purchase of a business for him in Upminster, 'subject to our committee not being held liable for more than £250 over and above a grant of £100 from the Contingency Fund.'[243]

The Morgans eventually moved to West Hartlepool in July 1905, where they stayed until 1908. In 1914 they were working in Tivetshall Monthly Meeting (Norfolk) where they commented on the 'difficulties attendant on working in an agricultural district'[244] a comment relevant to work in any rural area.

Phillips cannot be described as a leader at the level of the Yearly Meeting, but it would be foolish not to designate him as a Friend of some prominence and influence within Wales. His obituary in the *Radnor Express*, recognising his abilities, said of him that he 'had he been willing to leave Llandrindod Wells there is no doubt that he could have filled an important post anywhere in Great Britain' adding that he was 'A man of inexhaustible energy, he threw himself wholeheartedly and enthusiastically onto whatever he took up.'[245]

Without the investment and interest by the HMC it is doubtful that Llandrindod would have developed as it did. By 1915, the committee were apparently indicating that the help proffered might be withdrawn, 'in view of the many requests for help which were being received.'[246] Such a decision was not made.

Within Radnorshire, Phillips was a prominent Quaker, alongside John Owen Jenkins. The work of the two, and the efforts of B. J. Elsmere, ensured that from the 1890s Quaker witness was firmly re-established within the county, although even by 1913 Llandrindod Meeting noted concerns about its own vitality.[247] Phillips noted in 1934 that the war had changed and affected much that had been achieved:

> The Meeting (Llandrindod) has been slow in recovering from the dislocation of war times ... All meetings have been smaller since ... Advancing age of

243. HMECEC, M4, 6.2.1913.
244. HMECEC, M3, 1.9.1914.
245. *RE*, 30.11.1944.
246. LlWPM, M6, 8.2.1915.
247. LlWPM, M10, 1.5.1913.

faithful Friends, change in circumstances and many removals from the town have all played their part in making the path more difficult.[248]

Jenkins, who died in 1944, would probably have been the sadder man, his 'chapel' and meeting in Penybont closed, no meeting having been held there for twelve months prior to June 16th 1945.[249] The building was sold to his daughter Florence in 1945.[250]

John Edward Southall (1855–1928)

John Edward Southall was probably the only Quaker from England who sought to understand and identify with the 'Welsh soul.' He was fairly well known across Wales, and recognised as someone who strongly identified with the country, especially with regard to the future of the language; as one denominational paper said of him he was 'An Englishman who has not only learnt to speak Welsh well, but is also more fervent for the language than very many of the Welsh.'[251] Y Faner similarly paid tribute to his love of the language, saying of him that it was a very healthy thing to see an Englishman standing up zealously for the continuation of the old language.[252] Thus it was no surprise for the Western Mail to ask him to contribute his views about Wales, alongside other Welsh notables, at the time of Victoria's Jubilee in 1897.[253]

Southall is important because he represents a facet within Quaker life in Wales that was in many ways unique. His family were prominent in the life of Friends at local, regional and national level, and in the civic life of Herefordshire. His father, John Tertius Southall, served as Clerk to his Monthly Meeting and was the first Clerk of WQM, when so constituted in 1869, and was one of those who laid a cornerstone at the new meeting house in Llandrindod in August 1897, commenting affectionately that 'he had been told, and he believed correctly, that at one time Friends were the largest

---

248. Phillips, The Growth of Llandrindod, 1934, 3.

249. HRMM, M11, 16.6.1945.

250. HRMM, M7, 10.11.1945

251. Y Goleuad, 16.5.1900. ('Sais sydd nid yn unig wedi dysgu Cymraeg yn dda, ond hefyd yn fwy selog drosti na llawer iawn o Gymry').

252 YFAC, 26.10.1898 and 22.03.1899.

253. WM, 23.6.1897.

body of non-conforming Christians in Wales.'[254] Tertius had an obvious affection for Wales, reminiscing and romanticising about Friends in Wales at one Quarterly Meeting, his memory carrying him back to the time when there was an important body of Friends in Radnorshire and

> he believed that Friends occupy a place in Wales with regard to Christian doctrine, and the practical carrying out of those doctrines, which no other body similarly occupies, and he hoped that we should not shrink from fulfilling our part in upholding simple spiritual truth in the Principality.[255]

Indeed, Tertius and his brother Henry had an obvious concern for the plight of Quakerism in Wales. Both had supported the work at the Pales, feeling that Friends had not done their duty towards Wales, Henry quoting an old Welshman who had told him that, 'Friends have not done their duty, and so Calvinistic Methodists have stepped in.'[256]

Tertius was active in support of the Liberal Party, serving as a member and alderman of Herefordshire County Council, a member of the Leominster Board of Guardian and a Justice of the Peace for both county and borough. Aged 70 he contested the North Herefordshire constituency (Leominster) in the 1892 general election. To further his political interests 'he purchased the *Leominster News*, which was ably edited by his son, Arthur Trusted Southall.'[257] It was therefore no surprise that both his sons were involved in printing and publishing.

John Edward Southall was brought up in a family that took its religious and civic responsibilities seriously. His father's sentiments concerning Wales and their Welsh ancestry influenced him, such that in 1878 a minute of Neath Preparative Meeting records that he had

> expressed a desire to have one each of the duplicate Welsh copies now in Neath Library of Pugh's Salutation, Penn's Primitive Christianity, and the Compendium of Doctrine etc.[258]

254. *TF*, 6.8.1897, 517.
255. *TF*, 3.7.1896, 444.
256. *TF*, 24.12.1896, 851.
257. Celia Southall, *Records of the Southall Family* (private circulation, 1932), 125.
258. NPM, M12 11.7.1878. H. Bevington Gibbins was asked to send the books to him.

This indicates that by then he must have had enough Welsh to be able to read and make use of Welsh publications. Guto[259] thought that Southall was exposed to Welsh at home in Leominster because workers in the business and in the home would have been Welsh speaking. There is some evidence for this. One such employee was John Handyside Williams of Corris, who with his wife later became Quaker missionaries in Sohagpur, India. Both were convinced as Quakers in 1874 when Williams worked for the Orphans Printing Press in Leominster.[260] According to one author, Southall began learning Welsh as soon as he left his school at York.[261]

Southall was apprenticed as a printer to the Quaker John Bellows of Gloucester in 1871,[262] a Friend who challenged the Yearly Meeting through his support for intervention in the Boer Wars and, as already noted, becoming a prominent Liberal Unionist. Bellows' religious inclinations and sympathies were with conservative Friends, and he had written a personal defence of his position, that accusations were often

> lightly and frivolously bought against all who in the present day endeavour in their measure to walk in the same path that was trodden by the early Friends, and to be faithful to the same Spirit and Power which brought them into the inheritanceof great things by first exercising them in small things.[263]

Bellows also wore plain dress, and Southall noted that he did this as a witness for his religious principles especially when LYM in 1861 had changed aspects of the older Quaker disciplines, which some Conservative Friends found objectionable and which led to dissension and disagreement. The dress code was bad enough but the change in use of language apparently caused Bellows greater suffering.[264] It was in the shadow of these changes that some, under John Sargeant, established the independent Monthly Meeting at Fritchley in Derbyshire in 1870.[265] Punshon describes it as a

259. Dafydd Guto, 'John Edward Southall,' in *Y Casglwr*, No. 64, Christmas, 1998, 7.

260. *TF*, 27.1.1905, 59.

261. Arthur Mee, ed., *Who's Who in Wales* (Cardiff, *Western Mail*, 1921), 87.

262. Ifano Jones, *Printing and Printers in Wales and Monmouthshire*, 1925, 257.

263. *BF*, 5th month, 1881.

264. Waymarks, 1, 6th month, 1902, 86.

265. W. Lowndes, *The Quakers of Fritchley* (Fritchley, Derbyshire, Friends Meeting House, 1980), 18.

'schism'.[266] Bellows had contact with Sargeant, and in February 1872 met with him at Gloucester,[267] after which Sargeant visited other like-minded Friends within the Quarterly Meeting, such as Samuel Alexander of Leominster. Southall would then have been touched and influenced by Quakers with conservative leanings, compared to the evangelic sympathies of his family, to the point that he became a member of the Fritchley group. He set out their position and his sympathies in a letter in the *Daily News*, responding to a critical report in the same newspaper concerning a Quaker witness at an inquest who refused as a matter of principle to take off his hat in court. He set out the position of what he called 'the smaller body of Friends,' those repudiating the innovations in doctrine and discipline which had overtaken LYM, and argued that the Fritchley group had a 'better claim to represent the Quakerism of George Fox and Robert Barclay.'[268] By then he had already published parts of Sargeant's diary.[269]

The first public indication that Southall was challenged about the nature of Quakerism appears in an 1877 letter. This concerned the quality of tracts published and distributed by Friends. Tracts were produced locally, but the Friends Tract Association was a loose umbrella organisation to examine activity across the Yearly Meeting and met during it. Southall focused on the importance of having access to the writings of early Friends, so that readers

> become more spiritually exercised through hearing or reading of the dealings
> of God with some of His servants and faithful witnesses who bore the cross,
> and counted the cost of being real Quakers.[270]

By 1881 his position had become clearer. Writing in the *British Friend* on 'What is Quakerism?' he sought to reassure a perplexed parent, challenged by the problems of bringing up children as Quakers and having to explain to them the nature of their faith. Southall dismissed the modernism of

266. Punshon, *Portrait*, 1999, 190.
267. John E. Southall, *Selections from the Diary of John G. Sargeant, a Minister of the Society of Friends containing an account of his Labours and Travels in the Service of the Gospel and showing the Grounds of his ceasing to regard LYM as representing the Society of Friends* (Newport, John E Southall, 1885), 192.
268. *Daily News*, 8.1.1890.
269. Southall, *Selections*, 1885, 192.
270. *TF*, 7th month 1877, 193– 4. Emphasis added.

Quakerism as a changeable garment. It was 'a faith unchangeable, ever-lasting in its nature, woe be to him who adds to, or takes from it!' and as for the ancestors, their

> religious beliefs was grounded in a faith of the Spirit, not on opinion; if we are not with them it will be so with us, and we may boldly call ourselves their successors not otherwise! [271]

In the same letter he drew attention to the fact that Friends were now 'participating in the perpetuation of heathen or Popish feasts and fasts!' This complemented the actions of John Bellows who had allowed some of his workers to work on Christmas Day, contrary to the Factory Acts, and for which he was prosecuted by the Factory Inspectorate and fined forty shillings. Bellows stated in court that all he was doing was witnessing to the fact that 'no Act of Parliament had a right to order him to keep a Romish holiday.'[272] Interestingly, two years later Southall was fined twenty shillings with twenty eight shillings costs in the Police Court for employing three boys without keeping a register or having a certificate under the Factories Act to so employ, but there is no reference that this was done for any reason of principle. He kept his hat on in court.[273]

This change in Southall's spiritual understanding exercised his mother, given that her husband and his brother Henry were stout supporters of the HMC. Entries in her diary indicate considerable concern and worry about her son.[274] She was no doubt very agitated by one of his early tracts, since it was directed at her and her fellow worshippers within WQM:

> What is the faith of your fore-runners who went by the honoured name of Quakers, where is their zeal, their constancy, their clear testimony against evil in every form; are not you hand in hand with that which grieved their spirits and caused them to cry out aloud, and to lift up their voices in streets and markets, and steeple houses, – you who adorn the tombs of the prophets, but are not found following in their footsteps; who were planted as a wholly

271. *BF*, 3rd month 1881, 67–68.
272. Ibid.
273. *WM*, 31.07.1883.
274. HRO, BG 99/2/140. Extracts from the diary of Elizabeth (Trusted) Southall, (*ETS*).

right seed, a noble vine, how have you degenerated, lost your beauty, and become weak as other men?[275]

This was a harsh, judgemental and accusatory tract written with biblical flourish, reflecting the enthusiasm of a new convert. Its opening lines are clear; 'Hear the word of the Lord ye rulers of Sodom: give ear unto the Law of your God, ye people of Gomorrah.' His spiritual condition much perplexed his mother: she wrote of her 'poor son's unnatural strange ways' and the fact that he was 'still contemplating this miserable and mad connection'[276] with 'the Fritchley people the representatives of the very narrowest views unmixed with anything of Christian charity.'[277] In September 1880 John Bellows had visited her, the suggestion being that he was there to intercede on behalf of her son, but she commented that she

> was hardly prepared to enter fully into the painful business he came upon. I fear I was rather too excited to enter into the subject sufficiently cool and collected. I feel I ought to have looked entirely and faithfully for help from above.[278]

This might also be a reference to the fact that she objected strongly to John's intention to marry one Ann Berry. She does not elaborate on the reasons for this, but it was probably related to Ann's social status;[279] according to the marriage certificate she was originally from Stafford, the daughter of a dairyman, and that John's mother did not feel that her son could afford to keep a wife at that time. Ann was a convinced Quaker, joining through Westminster and Longford Monthly Meeting in April 1879. They had considered a minute from Dorking, Horsham and Guildford MM together with a letter from her, informing them that she had moved to live within their area, and that she wished her application for membership of the Society to be considered by them.[280] In accepting her into membership they noted

275. J.E. Southall, *A Faithful Warning to those Calling Themselves Friends, more particularly in Western Quarterly Meeting, England* (Gloucester, np, 1881).
276. *ETS*, 6.8.1880.
277. *ETS*, 22.11.1880.
278. *ETS*, 23.9.1880.
279. *ETS*, 19.8.1882.
280. WLMM, 16.1.1879.

that, 'None of her relatives are Friends and in consequence the religious views which she has felt it right to adopt have involved her in many trials.'[281] Ann and John married in September 1882 at Cardiff Meeting house; his parents did not attend, but his sister Lucy described the event to her mother. Lucy said that the event was dominated by 'four very broad brims'[282] a reference to the traditional broad brimmed hat which the conservative Quakers wore, and that it was 'sad to see poor John only surrounded by fanatics.'[283] Two of the hats would have been worn by Charles Allen Fox and Tonnes Andreasen who were the two legally required witnesses at the wedding.[284] Southall must have been similarly attired.

Southall's adherence to the conservative Friends never diminished. His mother noted that in WQM in December 1880, John had risen to challenge the words of their

> venerable friend S. Bowley as he [John] sat down at the bottom of the meeting with his so-called friends, poor and uneducated men whom he has strengthened in their false views, not the worse for being poor but their want of education makes them more easily converts to opinions. [285]

This was no doubt a reference to Charles Allen Fox and Tonnes Andreasen. Her diary entries indicate that John's contact with Charles Allen Fox[286] and with 'the man Anderson and his wife'[287] highlights the fact that by 1880 her son was part of a group of conservative Friends based on Cardiff meeting; indeed Andreasen and his wife Mary Ann had spent Christmas with Southall at Newport, since he would not go home to his family in Leominster; the tensions that this group caused within Cardiff Preparative Meeting have already been explored. At WQM in April 1882, she reports to her great surprise and sorrow, that 'poor John made his appearance … with J. Bellows, speaking very objectionably in which John Bellows took his

281. LSF, WLMM, M3, 17.4.1879.
282. *ETS*, 18.9.1882.
283. Ibid.
284. General Register Office, copy of an Entry of Marriage, 27.7.2006.
285. *ETS*, 1.12.1880.
286. *ETS*, 22.11.1880.
287. *ETS*, 1.1.1881.

part.'[288] The mother and daughter-in-law were however to be reconciled and the matriarch noted, with certain satisfaction, was, 'as far as we can see, much better suited than we at first saw and there is a comfort in his having someone to take care of him.'[289]

Southall applied for membership of Fritchley Meeting in 1881, but was not accepted amongst them until 1894,[290] through the Bournbrook (Birmingham) branch, described as 'a natural development of like-minded Friends who lived too far away from Fritchley to become fully involved in the life of the Meeting.'[291] Living in Newport, his attendance at Fritchley, and even at Bournbrook, would presumably have been spasmodic. The process of acquiring membership in the Fritchley group was prolonged possibly because he lived at such a distance. He was recorded as a minister with them in June 1901.[292] His stature amongst the schismatics was confirmed by the fact that from 1899 to 1906 he was Clerk to Fritchley General Meeting. According to Lowndes he pressed for the General Meeting to be held at Bournbrook, but this apparently developed into a personal quarrel, such that by 1912 Southall was removed from the list of recorded ministers.[293] In 1924 he was removed from membership amongst them, Lowndes describing him as an 'apparently turbulent and independent member'[294] and giving as part of the reason for his expulsion the fact that Southall ministered without the authority of the meeting both at home and abroad. Lowndes refers to Southall giving service in America,[295] which is incorrect. He never crossed the Atlantic, but he did give service in France in August/September 1915, where he 'was visiting Paris on religious service, holding meetings in a suburb ... and attending others amongst seekers after truth'[296] He was in Germany in November 1911 with Max Reich and Charles C. Gillet.[297] Lowndes provides only perfunctory

288. *ETS*, 19.4.1882.

289. *ETS*, 2.3.1883.

290. Lowndes, *The Quakers of Fritchley*, 1980, 159.

291. Ibid., 55.

292. *BF*, July 1901, 194.

293. Lowndes, *The Quakers of*, 1980, 61.

294. Ibid. 77.

295. Lowndes, *The Quakers of*, 77.

296. *TF*, 10.9.1915, 705.

297. *BF*, January 1912, 25 and *TF*, 15.12.1911, 816–818.

details about Southall's career with Fritchley, and his removal as a recorded minister came probably because he was involved with Reich and the 'Children of the Revival.' His removal from membership in 1924 is evidence that Fritchley moved exceedingly slowly!

There is no record to show that Southall ever, as a result of his membership with Fritchley, resigned his membership with his Monthly Meeting or that they took any initiative in this direction. Dual membership was then tolerated. Given Southall's connection with Mills, whose work he published, and with Charles Allen Fox, both of whom were disowned, it is somewhat surprising that his visible connection with Fritchley was so tolerated, especially since Cardiff meeting was much challenged by their behaviours, and that of Andreasen. However, the relationship between Fritchley and LYM may have been overall fairly relaxed; attendance by members of LYM at Fritchley's General Meeting was apparently common. Thus when the General Meeting was held in October 1901 half of those in attendance consisted of members of London, Dublin and Philadelphia Yearly Meeting and it was the 'largest ever known there as well as one of the most weighty and impressive' and the report went on:

> As the principles inculcated by the 'small body' are much nearer those accepted by Friends many years ago, than to those in vogue at present, it might be thought that a sprinkling of elderly birthright members would be present. As a matter of fact there were none such. The meeting was chiefly composed of persons in middle life, and a large number of young people, with a few elderly Friends from outside who had years ago been convinced.[298]

LYM was represented by Friends from Derby, Lincoln and Nottinghamshire Quarterly Meeting, Lancashire and Cheshire Quarterly Meeting 'sent the largest quota.' General Meeting Scotland was represented, but the South of England had 'shown very little appreciation of the Fritchley testimony to simplicity of life and worship.' In 1903, Frederick F.B. Sainty of Derby Meeting had travelled in the ministry with Thomas Davidson of Fritchley, apparently the first occasion of its kind.[299]

The fact that Southall was a scion of a well-respected family, and a wish

---

298. Report by Southall, in *BF*, 11th month 1901, 300–301.
299. *BF*, January 1903, 22.

not to cause his parents hurt, may have stayed the hand of Friends, and so he remained a member of LYM despite his Fritchley connection.

Southall was strong-willed, determined if not stubborn. In 1910 SWMM wanted to sell Trosnant meeting house in Monmouthshire Southall was a Trosnant trustee, but he refused to sign the relevant papers.[300] They turned to the QM for assistance, who called upon the 'refusing trustee to sign the conveyance [trusting] that when our Friend realised the terms under which he was appointed … he will see his way to do this.'[301] The outcome was that Southall signed and the sale took place in 1912, but only after extracting from the meeting an undertaking that interest on £100 from the sale, for twenty years, be earmarked for Monmouthshire meetings.[302] In July 1911 the MM made an appeal for £50 towards its depleted funds because of 'expenditure of £74 9s 2d in legal charges over the appointment of new trustees,'[303] which probably arose from the challenge inherent in the sale of Trosnant, and the need to establish new trust deeds.

Apart from this one reference to Trosnant, Southall's name hardly appears in the minutes of his Monthly or Quarterly Meetings, indicating that he was perhaps on the periphery. The exceptions relate to Southall's involvement with Henry Rees of Cardiff Meeting, reporting on suitable premises for worship in Newport[304] and another where the Meeting refused to reimburse Southall for 'removing and replacing glass at Newport meeting house,'[305] because he had not been authorised to undertake the work. Perhaps this was a sign that some in the Monthly Meeting might not have been sympathetic to him.

His involvement and interest in the Revival and with Reich in 1911 has already been noted. He was not closely involved in the work of the LYM, and given his interests in Welsh issues this was a loss, although it does not necessarily follow that he would have been a leader or opinion-shaper within the Yearly Meeting or WQM on such matters.

By 1880 Southall had established his business in Newport, Guto[306] noting

---

300. *SWMM*, M7, 2.3.1910.
301. *SWMM*, M3, 13.7.1910.
301. *SWMM*,17.1.1912,
303. *SWMM*, 3.8.1911.
304. *SWMM*, M12, 14.11.1889.
305. *SWMM*, M12, 13.11.1890.
306. Guto, 'Southall,' in *Y Casglwr*, 1999, 7–9.

that he was a man who ventured in publications, and much of his output was educational. His mother felt considerable uncertainties about his business,[307] although by November her concerns had been ameliorated, by her husband's assessment that 'John was applying to business and trade was as good or better than he expected and was so far satisfactory.'[308] Worries about his business and finances pepper her diary entries for some time, along with concern over 'such dismal surroundings at home.'[309]

Some of his editorial practices reflected his conservative Quaker viewpoint. Thus he refused, adhering to the traditional Quaker practice about titles, to use 'Saint' as a prefix in place names, or indeed to call 'any places built of stone and mortar Churches ... I believe that a religion which attaches any sanctity to PLACES, is nearly nineteen hundred years out of date, when an opportunity is afforded to know better.'[310] He adhered to this practice in much of his writings, and was attacked for his eccentricity: 'he has no right to alter Welsh geographical terminology so as to square with his religion. To guillotine St David's, St. Asaph's and other pretty names leaving us only such ugly trunks as 'Davids' and 'Asaphs' is an abomination.'[311]

In addition to being a publisher, he was a prolific author in his own right. A partial list of his output offers an insight into some of his interests, especially his passion for Wales and its language, and the cause of conservative Friends.[312] He was a propagandist for their viewpoint, writing and publishing many supportive leaflets. The most ambitious, but failed, enterprise in this direction was the publication of the short-lived journal *Waymarks*,[313] being 'A Religious and Literary Journal in Unity with the Testimony of the Early Quakers.' It was to rely on annual subscriptions to be sustainable. The first issue appeared in February 1902, the last in January 1904 when in a letter to all subscribers he informed them that it would cease

307. *ETS*, 30.3.1880.
308. *ETS*, 26.11.1880.
309. *ETS*, 9.10.1884.
310. J.E. Southall, *Wales and her Language: Considered from a historical, educational and social standpoint with remarks on modern Welsh literature* (Newport, J.E. Southall, 1893),iv.
311. *WM*, 31.5.1895.
312. See bibliography for a full list.
313. Jeremiah, 31, 21.

publication and that he would return subscriptions, adding, 'should any Friends feel inclined to contribute towards the expenses during the past year, I shall be pleased to hear from them.'[314] The fact that he referred to his health problems in the same edition may have had some bearing on the decision to cease publication. Southall's intention seems to have been to resume publication in 1905, but clearly costs were a factor in its demise. In all probability Southall wrote most of the copy. It was never meant to compete with the *Friend* or the *British Friend*, even though the 'realm of Christian experience is but lightly touched upon by these.'[315] It cannot have had a large subscription base, despite Southall's attestation to its warm reception, and the fact that a

> considerable number were sent to persons professing to belong to the Society of Friends. Those who have responded most warmly belong, as a rule to the obscurities of that Society and not to the celebrities: in other words, they do not belong to the official class.[316]

He wrote for the *Friend*, the *Friends Quarterly Examiner* and the *British Friend*, and so maintained a national profile within LYM, concerned about the issues that challenged it.

Southall proved to be an indefatigable public defender and proponent for the Welsh language; more than this, he wrote in the Welsh-language press, keeping abreast of its contents. He was also interested in the fate of Gaelic in Ireland. Between 1885 and 1893 he corresponded with the Society for the Preservation of the Irish Language in Dublin,[317] where he compared the position of Irish and Welsh and expressed concern about the Anglicising influence of education. As an English-born Quaker, he was exceptional. The only other Quaker so engaged was Tobit Evans, who was Welsh-speaking by birth. Southall's identity with the language was well known publicly, as testified to in one of his articles:

---

314. *Waymarks*, January 1905.
315. *Waymarks*, 1, 2nd month 1902, 1.
316. Ibid., 20
317. *Freeman's Journal and Commercial Advertiser*, 12.11.1885 and 16.5.1889, 10.9.1891, 12.5.1893).

Not many days ago, I had occasion to take the train to a station in the Wye valley, and had scarcely entered it when I heard myself accosted in Welsh, by a substantial tradesman belonging to one of the industrial districts of Monmouthshire.[318]

His first exploration of Welsh issues in a Quaker context was in an article in the *Friends Quarterly* in 1880[319] where he outlined his understanding of Wales as a distinct nation with a natural and historical claim, possessing strong religious susceptibilities, and, in certain directions, influenced by 'circum-stances unknown in England.'[320] An influence he elaborated else-where 'that from whatever source it springs, it is [a] diffusive, expansive, ethereal force subtlety propagating itself.'[321]

In his article in the *Quarterly* he was anxious to share his understanding with his fellow Quakers, and to examine the relationship of Friends to Wales. He noted that the Society was represented in Wales by comparatively few, many of whom were of English descent, and that there were perhaps only three or four individuals attending meetings who spoke Welsh. Indeed, he was clear that the Society had not paid sufficient attention to the particular conditions of Wales, although he felt that there was a kindly feeling towards Friends in the country. The contents reveal that he was well versed in Welsh Quaker history. Despite the tendency towards romanticism, the tenor of his article was serious and analytic. He noted the impact of migration on the language, quoting a speech given by Henry Richard, M.P. in Cardiff in 1897 about 'the flood of Anglo-Saxon influence rushing into our country.'[322] Not surprisingly he saw the need for Friends to publish in Welsh, since he was particularly aware of the sizeable amount of literature published and sold in Welsh, especially on religious affairs. The demand upon Friends was clear

[w]here have been those who would go and live among the people as part of themselves, sharing their sympathies, feeling with their feelings, speaking

318. J.E. Southall, 'The Middle Class and Quakerism,' in *The British Friend*, October, 1903, 296–97.

319. J.E. Southall, 'The Society of Friends in Wales,' in *Friends Quarterly Examiner*, 14, 1st Month 1880, 86–97.

320. Ibid., 86.

321. Southall, *Wales and her Language*, 1893, 334.

322. Southall, 'The Society of Friends ...' 1880, 97.

their grand old language, that echoes in the breast of many in whom the 'native fire' burns with such an indescribable thrill, and as occasion offers, instruct them in the way of God more perfectly?[323]

His concern, writing as a member of LYM, was that it had 'not sufficiently realised the conditions with which we are surrounded in Wales'[324] if Wales was to be won for Christ and all were to be gathered.

Southall became a leading member of SUWL. In 1903 and 1904 he was a member of its council,[325] which meant that he rubbed shoulders with some of the Wales' leading educationalists, and those favouring political action, such as Beriah Evans, secretary not only of Cymru Fydd but also of SUWL. This connection must have meant that Southall and Tobit Evans knew each other, their common interests, denomination and linguistic interests bringing them together.

In 1886 members of SUWL gave evidence before the Royal Commission on Education. In August 1888 Southall published a book made up of evidence given to it by nine leading witnesses, but they were not all in total unity with each other as to the nature of the issue or its solution. All of them however urged greater use of Welsh and the promotion of bilingualism.[326] His introduction reflected his own hopes and realism, at the same time condemning those who saw Welsh, as many did, as a vexatious obstacle to the unity of Wales:

Wales is too wide-awake and too keenly alive to her material interests, to believe that she can do without the English language or English influence; both are at present bound up in her life; but she has an individuality of her own, which some of her sons at this day believe had not been sufficiently developed in the past and that the nation has suffered in many ways in consequence.[327]

323. Ibid., 93.
324. Ibid., 94.
325. See *Cymru*, 15.10.1903, XXV, 147, 155–165 and 15.11.1904, XXVII, 160, 229–236.
326. John E. Southall, ed., *Bilingual Teaching in Welsh Elementary Schools or minutes of evidence of Welsh witnesses before the Royal Commission on Education in 1886–7 with introductory remarks* (Newport, John E. Southall, 1888).
327. Ibid., i.

He wished that everyone in Wales, through education, would have some grasp of Welsh, proposing the publication of bilingual reading books, which his company pursued.

In 1893 he published his first volume on the language, supported by some notable Quaker subscribers, notably Theodore Neild, head of Dalton College Manchester, and H. S. Newman of Leominster. In it he insisted on having quotations in Welsh without any English translations, feeling that

> if English people want to become acquainted with the Celtic genius as manifested in Welsh literature, they must learn the language ... they must in some way acquire the accent from living lips who know its power.[328]

He was adamant that Welsh should be used as a means of education, concerned that the 'deluge of English'[329] into the populous areas of Glamorganshire, Monmouthshire and Denbighshire would obliterate the language there, and for the rest of the country it would become a provincial and rustic feature rather than a national one. He argued that all children born into Welsh-speaking families should be taught the language at school, with the ultimate aim that everyone in Wales should be able to use Welsh and be bilingual. Reviewing the book, *The Times* felt that it was curious that it was an Englishman who was trying to stir the Welsh to defend their language, finding it to be a 'comprehensive review of the Welsh linguistic question in its modern phase.'[330] The *Friend* found the book burdensome, because Southall was too fond of detail; it advocated some 'pruning of the text,' and was far less enthusiastic than the author: 'We shall not perhaps so readily concur in advising the study of Welsh for its own sake. This must depend on circumstances.'[331] However, the book was warmly welcomed by others. Michael D. Jones was full of praise for Southall and of the Quakers:

> the eminent denomination to which he belongs is against all sorts of war, defensive as well as aggressive. The heart, as a rule, directs the mind, more than the mind directs the heart. The Quakers are a denomination of people whose feelings are commonly with the oppressed, and they look with

328. Southall, *Wales and her Language*, 1893, iii.
329. Ibid., 379.
330. TT, 28.7.1892.
331. *TF*, 7.10.1892, 670. No authorship.

Christian disdain on invaders who subdue nations ... the Christian heart of the Quakers is obvious in his book sympathising with the Welshman who is being oppressed ... John Southall had learnt the language, and it can be seen that he is zealous Welsh scholar.[332]

The results of the 1891 Census, and its linguistic analysis, confirmed Southall's pessimism. He outlined his concern in another book, that if the decline in the language was similarly reflected in the next census then it would die. He hoped that the Welsh-speaking areas of West Wales would be able to provide the energy to reverse this. He urged middle-class English families in Wales to hire Welsh-speaking nannies for their children, so that they could learn Welsh; such employees would be available, he felt, from Ceredigion and north Carmarthen.[333] He was therefore delighted when the Cardiff School Board conducted a plebiscite on the teaching of Welsh in its schools, and by a large majority parents voted in favour, without as he said 'any outside agitation being brought to bear on the case.'[334]

In October 1897, *Y Genninen* published an article by Ap Dewi Môn,[335] 'Is the Welsh Language Dying?' setting out his understanding of that fact, arguing indeed that this was to be welcomed.[336] He explained that multi-

---

332. Jones, *Oes a Gwaith*, 1903, 263–272. ('*Mae'r enwad anrhydeddus y perthyna iddo yn erbyn pob math o ryfel, amddiffynnol yn gystal ac ymosodol. Y galon, fel rheol, sydd yn cyfarwyddo y pen, yn fwy nag y mae'r pen yn cyfarwyddo'r galon. Y mae'r Crynwyr yn enwad o bobl ag y mae eu teimlad yn gyffredin gyda'r gorthrymedig, ac edrychant gyda dirmyg Cristionogol ar oresgynwyr yn darostwng cenhedloedd ... y mae calon Gristionogol y Crynwyr yn amlwg yn ei lyfr yn cydymdeimlo a'r Cymro sydd yn cael ei orthrymu ... y mae John Southall wedi dysgu'r iaith ei hunain, a gellir gweled ei fod yn Gymreigydd aiddgar.'*).

333. J.E. Southall, *The Welsh Language Census of 1891 with Coloured Maps of the 52 Registration Districts in to which Wales is Divided* (Newport, John E. Southall, 1895).

334. J.E. Southall, 'The Linguistic Plebiscite in Cardiff,' in *Young Wales*, 3, 33, 1897, 213.

335. The bardic name which translates as 'the son of Dewi Môn.' As will be seen, Southall exchanged articles with the father about Quakerism in the same magazine in 1901.

336. Ap Dewi Môn, 'A Ydyw y Gymraeg yn Marw,' in *Y Genninen*, October 1897, XV, 4, 266–268. ('*Ymdrechaf, yn y lle blaenaf, i ddangos fod trancedigaeth yr iaith Gymraeg yn beth i'w ddymuno; ac yn ail, fod y peth dymunol hwn yn prysur gymeryd lle.*'– 'I shall attempt in the first place to show that the death of the Welsh language is something to be welcomed; and secondly, that this desirable situation is already a fact.'). The editor of the magazine felt that the author did not actually believe what he wrote, and that his objective was to set out an argument for discussion.

plicity of language was a bad thing, English was the dominant language and that given the 'survival of the fittest' Welsh could not survive. In addition, he did not believe that its survival affected any sense of Welsh identity. He saw that the number of speakers was already declining, the quality of language deteriorating, the language of religion was being anglicised and that the 'mad, insane' efforts to save the language were merely evidence of its demise, highlighting the fact that the Welsh Language Society was created to promote the teaching of English through Welsh.

A year later Southall challenged these arguments. In defence, he strongly emphasised the importance of education, suggesting that every effort should be made to teach Welsh in every school in Wales. He recognised that the Welsh had not yet woken up to demand a bilingual education, and that a unilingual education in English was inadequate. Education was the saviour. He saw the extension in the teaching of Welsh in the schools as a 'a silent and serene national awakening.'[337] This was in an article which he wrote in Welsh, acknowledging his thanks to a friend who had translated parts of his article and corrected his Welsh in other sections. The survival of Welsh, he perceived, was a miracle given the conditions and attitudes surrounding it. He regarded the teaching of English as essential but this should not prevent Wales becoming bilingual. The language was the perfect instrument for national unity.

Interestingly, in defending the language, he could not but introduce his Quakerism. Outlining the success of Welsh speakers throughout the kingdom, especially as preachers and ministers in English pulpits, he added that, he could not 'as a Quaker approve arrangements for the pulpit; because it is my responsibility to uphold a spiritual and free ministry,'[338] a quiet judgment in itself on the Welsh pulpit. The editor of the *British Friend* in May 1906 referred to, and quoted from, an article published in *Y Genninen*, April 1906,[339] where the writer made the claim that Wales had no need for a paid professional ministry, that all were priests. It seems probable that it was

---

337. J.E. Southall, 'A Ydyw y Gymraeg yn Marw?' *Y Genninen*, October 1898, XVI, 4, 244.
338. Ibid. 245. ('*Rhaid i mi, er hyny, nodi nas gallaf fel Crynwr gymeradwyo trefniadau pwlpudaidd; oblegid fy nyledswydd i ydyw dal i fyny weinidogaeth ysbrydoledig a rhad.*').
339. Thesbiad, 'Y Diwigiad a'r Weinidogaeth, (The Revival and the Ministry)' in *Y Genninen*, xxiv, 2, April 1906, 127–132.

Southall who drew the editor's attention to the article, and translated it for him, since it was in accord with the Quaker view.

Southall's concern for the future of the language was evident. In 1897 he won a prize for an essay written in English at the Newport Eisteddfod, under the *nom de plume* Galar Gwent (The Lament of Gwent), on the use and teaching of Welsh in Gwent; his *nom de plume* a key to his sentiments.

In 1899, he read a paper, later published, on *The Future of Welsh Education*[340] to a meeting of the Cymru Fydd Society in London.[341] He was by then well known within its circles, because in 1898 he had had his second article published in their magazine, on modern languages in county schools.[342] This association with Cymru Fydd gives some indication as to his political sympathies. No doubt he would have agreed with the sentiments expressed in the first editorial of their magazine:

> everything points to the advent of the Welsh people to a national individuality and a fuller life. Our claim to a national individuality is no longer ignored or disputed, but, on the contrary, it is agreed that whatever goes to the making of a nation, be it history, race, language or soil, the Welsh people are fully entitled to the status and dignity of a true nation.[343]

He was already in touch with one of the principal founders of Cymru Fydd, T.E. Ellis M.P, writing to him in April 1894, recognising that Ellis, as government Chief Whip, was a person of some influence. Writing from Aberystwyth, he outlined his hopes about the teaching of Welsh in schools and his own publishing plans, welcoming appointments to the Education Inspectorate in Wales. He hoped that Ellis might be able to influence the senate of the University of London to allow a petition from the Normal College, Bangor, to allow Welsh as an optional subject for matriculation.[344]

Southall maintained correspondence with E.T. John, M.P. for East Denbighshire, an ardent supporter for Welsh Home Ruler who in 1914

340. J.E. Southall, *The Future of Welsh Education: being a review of some of the existing forces affecting education in Wales from the viewpoint of NATIONAL INDIVIDUALITY* (Newport, J.E. Southall, 1900).

341. *WM*, 29.4.1899.

342. J.E. Southall, 'Modern Languages in County Schools,' in *Young Wales*, Vol. 3, September 1897, 213–215 and Vol. 4, October 1898, 235–238.

343. *Young Wales*, 1, January 1895, 1.

344. NLW, T.E. Ellis 2, MS 3784, 14.4.1894.

introduced the Government of Wales Bill in the House of Commons. The thrust was again education and the language:

> I know thee by repute as an energetic Welsh nationalist ... I look on the Welsh language as a valuable national asset which even now is not sufficiently appreciated. For the mass of the population, it affords an avenue of culture, out of the reach of the corresponding classes in England.[345]

He outlined the need to ensure that monoglot English speakers became sympathetic to the language, 'Cymrecizing' them, and was concerned at the attitude of certain counties such as Denbighshire. He called for Welsh as a compulsory subject in all elementary schools, and as a requirement for certain public posts. His support for the Welsh National Education Council and a Welsh Civil Service marks him out as favouring home rule. Writing to John in 1921, again on Welsh in education, when John was no longer an M.P., Southall advocated and supported moves for an all-Wales conference on the future of the language within education.[346]

Given his interest in the language, and the commercial publication of books in Welsh, it is not surprising that he corresponded with leading Welsh literary figures. In May 1897 he wrote to Edward Anwyl who had been professor of Welsh at University College, Bangor, about the publication of a piece entitled *The Significance of Religion*, raising questions about how it should be circulated for purpose of sales.[347] He had contact with such figures as T. Gwynn Jones, poet and professor of Welsh at Aberystwyth, whom he approached for help with translations.[348] D. Rhys Phillips, the Welsh librarian at Swansea, was another correspondent; he was very much involved with the formation of the Welsh Bibliographical Society, of which Southall, for a time, was a member. Southall enquired about the organisation in 1906, but was unable by 1914 'to continue my *tanysgrifiad* (subscription) and must reluctantly relinquish it for the present.'[349] He is listed as an ordinary member in the Society's annual reports for 1925–7.[350] There was correspondence with

---

345. NLW, E.T. John 6, MS 1821, 15.1.1918.
346. NLW, E.T. John 9, MS 2906, 28.6.1921.
347. NLW, Anwyl Letters, MS 2404D and 2505D.
348. NLW, G MS 5312 –15, 24.10.1910 – 10.10.1921, T. Gwyn Jones Papers.
349. NLW, D. Rhys Phillips 2, 4621, letter 11.8.1914.
350. List of Members, *Journal of the Welsh Bibliographical Society*, Vol 3, 1–3.

J. Glyn Davies,[351] a writer now more fondly remembered for his poems for children, and with D. J. Williams, of Llanbedr, the author of many popular books for children.[352] In 1898 Williams had published a reader for children *Hanes â Chan*, but complained to T.E. Ellis that by January 1899 he had sold few, noting that 'one school in Aberdare has had some 46 copies but the Headmaster is a personal friend of mine.'[353]

Given Southall's outlook and his penchant to proclaim his brand of Quakerism, his article, in rather stiff Welsh, in *Y Genninen* entitled 'Why I am a Quaker'[354] is unsurprising. In it he made no effort to distinguish between the witness of Fritchley and LYM, and such a distinction would in any case have been lost on the readership.

In this article Southall was at pains not to describe Quakerism as a form of religion; rather for him it was a profession, an experience, drawing from the well of life, as described in scripture. He exalted the use of silence as the means whereby the voice of God could be heard and expressed, reliant on the One Priest (Christ) amongst the worshippers. He touched upon baptism in the Spirit as a saving mechanism, and explained that if the call was to obey Christ then this did away with all sacraments. In the next edition of the magazine, he was challenged by Dewi Môn, being the bardic name of the Rev. David Rowlands, principal of Brecon College, in an article entitled 'Why I am not a Quaker.'[355] He described his one experience, in a large English city, of worshipping amongst Friends; he had found the silence burdensome, describing those gathered as being like sheep on edge. One elderly lady had ministered briefly with the words, 'Let the whole earth be silent before the Lord of hosts,' and he felt the whole experience had been wasteful, since for him opportunities to praise and pray had been lost. Dewi Môn recognised the valuable contribution Friends had made to the life of the church, and their sufferings for it, but argued that they had now become so withdrawn as 'to make place for other denominations possessing more accurate understanding of the Christian faith.'[356]

351. NLW J. Glyn Davies, Correspondence MS 3679a–c.

352. NLW, D.J. Williams, Llanbedr, Box 3, 1909–1941, 5 and 15.12.1924.

353. NLW, T.E. Ellis 1, MS 1947, 27.1.1899.

354. J.E. Southall, 'Paham yr Wyf yn Grynwr' in *Y Genninen*, XIX, 3, 1901, 171–176.

355. Dewi Môn, 'Paham nad wyf yn Grynwr,' in *Y Genninen*, XIX, 4, October, 1901, 281–285.

356. Ibid.

The following January, Southall sought to address some of the criticisms levelled by Dewi Môn and was adamant that:

> so long as the churches occupy the minds of the people with the sound of words, rather than direct them to the still quiet voice, and so long as they rely on the form of the word rather than calling on the Divine power, so long as this state remains then they ignore the search for true worship.[357]

This was not a major theological disputation; the articles were relatively short but unusual. There are no other example of such writings in a Welsh-language periodical of the time about and concerning the Quakers, other than perambulations about the noble history of the Quakers in Wales by non-Quakers; for example, a series of articles by Edward Griffith of Springfield, Dolgellau, on the early Quakers of Dolgellau in *Y Genninen*, October 1899, January and April 1890. There are two articles of a more theological bent by the Rev. J. T. Alun Jones, of Bala, in *Y Drysorfa*, July 1917, and December 1917, entitled 'Y Crynwyr.'

Southall used his press to promote and encourage the use of Welsh within schools. He was not only an advocate but a propagandist, in the positive sense of being a persuader.[358] One of his last public acts in this regard was giving evidence in 1926, on behalf of those publishing in Welsh, to the commission on the use of Welsh in education and life.[359] No doubt he saw commercial opportunities in publishing material in Welsh, particularly for schools, but this never made him a fortune. His profuse output of Quaker tracts would similarly not be personally enriching, but must have given him considerable satisfaction. His sister, writing in 1924 and again in 1927 to their younger brother, echoes her mother in hinting that Southall may not have been competent financially, hinting at the fact that he relied for some of his income from trusts established by his parents.[360] When he died in 1928, his

357. J.E. Southall, 'Paham yr Wyf yn Grynwr' in *Y Genninen*, XX, 1, January, 1902, 78.

358. See Gareth S. Jowett and Victoria O'Donnell, *Propaganda and Persuasion* (Newbury Park, Ca., Sage, 1992).

359. *Welsh in Education and Life: Being the Report of the Departmental Committee appointed by the President of the Board of Education to inquire into the position of the Welsh Language and to advise as to its promotion in the educational system of Wales*, (London, HMSO, 1927).

360. HRO, BG 99/2/182. Letters, Lucy Hannah Southall, 4.2.1924 and 15.1.1928.

total estate was nevertheless worth over £5,239, leaving £2,000 in trust to Jessie Cameron, of Bucklyvire, Stirling, Scotland, to promote Quaker literature in foreign countries.[361] Around 1934 she transferred Southall's books to the care of the Newport Public Library, who later transferred them to the NLW.[362]

He remained a plain conservative Friend, his last pamphlet in their interest appearing in 1923. He died at his brother's home in Leominster in December 1928, a year after tragedy overtook him. In February 1927 he had found his wife dead in her bed asphyxiated by coal gas escaping from a jet gaslight.[363] Despite his loss Southall's tenacity of faith was confirmed. He objected to the form of the oath, saying that 'The whole truth is not easy to get at.' The coroner told him to tell the whole truth as far as he knew it, to which Southall agreed but later qualified his evidence with the remark 'So far as my memory serves' the coroner then commenting 'that, if all witnesses were as scrupulous as Mr Southall, they would avoid a good many misstatements.'[364] A report of his burial in the *Friend* is a true reflection of his contribution to his faith and his adopted country:

> A strongly convinced Quaker of the old school, he used his press from time to time for the spread of Quaker principles. He travelled a good deal in Wales, acquiring the Welsh tongue that he might reach those who could only speak their native language. He was indeed a Welsh scholar and had published Welsh textbooks which have been widely used.[365]

He was buried in the Quaker graveyard in Leominster, his wife rests in the public cemetery in Newport.

These three men are by now largely forgotten, but they are not lost to that 'enormous condescension of posterity' and are not mere casualties of history.[366] Their voices, within Welsh and Quaker history, are now subdued,

361. HRO, BG 99/2/219.
362. Private communication with Newport Library, and dedications in the frontispieces to Southall's books at NLW.
363. *SWDN*, 4.2.1927.
364. *SWDN*, 4.2.1927.
365. *TF*, 23.11.1928, 1058.
366. E.P. Thompson, *The Making of the English Working Class*, New York, 13.

but they were 'real' people existing in a vibrant context articulating to varying degrees 'the identity of their interests,'[367] according to their circumstances and positions. They each saw their Quakerism not only as faith but as a social and cultural influence and they as its agents in its life within Wales.

All three remained true to the dissenting tradition to which they belonged. Evans stood against tithes, and his political perambulations testify to a stubbornness of purpose even when it took him away from his radical roots. Phillips pledged for freedom of conscience in education concerning the 1904 Education Act, something that Evans would not since he supported the legislation, and Phillips resolutely defended the pacifist position in response to conscription in 1916. Southall attested to a minority view of 'true' Quakerism even though they eventually disavowed him because he retained his connection with the 'other' branch. True to his stand he seems not to have been publicly committed to any testimony other than the saving grace of Christ. He was the only one born into a Quaker family; the other two were Quakers by convincement, Phillips to be thoroughly immersed in the activities of the Society, while Southall remained true to his birthright. Evans must have been on the margins and it is doubtful that he attended Meeting with any regularity. His daughters were not introduced to the Society, and one was somewhat vague as to her father's allegiance. The family worshipped with the Anglicans. Indeed there is a hint that his membership of the Society was in some way a part of Tobit's rebel nature, joining a group that was far removed from the circles which surrounded him.

All three were writers, two prominent journalists, maintaining a long tradition amongst Friends as wordsmiths. Their writings, especially those of Southall and Evans, were 'evangelistic' in tone, albeit on different topics and issues, both sharing a love and concern for the use of Welsh. Southall was not politically involved, Evans was, seeing party politics as a means of salvation. Phillips turned his back on such politics, maintaining his mission of saving souls, serving his community faithfully and diligently.

367. Ibid., 9.

Chapter 6
'Yma o hyd'

Exploration and study of the life of LYM in Wales during the nineteenth and twentieth centuries is sparse, offering a clue as to the Society's standing in the country: commentators felt that there was little of consequence to address.

Where then, after 1860, do the Quakers fit into Welsh history? There are varying interpretations of the way religion affected Welsh history. Jenkins,[1] Jones[2] and Morgan[3] draw on the view that nonconformity, language and culture were heavily intertwined into the historical tapestry. For Williams[4] and Smith,[5] it is the discovery of an awakening proletariat that defines the direction and energy of modern Welsh life, Smith feeling that adjusting to linguistic change, inevitable given the scale of migration into Wales, did not negate a commitment to a Welsh identity; the dragon has two tongues as outlined by Glyn Jones in his ground-breaking 1986 study, with a fresh understanding of the way English and Welsh complement each other.[6] Cragoe[7] on the other hand is an apologist for Anglicanism swept aside by the Nonconformist hegemony, finding for it and 'other parties ... besides the radicals'[8] a place in a maelstrom of religious jealousies and misrepresentation. Price[9] and Hughes[10] and H.G. Jones[11] are significantly more nationalistic, with a history reliant on its own inner force and consciousness, and a

1. Jenkins, *Hanes Cymru*, 1933.
2. I.G. Jones, *Explorations*, 1981 and *Communities*, 1987.
3. Morgan, *Wales in British*, 1991.
4. Williams, *When Was Wales?*, 1995.
5. Smith, *Wales*, 1999.
6. Glyn Jones, *The Dragon Has Two Tongues*, 1968.
7. Cragoe, *Anticlericalism*, 2000.
8. Cragoe, *Culture, politics*, 2004, 272.
9. Price, *David Lloyd George*, 2006.
10. Hughes, *Cymru Fydd*, 2006.
11. Jones, *John Kelsall*, 1938.

dialectic refuting the 'British/English' identification.

It is difficult to see the Quakers in Wales fitting naturally with any of these interpretations. Allen[12] is right to talk of 'Welsh Quakers,' but after the 1830s it is far harder to sustain such a description. From the 1870s onwards 'Quakers in Wales' seems a better description.

By the nineteenth century LYM, as an institution, had no robust mechanisms whereby it could reflect on matters relating to the life of Wales. The number of Quakers in the principality meant that Wales, as a national entity, existed on its periphery, its name almost expunged from its structures. Additionally within Wales the Quakers, like the Jews, had 'little effect on social affairs and policy ... because of their small membership.'[13] The number of Quakers in Wales was too small to influence any debate that was specifically Welsh, not possessing that 'critical mass'[14] as to be able to affect affairs, enabling them to influence outcomes, even assuming that they were interested in issues that were of particular importance to the Welsh constituency.

Indeed, LYM had little to say about national identity, British, Welsh or otherwise. Extrapolating from Phillips' approach national identity for it was enshrined in crown and parliament, and particularly treasured in the imperial adventure.[15] Events around these attracted considerable attention amongst Quakers. Consequently, by default, LYM became an overtly English institution, but it did not dwell on this fact because there was no awareness that it was ever an issue. The problem of Welsh or British identity had no bearing on its life, even though by the 1880s, for most people in Wales, expressing their Welsh identity had acquired considerable potency.

This divergence can be seen in LYMs reaction to the principal issues dominating Welsh political life in the late 1800s. Much of this was embedded in the politics of dissent and expressions of the nonconformist conscience. The issues weren't unique to Wales, but there disestablishment and education were seen as 'national' issues which were embedded into the national psyche and politics. The debate about temperance, whether or not the solutions

---

12. Allen, *Quaker Communities*, 2007.
13. T. Brennan, E.W. Cooney and H. Pollins, *Social Change in South West Wales*, 1954, 75.
14. See Philip Ball, *Critical Mass: How one thing leads to another*, 2005, 285.
15. Phillips, *Friendly Patriotism*,1989.

proposed were effective, similarly took on a shape and an outcome that was distinctively Welsh. The interest and sympathy of LYM in all these matters cannot be questioned, but those particular elements within them, of particular concern to Wales, were not separately addressed or considered.

LYM remained largely silent on disestablishment which was a lost cause in England, but a powerful issue in Wales. Welsh education had acquired a distinctive character of its own that the 1902 Education Act was perceived to threaten. The scale of the 'Welsh Revolt' against the Act did not, however, materially influence the deliberations and actions of LYM, although it made clear its support for personal protest against the legislation; the other Welsh nonconformist denominations were loud in their general opposition.

LYM acted according to its ancient testimonies maintaining, in most matters, a liberal, moderate viewpoint but hardly challenged the status quo. Thus temperance was never about total abstention. The principal emphasis was on supporting individual witness. Collective action was only possible when LYM, in unity, collectively discerned the way forward. The discussion around the 1902 Education Act highlights the difficulties with this, especially when some Friends were adamant that LYM was not being true to its traditions in refusing to oppose the Act on grounds of conscience. In such circumstances it highlights the difficulty in distinguishing between 'religious motivation and political opportunism.'[16]

By 1918, LYM had restated its traditional testimony on war by challenging censorship, some of its officers being prosecuted and imprisoned for this. It was Welsh speaking academics and nonconformists and the socialists, that led public pacifistic activity in Wales after 1916 – there was a strong connection between the Fellowship for Reconciliation and the Independent Labour Party in Wales[17] – and Friends were not involved this forum. Across Wales Friends were never nationally visible in their challenge to the war. As in the rest of the YM some members and attenders stood for conscience once conscription was introduced, but the volunteer soldiers amongst them challenged long held assumptions. Friends in Wales were muted and did not visibly challenge the war, responding locally to acts of personal resistance.

In terms of Welsh political life there never was a Quaker voice, finding

16. Turner, *Revivals*, 1979, 383.
17. Gwynfor Evans, *Heddychiaeth Gristnogol yng Nghymru*, 1991, 21.

direct expression specific to Wales. LYM never developed a potent voice, in the sense that they were actively, seriously and consistently engaged with Welsh issues.

In terms of sustaining Quakerism in Wales the endeavours of the HMC proved to be crucially important. However, English in language, the HMC was also geographically specific. It focused on those areas where there was still a Quaker presence, Radnorshire, Glamorganshire and Monmouthshire, and succeeded in maintaining this presence even though the membership figures remained small. The efforts of such men as Hercules Phillips were partially vindicated, albeit directed by a committee in London, working in consultation with WQM. Despite its investment in Wales, Friends from ales were never prominent in its deliberations and decisions. Between 1882 – 1918 the HMC, and its inheritor body, no Quakers from Wales served on it.

F.J. Gibbins, a keen historian of Friends in Wales, addressed WQM in 1882. He was of the opinion that between 1800–75 only 25 Friends had come into membership by convincement within South Wales Monthly Meeting, and that the

> Society here has been chiefly replenished by the Settlement within its limits of Friends from other places, to such a large extent has this been the case that there is now scarcely a member whose grandparents were Welsh Friends.[18]

SWMM was therefore of a 'very migratory character' and its meetings had no members over 25 years of age who had belonged to it during the whole of their lives. Marwick, makes a similar point about Quakers in Scotland, saying that growth there in the late nineteenth century, 'seems explicable … partly to immigration from England, probably outbalancing emigration,' as in Wales the figures of membership in Scotland were low, 363 members in 1902.[19]

Mission endeavour through the work of the HMC in Wales developed between 1867 and 1910. Without its labours it is doubtful that Quakerism in Wales would have survived. Frederick Sessions was even more certain

---

18. NLW, MS 4859 C9.
19. William H. Marwick, 'Quakers in early twentieth century Scotland,' in the *Journal of the Friends' Historical Society*, 52, 1968–71, 211–8.

saying, not just about Wales, as he addressed the Annual Meeting of the HMC during Yearly Meeting in 1891 that it was

> hardly too much to say that WQM as it exists at present owes its very existence to Home Mission work ... Where should we have been as a Quarterly Meeting if we had not filled our depleted ranks by aggressive Christianity?... The proportions of our received, as against born members are tremendously pulled down by a few non-aggressive meetings we still have. There are three of our meetings that do not report one single attender and are non-aggressive and have no mission work.[20]

The success of home mission work is not so much reflected in the number of members, but by the fact that moribund meetings were resurrected, so that by 1918 the Society still had a foothold in the country. The HMC saw itself as the saviour of the YM and had proved

> to be the saving of several dying, and the resuscitation of some dead, congregations, besides being the means of propagating the doctrines and principles of Friends through widespread districts of England and Wales.[21]

In 1885 SWMM had 76 members and at its highest point, 1899, membership stood at 181, and by 1918, 132; comparing 1885 to 1918, there had only been a net increase of 56 members, not taking into account movement within the membership and transfers into the area. An examination of the numbers of transfers into south Wales from 1890 to 1918 shows a total of 207 transfers compared to membership by convincement of seventy-one, supporting Gibbins' evaluation. Associate members and attenders were an important element in the Monthly Meeting, as the figures between 1899 and 1918 show, but these were not overwhelming. There were 79 such recorded in 1900, but by 1918 this had diminished to 25. Figures used here are based on an examination of figures derived from an analysis of the annual tabular returns and reliant on a simplification of them (1861–1918), since the format of collection and collation changed over time, making comparison difficult.

---

20. TF, 6th month, 1891, 100.
21. TF, 1st month, 1887, 4–5.

There is therefore no attempt at precision and rounded figures provide indication of trends. The returns do not show how many of these associate members became full members. Indeed it is difficult to correlate convincements to number of attenders. The highest number of convincements shown in any one year, 1905, was eight contrasted to 44 attenders recorded for that year.

Whatever judgement might be made about the style, approach and efforts of the HMC without it Friends would have gently vanished from Wales. Despite this an examination of the minutes of the HMC indicates that Friends from Wales were not prominent in its deliberations and decisions.

The 1904–05 Revival in Wales was an international event that Friends could not ignore. Their pride was touched as they perceived elements of their own practices and disciplines permeating into Welsh religious life. Silent waiting with unprepared outpouring was a signal that possibly a Quaker renewal was imminent, but this never happened.

Perhaps Friends across Wales benefitted from the spirit of the 1905–06 Revival. If so it was minimal. Many seem to have deluded themselves about its nature, dwelling on the possibilities rather than the fact. W.G. Hall saw Evan Roberts as a Quaker since he had stated 'that his message was dictated to him by the Spirit of God, and that with regard to his future engagement, he was entirely in the hands of God' and under such circumstances, and his wish not to be fettered, he had 'evinced himself a Quaker instead of a Methodist.'[22] However, if Nonconformists in Wales assumed that the Revival gave them dominance in national life[23] the Quakers could make no such claim despite enthusiasm some might have had for its outcomes. Increasingly it was the loss of authority over Welsh life that was the issue for most nonconformists, given their past dominance, but this was not an issue that challenged Friends in Wales. Indeed the legacy of the Revival according to one source

> was to be found both in the explosion of small evangelical and Pentecostal sects, which were increasingly divorced from the lives of most Welsh people.[24]

22. *The Friendly Messenger*, February 1905, 10.
23. Pope, Building, 1998, 6.
24. Chambers and Thompson, *Coming to terms*, 2005, 340.

In 1912 the YM supported what was in effect a mission to reach such elements who might yet fulfil the initial Quaker optimism, an impossible aspiration as these disparate groupings drew away from mainstream nonconformity.

The Revival and its activities highlighted one particular issue in the minds of some Friends, as to why Quakerism had failed to root itself in Wales, when dissent was flourishing: the use of music and singing. Its hold on nonconformity was so powerful that during the Tonypandy riots of 1910 workmen sang hymns. Indeed Elsie Cadbury, writing about the revival, was clear about this element.

> We must recognise the power of song. 'This movement in Wales,' said an English minister to us, 'is Quakerism plus the liberty to sing, and I pray it may teach you Quakers something.'[25]

For Frances Thompson this was something to do with the Celtic temperament which was different to the 'Teutonic race' such that the Quakers in their 'quieter forms … [followed] the same spirit in its leadings.'[26] This issue of music and its role in Welsh religious life challenged many Friends because it was one explanation for their relative failure in Wales, 'The Welsh too are ardently fond of singing and make this a very prominent part of their services [and] very much miss this if they attend Friends' meetings.'[27] F.J. Gibbins reporting on the unveiling of a statue to Henry Richard at Tregaron could comment that 'Some fine Welsh singing formed a necessary part of the proceedings.'[28] One journalist commenting on the decline of Quakerism summed it up thus:

> A powerful contributory cause is the peculiar method of worship, which, in the Quaker community has hardly changed, with the passing of the years. Its quietude, its introspection, its abandonment of all emotion and beauty is

---

25. Cadbury, *The Welsh*, 1905, 319.
26. YMP, 1905, 392.
27. NLW, MS 4859C9, Paper 9, address by F. J. Gibbins to WQM.
28. TF, 25.8.1893, 546–7, emphasis added.

completely at variance with the method of worship to which the Celtic temperament responds.[29]

As already stated LYM did not give direct attention to questions of identity and nationality. It did see Wales as 'one organising principle,'[30] possessing a unique linguistic and cultural tradition, but never weighted Welshness in its activities against other social and economic factors. The English identity of LYM remained undisputed, reinforced by the attitudes of writers and correspondents in the two principal magazines. Many Friends would have concurred with the sentiment:

We are not inclined to become 'Little Englanders.' We heartily believe in the expansion of England. A vigorous, energetic, and industrious people, increasing rapidly in population like the Anglo-Saxons must expand.[31]

The sentiments were plain, 'England has had her own little wars – little because England's power is great, and the people she has sought to subdue are weak'[32] and expanding on this that, though Egyptian soldiers had been employed in the Sudan expedition, the officers and engineers were English-men, paid for by English money such 'that one result must be to rivet the claims of England on Egypt, and that the definite evacuation of that country by England is thereby postponed for years.'[33] It was, as *The Friend* observed, that 'The Society of Friends in England forges ahead ... and committees held in London clustering round Meeting for Sufferings ... show solid advance.[34] An editorial written in 1893 about the opening of the Imperial Institute in London by Queen Victoria is illustrative of this general tenor. It was 'The loyalty of the people of England' to the Queen and the Royal family that was highlighted.[35]

---

29. SWDN, 21.1.1928. 'The Quakers in Wales: Sidelights on Welsh Religious History' by George A. Greenwood.
30. M.J. Daunton, 'Book review of 'Re–birth of a Nation,' K.O. Morgan,' in *English Historical Review*, XCVII, January 1982, 161.
31. TF, 23.4.1897, 256.
32. TF, 1.1.1897, 3.
33. Ibid.
34. TF, 15.6.1906, 391.
35. TF, 19.5.1893, 305.

In January 1912, when Sufferings considered the strained relationship between 'England and Germany,'[36] such was the ire of one Scottish meeting that the Clerk of Dundee Preparative Meeting wrote on behalf of the meeting protesting at the 'grave error in heading the appeal England and Germany.' The magazine took note, and later in the month an article on the same issue was entitled 'Britain and Germany as Friends'[37] but another article, in the same issue, was still entitled 'England and Germany' within a whole section on 'Anglo-German Relations.' By October 1912 *The Friend* had reverted to the original 'England and Germany' with the qualification of the 'strained relations between the two great Teutonic people.'[38]

This insensitivity was part of the 'British' problematic, explained by Heyck by the fact that the

> English were quick to assume that what was good for England was good for the rest of Britain. They habitually said 'England' when they meant 'Britain'. On the basis of prejudice rather than science, they asserted that the 'Anglo-Saxon race' from which English men and women, allegedly descended, was far superior to the 'Celtic race' of Wales, Scotland and Ireland.[39]

Quakers reflected common usage of the time for which they cannot easily be blamed. They would similarly make generalised distinctions about the 'races' which was no more than an idea cobbled together during the thirteenth to sixteenth centuries, and imperfectly conceptualised with little regard to its 'political' impact. Many commentators, including Quakers and others such as J.S. Mill contributed to racial theory with little regard to its exegesis, and the complexities that this created.[40] The inherent prejudice shown in writings about African-Americans, similarly, cannot simply be construed as racist within modern usage of that term, but rather an expression of how the world was perceived and appraised at the time, however erroneously. Henry

36. TF, 09.02.1912, 80.
37. TF, 23.2.1912, 107–08.
38. TF, 11.10.1912, 652.
39. Thomas William Heyck, *A History of the Peoples of the British Isles: from 1860 to 1914,* 2002, 379.
40. Ivan Haanaford, in *Race: The History of an Ideal in the West,* 1996, 8.

Stanley Newman, after his 1890 visit to America could thus write about 'the coloured people' of Arkansas that they had not yet acquired the power to govern with discretion, that it was a slow development that 'has taken the Anglo Saxon a thousand years of training to learn how to govern.'[41]

Traditionally, for many Christians, the influence of the biblical nation has been important in the political and religious imagination, with concepts of the 'Holy Nation' and 'the chosen people' giving support to the idea that we live under a 'sacred canopy.'[42] For Welsh Nonconformists the relationship between God and the 'nation' and their own sense of identity was a central theme in their faith. Morgan explores this theme in his study of the Welsh and their bible as

> the force of civilisation which formed many of our characteristics as a people, whether or not we believe in it now or not ... with the coming of the Bible into our language, we were gradually Israelised ... totally in imagination and soul.[43]

The challenging question of how God works His providential governance, such that personal and 'national' destinies are fulfilled, was important. Yet an all-encompassing God showing preference to any group of adherents is a paradox, for surely the nation is an aberration, undermining the universality and transcendence of the deity, highlighting the struggle between universality and particularity, globalisation and nationalism?[44] Quakers in LYM were similarly touched by the providence of God in the life of the country, but not as vocally as it was within the Welsh setting where religion was the one

---

41. TF, 4th month, 1890, 91.
42. Peter Berger, *The Sacred Canopy*, 1990.
43. Derec Llwyd Morgan, *Y Beibl a'n Cymreictod* (The Bible and Our Welshness), 1988 (*'grym gwareiddiad a ffurfiodd lawer iawn o'n nodweddion fel pobl, pa un a gredwn ynddo bellach ai peidio* (1) ... *Gyda dyfod y Beibl i'n hiaith, yn raddol raddol fe'n Hisraleiddiwyd... yn bendifaddau ddychymyg ac enaid.'* (5)
44. See, for example, Douglas John Hall and Rosemary Radford Ruether *God and the Nations*, 1995.

issue that contributed most over the long term to the Welsh sense of identity (and) must surely be accepted as the most important factor in encouraging Welsh national feeling in the nineteenth century.[45]

LYM made no contribution to such an outlook. Bebbington is right to highlight the fact that 'in the absence of a nationalist party, religion gave rise to a form of surrogate nationalism in Scotland as well as in Wales,'[46] but their common Protestantism also bound them to England and British imperialism. Thus, as Cragoe proposes, Welsh radicals worked within the same ideological framework as their English counterparts, and leading figures in Welsh politics 'generally defined their own ideological positions in a thoroughly British context;'[47] as Phillips eloquently argues Quakers in LYM were part of the imperial venture.[48] Although many Quakers identified with Welsh radicalism, they were not visibly attached to Welsh or Scottish national feeling, even though as Hatton concludes, despite their English origins, Friends did identify with Ireland, considered themselves as Irish even 'when the term was pejorative and usually meant Catholic-Irish.'[49] A contradiction that surely has something to do with the fact that Ireland Yearly Meeting had a separate existence.

The Welsh language was a powerful aspect of Welsh identity, but it would be foolish not to recognise that, by its supremacy, English did displace minority languages. Organisations and bodies with an all-Britain mandate naturally gave precedence to the use of English, and LYM was no exception. It never truly acknowledged any responsibilities towards Welsh as a living language. Thus, Allen writing about LYM in an earlier period, described it as an English movement because it paid scant attention to the language.[50]

45. D.W. Bebbington, 'Religion and National Feeling in 19th Century Wales and Scotland,' in *Studies in Church History*, Vol. 18: *Religion and National Identity*, Stuart Mews ed., 1982, 496.

46. Ibid. 503.

47. Mathew Cragoe, 'Conscience or Coercion? Reply,' in *Past and Present*, 169, 2000, 208, 205–213.

48. Phillips, *Friendly Patriotism*, 1989.

49. Helen E. Hatton, *The Largest Amount of Good: Quaker Relief in Ireland: 1654–1921*, 1993, 10.

50. Allen, *Quaker Communities*, 2007, 188.

This becomes part of the ambivalence within the problem of what constitutes British identity and its discourse, the accommodation of minority languages. Although aware of the importance of Welsh, Hodgkin adopted what was no doubt a common attitude amongst many of his period, when writing about George Fox in Wales. He felt that Fox would have acted like 'a true Englishman (with) an instinctive feeling that English was the proper language for a reasonable being to use.'[51] Although, in his defence, Hodgkin in 1901 he had begun to study Welsh believing 'that the history of Britain ought not to be written from the purely Teutonic point of view.'[52]

Apart from Friends all denominations in Wales, at some point or another, published regularly in Welsh. Even the minority Unitarians published *Yr Ymofynydd*, and for a short time the Salvation Army published a Welsh version of *War Cry* (*'Gad Lef'*). The 1840–50 Mormon missions were so successful that they published their own Welsh-language newspaper, *Udgorn Seion* from 1853 until 1862, but then in 1849 they had about 4,500 members in Wales in ninety-five branches, and even by 1878 they still had 457 members.[53] Given their numbers and distribution Friends could make no such linguistic investment. Additionally there was no advocate for the use of Welsh once Wales YM disappeared, and no one who would echo the sentiments of the Chief Rabbi when he visited Swansea in 1899 that it was

> essential that [the Jews] should be taught the language spoken in the country of their adoption [that] in the principality they should cultivate the Welsh language, which would materially assist them into developing into worthy and useful citizens.[54]

It was not until 1994 that Welsh ever appeared in BYMs 'Book of Discipline.'

Yet, it was not as though Friends were insensitive to the broader issue of the importance of language. H. Stanley Newman in an account of his visit to Brummana (then a part of Syria), was clear about the importance of encouraging an indigenous 'Friends' Arabic Church' where the use of Arabic

---

51. Thomas Hodgkin, *George Fox*, 1896, 147.
52. Creighton, *Thomas*, 1917, 250.
53. T.H. Lewis, *Y Mormoniaid yng Nghymru*, 1956.
54. *South Wales Daily Post*, 6.5.1899.

could predominate. Perhaps for most Friends the proximity to England, and their own linguistic preferences, affected their attitude to the use of Welsh. Although not totally devoid of understanding its importance Welsh belonged to the fringes of their witness. A report on the funeral of Mary Bowen, a descendent of a branch of a well-known Quaker banking family, was performed according to the usages of Friends at Meysydd Bach, Swansea is illustrative in this respect: 'As the large following at the funeral was nearly all Welsh speaking people, the occasion was unique.'[55]

Some Quakers might have agreed with the sentiments of Principal T.C. Edwards, in his farewell address as moderator of the South Wales Association of the Calvinistic Methodists in 1884 that 'Methodism does not exist to keep the Welsh language alive. Our religion is more important than language,'[56] or as reported in his denominational newspaper, 'It is not the purpose of any denomination to keep language alive ... It is best to throw Welsh into the sea than endanger the soul of anyone; and many certainly are in a poor state.'[57] English might have been the language of educated nonconformity in Wales, but many would also have been writing in Welsh, whilst a great number of nonconformists would have been reading in Welsh. In 1884 Tobit Evans translated a general leaflet on Quakerism into Welsh for which he wrote a very short preface, referring to former meetings across Wales, their once greater numbers, especially in Merionethshire. Inevitably, he mentioned their persecution and their emigration such that by 1800 most meetings in north Wales had closed. Now, he went on

> the English have small meetings in Swansea, Neath, Cardiff, and the Pales
> (near Penybont), Radnorshire; these are all the meetings now held by the
> Friends in Wales. It is such a pity that a denomination of such fine people
> have died out in the Principality.[58]

55. TF, 8.12.1905, 818
56. YFAC, 22.10.1884. ('... nad yw Methodistaieth yn bod i gadw yn fyw yr iaith Gymraeg. Y
    mae ein Crefydd yn bwysicach na'n iaith.').
57. Y Goleuad, 18.10.1884. ('Nid amcan unrhyw enwad crefyddol ydoedd cadw yn fyw iaith ...
    Gwell bwrw y Gymraeg i'r mor na pheryglu einioes yr eneidiau; ac y mae rhai ohonynt yn
    sicr o fod mewn enbydrwydd.').
58. Cymdeithas y Cyfeillion a elwir yn gyffredin 'Crynwyr,' 1884, translated from the English
    by H. Tobit Evans. ('Y mae gan y Saeson gyfarfodydd bychain yn Abertawe, Castellnedd,

Evans' use of the term 'English,' indicates that for him these meetings had no Welsh-speaking Friends, conveying a representation that they were an alien denomination who had lost their Welsh roots and language; a perception that many in Wales would have concurred. The Welsh language had no place in the deliberations of LYM and no one well-placed in its life able to access the pronouncements of that constituency. McLeod's comment about not accessing Welsh language material for his historical studies because he cannot read the language is apposite.[59]

Part of the problem for Quakers in Wales was that the Welsh had already consigned them to history. Indeed H.D. Phillips' evidence to the Royal Commission on the Church in 1908 was guilty of this, dwelling as it did on the noble, golden suffering past. Quakers held particular fascination for Welsh antiquarians, such as Alcwyn C. Evans (1828–1902) who lived in the former meeting house in Carmarthen, George Eyre Evans, the Unitarian minister at Aberystwyth, and J.H. Davies, Cwrtmawr, Llangeitho. Reliance on past Quaker history and their 'Sufferings' became badges of honour, providing legitimacy to their role in Welsh life The two articles by the Rev. J.T. Alun Jones, in *Y Drysorfa*, 1917 reflects this over-romanticised tendency: 'And even though in comparison they are few in number, amongst the smallest of the Protestant tribes, their influence is great and important.'[60] Friends were comfortable with this. The sufferings of other sects, was not as dramatic, though this ignores the fact that the early Methodists in Wales also suffered even into the late eighteenth century.[61] HRMM's Triennial Report to the Quarterly Meeting in 1893 considered the past success of Quakerism in Wales, at the time of George Fox, and the current state of religious life in Wales, stating that:

Caerdydd, a'r Pales (ger Penybont), Maesyfed; a dyna yr holl gyfarfodydd a gynhelir gan y Cyfeillion yng Nghymru yn awr. Gresyn fod Cyfundeb o bobl mor rhagorol wedi marw yn y Dywysogaeth.).

59. McLeod, *Secularisation in Western Europe*, 16–17.
60. Jones, in *Y Drysorfa*, July 1917, no. 1041, 241–6 ('*A serch er ychydig mewn cymhariaeth yw eu rhif, a'u bod ym mhlith y lleiaf o'r llwythau Protestanaidd, mae eu dylanwad yn fawr a phwysig.*') and December 1917, No. 1046, 446–51.
61. See E.D. Evans, 'Methodist Persecution in Merioneth in the late eighteenth century,' in *Historical Society of the Presbyterian Church of Wales*, 28, 2004, 23–37.

Our own well known historical tradition as sufferers for liberty of conscience, and the whole tendency of religious Welsh aspirations, present a wide and open door for us to enter, and gather in a spiritual harvest.[62]

Friends never addressed that challenge. WQM dwelt rather on the 'sweet fragrance attaching to the name of Friends in some parts of Wales' and that 'their great service in the securing of religious liberty will never be forgotten.'[63] In this case the author being Hercules Phillips was not a disinterested party!

Heyck sees five main themes affecting Wales between 1860–1914 against which Friends can be measured.[64] First, they were not involved in questions concerning the land and poor relations between landlord and tenant; second, even though they were to be found within the 'dominance of nonconformity,' they had little authority within Wales. There was then the attachment of nonconformity to the British Liberal party which they never endorsed, and Friends' role in the Welsh cultural revival can best be described as decidedly muted if not non-existent. Finally, they were indisputably caught in the process of industrialisation in south Wales, largely before 1860, and part of its development. Within this matrix they retained some connection and influence, even though their own vibrancy depended on in-migration from England. By this analysis, however, they were detached, almost bystanders in the life of Wales. As one Quaker would have it they had 'failed to keep within the flow of Welsh life.'[65]

Isichei,[66] Kennedy[67] and Phillips[68] are amongst the few historians to have undertaken detailed research into the activities of LYM during the period of this study, but none pay any heed to Wales or Welsh issues. Isichei does refer to the almost total absence of Friends in Wales. Such an omission is understandable given the Anglo-centricity of their studies, a feature upon which they do not dwell and are not sensitive to its implications, similar

---

62. HRMM, 23.11.1893, Triennial report to WQM.
63. SWDN, 10.10.1921. 'Churches of Wales, Missions and Ministers No. 15: the Story of Quakerism.'
64. Heyck, *A History of*, 2002, 380.
65. Quoted by Jonathan Lloyd, *Y Crynwyr yng Nghymru*, London, BBC, 1947, 6. ('... *methu a chadw ynghanol ffrwd y bywyd Cymreig.*').
66. Isichei, *Victorian*, 1970.
67. Kennedy, *British Quakerism*, 2001.
68. Phillips, *Friendly Patriotism*,1989.

indeed to the way LYM behaved. Their perspective is singularly 'English' since it is through the mirror of English history that they analyse and saw the Yearly Meeting.

Kennedy is concerned for LYM as a religious community, irrespective of any national labels, describing the transformation in its life across Britain and thus reliant on national 'British' events. Apart from examining activities within Lancashire and Cheshire Quarterly Meeting before 1871, he ignores the implications of transformation at the regional and local levels – the local, Monthly and Quarterly meetings. His principal argument about transformation is important, but he could have paid more attention to the less well-publicised life of the YM to demonstrate that its life was not so dominated by the events as described by him. He refers to the disownment of Edward Trusted Bennett in 1873, for his unsound theological views, noting that 'he was the last British Quaker to be disowned for holding unsound views.'[69] It is however difficult not to consider the disownment of William Mills of Cardiff in 1893 as being comparable to Bennett's in importance, even though strictly speaking he was not cast out for heresy. Mills' disownment demonstrated the tenaciousness of Quietist views within the YM and the tensions arising from this. Mills was not however a figure of importance, and his expulsion was linked by his Monthly Meeting to his behaviour rather than to his pronouncements, even though these challenged the orthodoxy within LYM. Mills was also an ordinary workingman and the suggestion of class bias cannot be totally disregarded.

The transformation for Kennedy was part of an evolutionary unfolding of LYM into a more liberal organisation beginning around the 1870s and 1880s, an accommodation with modernity. Yet within Wales and WQM there is no sign that these undercurrents made much impression, Friends there remaining theologically orthodox. Friends in Wales did not take up the banner of liberal modernity with any vigour, and no such voice is heard from there. At the same time the 'Quietist' tensions in Cardiff can be largely ignored, not because they were irrelevant, but because they had no effect on the life of the Monthly and Quarterly Meeting, other than as an irritant contained locally, compared to agitations elsewhere.

69. Kennedy, *British Quakerism*, 2001, 82.

Kennedy highlights, as he sees it, the gulf between evangelicals and liberals,[70] particularly on the question of Home Mission, and appears exaggerated, since at the regional level a greater sense of balance prevailed. This might also be true to some extent at the national level. When for example the new HMC committee was established and met in 1894, it was unequivocal about its position. Its minute, whilst hinting at some disagreement, gave continued support for the work already being undertaken, indicating some element of unity amongst the committee:

> At this and at our previous sitting we have been engaged in a serious consideration of the present position of the work under our care, as well as of our future policy and methods of procedure. A proposal has been made for the entire discontinuance of the plan hitherto adopted of assisting Friends with a definite religious concern to reside more or less permanently in given centres of work. While earnestly desiring to meet the objections felt by some Friends to this portion of the Committee's service, it is felt that no course which would in any way interfere with entire freedom of service in any of those whom the Lord has called into His harvest field can be satisfactory. We cannot therefore, adopt the proposal.[71]

The role of mission was not affected, and it is after this that much of their activity took place in Wales. Whereas it is true that this was two years before the Manchester Conference, the direction of the HMC, even after this, were not so radically changed. Kennedy gives no credit for the way home mission saved many meetings, adding to the Society's resilience and vigour. From the Welsh perspective that gulf never existed.

Kennedy's contention that the Inward Light was for many nineteenth century Friends a 'delusion'[72] to be discarded seems somewhat strong especially since he places little reliance on Holiness activities within the YM, and ignores the importance of the Welsh Revival. He overstates his case. Both rekindled an understanding of the Inward Light, and those Friends who visited the Revival in 1904–05 saw this as a reawakening of that Light.

70. Ibid., 127.
71. HMC, M3, 4.5.10.1894.
72. Kennedy, *British Quakerism*, 2001, 428.

Perhaps the difficulty is how the Inward Light is understood. If it is about the reawakening of the presence of Christ in the heart, then the Revival cannot be ignored and was an important element that briefly touched the life of the Yearly Meeting, irrespective of its long-term impact.

Similarly, there was little activity amongst the Quaker Socialists in Wales. S.G. Hobson would undoubtedly have been active in the Socialist Quaker Society had he not resigned his membership before it was established within the YM. In this context Friends in Wales remained conservative in their social outlook. The minutes as highlighted already from Llandrindod Wells meeting are illustrative of this.

Kennedy sees the failure of LYM to uphold the peace testimony during the Boer War, as 'a spiritual debacle'[73] but in reality this loosened their corporate approach such that, when the First World War came, a more pragmatic and tolerant attitude prevailed across the Yearly Meeting, most certainly in Wales, even as others rediscovered the radical challenge of that testimony. This parallels, in part, the change that occurred in attitudes with regard to tithes in the previous century, which had become a compromised tenet of faith and an exaggerated grievance.[74] Both are indicators not of a loosening of faith, a compromise of principle, but rather a willingness to live in the world and meet its challenges openly whilst retaining a willingness to be radical and open. Even if Quakers in Wales retained a more conservative theology they were not so straight laced as to be intolerant of readjustment and compromise.

Phillips is concerned for the politics that surrounded LYM in the Edwardian period, remaining aloof from Welsh developments, and thus looses sight of important influences within the British polity. He gives no space to matters Welsh or Scottish, since his premise is that the life of LYM was, in its generality, in unity on political matters affecting the state. In terms of how the YM acted as a body this is largely correct, thus he can ignore any anomalies stemming from differences expressed outside of England. Since Friends in Wales and Scotland were largely in accord with such national sentiments, Phillips can hardly be accused of being partisan.

Phillips' thesis fits in well within a framework of a denomination

---

73. Ibid., 424.
74. See Evans, *The Contentious Tithe*, 1976.

comfortable, safe and bourgeois in its undertakings and accomplishments, loyal servants of crown and Imperial venture. This was also true of the Welsh except that they were also striving to recover their identity and national consciousness, concerns that were not as germane to England. The viewpoint of Friends was sympathetic to Welsh efforts but they were not actively engaged within them. They paid lip service, reported and reflected on them, but did not take up the issues publicly as did the other Nonconformist denominations, for whom it might be said that 'Nationalism [was] the philosophy of identity made into a collectively organised passion'[75] but not for the Quakers of Wales.

Isichei in her examination of LYM as a social institution remains detached from what were the realities affecting the political and social life of Wales. Yet her clear analysis of the class structure within LYM, as non-plebeian and elitist, is as relevant to Welsh society since that is what they were within Wales. Some care needs to be taken when looking at Radnorshire where, in this rural area, new converts to Quakers were in the main ordinary local people, as indeed were those attached to the Quaker mission meetings anywhere. Wales had few connections amongst the ordinary working classes, whatever their language, and with the monoglot Welsh they might as well have been aliens, since Friends really had no one to communicate within that community. Even amongst the bilingual and more educated populace their principal resonance was as memory of past endeavours and sacrifices.

Friends in Wales had long been overtaken by the dynamism and numbers of the other denominations dominating Welsh public life who helped steer the recovery of Welsh national identity well into the twentieth century. The absence of hymns, which 'provided the substance of much popular music,'[76] and of the sermon, with its 'nineteenth century princes,'[77] from the Quaker meeting further reinforced the class and cultural divide, especially since in Wales both were important elements in the shaping of the national character.

75. Edward Said, *Identity, Authority and Freedom: The Potentate and the Traveller*, 1991, 17.
76. Kenneth D. Brown, *A Social History of the Nonconformist Ministry in England and Wales 1800-1930*, 1988, 5.
77. Ibid., 234.

Both were common features of the Quaker mission meetings but never touched the traditional meeting or the life of the YM.

Punshon, writing the most recent 'short' history of Quakers, has five references to Wales ending with the eighteenth-century Methodist revival. He refers to John Wesley and George Whitfield,[78] but makes no reference to the fact that the Welsh Methodist revival had features unique to itself; neither does he feel the need to mention the 1904–05 revival. Nevertheless, but implicitly, he acknowledges that Wales, Scotland and Ireland were national entities. George Fox's tour of 1667–8 was 'through the whole nation [i.e. England] touching Wales and Scotland also'[79] and the early Quakers took 'their message beyond the confines of England.'[80] They, however, owed no allegiance to 'this world' were unmoved by political considerations, and any national or cultural attributes could be ignored, except that by default LYM acquired an English persona becoming an institution with an English core. In Scotland and Wales Friends were to remain a minority within scattered communities forming part of LYMs fringe. Implicitly Punshon recognises the Englishness of organisational Quakerism and makes no attempt to relate to issues of national diversity within Britain. He like many of the commentators who lived during the period covered by this thesis makes the Quakers to be spectators to Welsh national life, placing them on its margins, reinforcing their image as an institution best reflective of English attitudes and history. Dandelion on a broader and wider scholarly canvass similarly overlooks the nationalistic dimension to Quakerism across Britain.[81]

Irish affairs did trouble LYM, affecting many Friends individually, reflective of the mayhem evident at the Parliamentary level. This was not true for Welsh issues whose affairs remained comparatively lowly in the YM. How else does one explain the fact that the YM supported a petition for Sunday closing in Ireland but never mentioned the earlier Welsh equivalent?[82] It was not indifference, but in Ireland Quakers had a national voice and forum, which was not true of Wales, and the dominance of Irish

78. Punshon, *Portrait*, 1999, 148.
79. Ibid., 85.
80. Ibid., 69.
81. Pink Dandelion, *An Introduction to Quakerism*, 2007.
82. YMP 1888, 50.

Catholicism shaped attitudes, whereas in Wales, Friends were comfortable with its nonconformist dominance. Wales could be taken for granted; there was no 'Welsh question.'

Given the paucity of scholarly material about Quakers in Wales from 1830 almost to the present day, further work needs to be done on examining the overall development of Friends across the YM throughout this period. This study explores only part of that picture. There is a need for a comprehensive study of the development and successes of Home Mission across the whole of the YM. This could counterbalance some of the hagiography with which Kennedy and others[83] have endowed to the 1895 Manchester Conference, seen as the pivotal point when modernity gripped the YM. The work of the HMC and also of the FFDSA deserves fresh reappraisal, so that the transformation in the life of the YM in the twentieth century can be put in better perspective. Had Home Mission not happened then it is questionable whether Quakerism in Wales and elsewhere would have survived. Their activity within Wales and WQM is clear, but study of what happened in other Quarterly Meetings is necessary. Alongside this a clearer understanding of tension between evangelics and liberals at the local/regional level would be helpful, since that debate has tended to be dominated by national considerations. One of the most intriguing aspects pervading the life of LYM in the Victorian period, was the two or three way theological emphasis, with a[its problematic nomenclature, within it. The inter-relationship between these elements is important since it touched upon the life of meetings at every level. These viewpoints found expression in the pages of the *Friend*, and the *British Friend*, but further work is merited, particularly at the Quarterly Meeting level, to see how it was expressed there. One distinct issue, for example, is the actual relationship between Quakers in Fritchley Meeting and the rest of the YM, which has been poorly explored even though documentary evidence is scant; Lowndes does not explore this inter-relationship.[84]

Another element deserving attention is impact on the life of the Yearly Meeting of the split in the Liberal camp over Irish Home Rule and the Boer

83. See for example Roger Wilson, Manchester, Manchester and Manchester Again: from 'Sound Doctrine' to 'A Free Ministry' the theological travail of LYM throughout the nineteenth century 1990.

84. Lowndes, *The Quakers of*, 1980.

War, and the emergence of the Liberal Unionist. These point to conservative political attitudes within the YM, which affected discussion and decisions within it on domestic and theological affairs.

The standing of the Society across Wales was defined by its past, rather than by its contemporary contribution. No Quakers could be described as prominent figures affecting Welsh national consciousness on any level – politically, culturally or religiously. They were not commentators on Welsh life, and there was no leadership from where this could have come. The Wesleyans had the Welshman, the Rev. Hugh Price Hughes to lead and redirect them, and in England the Baptists would look to such figures as the Rev. John Clifford. In Wales most people would have recognised the names of leading ministers across the denominations, and the Unitarians, few as they were, could claim to be provide Welsh national 'leaders.'[85] In January 1900 the *Western Mail* described Charles Allen Fox, who had by then unbeknownst to the paper been disowned by his Monthly Meeting, as 'the leading Quaker in this district.'[86] No doubt this was much to the chagrin of many Quakers in the south Wales/Cardiff area. Fox was a great self-publicist, but nevertheless it is a comment that reflects on the general standing of Quakers in the community.

LYMs life in Wales was shaped not by the famous but by ordinary individuals none of whom grew to obvious national prominence. They exercised their influence and authority within what were essentially 'quiet processes and small circles,'[87] and reflected the way the YM, as a denomination, lived its witness in Wales. The three, whose lives are illustrated made such a contribution to the witness of LYM, even if it were not so consequential as to leave a significant footprint on Welsh history. They must be counted amongst Milligan's backbenchers, the lesser and unknown;[88] those neglected or overlooked in the Rowntree Quaker histories.

By 1914 Cardiff was the largest meeting in Wales. Yet, despite investment in Newport, Swansea and Radnorshire, the second largest meeting was

---

85. See D. Elwyn Davies, *Cewri'r Ffydd* (Giants of the Faith) 1999.
86. WM, 12.1.1900.
87. QFP, para. 24.56, quote from Rufus Jones.
88. Edward H. Milligan, 'Biography as a foundation of history' on http://www.quaker.org.uk/talks accessed 20.02.13.

Colwyn Bay. Colwyn Bay Meeting had had no direct input by the HMC, being reliant on retirees into the district. Neath continued its gentle decline. To-day, it has a membership of two, meets on two Sundays a month, the meeting house being in the care of the local council, with Friends allowed to use it. As the home mission workers retreated, so did much of the vitality of the meetings to which they had been attached. Even in Llandrindod, where Phillips remained in post until 1934, his presence could not compensate for that process of secularisation affecting the whole of religious life in Wales.

What then of Quakers in Wales from c.1860 to 1918? Any deconstruction of the life of LYM in Wales indicates that it was long alienated from its Welsh roots and beginnings, almost a relic clinging to the fabric of Welsh history, aloof from the national and communal life of Wales. Indeed one Welsh commentator in Y Faner felt that the 1895 Manchester Conference had generated an awareness that the

> Quakers as a denomination had kept themselves excessively apart, not taking the necessary steps to influence public opinion on the principal issues of the day.[89]

Within Wales they were confined geographically having no involvement of note in most of the country, absent from the populous valleys of south Wales. As a body they were few, feeble, and dominated by Friends who had moved primarily into south Wales, reflecting the demographic changes accompanying industrialisation. Even in Radnorshire the same characteristic is evident, although there the two mission meetings at Llanyre and Penybont provided a more local, native flavour. It is difficult to see the Quakers as being rooted in the national life of Wales. LYM, even had it aspired to, could not be construed as having a Welsh dimension, and its organisational structures did not allow for this. As such, Quakerism reflected 'a mere episode in the religious history of the principality.'[90] They were small in number 'almost all English settlers in Wales, with the exception of a section of Quakers in

---

89. YFAC, 16.11.1895. ('... fod y Crynwyr fel cyfundeb, wedi cadw eu hunain ar wahan yn ormodol, heb gymmeryd rhan ddyladwy yn ffurfiad barn y cyhoedd ar gwestiynau penaf y dydd.')
90. *Liverpool Mercury*, 5.4.1894.

Radnorshire, who are Welsh by descent, but quite Anglicised in speech.'[91]

There was no voice within LYM to speak on Welsh matters, nor indeed from amongst its members in Wales, and it was divorced from the mainstream of Welsh religious culture. Yet, this was a denomination that had contributed to the religious topography of Wales, and continued to be held in considerable esteem; Principal T.C. Edwards noted his sadness that Quakerism and its beauteous offering was in danger of disappearing – and not merely in Wales.[92] This was a group of believers who at a time of great turmoil, tenacious in their sufferings, had proved their metal in the past, an exemplar to be replicated. They were part of old Welsh dissent, with a voice that had influence within the ruling Victorian and Edwardian elites, such that they could not be ignored despite their small numbers across the UK, but they were never busy or closely involved in Welsh affairs and did not generate any activity at a Welsh national level. They were merely a drop of lubricant in the machinery of Welsh denominational witness.

The shallowness of LYMs concern and interest for Wales is evident, and thus denies it any claim to be representative of 'British' Quakerism. In its general and conceptual behaviour it represented 'English' Quakerism, and as such was it configured. Wales suffered from a form of 'benign neglect,' a gentle form of forgetfulness, and most Quakers would not have been as emotionally attached to those issues that gripped their fellow Nonconformists in Wales. The LYM was by default an English institution with its life shaped, unconsciously, by that fact. In Wales Quakers were but a remnant,

> In character and content, the Quakers in Wales were English rather than Welsh ... when the nineteenth century dawned, the Quakers yet stayed in some pockets in Wales – as snow in the shadow of the wall.[93]

91. Ibid.
92. *Y Goleuad*, 18.10.1884.
93. Jones, 'John Kelsall,' 1939, 87. ('*Mewn ffurf a chynnwys, Seisnig yn hytrach na Chymrieg oedd y Crynwyr yng Nghymru ... Pan wawriodd y Bedwaredd Ganrif ar Bymtheg, arhosai'r Crynwyr eto mewn ambell lecyn yng Nghymru – megis eira yng nghysgod clawdd.*').

Bibliography

Primary Material

Bangor University Archives
  Student record for Henry Tobit Evans

Borthwick Institute for Archives, York
  Medical details relating to William Jesper Sayce

Ceredigion Archives, Aberystwyth (CA)
  Log Book, Llechryd British School

Ceredigion Library Service, Aberystwyth
  Unauthored manuscript on Henry Tobit Evans

Glamorgan Record Office, Cardiff (GRO)
  A List of Members of the South Division of Wales Monthly Meeting in the County
  of Glamorgan, from 1837 to 1924 inclusive
  Minute Books Cardiff Preparative Meeting
  Minute Books Neath Preparative Meeting
  Minute Books South Division of Wales Monthly Meeting
  Minutes, Ministry and Oversight Committee, South Wales Monthly Meeting
  Minute Books Swansea Preparative Meeting
  Minute Book of Wales Yearly Meeting
  Register Cardiff First Day School
  Tabular Statement Returns, South Wales Monthly Meeting

Herefordshire Records Office, Hereford (HRO)
  Minute Book Hereford and Radnor Monthly Meeting
  Minute Book Leominster Preparative Meeting
  Minute Book, Ministry and Oversight Committee, Hereford and Radnor Monthly
  Meeting
  The Southall Family Archive

Library of the Society of Friends, London (LSF)
  Dictionary of Quaker Biography
  General Committee Minutes, Friends First Day School Association
  Meeting Records: Vol. 9–10
  Minute Books and Reports Meeting for Sufferings, 1860–2006.
  Minute Book Westminster and Longford Monthly Meeting
  Minute Books Home Mission Committee
  Minute Books Home Mission Executive Committee
  Minutes Home Mission and Extension Committee

Minutes Home Mission and Extension Committee, Executive Committee
Minutes Friends Tract Association
Minutes and Proceedings London Yearly Meeting
Minutes Parliamentary Committee

Lancashire Record Office, Preston (LRO)
Minute Books Lancashire and Cheshire Quarterly Meeting
Minute Book Women's Quarterly Meeting, Lancashire and Cheshire

National Library of Wales, Aberystwyth (NLW)
Anwyl Letters
Calvinistic Methodist Archives
D.R. Daniel Collection
Daniel Davies, Ton, Collection
O.M. Edwards Papers
T.E. Ellis Papers
Sir Samuel T. Evans Papers
J.R Hughes Collection
E.T John Papers
T. Gwyn Jones Papers
Llandinam Papers
League of Nation Union Papers
D. Rhys Phillips Papers
MS 1882B, Crosswood Papers 242, Copies of letters.
MS 2819C, David Samuel 9-14, Notes on Welsh Grammar.
MS 4859C, The Society of Friends in Wales.
MS 9511D, 'S.R' and 'C.R' Correspondence.
MS 14432B, Dr. J.H. Salter, Natural History, Journal 2.
MS 18114D, Letters etc to Henry Tobit Evans.
MS 18438C, Letters to Henry Tobit Evans.
MS 18618C, Letters to Henry Tobit Evans.

Powys County Archives Office, Llandrindod Wells (PCAO)
Minute Book Llandrindod Wells Preparative Meeting
Minute Book North Wales Monthly Meeting
Minute Book of the Pales Mission and Day School

Wellcome Institute Library, London
Sir George Newman Collection

Worcestershire Record Office, Worcester (WRO)
Minute Book General Meeting for Herefordshire, Warwickshire and Wales
Minute Books Western Quarterly Meeting
Minutes Western Quarterly Meeting Evangelistic Committee

Newspapers

Cambrian News
Carmarthen Journal
Daily Mirror
Daily News
Freeman's Journal and Commercial Advertiser
Liverpool Mercury
Manchester Guardian
Liverpool Mercury
Pembrokeshire County Guardian
Radnor Express
South Wales Daily News
South Wales Daily Post
Swansea and Glamorgan Herald and Herald of Wales
The Aberystwyth Observer and Merionethshire News
The Christian
The Crusader
The Friendly Messenger
The Guardian
The Times
Welsh Gazette
Western Mail
Y Cymro
Y Deyrnas
Y Faner ac Amserau Cymru
Y Genedl
Y Goleuad
Ye Brython Cymreig
Yr Undebwr Cymreig

Periodicals

Cymru
Friend's Quarterly
Friends Quarterly Examiner
Nature
The British Friend
The Builder
The Friend
The Friendly Messenger
Y Casglwr
Y Diwygiwr
Y Drysorfa

Y Dysgedydd
Yr Efrydydd
Y Genninen
Waymarks
Young Wales

Secondary Material

Allen, Richard C. 'The Society of Friends in Wales: The Case of Monmouthshire *c.*1654–1836,' unpublished PhD thesis, University of Wales, Aberystwyth, 1999.

Dandelion, P. 'A Sociological Analysis of the Theology of Quakers,' unpublished PhD thesis, University of Brighton, 1993.

Dobbs, Carol Anne. 'The Welsh Religious Revival of 1904,' unpublished B.A. dissertation, University of Birmingham, 1974.

Evans, O.G. 'Llain y Delyn, Fellowship House, Tymbl and its relation to the Quakers in Britain,' unpublished, M.Phil Thesis, Birmingham, 2001.

Griffiths, Eirwen. 'Monmouthshire and the Education Act 1902: The Welsh Revolt of 1902–05: A Study of Conflict between National and Local Government in the Field of Education,' unpublished M.Phil thesis, London, 1994.

Hibbert, Michael. 'Quaker Influences on Adult Education during the Victorian Era (1837–1901),' unpublished M.Ed thesis, University of Wales, Bangor, 1990.

Jones, H.G. 'John Kelsall: A Study in Religious and Economic History,' unpublished M.A. thesis, University of Wales, Bangor, 1938.

Llywellyn, Henry Byron. 'A Study of the Apostolic Church in Wales in the context of Pentecostalism,' unpublished M.Phil thesis, University of Wales, Cardiff, 1997.

Munson, J.E.B. 'A Study of Nonconformity in Edwardian England as revealed by the Passive Resistance Movement against the 1902 Education Act,' unpublished PhD thesis, Oxford, 1973.

Owen, J.A. Owen. 'A Study of Orality and Conceptuality during the Welsh Religious Revival of 1904–06,' unpublished PhD thesis, University of Birmingham, 1997.

Phillips, Brian David. 'Friendly Patriotism: British Quakerism and the Imperial Nation, 1890–1910,' unpublished PhD thesis, University of Cambridge, 1989.

Spencer, Carole D. Quakerism as Holiness: An Historical Analysis of Holiness in the Quaker Tradition, unpublished PhD thesis, University of Birmingham, 2004.

Turner, Christopher Ben. 'Revivals and Popular Religion in Victorian and Edwardian Wales,' unpublished PhD thesis, University of Wales, Aberystwyth, 1979.

Williams, M. Fay. 'The Society of Friends in Glamorgan, 1654–1900,' unpublished M.A. thesis, University of Wales, Aberystwyth, 1950.

Books:

Allen, Richard, *Quaker Communities in Early Modern Wales: From Resistance to Respectability* (Cardiff, University of Wales Press, 2007).

Amery, Julian, *The Life of Joseph Chamberlain: 1901–1903*, Vol iv (London, Macmillan, 1951).

Anderson, Benedict, *Imagined Communities: Reflections on the Origin and Spread of Nationalism* (London, Verso, 2002).

Andreasen, Tonnes, *Resignation of Membership in the so-called Friends Christian Fellowship Union* (Cardiff, 11th month 1880).

_____, *The Truth* (Cardiff, no date or publisher).

_____, *Where are the "Quakers' gone to?'* (Cardiff, J David, 1887).

_____, *A Guide to the Truth as held by the People (in scorn) called Quakers* (Cardiff, J. David, Steam Printer, 1889).

_____, *The Famine or the State of the Society of Friends at the present day, with extracts from Samuel Fothergill and Sarah (Lynes) Grubb* (Cardiff, J. David, Machine Printer, 203 Bute Road, 1890).

ap Nicholas, Islwyn, *Heretics at Large: The Story of a Unitarian Chapel* (Llandysul, Gomer Press, 1977).

Arnold, Mathew, 'On the Study of Celtic Literature,' in *Lectures and Essays in Criticism* (Manchester, University of Manchester Press, 1962) 258–290.

Arnot, R. Page, *South Wales Miners: A History of the South Wales Miners Federation (1898–1914)* (London, George Allen & Unwin, 1967).

Ashton, Philip, 'The Divided Ideals: The Religious Society of Friends and the Irish Home Rule Controversy 1885 to 1886,' *The Woodbrooke Journal*, N[o.] 6 (Birmingham, Woodbrooke Quaker Study Centre, Summer 2000).

Ausubel, Herman, *John Bright: Victorian Reformer* (London, John Wiley and Sons, 1966).

Baker, William King, *A Quaker Warrior: Life of William Hobson* (London, Headley Bros, 1913).

Ball, Philip, *Critical Mass: How one thing leads to another* (London, Arrow Books, 2005).

Ball, Stuart, 'The National and Regional Party Structure' in *Conservative Century: The Conservative Party since 1900* (Anthony Seldon and Stuart Ball eds., Oxford, Oxford University Press, 1994) 169–220.

Barclay, Robert, *Barclay's Apology in Modern English*, Dean Freiday ed., (Elberon, N.J., 1967).

Barnard, H.C., *A History of English Education from 1760* (London, University of London Press, 1964).

Bassett, T.M., *Bedyddwyr Cymru* (Abertawe, Ty Ilston, 1977).

_____, 'The Sunday School,' in *The History of Education in Wales*, Vol 1, Jac L.

Williams and Gwilym Rees Hughes eds., (Swansea, Christopher Davies, 1978) 70–82.

Bauman, Richard, *Let Your Words Be Few: Symbolism of speaking and silence among Seventeenth-century Quakers* (Cambridge, Cambridge University Press, 1983).

Bebbington, D.W., *The Nonconformist Conscience: Chapel and Politics, 1870–1914* (London, George Allen and Unwin, 1982).

_____, 'Religion and National Feeling,' in *19th Century Wales and Scotland in Studies in Church History*, Vol. 18, 'Religion and National Identity,' Stuart Mews, ed., (Basil Blackwell, Oxford, 1982) 489–503.

_____, *Victorian Nonconformity* (Bangor, Headstart History, 1992).

Bello, Walden, *Visions of a Warless World* (Washington DC, Friends Committee on National Legislation, 1986).

Bellows, Elizabeth, *John Bellows: Letters and Memoirs edited by his wife* (London, Kegan Paul, Trench, Trubner and Co. Ltd.,1904).

Berger, Peter, *The Sacred Canopy* (Anchor Books, London, 1990).

Bhabha, Homi, 'Introduction,' in *Nation and Narration*, Homi Bhabha, ed., (London, Routledge, 1995) 1–7.

Book of Christian Discipline of the Religious Society of Friends in Great Britain (London, Samuel Harris, 1883).

Boulding, Kenneth, *New Nations for Old* (Wallingford, Pendle Hill Pamphlets, 1942).

Braithwaite, William C., *The Beginnings of Quakerism*, ed. Henry J Cadbury, (Cambridge, Cambridge University Press, 1955).

_____, *The Second Period of Quakerism*, (York, William Sessions, 1961).

Brennan, T., E.W. Cooney and H. Pollins, *Social Change in South West Wales* (London, Watts and Co., 1954).

Breuilly, John, *Nationalism and the State* (Manchester, Manchester University Press, 1993).

Briggs, Asa, 'Past, Present and Future in Headlines: The 1890's,' in *Fins de Siècle: How Centuries End*, Asa Briggs and Daniel Snowman eds., (London, Yale University Press, 1996) 157-196.

Brockway, Fenner, *Bermondsey Story: The Life of Alfred Salter* (London, George Allen and Unwin, 1947).

Brown, Kenneth D., *A Social History of the Nonconformist Ministry in England and Wales 1800–1930*, Oxford, Clarendon Press, 1988.

Brown, Roger Lee, *A Pool of Spirituality – A Life of David Howell (Llawdden)* (Dinbych, Gwasg Gee, 1998).

Bruce, Steve, *A House Divided: Protestantism, schism and secularisation* (London, Routledge, 1990).

Burke, Peter, 'Overture: The New History, its Past and its Future,' in *New Perspectives on Historical Writing*, Peter Burke ed., (Oxford, Polity Press, 1997), 1–23.

Burnet, G.B., *The Story of Quakerism in Scotland: 1650–1850* (London, James Clarke and Co., 1952).

Butler, David M., *The Quaker Meeting-houses of Britain*, Vol II (London, Friends Historical Society, 1999).

Carlyle, Thomas, *Sartor Resartus and On Heroes, Hero Worship and the Heroic in History* (London, Macmillan, 1901).

Caedel, Martin, *Pacifism in Britain, 1914–1945: The defining of a faith* (Oxford, Clarendon Press, 1980).

Chambers, Paul, 'Social Networks and Religious Identity: An Historical Example from Wales,' in *Predicting Religion: Christian, Secular and alternative futures*, Grace David, Paul Heelas, Linda Woodhead eds., (Aldershot, Ashgate, 2003), 74-85.

_____, 'Religious Diversity in Wales,' in *A Tolerant Nation: exploring ethnic diversity in Wales*, Charlotte Williams, Neil Evans and Paul O'Leary, eds., (Cardiff, University of Wales Press, 2003), 125–38.

Charlton, C., 'Introduction,' in *A History of the Adult Education Movement*, J. Wilhelm Rowntree and Henry Bryan Binns, (Nottingham, University of Nottingham, republished 1985) iii–lxxiii.

Christian Doctrine, Practice and Discipline (London, Friends' Book Depository, 1861).

Christian Discipline of the Society of Friends: Church Government (London, Headley Bros., 1906).

Christian Life: Faith and Thought in the Society of Friends (London, The Friend's Bookshop, 1923).

Cohen, Robin, *Frontiers of Identity: The British and the Others* (London, Longman, 1994).

Colley, Linda, *Britons: Forging the Nation, 1707–1837* (London, Pimlico, 2003).

Conference on Home Mission Work in the Society of Friends held in London, 29–30 Eleventh Month, 1881 (London, FFDSA, 1881).

Conley, T.A.B., 'Changing Quaker attitudes to wealth, 1690–1950' in *Religion, Business and Wealth in Modern Britain*, David J. Jeremy ed., (London, Routledge, 1998) 137–52.

Conran, Tony, trans., *The Peacemakers: Waldo Williams* (Llandysul, Gomer, 1997).

Cooper, Wilmer A., *A Living Faith: An Historical Study of Quaker Beliefs* (Richmond, Ind., Friends United Press, 1990).

Cox, Jeffrey, *The English Churches in a Secular Society* (Oxford, Oxford University Press, 1982).

Cragoe, Mathew, 'Anticlericalism and Politics in Mid-Victorian Wales,' in *Anticlericalism in Britain c.1500-1914*, Nigel Aston and Matthew Cragoe eds.,

(Thrupp, Sutton Publishing, 2000), 179–97.

_____, *Culture, politics, and national identity in Wales, 1832–1886* (Oxford, Oxford University Press, 2004).

Craig, F.S., *British Parliamentary Election Results:1885–1918* (London, Macmillan, 1975).

_____, *British Parliamentary Election Results:1832–1885* (London, Macmillan, 1977).

Creighton, Louise, *Life and Letters of Thomas Hodgkin* (London, Longman, Green and Co., 1917).

Cronk, Sandra L., *Gospel Order: A Quaker Understanding of Faithful Church Community* (Wallingford, PA., Pendle Hill Publications, 1991).

Crook, John, *Egwyddorion y Gwirionedd, neu y pethau hynny ynghylch athrawiaeth ac addoliad a sicr gredir ac a dderbynir gan y bobl a elwir CRYNWYR (Quakers) sef yn mherthynas i grist ei ddioddefaint, marwolaeth, adgyfodiad, ffydd yn ei waed ef, y cyfri o'i gyfiawnder ef a'i sancteiddrwydd etc.* (Casnewydd (Newport), John. E. Southall, 1905).

Curtis, S.J., *History of Education in Great Britain* (London, University Tutorial Press,1948).

Daunton, M.J., *Coal Metropolis: Cardiff 1870–1914* (Leicester, Leicester University Press, 1977).

Davies, Dewi Eurig, *Diwinyddiaeth yng Nghymru 1927–1977* (Llandysul, Gwasg Gomer, 1984).

_____, *Byddin Y Brenin – Cymru a'i Chrefydd yn y Rhyfel Mawr* (Abertawe, Tŷ John Penry, 1988).

Davies, D.J., *Hanes Hynafiaethau ac Achyddiaeth Llanarth, Henfynyw, Llanllwchaiarn a Llandyssilio Gogo* (Caerfyrddin, W. Spurrell a'i Fab, 1930).

Davies, D. Elwyn, *Cewri'r Ffydd* (Llandysul, Gwasg Gomer, 1999).

Davies, E.T., *Religion in the Industrial Revolution in South Wales* (Cardiff, University of Wales Press, 1965).

_____, *Religion and Society in the Nineteenth Century* (Llandybie, Christopher Davies, 1981).

Davies, Gwilym, *Welsh School of Social Service 1911–1925* (Cardiff, *Western Mail*, 1926).

Davies, Horton, *Worship and Theology in England 1900–1965* (Princeton, Princeton University Press, 1965).

Davies, J.H., *Y Crynwyr yng Nghymru* (Merthyr, Pwyllgor Canolog Cynghrair Eglwysi Rhydd ac Efengylaidd Cymru, n.d).

Davies, John, *A History of Wales* (London, Allen Lane, 1993).

Davies, Richard, *An account of the convincement, exercises, services and travels of that ancient servant of the Lord* (London, Printed and sold by T. Sowle, 1710).

Davies, R.R., *The First English Empire: Power and Identities in the British Isles, 1039–1341* (Oxford, Oxford University Press, 2000).

Day, Graham, *Making Sense of Wales: A Sociological Perspective* (Cardiff, University of Wales Press, 2002).

Dell, Anthony, *The Church in Wales: A Complete Guide to the Disestablishment Question* (Westminster, P.S. King & Son, 1912).

Dieter, Melvin Easterday, *The Holiness Revival of the Nineteenth Century* (London, Scarecrow Press, 1996).

Dodd, Philip, 'Englishness and the National Culture,' in *Englishness: Politics and Culture 1880–1920*, Robert Colls and Philip Dodd, eds., (London, Croom Helm, 1986).

Dutton, David, *A History of the Liberal Party* (Basingstoke, Palgrave, 2004).

Eaton, Jack, *Judge Bryn Roberts* (Cardiff, University of Wales Press, 1989).

Edkins, Jenny, *Poststructuralist and International Relations: Bringing the Political Back In* (Boulder, Colorado, Lynne Rienner Publishers, 1999).

Ellis, John S., 'Pacifism, militarism and Welsh Identity,' in *Wales and War: Society, Politics and Religion in the Nineteenth and twentieth centuries*, Mathew Cragoe and Chris Williams, eds., (Cardiff, University of Wales Press, 2007) 15-37.

Epistles from the Yearly Meeting of Friends held in London, Vol. II (London, Edward Marsh, 1858).

Evans, Beriah Gwynfe, *Diwygwyr Cymru : sef, ymchwiliad hanesyddol i ddechreuad yr enwadau ymneillduol a'i brwydrau dros ryddid cydwybod* (Caernarfon, Gwenlyn Parry, 1900).

Evans, D. Gareth, *A History of Wales, 1815–1906* (Cardiff, University of Wales Press, 1989).

Evans, Eifion, *The Welsh Revival of 1904* (Bridgend, Evangelical Press of Wales, 1987).

Evans, Eric J., *The Contentious Tithe: The Tithe Problem and English Agriculture 1750–1850*, London, Routledge and Kegan Paul, 1976.

Evans, E.W., *The Miners of South Wales* (Cardiff, University of Wales Press, 1961).

Evans, Gwynfor, *Heddychiaeth Gristnogol yng Nghymru* (Llandysul, Cymdeithas y Cymod, 1991).

Evans, H. Tobit, *Y Berw Gwyddelig* (Llanarth, Cymdeithas y Wasg Undebol Gymreig, 1889).

—————, *Cymdeithas y Cyfeillion a elwir yn gyffredin 'Crynwyr,'* London, FTA, 1884, translated from the English by H. Tobit Evans.

—————, *Gwyddeleiddio Cymru* (Llanarth, Cymdeithas y Wasg Undebol Gymreig, 1889).

—————, *Rebecca and her daughters: Being a history of the Agrarian Disturbances in Wales known as 'The Rebecca Riots* (Cardiff, Educational Publishing Co., 1910).

Evans, L.W., *Education in Industrial Wales, 1700–1900: A Study of the Works Schools System in Wales during the Industrial Revolution* (Cardiff, Avalon Books, 1971).

Evans, Neil, 'Internal Colonialism? Colonisation, Economic Development and Political Mobilisation in Wales, Scotland and Ireland,' in *Regions, Nations and European Integration: Remaking the Celtic Periphery*, Graham Day and Gareth Rees, eds., (Cardiff, University of Wales Press, 1991) 235–64.

—————, 'Loyalties: state, nation, community and military recruiting,' in *Wales and War: Society, Politics and Religion in the Nineteenth and Twentieth Centuries*, Mathew Cragoe and Chris Williams, eds., (Cardiff, University of Wales Press, 2007) 38–62.

Fanon, Fritz, *Black Skins, White Masks* (Pluto Press, London, 1986).

_____, *The Wretched of the Earth* (New York, Grove Press, 1963).

Figgis, J.B., *Keswick from within* (London, Marshall Brothers, London, 1914).

Fox, Charles Allen, *George Fox: No precursor of the Salvation Army (so called, and that Sect no Quakers; its foundation tried and discovered to be on the sand; with a warning to all "Friends". In answer to G.R's "George Fox and his Salvation Army of 200 Years ago")* (Derby, James Harwood, Corn Market, 1881).

_____, *The Question of Compulsory Vaccination* (London, E.W. Allen, 1890).

_____, *Leaves of a Review of Life* (Weymouth, C.F. Warden and Co., 1911).

_____, *Of My Writings and of the Simple Life* (South Petherton, C.A. Fox, 1911).

Fox, George, *Journal of George Fox*, John L. Nickalls ed., (London, London Yearly Meeting, 1975).

_____, *The Works of George Fox*, Vols 7 & 8 (New York, AMS Press, 1975).

Friends Ambulance Unit, *List of Members and Addresses*, London, FAU, 1919.

Gardiner, A.G., *The Life of George Cadbury* (London, Cassell, 1923).

Garrard, Mary N., *Mrs Penn-Lewis: A Memoir* (London, Overcomer Book Room, n.d).

Gibbard, Noel, *On the Wing of the Dove: The international effects of the 1904–05 Reviva*, (Bridgend, Bryntirion Press, 2002).

Ginzberg, Carlo, *The Cheese and the Worms: The Cosmos of a Sixteenth–Century Miller* (Baltimore, John Hopkins University Press, 1992).

Glaser, Anthony, 'The Tredegar Riots of August 1911,' in *The Jews of South Wales: Historical Studies*, Ursula R.Q. Henriques ed., (Cardiff, University of Wales Press, 1993) 151–76.

Graham, John William, *Evolution and Empire* (London, Headley Brothers, 1912).

Gregory, Adrian, 'British 'War Enthusiasm' in 1914: a reappraisal' in *Evidence, History and the Great War: Historians and the Impact of 1914–18*, Gail Braybon ed., (Oxford, Berghahn Books, 2005) 67–85.

Gregory, Jeremy, 'The Making of a Protestant Nation' in *England's Long Reformation 1500–1800*, Nicholas Tyacke, ed., (Abingdon, Routledge , 1998) 307–33.

Greenwood, John Ormerod, *Quaker Encounters*, Vol. 1, Friends in Relief (York, Wm. Sessions and Sons, 1975).

Griffith, Stephen, *A History of Quakers in Pembrokeshire* (Llandysul, Milford Haven Preparative Meeting, 1990).

Griffiths, E.H., *Heddychwr Mawr Cymru*, Vol. 1 (Caernarfon, Llyfrfa'r Methodistiaid Calfinaidd, 1967).

_____, *Seraff yr Efengyl Seml*, Vol. 2 (Caernarfon, Llyfrfa'r Methodistiaid Calfinaidd, 1968).

Grigg, John, *The Young Lloyd George* (London, Eyre Methuen, 1973).

Grubb, Edward, *What is Quakerism? An Exposition of the leading Principles and Practices of the Society of Friends, as based on the experience of the 'Inward Light.'* (London, Woodbrooke Extension Committee, 1929 edition).

Grubb, Isabel, *Quakers in Ireland: 1654–1900* (The Swarthmore Press, London, 1927).

Haanaford, Ivan, *Race: The History of an Ideal in the West* (Washington D.C., Woodrow Wilson Centre Press, 1996).

Hackforth-Jones, Jocelyn, 'Re-Visioning Landscape, *c*.1760–1840,' in *Cultural Identities and the Aesthetics of Britishness*, Dana Arnold, ed., (Manchester, Manchester University Press, 2004) 35–52.

Hall, Basil, 'The Welsh Revival of 1904–05,' in *Popular Belief and Practice*, G.J. Cuming and Derek Baker, eds., (Cambridge, Cambridge University Press, 1972).

Hall, Catherine, *Civilising Subject: Metropole and Colony in the English Imagination 1830–67* (Cambridge, Polity Press, 2002).

Hall, Douglas John and Rosemary Radford Ruether, *God and the Nations* (Fortress Press, Minneapolis, 1995).

Hall, W.G., *Quaker Home Missionaries Past and Present: A Plea for the Return to the energetic Faith and Practice of the Founders of the Society of Friends. A paper read before the Home Mission workers in London*, Nov 3rd 1899 (London, Friends Tracts Association, 1899).

Hamm, Thomas D., *The Transformation of American Quakerism: Orthodox Friends 1800–1907* (Bloomington, Indiana University Press, 1992).

Harrison, Brian, *Drink and the Victorians: The Temperance Question in England 1815–1872* (London, Faber and Faber, 1971).

Harvey, John, *The Art of Piety: The Visual Culture of Welsh Nonconformity* (Cardiff, University of Wales Press, 1995).

Hastings, A., *The Construction of Nationhood: Ethnicity, Religion and Nationalism* (Cambridge, Cambridge University Press, 1997).

Hatton, Helen E., *The Largest Amount of Good: Quaker Relief in Ireland: 1654-1921* (McGill Queen's University Press, Kingston, 1993).

Haywood, John, *The Celts: Bronze Age to new Age* (Harlow, Pearson Longman, 2004).

Heathfield, Margaret, *Being Together: Our Corporate Life in the Religious Society of Friends* (London, Quaker Home Service, 1994).

Hechter, Michael, *Internal Colonialism: The Celtic Fringe in British National Development 1536–1966* (London, Routledge Kegan Paul, 1975).

Hempton, David, *Religion and Political Culture in Britain and Ireland: From the Glorious Revolution to the decline of Empire* (Cambridge, Cambridge University Press, 1996).

Henriques, Ursula R.Q., 'Introduction,' in *The Jews of South Wales: Historical Studies*, Ursula R.Q. Henriques ed., (Cardiff, University of Wales Press, 1993) 1-8.

Herbert, Sydney, *Nationality and its Problems* (London, Methuen and Co., 1919).

Heron, Alastair, *Quakers in Britain: a century of change, 1895–1995* (Kelso, Curlew Graphics, 1995).

_____, *Our Quaker Identity: Religious Society or Friendly Society* (Kelso, and Curlew Books, 1999).

Hess, Dale, *A Brief Background to the Quaker Peace Testimony* (Victoria, Australia, Victoria Regional Meeting, 1992).

Hewison, H.H., *Hedge of Wild Almonds: South Africa, the pro-Boers and the Quaker Conscience, 1890–1910* (London, James Currey, 1989).

Heyck, Thomas William, *A History of the Peoples of the British Isles: from 1860 to 1914* (London, Routledge, 2002).

Hill, Christopher, *The Experience of Defeat: Milton and Some Contemporaries* (London, Faber and Faber, 1984).

Hobson, S.G., *Pilgrim to the Left: Memoirs of a Modern Revolutionist* (London, Edward Arnold and Co., 1938).

Hodgkin, Thomas, *George Fox* (London, Methuen, 1896).

Hollis, Patricia Hollis, *Ladies Elect: Women in English Local Government, 1865–1914* (Oxford, Clarendon Press, 1987).

Holmes, Janice, *Religious Revivals in Britain and Ireland*, *1859–1905* (Dublin, Irish Academic Press, 2000).

Howard, Thomas Albert, *Religion and the Rise of Historicism: W M L de Watte, Jacob Burckhardt, and the theological origins of nineteenth century Historical Consciousness* (Cambridge, Cambridge University Press, 2000).

Howse, W.H., *Radnorshire* (Hereford, E.J. Thurston, 1949).

Hughes, Dewi Rowland, *Cymru Fydd* (Caerdydd, Gwasg Prifysgol Cymru, 2006).

Hughes, J. Elwyn, *Arloeswr Dwyieithrwydd: Daniel Isaac Davies 1839–1887* (Caerdydd, Gwasg Prifysgol Cymru, 1984).

Hughes, Trystan Owain, *Winds of Change: The Roman Catholic Church and Society in Wales*, *1916–1962*, (Cardiff, University of Wales Press, 1999).

Humphreys, Emyr, 'Arnold in Wonderland,' in *Miscellany Two* (Bridgend, Poetry Wales Press, 1981) 81–100.

_____, *The Taliesin Tradition* (Bridgend, Seren, 2000).

Humphreys, Melvin, *The Crisis of Community, Montgomeryshire*, *1680–1815* (Cardiff, University of Wales Press, 1996).

Hunt, N.C., *Two early Political Associations: The Quakers and the Dissenting Deputies in the Age of Sir Robert Walpole* (Oxford, Oxford University Press, 1961).

Hutton, Ronald, *Debates in Stuart History* (Basingstoke, Palgrave Macmillan, 2004).

Iggers, George G., *Historiography in the Twentieth Century; From Scientific Objectivity to the Postmodern Challenge* (Middletown, Connecticut, Wesleyan University Press, 2005).

Ingle, H. Larry, *First Among Friends: George Fox and the Creation of Quakerism* (New York, Oxford University Press, 1994).

Irvin, Dale T., 'Holiness Movement,' in *Encyclopaedia of Millennialism and Millennial Movements*, Richard A. Landes, ed., (New York, Routledge, 2000) 179-181.

Isichei, Elizabeth, *Victorian Quakers* (Oxford, Oxford University Press, 1970).

James, David B., *Ceredigion: Its Natural History* (Aberystwyth, Cambrian Printers, 2001).

James, E. Wyn, 'The New Birth of a People': Welsh language and Identity and the Welsh Methodists, c.1740–1820,' in *Religion and National Identity: Wales and Scotland c.1700–2000*, Robert Pope, ed., (Cardiff, University of Wales Press, 2001) 14–42.

Jenkins, David, *The Agricultural Community in South-West Wales at the turn of the Twentieth century* (Cardiff, University of Wales Press, 1971).

Jenkins, Geraint H., *Hanes Cymru yn y Cyfnod Modern Cynnar*, *1530–1760* (Caerdydd, Gwasg Prifysgol Cymru, 1983).

_____, *The Foundations of Modern Wales 1642–1780* (Oxford, Clarendon Press, 1987).

_____, 'Rhyfel yr Oen: Y Mudiad Heddwch yng Nghymru 1653–1816,' in *Cadw Ty Mewn Cwmwl Tystion* (Llandysul, Gwasg Gomer, 1990) 27–50.

Jenkins, Geraint, ed., *Language and Community in the Nineteenth Century* (Cardiff, University of Wales Press, 1998).

Jenkins, J. Austin and E. Edwards James, *The History of Nonconformity in Cardiff* (Cardiff, Wesleyan and General Book Depot, 1901).

Jenkins, Philip, *A History of Modern Wales 1536–1990* (London, Longman, 1992).

_____, 'Seventeenth-century Wales: definition and identity,' in *British Consciousness and Identity: The Making of Britain*, Brendan Bradshaw and Peter Roberts, eds., (Cambridge, Cambridge University Press, 1998) 213–35.

Jenkins, R.T. *Hanes Cymru yn y Ddeunawfed Ganrif* (Caerdydd, Gwasg Prifysgol Cymru, 1928).

_____, *Hanes Cymru yn y Bedwaredd Ganrif ar Bymtheg: Y Gyfrol Gyntaf 1789–1843* (Caerdydd, Gwasg Prifysgol Cymru, 1933).

Jones, Brynmor Pierce, *The Spiritual History of Keswick in Wales: 1903–08* (Cwmbran, Christian Literature Press, 1989).

Jones, Aled, *Press, Politics and Society: A History of Journalism in Wales* (Cardiff, University of Wales Press, 1993).

Jones, Aled and Bill Jones, 'The Welsh World and the British Empire, *circa* 1851–1939,' in *The British World: Diaspora, Culture and Identity*, Carl Bridge and Kent Federovich, eds., (London, Frank Cass, 2002) 57–81.

Jones, D. Gwenallt, 'Michael D. Jones (1822–1898),'in *Triwyr Penllyn* (Caerdydd, Plaid Cymru, 1956) 1–27.

Jones, D. Lloyd, *Goleuni ar Gyflwr Iwerddon* (London, The Liberal Unionist Association, n.d).

Jones, E. Pan, *Oes a Gwaith Y Prif Athraw Y Parch Michael Daniel Jones* (Bala, H. Evans, 1903).

Jones, Frank Price, 'Rhyfel y Degwm,' in *Radicaliaeth a'r Werin Gymreig yn y Bedwaredd Ganrif ar Bymtheg* (Caerdydd, Gwasg Prifysgol Cymru, 1975) 73–107.

_____, 'Gwerin Cymru,' in *Radicaliaeth a'r Werin Gymreig yn y Bedwaredd Ganrif ar Bymtheg* (Caerdydd, Gwasg Prifysgol Cymru, 1975) 196–206.

Jones, Gareth Elwyn, *Controls and Conflict in Welsh Secondary Education 1899–1944* (Cardiff, University of Wales Press, 1982).

_____, *Modern Wales: A Concise History* (Cambridge, Cambridge University Press, 1999).

Jones, Gareth Elwyn and Gordon Wynne Roderick, *A History of Education in Wales* (Cardiff, University of Wales Press, 2003).

Jones, Goronwy J., *Wales and the Quest for Peace* (Cardiff, University of Wales Press, 1969).

Jones, Gwilym Arthur, *Bywyd a Gwaith Owen Morgan Edwards, 1858–1920* (Aberystwyth, Urdd Gobaith Cymru, 1958).

Jones, Henry, *Y Diwygiad: A'r hyn eill ddod o hono: Araeth gan yr Athraw Henry Jones* (Caernarfon, Swyddfa'r Herald, 1905).

Jones, Ieuan Gwynedd, 'The Religious Condition of the Counties of Brecon and Radnorshire as revealed in the Religious Census of 1851,' in *Links with the Past, Swansea and Brecon Historical Essays*, Owain W. Jones and David Walker eds., (Llandybie, Christopher Davies, 1974) 185–214.

_____, 'The Liberation Society and Welsh Politics,' in *Explorations and Explanations: Essays in the Social History of Victorian Wales* (Llandysul, Gomer Press, 1981) 236–68.

_____, 'The South Wales Collier in Mid-Nineteenth Century,' in *Communities, Essays in the Social History of Victorian Wales* (Llandysul, Gomer, 1987) 105–136.

_____, 'Language and Community in Nineteenth Century Wales,' in *Mid-Victorian Wales: The Observers and the Observed* (Cardiff, University of Wales, Press, 1992).

Jones, Ieuan Gwynedd and David Williams, *The Religious Census of 1851: a calendar of returns relating to Wales*, South Wales, Vol. 1 (1976), North Wales, Vol. 2 (1981) (Cardiff, University of Wales Press).

Jones, Ifano, *Printing and Printers in Wales and Monmouthshire* (Cardiff, William Lewis Printers, 1925).

Jones, Merfyn, *The North Wales Quarrymen 1874–1922* (Cardiff, University of Wales Press, 1982).

Jones, R. Tudur, *Yr Undeb: Hanes Undeb yr Annibynwyr Cymraeg 1872–1972* (Abertawe, Gwasg John Penry, 1975).

_____, *Ffydd ac Argyfwng Cenedl* (Abertawe, Ty John Penry, 1982).

Jones, Richard, *Crynwyr Bore Cymru* (Abermaw, William Jones a'i Feibion, 1931).

Jones, Richard Wyn, R*hoi Cymru'n Gyntaf: Syniadaeth Plaid Cymru*, Cyfrol 1, (Caerdydd, Gwasg Prifysgol Cymru, 2007).

Jones, Rufus M., *Studies in Mystical Religion* (London, Macmillan, 1909).

Jones, Rev. T.J., *Some Thoughts on How to Improve the Condition of the Welsh Church* (Merthyr Tydfil, Frost and Smith, 1893).

Jones, Thomas, *Welsh Broth* (London, W. Griffiths, 1951).

Jones, William, *Quaker Campaigns in Peace and War* (London, Headley Bros., 1899).

Jowett, Gareth S., and Victoria O'Donnell, *Propaganda and Persuasion* (Newbury Park, Ca., Sage, 1992).

Judd, Denis, *Radical Joe: A life of Joseph Chamberlain* (Cardiff, University of Wales Press, 1993).

Kearney, Richard, *Postnationalist Ireland: Politics, Culture, Philosophy* (London, Routledge, 1997).

Kennedy, Thomas C., *British Quakerism 1860–1920: The Transformation of a Religious Community* (Oxford, Oxford University Press, 2001).

Kent, John, *Holding the Fort: Studies in Victorian Revivalism* (London, Epworth Press, 1978).

Kirby, M.W., *Men of Business and Politics: The Rise and Fall of the Quaker Pease Dynasty on North East England, 1700–1943* (London, George Allen & Unwin, 1984).

Knight, Frances, 'The National Scene,' in *The Welsh Church from Reformation to Disestablishment 1603–1920* (Cardiff, University of Wales Press, 2007).

Koss, Stephen, *Nonconformity in Modern British Politics* (London, B.T. Batsford, 1975).

Kumar, Krishnan, *The Making of English National Identity* (Cambridge, Cambridge University Press, 2003).

Lambert, W.R., *Drink and Sobriety in Victorian Wales* (Cardiff, University of Wales Press, 1983).

Larsen, T., *Friends of Religious Equality: Nonconformist Politics in Mid-Victorian England* (Woodbridge. Boydell Press, 1999).

Lawson, John and Harold Silver, *A Social History of Education in England* (London, Methuen, 1973).

Legg, Marie-Louise, ed., *Alfred Webb: The Autobiography of a Quaker Nationalist* (Cork, Cork University Press, 1999).

Lewis, T.H., *Y Mormoniaid yng Nghymru* (Caerdydd, Gwasg Prifysgol Cymru, 1956).

Liberal Party, *The Parliamentary History of the Education Act, 1902* (London, The Liberal Publication Department, 1903).

Lilley, Keith D., 'Imagined geographies of the 'Celtic fringe' and the cultural construction of the 'other' in medieval Wales and Ireland,' *Celtic Geographies: Old Culture, New Times*, David C. Harvey, Rhys Jones, Neil McInroy and Christine Milligan, eds., (London, Routledge, 2002).

Longford, Paul, *Englishness Identified: Manners and Characters 1650–1850* (Oxford, Oxford University Press, 2000).

Lord Aberdare, *The Welsh Sunday Closing Act: Lord Aberdare's Challenge to the* Western Mail (Cardiff, *Western Mail*, 1889).

Lord, Peter, *The Visual Culture of Wales: Imaging the Nation* (Cardiff, University of Wales Press, 2000).

Lowndes, W., *The Quakers of Fritchley* (Fritchley, Derbyshire, Friends Meeting House, 1980).

Mackintosh, William H., *Disestablishment and Liberation: The Movement for the Separation of the Anglican Church from State Control* (London, Epworth Press, 1972).

Macpherson, Trevor, *Friends in Radnorshire* (Llandrindod Wells, Verzon Books, 1999).

Mae'r Gan yn y Galon/Quakers in Wales To-Day (Llandybie, Meeting of Friends in Wales, 1997).

Manifesto of the Cymry Fydd Society (London, Cymru Fydd Society, n.d). [*circa* 1888]

Martin, George Currie, *The Adult School Movement: Its Origin and Development* (London, National Adult School Union, 1924).

Marwick, W.H., 'Epilogue', in G.B. Burnet, The Story of Quakerism in Scotland(London, James Clarke, 1952) 194–202.

McHugh, Paul, *Prostitution and Victorian Social Reform* (London, Croom Helm, 1980).

McLeod, Hugh, *Religion and the Working Class in the Nineteenth Century Britain* (London, Macmillan, 1984).

_____, *Religion and Society in England, 1850–1914* (Basingstoke, Macmillan, 1996).

_____, *Religion and the People of Western Europe, 1789–1989* (Oxford, Oxford University Press, 1997).

_____, *Secularisation in Western Europe, 1848–1914* (Basingstoke, Macmillan, 2000).

Mill, John Stuart, *On Representative Government* (London, Longmans, Green and Co., 1926).

Milligan, Edward, *Quaker Marriages* (London, Quaker Tapestry Booklets, 1994).

_____, Recorded lecture *Biography as a foundation of history* 14.2.2008, available on www.quaker.org.uk/audio/talk/ted/mp3 .

Mills, J. Travis, *John Bright and the Quakers* (London, Methuen and Co., 1935).

Mills, William, *A Testimony for the Welfare of Zion* (Cardiff, no publisher, 1889).

Minutes and Proceedings of the Yearly Meeting of Friends (BYM, published annually).

Misztal, Barbara A., *Theories of Social Remembering* (Maidenhead, OU Press, 2003).

Moore, Rosemary, *The Light in their Consciences: The Early Quakers in Britain 1646–1666* (University Park, Penn., Pennsylvania State University Press, 2000).

Morgan, D. Densil, 'The Welsh Language and Religion,' in *'Let's Do Out Best for the Ancient Tongue:' The Welsh Language in the Twentieth Century*, Geraint H. Jenkins, Mari A. Williams, eds., (Cardiff, University of Wales Press, 2000).

_____, 'Y Ffydd yng Nghymru yn yr Ugeinfed Ganrif: Profiadau 1900–1920,' in 'Ysbryd Dealltwrus ac Enaid Anfarwol:' *Ysgrifau ar Hanes Crefydd yng Nghymru*, W.P. Griffith ed., (Bangor, Canolfan Uwch-Efrydiau Crefydd yng Nghymru, 1999) 190–206.

_____, 'Diwygiad Crefyddol 1904-05,' *Cof Cenedl XX: Ysgrifau ar Hanes Cymru*, Geraint H. Jenkins, ed., (Llandysul, Gwasg Gomer, 2005) 167–200.

Morgan, Derec Llwyd, *Y Beibl a'n Cymreictod* (Caerdydd, Gwasg Prifysgol Cymru, 1988).

Morgan, J. Vyrnwy, *The Welsh Religious Revival, 1904–05: A Retrospect and a Criticism* (London, Chapman & Hall, 1909).

Morgan, K.O., *Rebirth of a Nation: A History of Modern Wales* (Oxford, Oxford University Press, 1981).

_____, *Wales in British Politics, 1868–1922* (Cardiff, University of Wales Press, 1991).

_____, *Modern Wales: Politics, Places and People* (Cardiff, University of Wales Press, 1995).

Morgan, Prys, ed., *Brad y Llyfrau Gleision* (Llandysul, Gwasg Gomer, 1991).

_____, 'The Hunt for the Welsh Past,' in *The Invention of Tradition*, E.J. Hobsbawm and Terence Ranger eds., (Cambridge, Cambridge University Press, 2002) 43–100.

Morgan, Prys and David Thomas, *Wales: The Shaping of a Nation* (Newton Abbott, David & Charles, 1984).

Moss, Howard, 'Language and Italian National Identity,' in *The Politics of Italian National Identity: A Multidisciplinary Perspective* (Gino Bedani and Bruce Haddock, eds., Cardiff, University of Wales Press, 2000) 98–123.

Muers, Rachel, 'New Voices, New Hopes,' in *Towards Tragedy/Reclaiming Hope: Literature, Theology and Sociology*, Pink Dandelion, Douglas Gwyn, Rachel Muers, Brian Phillips and Richard E Sturm, eds., (Aldershot, Ashgate, 2004) 108–23

Murray, Nicholas, *A Life of Mathew Arnold* (London, Hodder & Stoughton, 1996).

Myers, Arthur Cook, *The Immigration of the Irish Quakers into Pennsylvania, 1682–1750* (The Author, Swarthmore, Penn., 1902).

Newman, Harriet M., *Henry Stanley Newman* (London, FFMA, 1917).

Nicholls, James, ed. *Bro a Bywyd: Waldo Williams* (Llandybie, Cyhoeddiadau Barddas, 1996).

Nicholls, Reginald, 'Early Quakers in Monmouthshire,' in *Monmouthshire Medley*, Vol. 1, Reginald Nicholls, ed., (Risca, Starling Press, 1976) 79–88.

_____, 'More about Early Quakers in Monmouthshire,' in *Monmouthshire Medley*, Vol. 3, Reginald Nicholls, ed., (Risca, Starling Press, 1978) 58–74.

Nordeau, Max, 'Degeneration,' in *The Fin de Siècle: A Reader in Cultural History* circa *1880–1900*, Sally Ledger and Roger Luckhurst, eds., (Oxford, Oxford University Press, 2000) 13–17.

O'Broin, Leon, *Protestant Nationalists in Revolutionary Ireland: The Stopford Connection* (Dublin, Gill and Macmillan, 1985).

O'Leary, Paul, *Immigration and Integration: The Irish in Wales 1798–1922* (Cardiff, University of Wales Press, 2000).

Oldstone-Moore, Christopher, *Hugh Price Hughes: Founder of a New Methodism, Conscience of a New Nonconformity* (Cardiff, University of Wales Press, 1999).

Olsen, Ted, *Christianity and the Celts* (Oxford, Lion Publishing, 2003).

Owen, Alex, 'Occultism and the 'Modern' Self in Fin de siecle Britain,' in *Meanings of Modernity: Britain from the Late-Victorian Era to World War Two*, Martin Daunton and Bernhard Reiger, eds., (Oxford, Berg, 2001) 71 – 96.

Owen, Eluned E., *The Later Life of Bishop Owen: A Son of Wales* (Llandysul, Gomerian Press, 1961).

Parry, J.P., *Democracy and Religion: Gladstone and the Liberal Party, 1867–1875* (Cambridge, Cambridge University Press, 1986).

Parsons, Gerald, 'Liberation and Church Defence,' in Religion in *Victorian Britain*, II, Controversies, Gerald Parsons ed., (Manchester, Manchester University Press, 1988).

Peate, Iorwerth C., *Traditions and Folk Life: A Welsh View* (London, Faber & Faber, 1972).

Penn, William, 'Good Advice to the Church of England, Roman Catholick, and Protestant Dissenter,' in *The Political Writings of William Penn*, (Indianapolis, Liberty Fund, 2002) 330–76.

Phillips, H.D., *The Early Quakers in Wales* (Aberavon, Consultative Committee of the Federation of Evangelical Free Church Councils in Wales, n.d., 1912?)

Pope, Robert, *Building Jerusalem: Nonconformity, Labour and the Social Question in Wales*, 1906–1939 (Cardiff, University of Wales Press, 1998).

_____, *Codi Muriau Duw: Anghydffurfiaeth ac Anghydffurfwyr Cymru'r Ugeinfed Ganrif* (Bangor, Canolfan Uwchefrydiau Crefydd yng Nghymru, 2005).

_____, 'Christ and Caesar? Welsh Nonconformity and the State,' in *Wales and War: Society, Politics and Religion in the Nineteenth and Twentieth Centuries*, Mathew Cragoe and Chris Williams, eds., (Cardiff, University of Wales Press, 2007) 165–83.

Price, Emyr Wyn, *David Lloyd George* (Cardiff, University of Wales Press, 2006).

Punshon, John, *Portrait in Grey: A short history of the Quakers* (London, QHS, 1999).

Quaker Faith and Practice (London, Britain Yearly Meeting, 1994).

Raistrick, Arthur, *Quakers in Science and Industry* (Newton Abbott, David & Charles, 1968).

Randall, Ian M., *Spirituality and Social Change: The Contribution of F.B. Meyer* (1847–1929) (Carlisle, Paternoster Press, 2003).

Redfern, Keith, *Before the Meeting: A handbook for Clerks* (London, Quaker Home Service, 1994).

Rees, Ivor Thomas. *Welsh Hustings: 1885–2004* (Llandybie, Dinefwr Books, 2005).

Rees, Rev. T. Mardy, *A History of the Quakers in Wales and their Emigration to North America* (Carmarthen, W. Spurrell and Son, 1925).

Rees, Thomas, *History of Protestant Nonconformity in Wales from its Rise to the Present Time* (London, John Snow, 1861).

Reich, Max. I., *Maddeuant, Purdeb a Heddwch* (Newport, J.E. Southall, 1912).

Reid, T. Weymyss, *Life of the Honourable William Edward Forster* (London, Chapman and Hall, 1888).

Renan, Ernest, 'What is a Nation,' in *Narration and the Nation*, Homi K. Bhabha ed., (London, Routledge, London, 1995).

Reynolds, Joan, *The Book of Roland: Being the Life of Roland Exton Reynolds: Boy Lover and Scoutmaster 1871–1922* (written by his sister and her friend, Ashford, Headley Brothers, 1923).

Rich, Eric E., *The Education Act 1870: A Study in Public Opinion* (London, Longmans, 1970).

Roberts, Gwyneth Tyson, *The Language of the Blue Books: The Perfect Instrument of Empire* (Cardiff, University of Wales Press, 1998).

Robbins, Keith, *John Bright* (London, Routledge and Kegan Paul, 1979).

Rostow, W.W., *The Stages of Economic Growth: A Non-Communist Manifesto* (Cambridge, Cambridge University Press, 1960).

Sayce, J.S., *What the Society of Friends Believes, and Why* (London, E, Hicks, 1892).

Scotland, Nigel, *Evangelical Anglicans in a Revolutionary Age, 1789–1901* (Carlisle, Paternoster Press, 2004).

Scott, James C., *Domination and the Arts of Resistance: Hidden Transcripts* (New Haven, Yale University Press, 1990).

Searle, G.R., *The Liberal Party: Triumph and Disintegration 1886–1929* (Basingstoke, Macmillan, 1992).

Sessions, Frederick, *Two and a half Centuries of Temperance Work in the Society of Friends, 1643–1893* (London, E. Hicks, 1893).

Sharman, Cecil W., *Servant of the Meeting: Quaker business meetings and their Clerks* (London, Quaker Home Service, 1983).

Sheeran, Michael, *Beyond Majority Rule: Voteless Decisions in the Religious Society of Friends* (Philadelphia Yearly Meeting, Philadelphia, 1983).

Smith, Anthony, *Nationalism: Theory, Ideology, History* (London, Polity, 2001).

_____, *National Identity* (London, Penguin Books, 1991).

Smith, David, 'From Riots to Revolt: Tonypandy and the Miners' Next Step,' in *Wales: 1880–1914*, Trevor Herbert and Gareth Elwyn Jones eds., (Cardiff, University of Wales Press, 1988) 107-138.

Smith, Dai, *Wales: A Question of History* (Bridgend, Seren, 1999).

Smith, Iain R., *The Origins of the South African War 1899–1902* (London, Longman, 1996).

Snell, K.D.M., and Paul S. Ell, *Rival Jerusalems: The Geography of Victorian Religion* (Cambridge, Cambridge University Press, 2000).

Southall, Celia, *Records of the Southall Family* (Private circulation, 1932).

Southall, John E. (place of publication all Newport, publisher John E. Southall, unless otherwise stated.)

_____, *A Faithful Warning to those Calling Themselves Friends, more particularly in Western Quarterly Meeting, England* (Gloucester, 1881).

_____, *Selections from the Diary of John G Sargeant, a Minister of the Society of Friends containing an account of his Labours and Travels in the Service of the Gospel and showing the Grounds of his ceasing to regard LYM as representing the Society of Friends* (1885).

_____, *Anti-Christian Preaching: A curious fragment from an old original Manuscript, revised and published by George Pitt* (1886).

_____, *Bilingual Teaching in Welsh Elementary Schools or minutes of evidence of Welsh witnesses before the Royal Commission on Education in 1886-7 with introductory remarks* (1888).

_____, *The Theatre: An essay upon the non-accordance of stage plays with the Christian profession* (1890).

_____, *Wales and her Language: Considered from a historical, educational and social standpoint with remarks on modern Welsh literature* (1893).

_____, *The Welsh Language Census of 1891 with Coloured Maps of the 52 Registration Districts in to which Wales is Divided* (1895).

_____, *Quakerism as the one Universal Religion* (1895).

_____, *Quakerism as a factor in the World's History* (1894).

_____, *Quakerism as practical Christianity: showing the Excellency of a true Christian worship; walk and conversation* (1895).

_____, *Music in Worship and Frances T. Havergal's Dream* (1895).

_____, *Some Account of the Convincement of Religious Progress of John Spalding* (1897).

_____, *Gospel Simplicity Commended* (1897).

_____, *Paid Ministry* (1897).

_____, *Leaves from the History of Welsh Nonconformity (Life of Richard Davies, Cloddiau Cochion)* (1899).

_____, *Preserving and teaching the Welsh Language in English speaking districts: being the substance of an essay awarded as a prize at the National Eisteddfod* (1899).

_____, *The Future of Welsh Education: being a review of some of the existing forces affecting education in Wales from the viewpoint of NATIONAL INDIVIDUALITY* (1900).

_____, *The Welsh Language Census of 1901* (1904).

_____, *An Educational Need in Monmouthshire: Welsh Teaching: Testimony of Headmaster at Llanover* (1905).

_____, *The Appearing of the Grace: Its Teaching, and its Effects* (1909).

_____, *The Doctrine of the Two Seeds. As Foundation Stones of the Christian Faith* (1923).

_____, *The True Worship under Christian Dispensation* (n.d.).

_____, *Art Thou in Health My Brother* (n.d.).

Spencer, Carole D., 'Holiness: The Quaker Way of Perfection,' in *The Creation of Quaker Theory: Insider Perspectives*, Pink Dandelion, ed. (Aldershot, Ashgate, 2004).

Stead, Peter, 'Vernon Hartshorn: Miners' Agent and Cabinet Minister,' in *Glamorgan Histories*, Vol. 6, Stewart Williams, ed. (Cowbridge, D.Brown and Son, 1968) 83–94.

Steere, G.R., *A New England? Peace and War, 1886–1918* (Oxford, Clarendon Press, 2004).

Sturgis, James L. *John Bright and the Empire* (London, The Athlone Press, 1969).

Swift, David E., *John Joseph Gurney: Banker, Reformer and Quaker* (Middletown, Connecticut, Wesleyan University Press, 1962).

Thomas, Anna Lloyd Braithwaite, *The Quaker Seekers of Wales: A Story of the Lloyds of Dolobran* (London, The Swarthmore Press, 1924).

Thomas, Malcolm, 'The Committee on General Meetings 1875–83,' in *A Quaker Miscellany* for Edward H. Milligan, David Blamires, Jeremy Greenwood and Alex Kerr eds., (Manchester, David Blamires, 1985) 133–144.

Townshend, Charles, *Political Violence in Ireland: Government and Resistance since 1848* (Oxford, Oxford University Press, 1984).

_____, *Easter 1916: The Irish Rebellion* (London, Penguin, London, 2005).

Trott, A.L., "The British School Movement in Wales, 1806–1846,' in *The History of Education in Wales*, Vol. 1, Jac L. Williams and Gwilym Rees Hughes eds., (Swansea, Christopher Davies, 1978) 83–104.

Trumpener, Katie, *Bardic Nationalism: The Romantic Novel and the British Empire* (Princeton, Princeton University Press, 1997).

Turner, Christopher B., 'Revivalism and Welsh Society in the Nineteenth Century,' in *Disciplines of Faith: Studies in Religion, Politics and Patriarchy*, Jim Obelkevich, Lyndal Roper, Raphael Samuel eds., (London, Routledge & Kegan Paul, 1987) 311–23.

Unity in the Spirit: Quakers and the ecumenical pilgrimage (London, CCR, 1979).

Vipont, Elfrida, *George Fox and the Valiant Sixty* (London, Hamilton, 1975).

Walters, Huw, *Y Wasg Gyfnodol Gymreig 1735–1900/The Welsh Periodical Press* (Aberystwyth, Llyfrgell Genedlaethol Cymru, 1987).

Walvin, James, *The Quakers: Money and Morals* (London, John Murray, 1997).

Waring, Elijah, *Recollections and Anecdotes of Edward Williams: The Bard of Glamorgan or, Iolo Morgannwg, B.B.D* (London, Charles Gilpin, 1850).

Warner, Stafford Allen, *Yardley Warner: The Freedman's Friend* (Didcot, The Wessex Press, 1957).

Weber, Max, 'The Sociology of Charismatic Authority,' in *From Max Weber: Essays in Sociology*, H.H. Gerth and C. Wright Mills eds. (London, Routledge & Kegan Paul, 1970) 345–252.

West, Shearer, *Fin de Siècle* (London, Bloomsbury, 1993).

Wigham, Maurice J., *The Irish Quakers: A Short History of the Religious Society of Friends in Ireland* (Dublin, Historical Committee of the Religious Society of Friends in Ireland, 1992).

Williams, Chris, 'Problematising Wales: An Exploration in Historiography and Postcoloniality,' in *Postcolonial Wales*, Jane Aaron and Chris Williams eds., (Cardiff, University of Wales Press, 2005) 3–22.

Williams, Glanmor, 'Religion, Language and Nationality in Wales,' in *Religion, Language and Nationality in Wales* (Cardiff, University of Wales Press, 1979) 1–33.

_____. 'Fire on Cambria's Altar: The Welsh and their religion,' in *The Welsh and their Religion* (Cardiff, University of Wales Press, 1991) 1–72.

Williams, Gwyn A., *When Was Wales? A history of the Welsh* (London, Penguin Books, 1985).

Williams, Howell, *The Romance of the Forward Movement of the Presbyterian Church of Wales* (Denbigh, Gee, n.d).

Williams, J. Gwyn, 'Crynwyr Cynnar Cymru: Cipolwg,' in *Y Gair a'r Genedl: Cyfrol Deyrnged R. Tudur Jones*, E. Stanley John, ed., (Abertawe, Ty John Penry, 1986) 126–271.

Williams, Tim, 'Language, Culture, Religion,' in *Wales 1880–1914*, Trevor Herbert and Gareth Elwyn Jones eds., (Cardiff, University of Wales Press, 1988) 73–106.

Wilson, Roger, *Manchester, Manchester and Manchester Again: from 'Sound Doctrine' to 'A Free Ministry' the theological travail of LYM throughout the nineteenth century* (London, Friends Historical Society, 1990).

Wright, Sheila, *Friends in York: The Dynamics of Quaker Revival 1780–1860* (Keele, Keele University Press, 1995).

Young, Robert J.C., *Colonial Desire: Hybridity in Theory, Culture and Race* (London, Routledge, 1995).

Journal Articles

Allen, Kerri, 'Representation and Self-representation: Hannah Whitall Smith as family woman and religious guide', *Women's History Review*, 7, 2, 1998, 227–39.

Allen, Richard C., 'An Example of Quaker Discipline: The Case of Dr Charles Allen Fox and the Cardiff Quakers', *The Journal of Welsh Religious History*, 1, 2001, 46–73.

_____, 'In search of a New Jerusalem: A preliminary investigation into the causes and impact of Welsh Quaker emigration to Pennsylvania', *Quaker Studies* 9/1, 2004, 31–53.

ap Dewi Môn, 'A Ydyw y Gymraeg yn Marw', *Y Genninen*, October 1897, 4, XV, 266–8.

Bebbington, D.W., 'Nonconformity and Electoral Sociology, 1867–1918', *Historical Journal*, 27, 1984, 633–56.

Bevir, Mark, 'Labour Church Movement, 1891–1902', *Journal of British Studies*, 1999, 38, 2, 217–45.

Blamires, David, 'The Context and Character of the 1895 Manchester Conference', *The Friends' Quarterly*, 30, 2, April 1996, 50–7.

Brent, Richard, 'The Whigs and Protestant Dissent in the Decade of Reform: the case of Church Rates, 1833–1841,' *English Historical Review*, 102, 405, 1987, 887–910.

Cadbury, Elsie M., 'Friends' Census and the Revival – The Revival', *Friends Quarterly Examiner*, 34, 1905, 316–21.

Chambers, Paul and Andrew Thompson. 'Coming to terms with the Past: Religion and Identity in Wales', *Social Compass*, 52, 3, September 2005, 337–52.

Clark, J.C.D., 'English History's Forgotten Context: Scotland, Ireland, Wales', *The Historical Journal*, 32, 1,1989, 211–28.

Cragoe, Mathew, 'Conscience or Coercion: Clerical Influence at the General Election of 1868 in Wales', *Past and Present*, 149, Nov. 1995, 140–69.

_____. 'Conscience or Coercion? Reply', *Past and Present*, 169, 2000, 205–13.

Daunton, M.J., 'Book review of 'Re-birth of a Nation,' K.O. Morgan,' *English Historical Review*: XCVII, January 1982, 160–1.

Davies, J.H., 'Bibliography of Quaker Literature in the English Language relating to Wales', *The Journal of the Welsh Bibliographical Society*, 1, 7, August 1914, 203–25.

Davies, Jonathan S. and Mark Freeman, 'A case of political philanthropy: The Rowntree Family and the campaign for democratic reform', *Quaker Studies*, 9, 1, 2004, 95–113.

Davies, R.R., 'Colonial Wales', *Past and Present*, 65, November 1974, 3–23.

Dellheim, Charles, 'The Creation of a Company Culture: Cadburys, 1861–1931', *The American Historical Review*, 92, 1, February 1987, 13–44.

Dewi Môn, 'Paham nad wyf yn Grynwr', *Y Genninen*, No 4, Vol XIX, October, 1901, 281–5.

Dodd, A.H., 'The Background of the Welsh Quaker Migration to Pennsylvania', *Journal of the Merioneth Historical and Record Society*, Vol III, Part II, 1958, 111–27.

Doyle, Barry M., 'Who Paid the Price of Patriotism? The Funding of Charles Stanton during the Merthyr Boroughs By-Election of 1915', *The English Historical Review*, 109, 434, Nov. 1994, 1215–22.

Ellis, John S., 'Reconciling the Celt: British National Identity, Empire, and the 1911 Investiture of the Prince of Wales', *The Journal of British Studies*, 37, 4 Oct. 1998, 391–418.

Eurig, Aled, 'Agweddau ar y Gwrthwynebiad i'r Rhyfel Byd Cyntaf', *Llafur*, 4, 4, 1986, 58–68.

Evans, E.D., 'Methodist Persecution in Merioneth in the late eighteenth century', *Journal of the Historical Society of the Presbyterian Church of Wales*, 28, 2004, 23–37.

Evans, H.T., 'Atgofion am y Parch. D.S. Davies', *Y Genninen*, July 1899, No 3, Vol. 18, 196–7.

Fraser, P., 'The Liberal Unionist Alliance: Chamberlain, Hartington, and the Conservatives 1886–1904', *The English Historical Review*, 77, 302, Jan., 1962, 53–78.

Grubb, Edward, 'The Evangelical Movement and its Impact on the Society of Friends (Presidential Address to the FHS, 1923)', *The Friends Quarterly Examiner*, 1924, 1–34.

Grubb, Mollie, 'The Beacon Separation', *The Journal of the Friends' Historical Society*, 55, 6, 1988, 190–9.

_____, 'Tensions in the Religious Society of Friends in England in the Nineteenth Century', *The Journal of the Friends' Historical Society*, 56, 1, 1990, 1–14.

Gruffydd, Pyrs. 'A Crusade against Consumption:' environment, health and social reform in Wales, 1900–1939', *Journal of Historical Geography*, 21, 1995, 39–54.

Gullifer, N.T., 'Opposition to the 1902 Education Act', *Oxford Review of Education*, 8, 1, 1982, 83–98.

Guto, Dafydd, 'John Edward Southall', *Y Casglwr*, 64, Christmas, 1998, 7–8.

_____, 'John Edward Southall', *Y Casglwr*, 65, Easter, 1999, 7–9.

Harvey, J., 'Spiritual Emblems: The Visions of the 1904–05 Welsh Revival', *Llafur, Journal of Welsh Labour History*, 6, 2, 1993, 75–93.

Hergest, Leighton, 'The Welsh Educational Alliance and the 1870 Elementary Education Act', *Welsh History Review*, 10, 1980–1, 172–205.

Holmes, Colin, 'The Tredegar Riots of 1911: Anti Jewish Disturbances in South Wales', *Welsh History Review*, 11, 1982–3, 214–25.

Hopkins, Deian, 'The Llanelli Riots, 1911', *Welsh History Review*, 11, 1982–3, 488–511.

Horridge, G., 'The Salvation Army in Wales', *The Journal of Welsh Ecclesiastical History*, 6, 1989, 51–70.

Hughes, Trystan Owain, 'An Uneasy Alliance? Welsh Nationalism and Roman Catholicism', *North American Journal of Welsh Studies*, 2, 2, Summer 2002, 1–6.

Jenkins, T.A., 'The Funding of the Liberal Unionist Party and the Honours System', *The English Historical Review*, 105, 417, 1990, 920–38.

'John ap John and Early Records of Friends in Wales, Compiled by William Gregory Norris', *Journal of the Friends' Historical Society*, Supplement 6, 1907.

Jones, E.D., 'The Journal of William Roberts, ('Nefydd') 1853–1862', *The National Library of Wales Journal*, IX, 1955–6, 93–101.

Jones, Emyr Wyn, 'William Jones: Quaker and Peacemaker', *The National Library of Wales Journal*, XXVI, 4, 1990, 401–26.

Jones, Gareth Elwyn, 'The Welsh Revolt Revisited: Merioneth and Montgomeryshire in default', *Welsh History Review*, 14, 3, June 1989, 417–38.

_____. 'Policy and Power: One Hundred Years of Local Education Authorities in Wales', *Oxford Review of Education*, 28, 2/3, Jun–Sept 2002, 343–58.

Jones, H.G., 'Dyddiau Olaf y Crynwyr yng Nghymru', *Y Traethodydd*, viii, 1939, 78–87.

Jones, Rev. J.T. Alun, 'Y Crynwyr', *Y Drysorfa*, July, 1917, 1041, 241–6 and December 1917, 1046, 446–51, 1917.

Jones, John Gwynfor, " 'Ebychiad mawr olaf anghydffurfiaeth yng Nghymru': Diwygiad 1904–05", *The Transactions of the Honourable Society of Cymmrodorion*, 11, 2005, 105–43.

Kennedy, Thomas C., " 'What hath Manchester wrought?' Change in the Religious Society of Friends, 1895–1920", *Journal of the Friends' Historical Society*, 57, 1994–6, 277–301.

_____, 'An Angry God or a Reasonable Faith: The British Society of Friends', *Journal of the Friends' Historical Society*, 57, 2, 1995. 183–98.

Koss, Stephen, 'Lloyd George and Nonconformity: the last rally', *The English Historical Review*, 89, 350, January 1974, 77–108.

Lambert, W.R., 'Some Working-Class Attitudes towards organised religion in nineteenth-century Wales', *Llafur*, 2, 1, 1976, 3–17.

Lewis, T.H., 'Y Mudiad Heddwch yng Nghymru, 1800–1899', *The Transactions of the Honourable Society of Cymmrodorion*, 1957 Session, 87–127.

Light, Julie, " '...mere seekers of fame'? Personalities, power and politics in the small town: Pontypool and Bridgend, *c*.1860–95", *Urban History*, 32, 1, 2005, 88–99.

Lloyd, Tecwyn, 'Welsh Public Opinion and the First World War', *Planet*, 10, 1972, Feb/March, 25–37.

Manton, Kevin, 'The 1902 Education Act', *History Today*, 52, 12, December 2002, 18–9.

Marwick, William H., 'Quakers in early twentieth century Scotland,' *The Journal of the Friends' Historical Society*, 52, 1968–71, 211–8.

Milligan, Edward H., 'The Ancient Way: The Conservative Tradition in Nineteenth Century British Quakerism,' *The Journal of the Friends' Historical Society*,57, 1, 1994, 74–101.

Morgan, Gareth, 'Rugby and Revivalism: Sport and Religion in Edwardian Wales,' *International Journal of the History of Sport*, 22, 3, May 2005, 434–56.

Morgan, K.O., 'Cardiganshire Politics: The Liberal Ascendancy, 1885–1923', *Ceredigion*, V, 1964–67, 311–39.

Morris, E.R., 'The Dolobran Family in Religion and Industry in Montgomeryshire', *The Montgomeryshire Collections*, 56, 1959–60, 124–47.

_____, 'Llanwddyn Quakers', *The Montgomeryshire Collections*, 66, 1978, 46–59.

_____, 'Quakerism in West Montgomeryshire', *The Montgomeryshire Collections*, 56, 1959–60, 45–65; 57, 1961–2, 17–22.

Munson, J.E.B., 'The Unionist Coalition and Education 1895–1902', *The Historical Journal*, 20, 3, 1977, 607–45.

Newman, Edwina, 'John Brewin's Tracts: The written word, evangelicalism and the Quaker way in mid-nineteenth century England,' *Quaker Studies*, 9, 2, 2005, 238–48.

Osmond, John, 'Whose Bill of Rights?', *Planet*, 75, June/July 1989, 16–21.

Owen, Bob, 'Cymru a'r Mudiad Heddwch, 1814–1824', *Y Genninen*, xliii, 1925, 201–10.

Peate, Iorwerth C., 'Diwylliant Gwerin', *The Transactions of the Honourable Society of Cymmrodorion*, 1938, 241–50.

Pierson, Stanley, 'John Trevor and the Labour Church Movement in England, 1891–1900,' *Church History*, 29, 4 Dec. 1960, 463–78.

Pocock, J.G.A., 'British History: A Plea for a New Subject', *Journal of Modern History*, 4, 4, 1975, 601–28.

Roberts, Harri, 'Embodying Identity: Class, Nation and Corporeality in the 1847 Blue Books', *The North American Journal of Welsh Studies*, 3, 1, 2003, 2–21.

Painting, David, 'Swansea and the Abolition of the Slave Trade', *The Swansea History Journal*: Minerva, 15, 2007–08, 10–18.

Packer, I., 'Religion and the New Liberalism: The Rowntree Family, Quakerism and Social Reform', *Journal of British Studies*, 42, 2003, 236–57.

Phillips, H.D., 'The Beginnings of Quakerism in Radnorshire', *The Transactions of the Radnorshire Society*, xi, 1941, 31–6.

Phillips, Rev W.F., 'Arwyddion Dirywiad Cenedlaethol', *Y Traethodydd*, 2, 8, October 1914, 321–34.

Pope, Robert, 'Evan Roberts in Theological Context', *The Transactions of the Honourable Society of Cymmrodorion*, 11, 2005, 144–69.

Pryce, Huw, 'National Identity in Twelfth Century Wales', *English Historical Review*, September 2001, 775–801.

Robbins, Keith G., 'Wales and the 'British Question' in *Transactions of the Honourable Society of Cymmrodorion*, 2002, New Series, 9, 2003, 152–61.

Richards, N.J., 'Religious Controversy and the School Boards 1870–1902', *British Journal of Educational Studies*, 18, 2, 1970, 180–96.

_____, 'The Education Bill of 1906 and the Decline of Political Nonconformity', *Journal of Ecclesiastical History*, XXIII, 1, January 1972, 49–63.

Roderick, Huw, '"A Fire Made of Shavings': The 1904 Revival in Cardiganshire', *Ceredigion*, XV, 1, 2005, 107–38.

Rowlands, Daniel, 'Y Fasnach Feddwol', *Y Traethodydd*, xxxvi, 1881, 336–50.

Russell, Conrad, 'The British Problem and the English Civil War', *History*, 72, 1987, 395–415.

Sessions, Frederick, 'A Home Missionary's Experiences', *Friends Quarterly Examiner*, 1893, 27, 181–99.

Shandler, Jeffrey, 'Imagining Yiddishland: Language, Place and Memory', *History and Memory*, 15, 1, Spring/Summer 2003, 123–49.

Smith, Robert, "'Cadw'r Iaith yw Cadw Crefydd Cymru:' Yr Enwadau Ymneilltuol a'r Iaith Gymraeg, 1918–1939", *Llen Cymru*, 25, 2002, 105–29.

_____, 'Methodistiad Calfinaidd a Gwleidyddiarth Cymru: 1918–1939', *Historical Society of the Presbyterian Church of Wales*, 26–7, 2002–03, 49–66.

Snell, K.D.M., 'The Sunday-School Movement in England and Wales: Child Labour, Denominational Control and Working Class Culture', *Past and Present*, 164, August 1999, 122–68.

Southall, J.E., 'The Middle Class and Quakerism', *The British Friend*, October, 1903, 296–7.

_____, 'The Society of Friends' in Wales', *Friends Quarterly Examiner*, 14, 1st Month 1880, 86–97.

_____, 'The Linguistic Plebiscite in Cardiff', *Young Wales*, 3, No 33, 1897, 213–15.

_____, 'Modern Languages in County Schools', *Young Wales*, 3, September 1897, 213–5 and Vol 4, October 1898, 235–8.

_____, 'A Ydyw y Gymraeg yn Marw?' *Y Genninen*, October 1898, No 4, Vol XVI, 243–6.

_____, 'Paham yr Wyf yn Grynwr', *Y Genninen*, No. 3, Vol XIX, 1901, 171–6.

_____, 'Paham yr Wyf yn Grynwr', *Y Genninen*, No. 1, Vol XX, January, 1902, 77–9.

Stevenson, Charles, 'Germs of Good: The Growth of Quakerism in Australia', *Journal of the Friends' Historical Society*, 59, 1, 2000, 55–66.

Taylor, Tony, 'The Politics of Reaction: The Ideology of the Cecils and the Challenge of Secular Education 1889–1902', *Educational Administration and History Monographs*, 20, 1997, School of Education, University of Leeds.

Thesbiad (*nom de plume*), 'Y Diwigiad a'r Weinidogaeth', *Y Genninen*, No. 2, Vol xxiv, April, 1906, 127–32.

Trevett, Christine, '"Not Fit To Be Printed": The Welsh, the women and the Second Day Morning Meeting', *The Journal of the Friends' Historical Society*, 59, 2, 2001, [Issued 2004], 115–44.

Whiting, Evelyn S., 'The Yearly Meeting for Wales 1682–1797,' *The Journal of Friends' Historical Society*, 47, 1, 1955, 57–70.

Williams, C.R., 'The Welsh Religious Revival, British,' *Journal of Sociology*, 3, 1952, 242–59.

Williams, Emyr Wyn, 'Liberalism in Wales and the Politics of Welsh Home Rule 1886–1910,' *Bulletin of the Board of Celtic Studies*, 37, 1990, 191–207.

Williams, H.G., 'The Forster Education Act and Welsh Politics,' *Welsh History Review*, 14, 2, 1988, 242–68.

Williams, J., 'Cofrifiad Ieithyddol Cymru 1901,' *Y Traethodydd*, Vol LIX, 1904, 452–9.

Williams, J. Gwynn, 'The Quakers of Merioneth during the Seventeenth Century', *Journal of the Merioneth Historical and Record Society*, VIII, 1978, 122–56 and 1979, 312–39.

Williams, T.M., 'Yr Enwadau Crefyddol a Dirwest', *Y Traethodydd*, xxxvi, 1881, 459–63.

Wilson, Roger, 'Friends in the Nineteenth Century', *Friends Quarterly*, October 1984, 23, 8, 353–63.

Zangerl, Carl H.E., 'The Social Composition of the County Magistracy in England and Wales', *The Journal of British Studies*, 11, 1, Nov 1971, 113–25.

Unpublished papers

Jenkins, Florence, 'John Owen Jenkins 1856–1944,' Private paper, edited and printed by Martin Williams, Llandrindod Wells, 1992.

Phillips, H.D., 'The Growth of Llandrindod Wells Society of Friends Meeting,' *circa* 1934.

_____. 'The Personal Story of H. D. Phillips and the Growth of Llandrindod Wells', Society of Friends Meeting, unpublished manuscript, 1941.

Williams, Martin, 'Evangelical Friends in Radnorshire from the late 19th Century,' Hereford and Mid-Wales Monthly Meeting, 1992.

_____, Evangelical Friends in Radnorshire from the late 19th Century, 28.11.1995.

A Report to Meeting for Sufferings from Meeting for Sufferings Committee Working Group on the Decision-Making Process of Meeting for Sufferings, Paper M06/10 D, Meeting for Sufferings 4.11.2006.

Biographical Notes on H T Evans: unpublished handwritten manuscript at Aberystwyth Town Library, n.d.

Government Papers

Digest of Welsh Historical Statistics, John Williams, ed., Pontypool, Welsh Office, 1985.

Royal Commission on Land in Wales and Monmouthshire: Minutes of Evidence, 1895, Cmd. 7661.

Royal Commission on the Church of England and other Religious Bodies in Wales and Monmouthshire, 1910, Cmd. 5432.

The Welsh Sunday Closing Act: Evidence: Report of the Royal Commissioners appointed to enquire into the operation of the Sunday Closing [Wales] Act 1881, 1890, Cmd. 5994.

Welsh in Education and Life: Being the Report of the Departmental Committee appointed by the President of the Board of Education to inquire into the position of the Welsh Language and to advise as to its promotion in the educational system of Wales, London, HMSO, 1927.

Other

Annual Report, National Library of Wales, 1919–1920.

Conference on Home Mission Work in the Society of Friends held in London, 29–30 *Eleventh Month, 1881*, London, FFDSA, 1881.

Encyclopaedia Britannica, London, Encyclopaedia Britannica (UK) Ltd., 2006.

Gwyddionadur Cymru, Yr Academi Gymreig, Caerdydd, Gwasg Prifysgol Cymru, 2008.

List of Members and Attenders, Meeting of Friends in Wales, February 2007.

Monbiot, George, 'A Life with no purpose', the *Guardian*, 16.08.2005.

Sundays in Wales: Visits to the places of worship of the Quakers, the Unitarians, the Roman Catholics, and the Jews by a Week-Day Preacher, Swansea, Pease and Brown, 1859. n.a.

Report of the Proceedings of the Conference held at Manchester from the eleventh to fifteenth of eleventh month 1895, LYM, 1895

Tomalin, Claire, 'Nothing matters, and everything matters', the *Guardian*, 16.09.06.

Who's Who in Wales, Arthur Mee, ed., Cardiff, *Western Mail*, 1921.

Who's Who in Wales, 1933, London, A. Reynolds, 1933.

Who's Who in Wales, London, The Belgravia Publications, 1937.

Y Bywgraffiadur Cymreig hyd 1940, Cymdeithas y Cymmrodorion, Llundain, 1953.

Electronic sources

Williams, M. Fay, 'The Society of Friends in Glamorgan, 1656–1900', Swansea Quaker Meeting, Presented as an M.A. Thesis, April 1950, Published electronically by Swansea

Quaker Meeting, First published 2005, V1.0, 2005 with editorial additions by Martin Willson (private circulation).

www.asanet.org

http://a-day-in-the-life.powys.org.uk/eng/civ/ec_hdphil.php

www.apostolic-church.org

www.archivesnetworkwales.info/cgiin/anw/search2?coll_id=11276&inst_id=35&term=Dillwyn

www.banneroftruth.org

http://www.british-history.ac.uk/report.asp?compid=16605#s1-32

www.christianendeavour.com

www.elim.org.uk

www.1919encyclopedia.org.

www.gutenberg.org/catalog

www.hereford.uk.com/history

www.history.powys.org.uk/school1/llandrindod/cefnpop.shtml

www.isle-of-man/manxnotebook/people/antiqarn/awmoore.htm

http://www.lambethpalacelibrary.org/holdings/depositedarchives.html

http://mmm.moody.edu/GenMoody/default.asp

http://yba.llgc.org.uk/en/index.html (Welsh Biography Online)

www.oxforddnb.com (Oxford Dictionary of National Biography)

www.quakersocialaction.com

http://search.eb.com

www.umanitoba.ca/colleges/st_pauls/ccha/Back%20Issues/CCHA1973/Olsen.html.

www.welshcoalmines.co.uk

http://wesley.nnu.edu/wesleyan_theology/theojrnl/06-10/09-2.htm

www.williamhaslam.org/board/viewtopic.php?t+211highlight+Keswick

Index